The Atkinson Family

IMPRINT IN HIGHER EDUCATION

The Atkinson Family Foundation has endowed this imprint to illuminate the role of higher education in contemporary society.

The publisher and the University of California Press Foundation gratefully acknowledge the generous support of the Atkinson Family Foundation Imprint in Higher Education.

Ethnic Studies at the Crossroads

AMERICAN CROSSROADS

Edited by Earl Lewis, George Lipsitz, George Sánchez, Dana Takagi, Laura Briggs, and Nikhil Pal Singh

Ethnic Studies at the Crossroads

George Lipsitz

UNIVERSITY OF CALIFORNIA PRESS

University of California Press
Oakland, California

© 2026 by George Lipsitz

All rights reserved.

Library of Congress Cataloging-in-Publication Data

Names: Lipsitz, George author
Title: Ethnic studies at the crossroads / George Lipsitz.
Other titles: American crossroads 76.
Description: Oakland, California : University of
   California Press, [2026] | Series: American crossroads ;
   76 | Includes bibliographical references and index.
Identifiers: LCCN 2026003746 (print) | LCCN
   2026003747 (ebook) | ISBN 9780520413368
   cloth | ISBN 9780520413375 paperback | ISBN
   9780520413382 ebook
Subjects: LCSH: Minorities—Study and teaching—United
   States | Ethnicity—Study and teaching—United States
Classification: LCC E184.A1 L554 2026 (print) |
   LCC E184.A1 (ebook)
LC record available at https://lccn.loc.gov/2026003746
LC ebook record available at https://lccn.loc
   .gov/2026003747

GPSR Authorized Representative: Easy Access System
Europe, Mustamäe tee 50, 10621 Tallinn, Estonia, gpsr.
requests@easproject.com

35 34 33 32 31 30 29 28 27 26
10 9 8 7 6 5 4 3 2 1

Contents

	Introduction: Ethnic Studies at the Crossroads	*1*
1.	Ethnic Studies as Opposition and Opposition to Ethnic Studies	*23*
2.	Ethnic Studies as Incorporation	*53*
	A Bridge for This Book: Ethnic Studies: The Crossroads, the Caduceus, the Archive, and the Repertoire	*80*
3.	Ethnic Studies as Accompaniment: Autonomous Learning Circles	*108*
4.	Ethnic Studies and Intersectional Justice	*134*
5.	Ethnic Studies as Inquiry and Instruction	*166*
6.	Ethnic Studies and the Current Crisis	*199*

Acknowledgments	*217*
Notes	*219*
Bibliography	*247*
Index	*267*

Introduction

Ethnic Studies at the Crossroads

Eduardo Galeano argues that dominant institutions in education, politics, and popular culture, what he calls "the looking glass school," create an upside-down curriculum that suppresses intellect and agency while producing despair and resignation. "The looking glass school teaches us to suffer reality, not change it," he argues; "to forget the past, not learn from it; to accept the future, not invent it. In the halls of criminal learning, impotence, amnesia, and resignation are required courses." Yet Galeano proposes that the world brought into being by the looking glass school can also provoke people to refuse unlivable destinies: "Perhaps—who can say—there can be no disgrace without grace, no sign without a countersign, and no school that does not beget its counterschool."[1] Despite their pervasive power, the mechanisms of domination can be subverted and inverted as they impel people to rise above their training, to learn from the past, to invent the future, and to build a better world.

This book describes and analyzes the peril and promise for ethnic studies in a world shaped by the practices of the looking glass school. *Ethnic studies* is a name applied to an academic research and teaching project that takes place in classrooms, conferences, journals, and books; yet it is also a key participant in a more widely dispersed antiracist social formation, one made necessary because of the failures of existing institutions to explain—much less constrain—the pervasive practices that *turn perceptions of difference into justifications for domination.* Seen in this way, ethnic studies is not a narrowly bounded research and teaching practice but rather a portal into critical reflection on the mechanisms that subject aggrieved individuals and groups to displacement, dispossession, demonization, exploitation, and exclusion. Initially addressing racism as a mechanism that deployed fears of difference as an excuse for domination, ethnic studies participants have gradually and increasingly come to see affinities and parallels with the ways in which fears of difference get deployed to dominate people because of class, gender, sexuality, disability, citizenship status, language, and other socially constructed categories of exclusion and subordination.

Ethnic studies research has shown that racism is not an aberration in an otherwise just society that affects only its direct targets. As Daniel Martinez HoSang explains, racism is "the necessary structuring condition of the corporate economy. It organizes labor markets and shapes the gendered division of labor that is crucial to the functioning of the economy. It is the main precondition of state violence. It undergirds our deeply hierarchical system of education, rooted in distinctions of status and innate intellectual ability. The abolition of racism requires the fundamental reorganization of all these structures."[2] Yet as explained in this book, especially in chapters 3 and 4, racism is not the only form of segregating, suppressing, shunning, and silencing people.

Racism provides the property system with a way to shift blame away from its failures and injustices by mobilizing hatred against aggrieved groups targeted as despised "others." As has long been the case, racist mobilizations blame and shame powerless victims for the crimes committed by the powerful. They divide the constituencies that might generate oppositional practices and processes. Yet as delineated clearly in the pioneering scholarship of Destin Jenkins, Andrew Kahrl, and Louise Seamster, under late capitalism, racism is not merely a strategy for ideological legitimation but also a key mechanism of capital accumulation enacted through racially targeted practices in the bond market, the tax system, and the construction and redrawing of municipal and utility service boundaries. These scholars show that the maldistribution of wealth between white and nonwhite communities is not simply a paradox but instead a causal relationship shaped by capital and resource extraction from aggrieved communities along with amenity and opportunity hoarding in racially privileged places.[3]

Thus white supremacy in the US is not merely the vestigial remnant of past histories of Indigenous dispossession, slavery, segregation, coloniality, and labor exploitation; rather, it gets reenacted, reproduced, and reinforced every day through a wide range of practices, processes, structures, systems, ideologies, and institutions.[4] Gloria Anzaldúa reminds us that "we are collectively conditioned not to know that every comfort of our lives is acquired with the blood of conquered, subjugated, enslaved, or exterminated people, an exploitation that continues today."[5]

The generations that built ethnic studies and continue its work have been confronted again and again by crises that are expressly racist in nature, such as impunity for police officers and vigilantes who kill Black people, and Supreme Court decisions that outlaw voluntary school desegregation programs and void key aspects of the Voting Rights Act while banning affirmative action. Crises come to us as mass shootings by racists targeting Black church members in Charleston, Latinx shoppers in El Paso, and Asian American women workers in Atlanta. Yet open racist intent is not necessary to produce racist effects. Crises that might seem to have no racist specificity because they affect the public at large often enact disproportionate damage on aggrieved communities of color. Floods related to hurricane damage and climate change along the coast of the Gulf of Mexico hit hardest in racially segregated neighborhoods, neighborhoods that then receive fewer resources for rebuilding than bastions of white settlement. The COVID-19 pandemic and syndemic produced disproportionate numbers of infections and deaths among people concentrated in positions most likely to be held by racialized workers: farmworkers, house cleaners, bus drivers and passengers, and frontline retail sales persons. The 2008 mortgage lending crisis damaged the entire economy and led to bankruptcies among major financial institutions, but the largest amount of suffering it caused came in the loss of wealth among US Black and Latinx homeowners who received sparse to nonexistent relief from the government agencies that bailed out the banks and speculators who had caused the crisis in the first place.[6] The abandonment of long-established principles of civil liberties in response to the attacks on the World Trade Center and the Pentagon in 2001 instigated moral panics and new security measures in many places but enacted an especially vicious reign of terror waged by government agencies and vigilantes against Muslims and all South Asian and Middle Eastern people perceived to be Muslim.

These crises have been all too real, but treating them as *states of exception* evades the harsh realities that face aggrieved communities in times when no general crisis is acknowledged. Walter Benjamin wrote that "the tradition of the oppressed teaches us that the 'state of exception' in which we live is not the exception but the rule."[7] It is tactically necessary and morally imperative to do what we can to oppose these states of emergency and stand with those most victimized by them. But Benjamin notes that the traditions of the oppressed also teach us that it is equally important to identify, address, and transform the taken-for-granted social practices and processes that originally produce hate, hurt, and fear—that make spectacular violence, exploitation, and oppression seem natural, necessary, and inevitable. This is the role that ethnic studies frequently has played and can continue to play in the world. Participants in the ethnic studies project and the broader antiracist formation to which it is tethered recognize in times of crisis that the survival strategies of historically oppressed people contain ways of knowing and ways of being that reveal the too often occluded causes and consequences of social crises. They teach that returning to the imagined state of normalcy that preceded the crisis will not suffice because the normal ways society operates are the cause of these problems, not their cure.

Equipped with the understanding that injustice did not start yesterday and will not end tomorrow, ethnic studies adherents and allies have developed tools for confronting crises and exposing their long-term causes. The decades of revanchist white supremacy that have caused so much unnecessary suffering have also generated powerful forms of opposition through social movements aiming toward liberation. People with their backs against the wall—and people whose backs are being pushed through the wall—have staged marches on behalf of immigrant and reproductive rights, mobilized campaigns to rein in and reverse predatory policing and mass incarceration, developed healing justice strategies on behalf of reproductive rights, and mounted resistance to pipeline construction and resource extraction schemes that violate Indigenous sovereignty.

Culminating in the massive demonstrations in 2020 protesting the police killings of Breonna Taylor and George Floyd, some of the largest and most widespread demonstrations in history have taken place during the past two decades. From the Idle No More insurgency in Canada to the Arab Spring in the Middle East, from mobilizations by and in support of the Zapatista movement in Chiapas to the coalitions organized in support of the Standing Rock Sioux Tribe water protectors, all around the world people who have been silenced, segregated, subordinated, and suppressed have been waking up, standing up, stepping up, and speaking up for justice.

The emergence of these oppositional mobilizations signals widespread desires for a new and better world. But these mobilizations also provoke vicious reaction and repression on the part of those eager to maintain and expand the benefits they derive from the increasingly indecent and unjust social order. The present moment parallels the situation in Europe in the 1920s and 1930s when fascism was on the rise: a period that Antonio Gramsci—who was locked up in prison by Benito Mussolini's dictatorship in Italy—described as a moment when the old was dying but the new could not quite be born. The recent mobilizations during the first decades of the twenty-first century have raised consciousness about the injustices of racial capitalism, but the power structure has acted quickly in response to repress, co-opt, and contain their radical impulses.

In the US, the mass demonstrations in 2020 insisting on the value and sanctity of Black lives provoked people situated inside many different circumstances to make sincere efforts to reckon with the pervasive presence of structural and systemic racism in society. They demanded justice but all too often were offered merely modest adjustments in the already-existing unjust racial order. Their radical desires met with powerful forces intent on containing, constraining, and co-opting them. They won concessions, but too many of those focused on *prejudice* rather than on *power*, on combating openly declared racist *intentions* rather than systemically structured *racist effects*, and on including more people from aggrieved groups in existing structures and systems without interrogating how forms of racist subordination remained embedded inside them. These concessions treated racialized exclusion and deprivation as anomalies in an otherwise just system, rather than as evidence that racism is a key constitutive element in all of the existing unjust structures of society. They sought to make institutions appear more welcoming to traditionally excluded people and to expand promises of access to resources without recognizing the ways in which uninterrogated assumptions within the institutions of law, medicine, policing, politics, and economics as currently conceived routinely reinforce rather than resist racist rule.

The concessions granted in the wake of antiracist upheaval entailed reforms such as calling for more Black students in law and medical schools but not radically reassessing legal and medical education and practice. They involved promises of expanded access to home mortgage loans and medical insurance without acknowledging how the practices of racialized risk assessment guarantee that most of the inclusion that has taken place in the past and is likely to occur in the future has been and will be limited, subordinate, and even predatory.[8] The issuance of antiracist proclamations has rarely led to actual antiracist practices.

WHAT IS ETHNIC STUDIES?

The word *studies* can evoke images of detached individual learning. Yet the etymology of the word also connects it to practices of active engagement. Meanings attached to the term as early as the twelfth century connoted striving, cultivating, applying, pressing, and thrusting toward. Only later did *studies* start to refer to the acquisition of knowledge through classroom instruction and individual attention and reflection. When Martin Luther King Jr. declared his opposition to the Vietnam War in 1967, he concluded his remarks by gesturing toward the prophet Isaiah and quoting the refrain of the spiritual "Down by the Riverside" that states, "I ain't gonna study war no more." Declining to "study" war in this articulation does not mean rejecting reading about it but rather refusing to prepare for it and participate in it.

The implication that *to study* means intending to act remains embedded in the word to this day. In imploring Black studies participants to connect campus learning to community concerns, Robin D. G. Kelley confides that he keeps in the top drawer of his desk a small scrap of paper with the words "Love, Study, Struggle" inscribed on it. This phrase reminds Kelley that Black study and resistance must begin with a love for the people that is mobilized through what he calls "relentless struggle, deep study, and critique" across different spheres of ideas and actions.[9] *Struggle* denotes an effort to be free from restrictions and constraints, a quality that makes it a logical partner to *study*. Moreover, as Eduardo Galeano asserts, "The first condition for changing reality is to understand it."[10]

The institutionalized ethnic studies classes, curricular initiatives, programs, and departments that later came into existence in classrooms on campuses made up only a small part of a broader antiracist social formation forged from widely dispersed acts of solidarity and cocreation across social spheres. The academic field named ethnic studies did not enter educational institutions because deans, chancellors, and regents woke up one day and decided they wanted more knowledge about race and ethnicity. Ethnic studies started in the streets, in mass mobilizations and insurrections waged by aggrieved groups opposed to the oppressive and exploitative social orders that bounded their lives. Struggles for resources, rights, and recognition generated opposition to what Black Power theorist and activist Stokely Carmichael (later Kwame Ture) described as "the dictatorship of definition, interpretation, and consciousness" that excused, justified, and naturalized exclusion, exploitation, and domination.¹¹ The egalitarian and democratic social movements of the mid-twentieth century developed their own versions of ethnic studies by turning mass meetings and small study groups into autonomous learning circles and alternative academies. These helped create, nurture, and sustain an expanded public sphere where education proceeded in large part without classrooms or books—in grassroots-created music, dance, theater, and poetry performances, in underground newspapers and community radio broadcasts, in art galleries, in street corner speeches, in wall murals and museums, in trade union caucuses, in neighborhood political associations, and in study groups in libraries, youth centers, and houses of worship.

The ethnic studies focused on in this book, then, refers not only to the interdisciplinary project of teaching, research, professional dialogue, and publication that bears its name but also to the broader social formation built from grassroots collective efforts to cultivate and deepen antiracist capacities and dispositions. The interrelationships linking campus and community concepts and strategies are profound, though often unacknowledged. For example, the many currents that flowed through the queer feminist of color anthology *This Bridge Called My Back* had origins in and effects on art and activism, as well as academic research and teaching. Aurora Levins Morales, a contributor to that volume, recalls its publication and dissemination as causing "a tectonic shift in a bedrock of silencing," noting that "our collective shout unlocked thousands of other voices."¹²

Concepts that have emerged from antiracist struggle and been honed and refined inside ethnic studies—such as intersectionality, abolition, coloniality, disidentification, borderlands/*nepantla,* hybridity/*mestizaje,* healing justice, *conocimiento,* racial formation, and social formation—now appear prominently in both academic discourse and popular struggles. They help clarify the ways in which the social construction of categories representing despised racial and ethnic "others" fuels and justifies the deadly and dreadful structural practices of residential and educational segregation, labor exploitation, mass incarceration, immigrant deportation, sex and gender discrimination and abuse, predatory policing, and wars without end as routine and scarcely debated or contested ventures. Investigation of new research objects and deployments of new research methods have led scholars engaged in interdisciplinary ethnic studies to formulate fundamentally new, true, and useful challenges to the hidden assumptions and unexplored ramifications of prevailing disciplinary and professional conceptions of medicine, language, law, labor, economics, crime, punishment, geographic scale, the nation-state, sovereignty, the natural world, and expressive culture.[13]

Links between ethnic studies as a project and the broader antidomination social formation can be conceived fruitfully through a metaphor advanced by artist and activist Ricardo Levins Morales. In a formulation drawn from advanced currents of botanical research, he noted that seeds require nutritious soil to survive and thrive. Even the best seed will not grow in nutrient-depleted soil. Inside study and struggle, Levins Morales describes the "soil" as the "compost of beliefs, ideas, values, and narratives that create the environment in which we're working." To be successful cultivators, people need to "plant the seed of the tree that one day we want to live under. We need to be preparing the soil in which the tree can grow."[14] The ethnic studies project and the broader antidomination social formation thrive when they are interdependent, when each is strong and helps nurture the other. Even inside their own spheres, their work entails enriching the soil to support the work we do and the work done by others.

Understanding racism entails grappling with the alternative archives, imaginaries, epistemologies, and ontologies of aggrieved communities. It enables developing and deploying new ways of asking and answering research questions and experimenting with new social relations of research. Perhaps most important, the ethnic studies project and the antiracist social formation to which it is tethered present explorations of embodied racial identities (and many other social identities) not as the culmination of scholarly research or social action but as a starting point from which to ask new original and generative general questions about difference and domination, knowledge and power, exclusion and inclusion, exploitation and expropriation.

The past, present, and future of ethnic studies as an academic project that is institutionalized in campus classrooms, departments, and programs can be chronicled within a genealogy of origins and development focusing on the first uses of the name for departments, the emergence of the field's first or most prominent journals and professional organizations, and the series of texts by famous authors who have most decisively shaped the trajectory of the field. This is an important history with a rich archive that has been explored productively by many researchers, but it is referenced only sporadically throughout this book.[15] References to and discussions about distinguished scholars, esteemed academic centers, notably transformative publications, and innovative curricular and pedagogical models do appear in many of the chapters that follow. It is important to remember, however, that these works reflect as well as shape antiracist study, struggle, and love in a broader social formation. They are neither more nor less important than the ethnic studies forged outside the academy—for example, by women of color and Deaf domestic violence and reproductive health collectives in East Harlem and Albuquerque, Duluth, Denver, and the Rosebud Reservation in South Dakota and Seattle; by antiracist arts-based community-building projects in Michigan City (Indiana), Houston, and East Los Angeles; in sites offering sanctuary to undocumented immigrants in Ohio and Arizona; or in worker education and mobilization circles in Mississippi and Florida.[16] While visible manifestations of the ethnic studies project appear in elite universities, library catalogs, and rosters and programs of professional organizations, key sites for the broader social project have been the streets of Ferguson and Minneapolis where uprisings against police killings took place, and the territories in the Dakotas where Indigenous water protectors—resisting violations of their sovereignty and assaults on their environment—battled against armed agents in service to the greed of corporations that profit from extraction (and destruction) of natural resources. These fights for racial justice inside the United States are part of a global struggle for a decent and democratic future waged by activists around the world, for example in the public protests by mothers of children "disappeared" by military and vigilante violence in Argentina, Mexico, Iran, Honduras, China, and El Salvador.[17]

INSTITUTIONALIZED ETHNIC STUDIES

In its slightly more than half century of formal institutional existence in college and K-12 education, ethnic studies has emerged as a key site for the discovery, invention, and dissemination of critical concepts that have opened doors to new ways of knowing and being. Institutionalization has made much of this success possible. Actions by students, professors, department chairs, faculty committees, deans, alumni, and community members have produced insubordinate spaces on and off campuses. These spaces have been sites for the generation of ideas, analyses, theories, and actions that have been needed most immediately and urgently by aggrieved social groups but ultimately have been of enormous value to many other people. While initially focused largely on race and ethnicity, ethnic studies has become a crucible for the creation and cultivation of analyses of a broad range of socially constructed and consequential identities, identifications, affiliations, and associations. It has informed and been informed by parallel and intersecting projects engaged in critical reflection and action in response to coloniality, language discrimination, misogyny, homophobia, transphobia, Indigenous dispossession, imperialism, labor exploitation, ableism, and many other forms of differentiation, exploitation, and exclusion.[18]

The ethnic studies project that once struggled for survival at the margins of academic and public life has now achieved significant levels of visibility and validation, influence, and impact. Departments, programs, and courses organized around the aims and ideals of ethnic studies are now well established in colleges and universities. New programs and departments are emerging rapidly in institutions as diverse as the University of Chicago and Antelope Valley Community College. Ethnic studies topics hold prominent places inside the curricular and research agendas of the full range of humanities and social science disciplines, and they have increasingly become prominent in professional schools of law, medicine, education, and urban planning. The field features its own journals, and studies of social identities and power now pervade articles in major scholarly publications and presentations at professional conferences and colloquia.

Scholars affiliated with ethnic studies win prestigious book prizes, fellowships, honors, and awards. Some specialists in the field hold endowed chairs at elite institutions. Others have been elected to lead prominent and prestigious professional organizations. The validation attached to professional credentials has enabled thousands of ethnic studies scholars to serve as expert witnesses in court cases about fair housing, fair hiring, educational inequality, book bans and classroom censorship, affirmative action, voting rights, environmental racism, gang injunctions, predatory policing, immigrant rights, and language discrimination. As writers of letters of support and members of advisory boards, people with training and credentials in ethnic studies have helped a vast array of educational, arts, and social justice organizations and initiatives secure funding for internal organization and public programming.

Ethnic studies researchers have proved themselves to be far more perceptive and prescient about pressing public issues than their counterparts in the traditional disciplines. They were more accurate than the dominant voices in political science, criminology, natural sciences, and economics in identifying and analyzing what would transpire from deregulating the banking and mortgage loan industries, from allowing fossil fuel companies to stymie responses to climate change, from waging wars in Iraq and Afghanistan and launching drone strikes around the world, from militarizing the policing of petty nonviolent offenses and incarcerating huge numbers of people, from privatizing education and other public institutions, from establishing international agreements that encouraged capital to move freely while containing labor, and from building an economy that allocates wealth upward while imposing artificial austerity on the majority of the people. Some of these insights came from scholarly engagement, yet they also drew inspiration and guidance from grassroots social movements battling over what Roderick Ferguson—drawing on Jacques Rancière—calls the "distribution of the sensible," by which they mean the political and aesthetic taken-for-granted assumptions, premises, and theories that allow some people to participate in making meaningful decisions that affect their lives while prohibiting others from doing so.[19] The communities central to the ethnic studies project have developed new knowledge from challenging dominant explanations of the causes and consequences of lead poisoning, sickle cell anemia, valley fever, AIDS, climate change, domestic violence, broken windows policing, and predatory lending. The establishment and expansion of ethnic studies inside educational institutions has made a difference in society. It produces an important public sphere—one of the few places in society where the origins, evolution, causes, and consequences of difference turned into domination can be evaluated critically and responded to creatively.

While the achievements of ethnic studies have been impressive and important, trying to resist racism in a society founded on racist subordination entails costs and compromises. The ethnic studies project has been riddled with contradictions from the start, and it remains shaped by them to this day. As delineated more fully in chapters 1 and 2, hard-won successes have provoked both opposition and co-optive incorporation. Reactionary attacks on critical race theory and on diversity, equity, and inclusion initiatives now prevent many instructors from presenting true and useful evidence and arguments about the existence of past and present racisms. Yet even the inclusion in the academy of previously excluded topics and demographic groups that signified victory for the ethnic studies project may not be an unadulterated victory for the broader antiracist project because it can come at the cost of isolating antiracism inside institutions structured in dominance, allowing institutionalized ethnic studies to do relatively well while ethnic peoples outside the academy continue to suffer terribly.

The research, teaching, and learning activities that take place inside educational institutions include a wide array of greatly needed and even necessary work. Education at all levels plays a crucial role in shaping what people know, imagine, and do. Yet formal status inside institutions can make ethnic studies sites into places where people in power defuse oppositional movements by offering subordinate inclusion to a few members of aggrieved groups—validating these individuals as exceptional—in order to justify treating the masses as disposable. As Roderick Ferguson argues, seemingly democratic and inclusionary policies by universities and other significant institutions can accommodate and advance the desires of some leaders of government and business to recognize social diversity in order to manage and discipline it, to smooth off its rough critical edges. Participants in ethnic studies constantly negotiate the contradictory intersections of insurgency and incorporation and find themselves forced to decide whether their work seeks to reform and therefore reinforce existing institutions or to transform them into venues for the generation of new democratic practices, processes, imaginations, and aspirations.[20] At times it is necessary to do both—to secure as much protection and support as can be granted by formal institutions while at the same time engaging in a number of oppositional initiatives that schools may tolerate but do not endorse.

Institutionalization can lead to incorporation and co-optation. Ethnic studies began as a grassroots project demanding relevant, culturally sensitive, and useful education and analysis, but it also quickly became a project manipulated by the state and capital to recognize difference in order to manage it, to create a leadership group among aggrieved populations separated from the grassroots, and to deradicalize opposition to racism by focusing on racial difference rather than racist domination. Institutionalized ethnic studies tends to emphasize race as a personal embodied quality, a special interest, an identity in competition with others for scarce resources, and a credential offering an alternative career path to upward mobility and success. Incorporation is a structural reality; it is not the result of the personal shortcomings of individuals, and it cannot be overcome or even meaningfully moderated by virtuous individual behavior.

In higher education, the field's mission to connect campus knowledge to community concerns frequently becomes overshadowed by the demands of professionalization. Radical demands to transform the system are deliberately and strategically misheard as requests for inclusion in it. Expressions of collective aspirations for dignity and freedom become translated into pleas for individual visibility and upward mobility. Analyses of Indigenous dispossession, of what the Supreme Court in 1968 called "slavery unwilling to die,"[21] of coloniality, and of imperialist war become framed as acknowledging racism but only as an aberrant flaw in an otherwise fully functioning democracy.

WHO SPEAKS?

This book is neither memoir nor manifesto. It is not an ethnic studies informed response to the crises surrounding its moment of publication such as the war in Gaza; the paramilitary kidnapping, brutalization, and deporting of immigrants; government policies immersed in white Christian nationalism; attacks on reproductive rights and disability justice; the demonization of trans adults, children, and those who care for them; or efforts by the US government to take full control over universities, law firms, media outlets, private businesses, and public health agencies. Analyses of these crises by people with specialized expertise about them have appeared and will continue to appear in ethnic studies journals, book series, and online posts.[22] These are urgent issues that other writers grounded in ethnic studies and other frameworks are taking on courageously. This book speaks to a different temporality. It proposes *a moment's pause* to explore ways in which ethnic studies can strengthen its capacities for connecting research and classroom instruction to community knowledge and concerns. Musicologist Nina Eidsheim describes the *pause* as an interruption, a practice through which we can take stock of how we have been trained to hear and mishear. The pause enables a fuller presence of mind. It recognizes many competing currents and many possible meanings in things we generally treat as firmly fixed and finite. The pause offers an opportunity to stop, look, learn, and listen as preparation for the challenges posed by current crises and the ones that are sure to follow it.[23]

This book focuses on deepening the capacity of ethnic studies to function as a source of critique and opposition, to fulfill its potential to be a site where a counterculture of accompaniment connects campus knowledge to community concerns. It is written in hopes of contributing to the continuation and augmentation of an infrastructure of critique, care, and contestation. The book joins a dialogue already in progress by a wide range of imaginative, inventive, and generative thinkers for whom I have great respect and admiration. I am seeking to add to this conversation already in progress by focusing particularly on the contradictions of the ethnic studies project and broader antiracist social formations, as they produce incorporation as well as opposition, collaboration as well as critique. The key question it attempts to answer is not *if* more crises will occur. It assumes they will. It seeks instead to explore options for preparing the ethnic studies polity to discern, analyze, and begin to resist crises before their full force becomes immediately evident.

My hope is that this book will stage in print a "town meeting" that cannot take place in person. People who long to live in a morally just world might through this book "meet" kindred spirits and learn with them and from them. Inside what Benjamin describes as the "tradition of the oppressed," the meeting has a long and honorable history as a nexus of engagement, energy, and empowerment. Mass meetings played key roles in the Black freedom struggle of the mid-twentieth century by enacting a new vision of community called together to engage in continuous social commentary, deliberative talk, and decisive action.[24] These meetings drew on a long history dating back to the midnight meetings in clearings known as "brush arbors" among enslaved people before emancipation. Gospel and folk music preserved the meaning of these meetings through songs that called people together to pray, sing, and solve collective problems. Songs like "There's a Meeting Here Tonight," "Oh What a Meeting," and "We're Going to a Meeting" described being reunited with loved ones in heaven but also issued invitations to church and community meetings on earth. Churches billed themselves as meetinghouses. In the 1960s when the college-educated performers associated with the Free Southern Theater staged plays followed by discussions in barns, churches, and clearings in the wild as part of organizing for Black freedom in Mississippi, they found that what they called plays the sharecroppers, day laborers, and domestics in the audience called meetings.[25]

The powerful tradition of the meeting in Black culture has parallels inside and across other aggrieved and racialized communities. Chicana intersectional feminist Cherríe Moraga recalls being deeply moved by her first meeting with Black intersectional feminist Barbara Smith, an encounter that provided Moraga with an experience she wished to repeat again and again because of "the pain and shock of difference, the joy of commonness, the exhilaration of meeting through incredible odds against it."[26] Meetings are not free of contradictions. As writings by Indigenous intersectional feminist Lee Maracle demonstrate, they can be fraught with antagonisms, exclusions, and aggressions. Yet those very problems imbue meeting participants with provocations to develop advanced capacities for discernment, presence of mind, imagination, and improvisation.[27]

Art activists in East Los Angeles stage music and art meetings that call a community into being guided by the practice that they name *convivencia*. Blending the Spanish word *con*, meaning "with," and *vivir*, meaning "to live," the *convivencia*, according to *artivista* Martha Gonzalez, "is the mindfulness of presence with others" that entails "being present and engaging together in mind, body, and spirit via participatory music and art practice" and establishes its own code of ethics as part of a practice of social change.[28] Conversations among friends meeting to discuss important issues are known in New Mexico as *la resolana;* the name references the ways in which the sun's rays on the south wall of a building—shielded from the east and west winds—produce warmth that is conducive to conversation. *La resolana* functions much like the conversations known as "groundings" on the gully corners and near the rubbish dumps in Jamaica and the *lakou* meetings in Haiti and Guadeloupe.[29] From the Native American powwow to the Bon Odori dance in the Japanese Obon ceremony and in Mexican fandango and *huapango arriebeno* gatherings, meetings enable people to think of *we* as well as *me* and to forge friendly and reciprocal relations of respect and accountability. I view this book as an invitation to readers to encounter an array of people, projects, politics, and possibilities emerging from the work of artists, activists, academics, and other dreamers and doers whose work in the world today envisions and enacts the outlines of a more just world.

I know that my experiences and observations form only a small part of a larger picture, that my arguments are partial, perspectival, and interested. The ethnic studies I describe may be very different from the one that others see. Every academic, artist, and activist mentioned in this book is one voice in a larger choir. Every action for social justice is one link in a larger chain. My embodied identities as a white, cisgender, heterosexual, monolingual English-speaking settler male with citizenship status and no apparent disabilities imbue me with a particular view of the world that is doubly partial. It is partial in the sense that it is incomplete because of the limits of my experiences, education, and abilities. It is also partial in the sense that it is not neutral or disinterested; it seeks to take stands and advance ideas intended to help solve the crises of our time. I make no claim that this volume is encyclopedic or comprehensive. It does try, however, to identify and analyze some practices, processes, and problems pervasive in the field, their attendant areas of engagement and concern, and to suggest some possible decolonial options ready for use.

The relative privileges inevitably attached to my identities will likely lead me to miss some dimensions of the fatal couplings of social identities and power that are life-and-death issues for members of more aggrieved groups whose struggles, sacrifices, aspirations, and ideas have been central to the emergence of ethnic studies, its attendant fields, and the larger antiracist and social justice formation that it both reflects and shapes. There will almost certainly be mistakes of commission and omission in the choices I make in selecting and presenting evidence and arguments. But even mistakes can be generative. They can provoke others to offer suggestions for how to make more true and more useful claims. If exposing my errors advances the cause of social justice even a little bit, no one will be more grateful for those exposures than me. We profit from our disagreements as much as—or even more than—from our agreements. All writing contains elements of experiment and error that can lead to discovery of previously unasked and unanswered questions that need to be worked out collectively outside of our narrow silos. Mistakes can be corrected, but silence on matters of overwhelming political, intellectual, social, and moral significance is inexcusable.

I have been affiliated with ethnic studies academic departments, book series, journals, and campus-community collaborations for thirty-five years. I have held tenure in departments of ethnic studies and Black studies as well as in departments of sociology and American studies with strong emphases on racial formation and racial projects. I have coedited and edited ethnic studies book series, journals, and anthologies and have been a reviewer and editorial board member for a wide array of presses and journals. My work inside academic circles has been enhanced, augmented, and uplifted consistently by connections to parts of broader antiracist formations off campus. I have attempted to form my research questions and research contributions in dialogue with the needs and profound wisdom of activist groups with which I have been in accompaniment.

The future of ethnic studies cannot be prescribed by any single author. It needs to be worked out collectively through widespread, large-scale, and often contradictory and unruly conversations and communications that reflect both conflict and coalescence among differently situated people and groups. The academic ethnic studies project and the broader antiracist formation with which it is associated vary from time to time, place to place, generation to generation, group to group. They can never be captured adequately by one story told from one point of view. It is a good thing that we are not of one mind and that we see things from different standpoints and perspectives. My observations and arguments are offered in the hope of illuminating options: They are posed as suggestions, not proffered as mandates.

THE PLAN OF THIS BOOK

This book argues that participants in the ethnic studies project can help turn the imperiled present into a fulfilled future by exploring options and taking actions consistent with the following perspectives:

1. Connecting the project of academic ethnic studies to broader antiracist, inclusive, egalitarian, and democratic social formations. Treating the mission of ethnic studies as necessarily blending classroom instruction and scholarly research with the pedagogies and practices of community autonomous learning circles established by artists and activists.
2. Recognizing racism as excuse, justification, and compensation for the social misery produced by neoliberal racial capitalism, especially its distributions of vulnerability, dependency, loneliness, and lack of efficacy.
3. Understanding that declared racist intent is not needed to produce racist effects.
4. Working with the metaphors of the "caduceus" and the "crossroads" described in the Bridge section as central frames for understanding the contradictory challenges and resources of ethnic studies and advancing its emancipatory aims.
5. Treating struggle and study as mutually constitutive rather than mutually exclusive.
6. Connecting antiracism to the ways in which perceived differences of class, gender, sexuality, disability, language, and citizenship status are used to produce and justify domination.
7. Developing ethnic studies as a practice that takes place at scenes of argument and accompaniment that require conscious strategies of display and conscientious commitments to helping change the world, not just occupying an oppositional space within it.
8. Acknowledging and appreciating the successes of ethnic studies while remaining fully aware of their shortcomings and the need to do more and better work in the future.

9. Recognizing the need to combat the pervasive presence of neoliberal individualism and competition in the structures of academic recognition and reward by creating a collective counterculture of mutual respect and accompaniment.
10. Dealing with the incorporation of ethnic studies and antiracism inside institutions structured in dominance that promote complicity with the forces they purport to oppose.

Chapter 1, "Ethnic Studies as Opposition and Opposition to Ethnic Studies," explores the centrality of ethnic studies, critical race theory, and diversity, equity, and inclusion programs as foils for the mobilization of revanchist right-wing racism. I argue that the coordinated campaign against the fabricated threat of "wokeism"—a catchall slur uttered to discredit all efforts to combat injustice and even to display any empathy for others—functions as a key component of a reactionary strategy to preserve the unearned privileges of whiteness and to monopolize its access to property and power while criminalizing non-normative ideas and identities. This chapter notes the particular importance of social movement mobilization by both the opponents and proponents of critical race theory and other antiracist projects.

Chapter 2, "Ethnic Studies as Incorporation," reveals the very real benefits yet significant dangers of incorporation of ethnic studies inside institutions structured in dominance. The power of antiracist social movement activism has impelled universities, corporations, and philanthropists to issue proclamations that promise to augment outreach and inclusion efforts, to develop policies that purport to lessen inequality, and to proclaim intentions to desegregate the ranks of faculty, students, workers, customers, and grant recipients. Sometimes valuable concessions can be extracted from those in power because of these pronouncements, but most often they offer only the illusion of inclusion through policies more intent on producing peace and quiet than peace and justice. Incorporation enables some advances but inhibits others. It is especially relevant today as colleges and universities are increasingly surrendering decision-making to wealthy funders and members of their boards of directors on a wide range of issues, while meekly complying with demands by legislators, pressure groups, and the executive branch of the federal government to silence dissenting ideas inside classrooms and across campuses.

The Bridge section, "A Bridge for This Book: Ethnic Studies: The Crossroads, the Caduceus, the Archive, and the Repertoire," interrupts the narrative arc of the book to introduce the crossroads and the caduceus—the symbol of a stick with two snakes entwined around it—as key concepts for ethnic studies work. Grounded in the survival strategies and epistemological traditions of historically aggrieved groups, these two metaphors call attention to how hegemony can be turned on its head, how poison can be transformed into medicine, and how toxic conditions can contain the raw materials needed for tonic relief. Throughout the Afro-diasporic world, the metaphor of the crossroads signifies the importance of making difficult choices at confounding intersections. The crossroads is the site where paths come together, where it is possible to see and head out in more than one direction. Choices need to be made at the crossroads because collisions can occur at them and choosing the wrong path can lead to disaster. Afro-diasporic cosmologies teach that action at the crossroads requires forging a unity out of opposites. In European history, the symbol of the caduceus serves to highlight the links between poison and medicine, to stand for the ways in which entities that can kill can also cure if used in the right doses and deployed in the right ways. These concepts capture the contradictory yet dialectical nature of antiracist study and struggle. Within ethnic studies as both academic project and social formation, the epistemologies enabled by the caduceus and the crossroads offer the possibility of making a way out of what seems to be no way.

The Bridge section also delineates the importance to ethnic studies of archives—both formal repositories of credentialed knowledge and improvised informal collections that members of aggrieved groups assemble covertly to document their experiences and aspirations. Fighting to expand the archives and creating new ones forms a central mission of ethnic studies. Yet the Bridge section also shows the indispensable work performed outside (although sometimes in tandem with) the archive by repertoires of embodied memory. These repertoires create, convey, and continue lessons learned through embodied presence in collective actions.

Chapter 3, "Ethnic Studies as Accompaniment: Autonomous Learning Circles," identifies the powerful roles played by autonomous learning circles in antiracist education and action. This chapter points specifically to the pedagogical innovations created by the Alliance for California Traditional Arts in East Los Angeles, Students at the Center and Free-Dem Foundations in New Orleans, and Asian Immigrant Women Advocates in Oakland. These pedagogies contain more than novel techniques of classroom organization and instruction; they are experiments implementing grassroots theories of social change. Autonomous learning circles and other new forms of collaboration, critique, and collective mobilizations play a valuable role in reimagining how ethnic studies work is being carried out in the present and might be expanded in the future.

Chapter 4, "Ethnic Studies and Intersectional Justice," explores intersectional activism and affiliation as key mechanisms within ethnic studies for finding families of resemblance among differently situated aggrieved groups. Movements for gay liberation, disability justice, migrant dignity, reproductive healing justice, and immigrant sanctuary reject single-axis approaches to injustice and find new democratic practices and possibilities emerging from the collective intelligence of individuals and groups deemed by the dominant society to be deviant, deficient, dysfunctional, and out of place.

Chapter 5, "Ethnic Studies as Inquiry and Instruction," reveals how Enlightenment traditions of binary oppositions and reliance on what Michel-Rolph Trouillot calls the "savage slot" make oppositional scholarship appear unacceptable and often even illegible to many reviewers. The chapter explores how the traditional disciplines and their divisions of scholarly labor impede holistic interdisciplinary analysis. It concludes with descriptions and evaluations of ethnic studies work that overcomes these obstacles.

Chapter 6, "Ethnic Studies and the Current Crisis," surveys the promise and peril of ethnic studies in the context of the dire crises facing the world at this moment of extreme danger. It draws on the history of the labor movement of the 1930s and the civil rights movement of the 1960s to speculate about the viability of ethnic studies in the future.

The road to social justice is long and the way is hard. Disappointments and defeats come more often that triumphs and successes. Yet the experiences we share and the worlds we help bring into being offer a taste of freedom that makes us long for more. Racism and the many other forms of discrimination and domination associated with it are not aberrations in an otherwise fair and just society. They are the logical outcomes of ways of knowing and ways of being that value products more than people, that create avaricious and acquisitive ego-centered subjects who view other humans and what we call the natural world as objects to be conquered and manipulated, and that mobilize hate, hurt, and fear to deny the interdependence upon which collective survival depends.

Ethnic studies is one of the places where alternatives to the madness, meanness, and mendacity of contemporary society can be forged. In a world drowning in its own contradictions and trapped in a downward spiral of violence and destruction, it will not suffice to demand equal entry into the realms of the pain inflictors. Antiracism requires the cocreation of a powerful counterculture that can enact a radical revolution in values. The dominant culture suppresses and even criminalizes empathy, altruism, hospitality, and commitments to the common good that defy market logics. If meaningful change is to come about, it will come from the bottom up, from the culture, creativity, courage, and conviction of people willing and able to create a better world. Ethnic studies can be one place where creative misalignment with the affective appeals of the dominant society can generate alignment with ideals and aspirations oppositional to it, especially by replacing individual self-interest and competition with convivial collaboration and caretaking relations. *Ethnic Studies at the Crossroads* offers an assessment of that possibility by exploring the field's and the formation's roles in generating opposition, fending off incorporation, and assembling accompaniment.

Abolishing racism is not merely an idealistic goal that might make society better; it is an urgent need in a world where open acts of racial hatred and subordination increasingly serve as justifications, rationales, and excuses for many different forms of domination and exploitation. Crises confronting the economy, the environment, and the educational and electoral systems evidence the systemic breakdown of key social institutions.[30] Both housing and health care have become unaffordable and inaccessible, held hostage by highly concentrated monopolies that control their supply and terms of sale. The people and corporations that hold power cannot fix the things they have broken; they cannot correct the harms they have inflicted on the planet and its people. They need to disavow both that racism exists and that it matters while at the same time deploying racism relentlessly to mask, excuse, and justify inequality and injustice.

In these vexed, vile, and violent times, people engaged in ethnic studies face painful contradictions. Like the broader struggles for dignity, democracy, and social justice to which it is tethered, the ethnic studies project today provides reasons for both joy and despair. Because of ethnic studies and related endeavors, people increasingly realize that social identities associated with race, gender, sexuality, language, and disability are not merely private and personal embodied qualities but rather evidence of socially constructed systems that produce artificial, arbitrary, and irrational forms of subordination and suffering. When members of aggrieved groups and their allies mobilize for social justice, their victories can generate convivial joy. Yet the giddiness that comes from victory can set the stage for frustration and despair when defeats occur. The same dynamics that enable progress provoke reaction. Ethnic studies specifically and antiracism more generally now confront vehement and violent opposition. As antiracism becomes more viable, deeply rooted racisms become more visible. Mobilizations for racial justice attract adherents and win victories that in turn cause deeply rooted racisms to be reasserted and revived. Participants in ethnic studies projects and broader antiracist formations can feel themselves careening between the polarities of exuberant optimism and paralyzing despair.

As Diana Taylor argues about performance studies, the importance of ethnic studies resides less in what it *is* than in what it *allows and enables* people to do.[31] The imagination, artistry, and activism explored in this book highlight the importance of cultivating the presence of mind required to recognize the urgent need for action and developing and deploying the skills to improvise endlessly as circumstances demand. People are developmental beings, each of us a work in progress. *Ethnic Studies at the Crossroads* does not aspire to be the first word or the last word about the way to liberation, but perhaps it will be a useful middle word that can help participate in what Dr. King so aptly described as "the long and bitter—but beautiful—struggle for a new world."[32] The bitterness cannot be wished away. It is here to stay. But it can be managed and manipulated into serving as an incentive to build something that is also beautiful.

1

Ethnic Studies as Opposition and Opposition to Ethnic Studies

Performance theorist Diana Taylor poses a question with crucial import at this time. She asks, "What can we do when apparently nothing can be done, and doing nothing is not an option?"[1] This is no ordinary time for ethnic studies and for the broader antiracist social formation to which it is attached. Participants in these projects face daunting problems in a time of danger when difficult decisions need to be made.

Claude Debussy once quipped that the music created by his composer predecessor and rival Richard Wagner was a sunset masquerading as a sunrise. For Debussy, Wagner's music, rather than signaling the emergence of a new order, merely marked the final culmination of a soon-to-be-obsolete approach to composition. The power of Debussy's metaphor rests in the ambiguity of sunsets and sunrises, the ways in which these two opposite entities could appear the same in photographs or paintings. The current state of ethnic studies might be assessed similarly. Its visibility in campus and community life and its presence in political discourse and social life could be read as a sign of the triumph of its oppositional ideas and practices. At the same time, organized attacks against antiracism and what its opponents call "wokeism" might portend the destruction of ethnic studies and the broader social formation from which it emerges and which it serves. At this crossroads, it is hard to discern whether ethnic studies is experiencing a sunrise of new possibilities or encountering the sunset of its long-cherished aims and hopes.

The police killings in 2020 of Breonna Taylor in Louisville and of George Floyd in Minneapolis sparked one of the largest mass mobilizations in history. Millions of people took to the streets to protest the killings and frame their mobilizations as products of a long-overdue reckoning with the pervasive presence and power of anti-Blackness in society. A surge of antiracist proclamations emerged from the upheaval as governments, schools, professional organizations, religious congregations, and even businesses pledged new antiracist initiatives. Proclamations do not automatically produce new policies, however. In fact, they can serve as substitutes for them. Increased *visibility* for antiracism does not necessarily increase its *viability*. "Black Lives Matter" emerged as a slogan, a hashtag, and an organization. The movement mobilized in support of it recognized accurately the homicidal fervor of anti-Blackness. Black people found themselves compelled to make the simple claim that they should not be killed and that their untimely deaths were worth grieving, only to find that even those modest assertions were too much for their enemies to concede. Activists framed the killings of Taylor, Floyd, and many others as evidence of a radical conjuncture in history, a moment that encapsulated, distilled, and crystallized things they had long felt about the precarity and vulnerability of Black lives. These killings made clear the calculated cruelty, malice, and mendacity of white supremacy. The deaths were seen as injuries that portended unlivable destinies, as insults that required a collective response.

The movement provoked vehement opposition. Even its putative allies worked to channel it along lines designed to contain its critique and co-opt its oppositional impulses. Reactions to the mass outpourings of grief, rage, and demands for change largely confirmed its participants' greatest fears. A large segment of white society responded by insisting that Black lives in fact *do not* matter. They supported the exculpation of the killers, allocated funds to expand militarization of the police, and circulated vile and vulgar racist memes and messages in support of white supremacy. Reactionary responses to the demonstrations of 2020 soon coalesced with and compounded long-standing nativist hatred of immigrants, religious bigotry against Muslims, displays of toxic masculinity and misogyny, and denial of Indigenous sovereignty and treaty rights. Campaigns coordinated by right-wing think tanks and their political apparatchiks attempted to criminalize ethnic studies, critical race theory (CRT), and diversity, equity, and inclusion (DEI) initiatives.

This chapter examines the origins, evolution, significance, and stakes of the campaign to outlaw CRT as an example of how the oppositional ideas and practices of the ethnic studies project and related efforts in the broader antiracist social formation have led the defenders of the existing social order to organize a social movement aimed at the eradication from public life of the analyses, aspirations, and assertions of self-definition and self-determination by members of aggrieved social groups. I argue that countering the social movement propelling this revival of racism and other forms of demonizing difference requires ethnic studies to reckon with the necessity of connecting with existing and emerging active oppositional social movements fighting for a decent, dignified, and democratic future for all people.

CRITICAL RACE THEORY AND THE RACIAL CONTRACT

Six weeks before he died of cancer in September 2021, philosopher Charles Mills responded to an invitation by American Sociological Association (ASA) president Aldon D. Morris to speak about the coordinated campaign demonizing CRT. Speaking on a panel at the ASA annual meeting, Mills identified the attacks on CRT as manifestations of the concept of the "racial contract" that he had established and developed extensively in a generative series of writings published over the preceding quarter century.[2] In those publications, Mills argues that white supremacy is not an aberrant or anomalous departure from the principles of European humanism but the logical result of centuries of thought and action grounded in the premise that European humanism requires seeing only white Europeans as fully human, while consigning people perceived to be nonwhite to the status of subpersons judged to be not yet fit for freedom.

Mills asserted in his presentation at the 2021 ASA panel that the campaign against CRT—with its claims of white injury and white innocence coupled with insistence on white immunity from accountability for racial subordination—was not a dangerous new development. It evidenced according to Mills only the latest manifestation of patterns of thought and action at the heart of social structures and systems that have long produced white supremacist *effects* without having to declare white supremacist *intent*. The campaign against CRT purported to be a reaction against new lessons taught and new kinds of books assigned in classrooms. In reality, however, it replicated and continued the long-standing social pedagogy of a centuries-old whiteness protection program. It sought to turn back the clock and restore racist rule while serving as a stalking horse for even more draconian efforts to expunge access to the ideas, experiences, aspirations, and analyses of people who are not white from classrooms specifically and from US society more broadly. Mills noted that it portended disastrous pedagogical and epistemological consequences for all students, because banning CRT substitutes indoctrination for education, kills curiosity, and leaves those it miseducates completely unprepared for living in the multiracial, multilingual, and multinational world they inhabit, one that is augmented rather than diminished by recognition of socially constructed differences.

Roderick Ferguson shows how defenders of racial segregation have long justified discrimination as moral protection of children against social and biological taboos. In turn, racial segregation has served as a central mechanism for preserving dominant gender and sexual norms, for protecting the properly gendered and property-owning patriarchal white family from loss of privileges and preferences. The transgression of social norms attached to changes in the racial order takes on augmented affective power by being represented as an unnatural and deviant physical, biological, and health transgression. The massive and successful resistance to desegregating schools in both the North and the South in response to the Supreme Court's *Brown v. Board of Education* decision never openly admitted its aim to preserve white people's preferential access to educational resources and opportunities. Instead, it put forth a discourse of child protection, of saving presumably "innocent" white children from having to sit next to Black classmates (children portrayed as dirty, diseased, and sexually licentious) and from having to endure the newly discovered horrors of having to ride a bus, though only when that bus was headed toward an integrated school.[3]

The preferences and privileges of the propertied, properly gendered, heteronormative, white, nuclear family are passed down across generations through economic and social inheritance. What Sara Ahmed calls "defense against an imagined loss of future line" motivates white parents to insist that the children who will inherit their money and property and carry on their name will remain faithful to the disavowal of the racial privilege that their parents work furiously to preserve and protect. Ahmed cites Elizabeth Spelman's observation that whiteness is an "investment" not only in the sense of investing as a practice that generates expected profitable returns but also in the sense of putting on a vest, a protective outer layer covering the body, fending off cold and providing reassuring warmth.[4]

Three years after Mills delivered his remarks to the ASA meeting, Donald Trump won reelection as president of the United States. Exit polls and other early assessments indicated that Trump secured approximately the same number of votes in victory as he did in defeat in 2020. The Democratic nominee, Kamala Harris, and candidates running for election to Congress on her ticket suffered a massive vote decline compared to 2020, when they benefited from the activist energy emanating from the Movement for Black Lives and the huge constituency it attracted. There is never only a single reason why one candidate triumphs over another, but it would be an egregious error to ignore the importance of racism as a key factor in the Republican victory. The Republicans responded to the mass demonstrations in support of the Movement for Black Lives in 2020 by organizing their constituents into active mobilizations against affirmative action, school desegregation, what was termed "wokeism" (an umbrella term venting resentment against all efforts to identify and rectify injustice), CRT, and DEI programs. Legislators at the municipal and state levels introduced nearly seven hundred bills that called for banning educational content and classroom discussions related to race and racism as well as to sexual orientation and gender identity.[5]

The polity activated and energized by these campaigns helps explain why an estimated 80 percent of 2024 Trump voters were white and why the first actions of the new administration in 2025 included revoking the executive branch's ban on race and gender discrimination, placing openly admitted white supremacists in powerful positions, offering white South African immigrants preferential access to citizenship, issuing an order that made the air force stop showing a film about the heroism of the Black Tuskegee airmen during World War II, and cutting off federal funds to all institutions that proclaimed diversity, equity, and inclusion as worthwhile goals.

While the Republicans mobilized white resentment and revanchist racism, the Democrats worked relentlessly to demobilize the masses who had flocked into the streets in 2020. They responded to proposals to shift funds away from policing and toward social services by doing the opposite—endorsing expanded expenditures for even more militarized police forces. The Black woman at the top of the Democratic ticket stayed silent on issues of race and gender justice but proudly touted her record as a prosecutor while boasting about the Biden administration's closing of the border to asylum seekers. She proclaimed herself a capitalist who owned a gun and stood ready to use it. The Democrats offered little to their supporters from aggrieved racialized groups except the promise of a government mounting a slightly less inhumane form of inhumanity than its electoral opponents. They may have been surprised by increased support for Trump by voters of color. They failed to see how the Democrats' decades of uncritical support for wars overseas, predatory policing, mass incarceration, and brutal and cruel border enforcement directed Latinx, Asian American, and Black job seekers into the military, the police, prison guarding, and border patrolling. These jobs gave them material stakes in the punitive practices that Trump proposed to augment, practices that built on a bipartisan public pedagogy promising security through sadistic punishment of demonized others. Moreover, the Democrats failed to see that neglecting enforcement of minimum-wage laws and statutes that protected safety conditions and limited work hours made new immigrants a force whose desperation for work could be exploited by employers to lower wages and worsen working conditions.[6]

While the Republicans created an active and engaged online and participatory public sphere with endless opportunities for action, the Democrats told their followers to wait for the results of special prosecutors' investigations, for court decisions that might go their way, and for the next time they would be asked to make donations to and cast votes for the elected officials and candidates who had told them to say silent. Failure to build on the mobilizations of 2020 lowered voter turnout in racialized communities and accounted for part of the massive decline in votes for the Democrats compared to 2020. The activism of the Republicans and the passivity of the Democrats bore out the observation that Julian Bond had offered years ago: While Republicans are *shameless* in exploiting racist sentiments, Democrats are *spineless* in confronting them.[7] By remaining silent, the Democrats ceded discussions of race in the public sphere to fear-mongering appeals to white entitlement. By failing to mobilize opportunities for participatory democracy, the Democrats allowed the Republicans to act unimpeded in mobilizing a constituency for participatory plutocracy grounded in white entitlement.

Trump's victorious campaign relied on racist demonization of immigrants, touted opposition to fair housing laws, and pledged to ban race relations training, CRT, and DEI programs. It sought to portray perceived impingements against the privileges of the white patriarchal nuclear family as biological transgressions against nature, cleanliness, and normativity by attacking trans youths and their parents and doctors, by portraying public school teachers and librarians as pedophiles grooming new victims, and by describing hardworking Latinx and Black immigrants both as lazy and passive parasites on welfare and as vicious and active savages committing rapes and robberies. Stories about immigrants capturing and eating white people's pet animals were featured in the campaign even though the people capitalizing on these stories admitted that the whole scenario was made up. Ambitious politicians like Florida governor Ron DeSantis and Texas governor Greg Abbott attempted to out-Trump Trump by staging cruel stunts against immigrants and encouraging their followers to excise antiracism from the public sphere by banning books, firing teachers and librarians, censoring class lessons that revealed the true history and current presence of racism, and making it criminal under state law to teach that systemic racism exists or has ever existed in the United States.

In keeping with the long and ignoble history of self-serving colorblind pretensions as protective cover for unjust color-bound conditions, the campaign to ban CRT in education claims that it is legitimate to ban recognition of racism but illegitimate to expose racist rule. It maintains that the mere mention of race is racist. It pretends that critiques of racism are personal attacks on white people. It enforces what Mills calls the "epistemology of ignorance" by claiming that facts should not be taught in schools if they have the potential to make white students uneasy about the privileges hoarded by their parents because of the existence of whiteness as a social force and structured advantage. The campaign rules inadmissible in advance any testimony that might reveal the true nature of systemic and institutionalized racism.

Yet in their attempts to hide whiteness, the opponents of CRT only make it more visible. Passing laws to protect the imagined hurt feelings of white students identifies them as members of a group rather than as individuals. Banning recognition of whiteness does not include banning recognition of other races when that recognition generates an endless stream of phobic fantasies rooted in representations of people of color as monstrous. Making whiteness synonymous with humanness relies on what Mills calls a "contrapuntal ensemble"—an interplay of opposites that contrasts allegedly innocent and virtuous whiteness with savage, uncivilized, and uncontrollable subpersons who are not white. This establishes the position of white people as the primary and necessary defenders of civilization. In an inversion familiar to Indigenous people around the world, this discourse portrays vicious aggression as frontier defense.

These practices can create expansive understandings of time. As Mills argues in his article "White Time," the racial contract compels those under its jurisdiction to inhabit the temporality of white history in which the peoples of Asia, Africa, and Latin America are presumed to have had no meaningful past before Europeans conquered them, to be lagging behind in development, and consequently to be rationally and ontologically deficient and in need of modernization. When evidence emerges that shows nonwhite people to not be free, the racial contract instructs its beneficiaries to say with condescension that their victims are simply not *yet* free but should appreciate all that the dominant culture is doing to move them gradually toward freedom in the future.[8] Mills notes with approval Michael Hanchard's claim that affirmations of Black humanity have frequently staked claims to oppositional temporalities and chronologies: to a history in which deceased ancestors are still present and owed respect, to calculations about the tempos of work and leisure not tied to the labor demands of industry, and to imperatives for creating time-specific improvisations that disrupt power relations in the present rather than merely accepting promises of better days in the future.[9]

Mills explains that the affect generated by the racial contract precludes empathy for nonwhite suffering, yet it cultivates self-pitying hypersensitivity to the point of outrage over policies such as affirmative action or DEI initiatives designed to diminish the overrepresentation of white interests in society and to narrow the differential advantage that whites enjoy at the expense of other groups.[10] These campaigners seem to have not noticed how feeble and ineffectual racial liberalism has been. Affirmative action initiatives do more affirming than acting, while DEI proclamations appear largely through unfilled promises to remedy the pervasive and uncontested presence of homogeneity, inequity, and exclusion. By making people accustomed to treating aggrieved racialized groups as if they are subhuman, the racial contract prepares its adherents to wage war against a wide array of designated others: immigrants, Muslims, women, the disabled, and people who are queer and trans. These hatreds take material form in campaigns to ban books about gender nonconformity from libraries and classrooms, to attack and incarcerate immigrants who are not white, and to criminalize forms of marriage and medical care needed by members of those groups.

The people who formulated and funded the public frenzy about CRT freely admit they neither know nor care what it actually is.[11] One of its most visible publicists confessed, "The goal is to have the public read something crazy in the newspaper and immediately think 'critical race theory.' We have decodified the term and will recodify it to annex the entire range of cultural constructions that are unpopular with Americans."[12] CRT thus functions as a floating signifier, as a term that can be used to tap anxieties about whiteness and sexual normativity. The fervent opposition to CRT followed a well-worn historical path prefigured by massive resistance to integration in the 1950s, to busing for school desegregation in the 1960s and 1970s, to affirmative action in the 1980s and 1990s, to voluntary school desegregation policies in the 2000s, and to the Voting Rights Act in the 2010s.

Once affirmative action was invalidated by the Supreme Court and CRT lost its luster as privileged villain, it quickly became supplanted by opposition to DEI programs. Beneath the surface, this succession of moral panics about an imaginary "reverse racism" entails opposition to the project of ethnic studies and indeed to any visible manifestation of larger antiracist social formations. It is not that nothing ever changes in history, but that when it comes to racism the changes are often more cosmetic than substantive. W. E. B. Du Bois compared white supremacy in the US to a crack in a plate that was once broken but had been patched up. Whenever the plate was dropped again, it broke along the lines of the patched-up crack because the weakness was structural, not surface.

The collective assertion of Black subjectivity and its concomitant affirmation of Black humanity in the mass demonstrations and mobilizations in 2020 struck many white people as an unforgivable offense, a repudiation of the racial contract.[13] The only racial injury that the opponents of CRT are willing to recognize is the prospect that antiracism will make white people feel uncomfortable, as if white feelings alone are to be protected.[14] Thus, the opponents of CRT seek to establish as a matter of law that white vanity is to be more respected than nonwhite humanity.

The arguments against CRT in the United States advanced by the apparatchiks of conservative think tanks and their allies in politics helped construct a social movement grounded in what can most charitably be described as a series of distortions but are in fact intentional lies. The campaign promoted moral panics through allegations that CRT is a form of indoctrination that defames innocent white people as perpetually guilty of personal racism simply because of their biological makeup. These charges misrepresent the actual arguments made within CRT, which hold (1) that race is a social and legal construction, not an immutable embodied property of individuals; (2) that whiteness is a socially performed, historically constructed, and legally administered systemic structural advantage perpetuated not primarily by individuals but by deeply ingrained practices and powerful institutions; and (3) that *whiteness* is not the same as *white* people, that while all white people benefit from the racial contract, not all have been, or wish to be, signatories to it.[15] As Gloria Anzaldúa observes, "Some members of a racial or ethnic group do not necessarily stay with the consciousness and conditioning of the group they're born into, but shift momentarily or permanently. For example, some whites embody a woman-of-color consciousness, and some people of color, a 'white' consciousness."[16] CRT assumes that people do not choose their parents or their pigments. Rather, it encourages people to make better choices about their politics and their principles.

The critics of CRT display projection when they map onto CRT the racist impulses and beliefs central to their own identities. They allege, counterfactually, that CRT claims that each member of a group is responsible for wrongdoing by any member of that group and that recognizing difference requires domination by one group over others. The campaign against CRT has led to laws, educational policies, and proposals to make it illegal for students to learn that Indigenous dispossession, coloniality, slavery, and segregation ever existed—or amounted to anything other than aberrations from an imagined race-free history. A proposed bill in Kentucky mandated withholding $5,000 per day from school districts if teachers were found to be using materials that *any* group of parents or the state's attorney general found objectionable.[17] The state of Florida imposed a curriculum of indoctrination on its teachers that mandated describing slavery as a benign institution providing marketable skills to enslaved people that could prove useful in the event that they eventually achieved a freedom their oppressors never intended to give them. The perpetrators of this white supremacist curriculum do not make the case for it on the basis of historical facts or reasoned arguments but instead use the power of the state to make sure the argument does not even take place. They do not refute or even respond to the CRT analysis that neighborhoods, schools, and jobs remain unjustly racially segregated; that vote dilution, voter suppression, and gerrymandering artificially augment the political power of white people; and that civil rights laws offer completely inadequate remedies for the harms perpetuated by environmental, medical, and transit racism, as well as by the racist violence of police officers and vigilantes.[18] Instead, they dictate as a matter of law that the present racial order must be viewed as an unquestionably just baseline norm not to be disturbed. US society is portrayed as innocent of any racial injustice, and the campaign deems that saying otherwise is a criminal act. The opponents of CRT deploy state power to ban a conclusion based on evidence—that racism is systemic and structural rather than aberrant and incidental. They do so not because the conclusion is untrue but because its veracity makes them uncomfortable and because they worry that it threatens to make white children disloyal to the racial projects that many of their parents support and from which they profit.[19]

The attacks on CRT are factually flawed and internally inconsistent. They make no sense as intellectual critique. Yet they contain great utility as a social movement strategy because they recognize the hold that fidelity to the racial contract has on individuals and institutions. Making CRT and other studies of social identities illegal in schools is less a utilitarian project than an expressive one. It establishes that the privileges of whiteness mean never having to take antiracist arguments seriously. Exposing the lies and fabrications of the campaign will not discredit it, because it is at heart an exhibitionist exercise in white impunity. Flaunting lies and evading accountability for implausible arguments produces its particular pleasures and accounts for its appeal. Like the claim that the 2020 presidential election was stolen from the true winner, the attacks on CRT actually *need* to treat lies as truths, because it is precisely getting away with lies and relishing the power to make others knuckle under to them that provides the movement with its deeply sadistic yet affectively satisfying allure. The campaign against CRT reaffirms the existence of the racial contract as an open secret, as a widely denied yet near universally applied social practice. Under these conditions, the racial contract is more than an epistemological position; it fulfills for the racial contract the kind of performative function that Rita Segato finds in the impunity offered to killers who get away with murdering Indigenous and poor and working-class women in Mexico. She says that these unprosecuted killings function to create and sustain "a deep symbolic structure" that teaches perpetrators to revel in their impunity.[20] Moreover, like the repeated attacks on school desegregation, affirmative action, and efforts to enforce fair housing laws, the attacks on CRT, while purporting merely to correct the unwarranted excess zeal of civil rights advocates, in actuality aim at the full repudiation and repeal of all of the modest concessions made to the targets of racism by the legal and political reforms of the 1960s and 1970s. They seek not only to end the laws and policies that might diminish the overrepresentation they have come to expect as a natural reward for whiteness but also to enact revenge against the people whose struggles produced those reforms in the first place. Even an unfunded and almost always unimplemented promise to pursue DEI is more than the defenders of white privilege can bear.

In order to sustain the concocted fictions of the campaign against CRT, the "conservatives" attacking it violate nearly all the principles they have purported to believe in for the past half century. Conservatives have attributed their opposition to school desegregation to a principled belief in local control of schools. They have portrayed their rejection of laws protecting labor, the environment, and civil rights as expressions of a faith in small government and a manifestation of their belief that only firm family values can instill in people the capacity to solve problems by themselves. They have belittled as whiners and professional victims people who point out that their membership in an aggrieved group deprives them of access to jobs, business contracts, and political representation, advising them to treat any collective consciousness or remedies as a group spoils system and instead to persevere as individuals. They have claimed that they do not "see color" and would be color-blind were it not for civil rights laws that force them to notice race.

In the campaign against CRT, however, the self-proclaimed proponents of local control of schools use their dominance over state governments (gained through gerrymandered nonwhite vote dilution and voter suppression as well as artificially augmented white overrepresentation) to prevent local teachers, parents, administrators, and school boards from making decisions about curriculum and instruction materials. The purported opponents of big government turn immediately to the state to declare *illegal* ideas that they *cannot refute*. They enact laws that mandate thought control, that ban teachers and textbooks from using certain words and phrases such as *diversity, cultural competence,* and *implicit bias*. The president they support issues executive orders that compel schools to pretend that racism does not exist. In testimony before the education committees of the Wisconsin legislature, one of the coauthors of the bill to ban CRT proposed to make it illegal for teachers to utter any one of a list of ninety words and concepts, a list that included *antiracism, anti-Blackness, conscious bias, unconscious bias, critical self-awareness, cultural relevance, educational justice, equity, intersectionality, multiculturalism, racial justice, structural racism,* and *whiteness*.[21] People who have argued incessantly that property rights are sacred now seek to prevent privately owned businesses from choosing to provide diversity training for their workforce. Conservatives who have long condemned the idea that group identities exist and who have extolled the importance of individual accountability now use the power of the state to protect the settled expectations and interests of whites as a group, to absolve white perpetrators of racist acts by not allowing their deeds to be mentioned, and to imagine that all white students are incapable of critiquing evil acts performed by people of their phenotype and color. If the opponents of CRT really wanted people to be treated as individuals and not as part of groups, they would oppose racial profiling by police forces and by immigration and customs enforcement thugs, fight against insurance and mortgage redlining, ban home appraisal discrimination, and act against the many other forms of systemic institutionalized racism that CRT and ethnic studies have identified.

Claims that bans on CRT protect defenseless children fall apart when the actual bans deny library patrons of all ages access to books by Toni Morrison, Ta-Nehisi Coates, and Maya Angelou; when the secretary of defense orders the Naval Academy to remove nearly four hundred books from its shelves, including writings by Martin Luther King, while retaining for circulation Hitler's *Mein Kampf;* when a biography of Roberto Clemente is pulled from the shelves of Florida school libraries because it describes accurately the racism he experienced in the 1950s as a Black Puerto Rican in the legally segregated South and the de facto segregated North. Proclamations about the importance of family values and parental authority become exposed as hypocritical pretexts when legislators deny children from aggrieved racialized groups books about racism that their parents would like them to read, and when legislators pass laws and issue administrative rulings that define as child abuse efforts by loving parents to provide gender-affirming medical care for their transgender children. Claims of color blindness disappear when the opponents of CRT assume that the color-blind children of color-blind parents will be made uncomfortable by learning about the history of slavery, segregation, lynching, and repression of the Black freedom movement, assuming that these children will automatically identify with the oppressors whose skin color resembles their own rather than with the content of the character of the freedom fighters, even though some of those—like John Brown, Anne and Carl Braden, Bob Zellner, Joan Trumpauer, and Gail Cincotta—were white.

The campaign against CRT thus makes clear that conservatives never believed any of the arguments they have been making for decades, that their "principles" were mere pretexts to foment racist resentments and defend the unfair gains and unjust enrichments that white people derive from the racial contract. Those of us who have made structural racism a focal point in our research and teaching assumed that our opponents would attempt to counter our arguments with a defense of the existing racial order and objections to our portrayal of it. We did not expect that they would simply cede the argument to us but make our descriptions, analyses, and interpretations illegal. The campaign against CRT does not tell scholars, teachers, students, and parents concerned about the depths, dimensions, and duration of structural racism that they are wrong; it simply uses the power of the state to make them shut up in hopes of making them go away.

The demonization of CRT—and by extension ethnic studies and other elements of the antiracist formation—relies on *countersubversion* as its affective and strategic heart. Michael Rogin's account of the long history in US politics and culture of demonized representations of alleged pagan Natives, Catholic and Jewish conspirators, Mexican bandits, Black rapists, and sexual perverts helps explain today's attacks on Black history, queer and trans individuals, and immigrants. Rogin explains, "The countersubversive needs monsters to give shape to his anxieties and to permit him to indulge his forbidden desires. Demonization allows the countersubversive, in the name of battling the subversive, to imitate his enemy."[22] Mills argues that the beneficiaries and supporters of whiteness are recruited perpetually to repress nonwhite resistance, to "employ massively disproportionate retaliatory violence" against it.[23] The attack on CRT deploys what Mills identifies as the racial contract's core strategies of insisting on a "sanitized, whitewashed, and amnesiac account of European imperialism and settlement,"[24] masking its aggressions against people of color as defending civilization from the alleged subversion posed by demonized "others" imagined to be subhuman.[25] This sanitized version of the past not only is inaccurate but also conveys the impression that the only way to understand the past is via what Eduardo Galeano calls "power's self-sacralization."[26]

Some of the attacks on CRT argue that antiracism is no longer needed because the *Brown v. Board of Education* ruling by the Supreme Court and the 1964 Civil Rights Act ended de jure segregation. Celebrating this version of history hides how massive white resistance neutralized the *Brown* decision and all subsequent civil rights laws.[27] It is important to remember that Derrick Bell first formulated CRT's stance on the impregnability of white supremacy precisely out of his experiences litigating cases covered by *Brown v. Board of Education* and witnessing how its implementation was thwarted by those determined to keep segregation intact.[28]

Countersubversion plays a necessary role in the racial contract because, as Mills argues in a wonderfully insightful passage, white supremacy lives in dread of "the cognizers whose mere presence in the halls of white theory is a cognitive threat, because—in the inverted systemic logic of the racial polity—the 'ideal speech situation' requires our absence, since we are, literally, the men and women *who know too much*, who—in that wonderful American expression—*know where the bodies are buried* (after all, so many of them are our own)."[29] The concept of the racial contract helps explain why censoring schoolbooks and classroom lessons is an imperative for the defenders of whiteness. It reaffirms their group's favored racial position, yet enables them to deny that they even notice race. The production, validation, and dissemination of false knowledge all support the social practice of white supremacy just as the mechanics of oppression distort and undermine cognition. The toxic blend of racial contract theory and racial subordination produces an epistemology that renders people incapable of understanding the world in which they live, an incapacity that is on full display in the campaign against CRT. As W. E. B. Du Bois argued about the postbellum South in the 1870s, racism is a form of *intellectual enfeeblement* that foments "an intolerance fatal to human culture" and recruits people who "listen to only one side of the question," who are childish and furious when criticized, and who interpret all disagreements as personal attacks.[30]

THE ROLE OF RACISM IN THE CURRENT CRISIS

The presidential elections of 2016 and 2024 and the emergence of right-wing mobilizations against CRT, DEI, ethnic studies, and the totality of the antiracist social formations are not evidence of the strength of racial capitalism but instead symptoms of its deep and insolvable crises. Racist fervor is needed to mask—but also to prop up—unjust distributions of wealth and opportunity, to preserve a property system increasingly reliant on dispossession and debt, to obscure industrial and consumer practices that destroy the environment, and to hide that political systems are now powerless to stop the depredations of avaricious multinational corporations and financial institutions. As Barbara Tomlinson and I argued more than a decade ago, neoliberal economics, politics, and culture have ushered in the chaotic breakdown and systematic disintegration of an entire way of life. It is no longer a question of *whether* radical changes will occur but rather of *which* changes will be made and whose interests they serve.[31]

The revanchist racism of the right builds on and exacerbates the culture that neoliberalism creates, a cruelly competitive ethos filled with envy, avarice, rancor, and resentment. Toxic masculinity, misogyny, homophobia, transphobia, and religious and racial bigotry have long histories, but they have been regenerated and reinforced in cultures shaped by decades of war without end, militarized policing, and incarceration designed for punishment rather than public safety or rehabilitation. High-paying secure jobs with health and retirement benefits have been replaced by part-time casual employment with no security that pays wages too low to secure health care or housing. As privatization and public-private partnerships eliminate jobs for public workers in education, transportation, sanitation, and health care, employment opportunities abound in the border patrol, police forces, and the military, all of which offer fertile ground for recruits for militias and armed vigilante groups. New technologies that could ease the burdens of labor and create new connections among physically dispersed peoples become mechanisms for cyber-fraud, cyberstalking, identity theft, doxing, and public vituperation. Recreational hate against people designated as other helps fill the emptiness of lives marked by addiction to alcohol, gambling, opiates, and pornography. Celebratory collection and display of guns and violent fantasies about using them to eliminate perceived enemies rehearse in advance the apocalyptic violence that racists predict and pursue.

The rise of revanchist racism in the twenty-first century has eerie and frightening resemblances to what philosopher Ernst Bloch witnessed with the rise of Nazism in Hitler's Germany. He saw the nation succumb to fascism by channeling the discontent of owners of small businesses and marginally situated workers against perceived racialized others. Bloch described people "fond of the fist clenched in the pocket" ready to "lash out in the direction of least resistance," always against an innocent victim.[32] Fascism aroused hope within people who were not against exploitation per se but merely resented not being among the ranks of the exploiters. It stoked desires to maim and kill through "cruel wishful images" with dreams of the "gallows at the end" and through imperialist wars that staged a "frenzy of destruction now raining down on others" to divert attention away from the frustrations and blasted hopes of bourgeois existence.[33] Incidents of bloodshed in wars, police killings, and mass shootings are not regrettable departures from normal life for fascists but rather sources of titillation and excitement that justify even more brutality. As artist Claudia Bernardi explains about the Dirty War waged by Argentina's military in the 1970s and 1980s, "What they wanted was not to kill so many thousand people.... It was to create an atmosphere to last into the future, an atmosphere of bleak individuality, of hopelessness, ugliness, even a lack of remembering what integrity is about. And they almost succeeded."[34] One method pursued to produce those ends by the dictatorship in Argentina looms large in the tactics of the Trump administration—enforcing repression in an arbitrary manner, punishing people never accused or even suspected of crimes—in order to paralyze the population with fear and create what Eduardo Galeano terms "a society of sleepwalkers."[35]

Bloch viewed fascism in 1930s Germany as inordinately fixated on bodies, on the disciplined ascetic body of the ideal Nazi contrasted with the despised non-normative body of the racialized other.[36] The attacks on disabled people, people who are trans, individuals with autism, and those who give birth to nonwhite children conform to this obsession with bodily normativity, some of it promulgated by members of Congress whose websites feature their fitness videos. Yet these self-presentations of strength only reveal weakness. In Hitler's Germany, according to Bloch, participation in mass movements and violent actions against dehumanized enemies compensated participants for their "factual powerlessness and degradation."[37] Fascist fervor fomented what Bloch calls "an orgiastic hatred of reason" because it possessed the potential to diminish the processes of vengeful violence.[38]

The hatred of reason endemic to fascism helps explain the fervor directed against K-12 classes, curricula, and instructors. As Alvin Gouldner observes, schooling produces a public sphere that can lessen the power, prejudices, and authority of the patriarchal family. Education can encourage critical thinking, lifelong learning, and creative problem-solving. When it is successful, education enables students to recognize unstated assumptions, to master abstract thinking, and to resist dogmatism, ethnocentricity, and authoritarianism.[39] Education about threats to the environment, infectious diseases, or the cumulative and continuing costs of white supremacy makes clear the limits of individual action and the need for interconnected people to build social unity and solidarity. The insistence by the opponents of CRT on an uncritical, exculpatory, and celebratory version of national history makes up part of a larger worldview that refuses all accountability and responsibility. As Jennifer Sandlin and Alan Gomez explain, American exceptionalism "provides an excuse not to sign international agreements or be held accountable for patterns of war crimes, to not respect other countries and cultures as international tourists, to blithely make and break treaties with Indigenous Peoples, to be anti-intellectual, or to find it unthinkable to not consume a disproportionate percentage of the earth's resources in relation to per capita population."[40]

Ethnic studies classrooms provide a public platform for exposing and critiquing the assumptions and presumptions that the opponents of CRT hold dear. In recent years especially, ethnic studies topics and methods have started to secure footholds in K-12 curricula and classrooms. Grassroots mobilizations such as the Ethnic Studies Now coalition have persuaded school districts and state boards of education to launch initiatives that make ethnic studies courses requirements for high school and college graduation. As Christine Sleeter and Miguel Zavala observe, these campaigns go beyond producing a constellation of educational offerings by connecting classroom instruction to community knowledge. Fights for culturally sensitive, relevant, and accurate classes and curricula inside schools inevitably lead to mining the rich resources of knowledge and mechanisms of creative problem-solving embedded in the survival strategies of aggrieved racialized groups.[41]

Although making ethnic studies a required course can lead to watering down antiracism rather than building it up—a dynamic that will be discussed in chapter 2—the work performed by dedicated instructors has made major contributions to schooling by expanding classroom objects of study as well as changing the relations of study in K-12 education. Scholars in schools of education have formed collectives to work closely with K-12 teachers, parents, and students for social justice in education.[42] The journal *Ethnic Studies Pedagogies* emerged in 2023 as a forum for educators to explore how studies of race and ethnicity are superbly positioned for forms of classroom instruction that are interactive, student centered, socially accountable, and well suited for encouraging participants to be active thinkers rather than passive receivers of sanitized and whitewashed curricula.[43]

While the book banners, censors, and suppressors of knowledge about racism claim to be protecting white children from feeling uncomfortable in the classroom, they mandate Eurocentric renditions of history and society that devalue the experiences and knowledges of children from aggrieved groups and that blame and shame them and their parents for not being included in the rewards of whiteness. Michael Yellow Bird (Mandan, Hidatsa, and Arikara) recalls the injuries inflicted on him as an Indigenous youth being force-fed a Eurocentric education. He recalls, "We learned that we did not know anything of value, nor did we have anything important to contribute from our culture unless it supported the myths of white supremacy. In junior high school we continued to learn we were primitive, superstitious people who should be thankful that God was on the side of the white people who came to the 'new world' to settle and help us have a better life."[44] Chicano painter José Delgado Zúñiga describes the training he received while pursuing a college degree in fine arts as a sustained "indoctrination in self hate."[45] Schooling routinely provides Black children with what novelist James Baldwin remembers as the great shock of realizing at the age of five or six or seven that the flag you pledge allegiance to has not pledged its allegiance to you.[46]

The culturally sensitive education that ethnic studies provides counters this kind of curriculum and pedagogy by respecting and building on the knowledge, experiences, and analyses of aggrieved groups. In some places it enables Indigenous students to learn tribal languages and master non-Western knowledge systems instead of sitting through instruction that treats the mass murders, displacements, and dispossessions of their people as triumphs for progress. Children from all groups designated by the school system as "disadvantaged" can learn how their kinfolk and skin folk have been and continue to be taken advantage of by systemic racism, but they can also be connected to powerful survival strategies that arm them with intellectual and psychic advantages of broad utility for all people dominated by neoliberal racial capitalism.

Children of all races are harmed by having facts about their worlds hidden from them. All students are helped, moreover, by the pedagogical innovations advanced inside ethnic studies K-12 classes. Building on concepts articulated by Paolo Freire, bell hooks, and others, these classes are in the vanguard in offering practice-based, participatory, student-centered lessons that treat students as discovers of knowledge and formulators of interpretations they craft for themselves rather than as passive recipients of conclusions crafted by others and required to be learned by rote from textbooks. They engage in exercises and projects that build their skills as researchers, documentarians, and analysts. These give them abilities and dispositions they can use inside classrooms and beyond them. They nurture, hone, and refine students' skills for identifying problems, collecting evidence, conducting interviews, mapping community assets, and presenting their findings in written reports, collectively authored books, art exhibitions, and public oral presentations.[47]

Interactive, practice-based, student-centered discovery education exists inside K-12 and college education in endeavors other than ethnic studies but holds a special place in that discipline. The field has become a prime laboratory for developing, implementing, and improving this approach to learning. Instructors in all subjects can benefit from these pedagogical innovations. This way of learning improves students' attendance and engagement in school, makes classrooms sites of convivial cocreation, and connects young people to the communities from which they come and to which they return every day. It also improves basic skills. Peer-reviewed studies by education researchers find that students in ethnic studies classes improve their grade point averages and test scores, become more likely to graduate and attend college, and make greater improvements on standardized tests than students not exposed to ethnic studies.[48] Test results that make students from aggrieved groups appear deficient receive great attention and dissemination. The consistent body of evidence that shows how ethnic studies improves school performance is routinely ignored and dismissed.

Like CRT, K-12 ethnic studies innovations make convenient foils for revanchist racism, not because they are unfounded, unreasonable, or unkind to white people, but because their successes have undermined the ways of thinking and ways of knowing upon which unjust social relations rest. The campaign against CRT is intellectually insupportable and pedagogically disastrous, but it makes perfect sense as an efficient and effective way of mobilizing a social movement in support of the racial contract. It promises psychic compensation and material reparations for the damages done to individuals and society by neoliberal racial capitalism. When it fails to deliver on these promises—as it always does—it demands even more draconian measures in support of its social vision. Countersubversion against imagined enemies protects the dominant racial order without having to justify it. It diverts attention away from the ever-increasing share of wealth monopolized by people who are rich, encourages whites who fear falling economically (or simply not rising to the wealth level of their expectations and desires) to take out their frustrations and fears on demonized racial others. It gives its adherents what seems like purposeful work to do, and it offers a sense of social connection for people wounded daily by competitive individualism and the isolation it produces. It provides the affective pleasures of vicariously wielding symbolic power to people who increasingly recognize correctly that they are otherwise powerless to influence the decisions that shape their lives.

Decades of policies that have systematically channeled riches and resources to the wealthiest portion of the population, that reconfigure public spaces to cater to the whims of rich investors and high-end consumers, that shred the social safety net, and that raise the costs of health care, housing, transportation, and education leave vast numbers of people feeling vulnerable. Judith Butler argues that the attacks on the World Trade Center and the Pentagon on September 11, 2001, produced an intensified sense of vulnerability that many US residents found intolerable. In response, they embraced a violent and self-centered subject position that "seeks to reconstitute its imagined wholeness, but only at the price of denying its own vulnerability, its dependency, its exposure, where it exploits those very features in others, thereby making those features 'other' to itself."[49] Psychologist Lynne Layton contends that fomenting and mobilizing hatred against despised and demonized others provides victims of these policies with targets for their resentments and symbolic enactments of the power they fear they have lost forever.[50] Perceiving themselves as having been hurt, they seek to hurt others. The hatred they express and their threats of violence—and sometimes the actual violence they perpetrate—do not function merely as *means* to an end but serve as *ends* in themselves. They are mechanisms for forging orgies of bonding around the affective pleasures of cruelty and contempt. Fear of vulnerability and frantic desires to impose it onto others have long been seeds of fascism. They permeate much of popular culture and political discourse today. As C. L. R. James observed about the 1930s in a comment that anticipates the rise of Donald Trump or someone like him, "Impotent rage, anger, and frustration which can find expression only in a popular art of blood, destruction, torture, sadism; and an outlet for cheated, defrauded personality in vicarious living through a few striking personalities, these are the basic results in the only field where the masses are not free but at least have some choice in deciding."[51] Campaigns against CRT specifically and ethnic studies more generally are self-perpetuating entities. They seek to relieve themselves of accountability for unjust racist hierarchies by making it illegal to mention them. Yet, as activists in Haiti say, breaking the thermometer will not cure the fever. Attempting to silence antiracist formations does nothing to diminish the powerful forces that create them.

WHY SOCIAL MOVEMENTS MATTER

Although the revanchist racists deliberately distort nearly everything about the premises, principles, and practices of CRT and ethnic studies, about elementary historical facts, and about the nature of classroom pedagogy and instruction, they do get one thing right: They recognize the importance of social movements in shaping social structures and social relations. Of course their movement differs markedly from the principles and practices of the freedom movements of the twentieth century whose gains they seek to reverse. Their movement is a top-down mobilization funded by wealthy donors whose influence and power guarantee them fawning coverage in the *Wall Street Journal* and on Fox News. Campaigners against CRT are coaxed, coached, and coddled by officeholders from the Republican Party. The details of their campaigns are orchestrated out of right-wing propaganda "think tanks" such as the Manhattan Institute, best known for promoting claims by Charles Murray that Black people are intellectually inferior to whites and that therefore no money should be expended on their education and well-being. Even when these campaigns fail to get books banned, teachers fired, and true histories excised from classroom instruction, they frame the terms of debate. Just as the mass uprising of 2020 compelled attention to the disposability of Black lives and the durability of white privilege, revanchist racist mobilization directs attention to debates about whether "wokeness" *has gone too far* rather than whether injustice *has lasted too long*.

The process of mobilizing through the slogan Make American Great Again (MAGA) offers rewards to participants that do not depend on realization of their goals. The organized campaigns of revanchist racism acknowledge that things are very wrong in society. They mobilize people to act for change. They create an active and engaged public sphere. They promote a shared sense of connection to others bound by a common purpose and offer identification with a strong leader and participation in a grand endeavor as compensation and reparation for the smallness of lives fixated primarily on material gain. They speak to the frustrated owners of failing small businesses, the men who feel inadequate and threatened on account of a perceived loss of male privilege and entitlement, and the military combat veterans suffering post-traumatic stress. Perceiving themselves as victims, MAGA supporters are eager to victimize others. They provide fertile ground for entrepreneurs to make money by selling T-shirts, statues, flags, and bumper stickers deifying their leader and demonizing those they despise as other. The point of these campaigns is not necessarily to win. Win or lose, they succeed by setting the terms of public debate, training supporters to organize and take action, intimidating opponents and bystanders, demonizing targeted opponents, and solidifying the immunity and impunity of whiteness.

People steeped in cynicism but frustrated by blocked avenues to wealth find the MAGA movement a rich source of opportunities for grifting. Steve Bannon, Brian Kolfage, and Timothy Shea, claiming to seek funds to build a wall on the southern border to keep out immigrants and asylum seekers, raised $25 million from gullible Trump supporters. No wall was built. The funds they raised paid for jewelry, boats, and cosmetic surgery for the promoters of the project. Nevada Republican politician Michelle Fiore attracted the attention of MAGA supporters by sending out a Christmas card featuring herself, her parents, and her children (including her five-year-old son) brandishing machine guns and automatic pistols. In 2024 Fiore was convicted of wire fraud for a scam that raised $70,000 purportedly intended to erect a memorial to a police officer killed in the line of duty. Fiore took all the money she had raised to pay for plastic surgery, rent, and her daughter's wedding. Lest anyone think that this grifting of their own supporters goes against the principles of the MAGA movement, one of Donald Trump's last official acts in his first term as president was to issue a full pardon to Bannon, and one of his first official acts in his second term was similarly to give Fiore a full pardon.[52]

The revanchist right gets its proponents to take actions in public, often in despicable ways. They disrupt school board meetings, threaten teachers and administrators, harass librarians, make bomb threats to hospitals and clinics, and increasingly enact actual violence against defenseless others. These are actions to be condemned rather than emulated, but their focus on action contains valuable lessons. The energy and momentum of a social movement cannot be stopped by voicing condemnations of it; a social movement can be defeated only by opposition from an equally intense and engaged countermovement.

The ethnic studies project and the broader antiracist formations attached to it are oppositional to powerful interests and therefore should expect to encounter opposition. Their survival and chances for success depend on responding to the forces arrayed against them with direct action, education, and mass mobilization. Participating in—and giving assistance to—social movement mobilizations can connect the relatively small project of ethnic studies to the much larger social formation of liberation struggles. Some of that formation appears inside visible and audible organizations that conduct campaigns, issue statements, and enroll members. But movements always entail more than the organizations that act in their names. Black Lives Matter is a malleable sign that can refer to a popular hashtag, a general slogan, a particular critique of white supremacy, a specific historical moment, a formal organization, or a collectively crafted conclusion and commitment. As Toni Cade Bambara explains, "The movement is exactly what the word suggests, a motion of the mind."[53]

Social movements do not solve social problems simply by their existence. They contain contradictions and confront internal conflicts.

Sometimes these conflicts inhibit movement, but on other occasions they generate powerful forms of organizational learning that recognize differences as evidence of questions previously unasked that need to be answered. The New York Young Lords started out with an uncritical embrace of male privilege and swagger but became a group with profound commitments to gender justice because of mobilization by women within the group.[54] Social movements shake up social life; they envision and enact new social practices and new social relations, as evidenced by their long-standing relationships with ethnic studies.

Ethnic studies ideas and actions have long drawn inspiration, explanation, and understanding from active social movements. Charles Mills developed his theories about the racial contract in part through his participation in activism. Sociologist Neda Maghbouleh notes with respect to the continuing influence and impact of *The Racial Contract* that Mills frequently described himself as a Third World/global South subject from Jamaica who was called to consciousness initially as a teenager by the protest campaigns and riots opposing the expulsion of Walter Rodney from that country in 1968.[55] That early life awakening prepared Mills for the extra-academic education he received as a graduate student in Toronto, where he participated in challenges to the neocolonial order by Anglo-Caribbean activists that drew him into support groups, forums, rallies, discussions, and lectures. He turned to philosophy in hopes of getting "a big picture overview" of the injustices he observed and fought against.[56] As will be explained more fully below, the scholars who created CRT and disseminated its key ideas also emulated previous social movements in their work and formulated their project as a social movement in itself.

Although most often treated by scholars and journalists as if it were merely a theoretical framework, CRT emerged from a nexus of actions by past and contemporary social movements. From the start it produced present and future forms of collective mobilization and struggle. Its fate has always rested on the ability of its proponents to mobilize people, to offer supporters important things to do rather than merely novel things to think, to engage in collective mobilizations that deepen the capacity for democratic deliberation and decision-making. Mills's formulations about the racial contract pave the way for recognizing CRT as a *vortex of action* that originated inside social movements for race, gender, and class justice. As Kimberlé Crenshaw summarizes its history, CRT was "dynamically constituted by a series of contestations and convergences pertaining to the ways that racial power is understood and articulated in the post-civil rights era."⁵⁷ Its emergence testifies to the accuracy of Robin Kelley's insight that "social movements generate new knowledge, new theories, new questions. The most radical ideas often grow out of a concrete intellectual engagement with the problems of aggrieved populations confronting systems of oppression."⁵⁸

CRT gained its first articulations in the 1980s among students from aggrieved racialized communities who were enrolled at Harvard Law School. Black students had lived in places where neighbors and siblings fixed their hair in "natural" styles, wore dashikis, and placed photographs on their bedroom walls of John Carlos and Tommy Smith raising clenched fists cloaked in black gloves in their protest against racism at their medal awards ceremony at the 1968 Olympics. In their neighborhoods and homes, students from aggrieved racialized groups read oppositional newspapers including *The Black Panther, Muhammad Speaks, El Grito del Norte, Palante,* and *Gidra*. They listened to music by Gil Scott-Heron and Nina Simone. They learned about history, race, and power from murals on neighborhood buildings and posters inside their homes. Some of them were among the first cohort of Black students to desegregate previously nearly all white institutions of higher learning. Others had been enrolled as undergraduates in ethnic studies courses like those taught by James Turner at the Africana Studies and Research Center at Cornell University. Some tutored inner-city school children and worked to help nonwhite candidates win elective offices for the first time. In their communities they were exposed to arts groups and musical ensembles that connected them powerfully to what Cedric Robinson has aptly named "the penetrative comprehension of Black opposition."⁵⁹ As Nelson Maldonado-Torres points out, "It was not only bodies of color who were now entering the privileged spaces of white education, but also their minds, memories, aspirations, questions and concerns."⁶⁰

The prehistory of CRT and its conditions of possibility emanated from grassroots groups working for self-defense, self-definition, and self-determination built on long histories of community conservatories and alternative academies. The Black freedom movement of the mid-twentieth century created citizenship schools, cooperative farms, community land trusts, alternative electoral systems, political parties, medical testing and treatment centers, trade union caucuses, poor people's movements, welfare rights organizations, community action patrols monitoring police misconduct, and a wide array of other self-defense and "serve the people" organizations.⁶¹

These parallel institutions prefigured how a just society might work by enacting the social relations they envisioned. They filled needs that were not being met by dominant educational, economic, electoral, medical, and public safety institutions. They responded to the radical divisiveness caused by racism and poverty by establishing sites of exuberant solidarity where strangers could become friends and antagonists could become allies. By inviting participants to recognize their linked fates without succumbing to fatalism, they worked together for change.[62] The parallel institutions resisted resignation and despair while promoting the self-confidence and self-activity that flow from convivial collaboration. They started to build in the present a tangible prefiguration of the world they wished to inhabit in the future, without having to ask or wait for permission from their oppressors to do so.

Ethnic studies in general and CRT specifically came into being as yet another parallel institution. The law students who created CRT challenged their teachers' expectations of how to make normative progress through three years of law school. They rejected the curriculum's distortions of the history of abolition democracy and the law's pretensions of timeless universality. They insisted on adding true histories of racist subordination and antiracist resistance to class syllabi and course listings. They brought with them to the law school memories of past histories of struggle against injustice that had shaped their consciousness. They sought to craft a future that could produce collective liberation as well as personal professional success. They did not view themselves as living in a time of gradual yet certain triumphant progress toward a socially just future but instead chafed against the injuries inflicted by dreams deferred.

The *study* of law conflicted with the lessons of *struggle* that these students had observed in their communities. They had witnessed brutal repression of social justice movements by the forces of "law and order." These social movement mobilizations suffered from state-implicated assassinations and systematic incarceration of a generation of antiracist activists. The law school curriculum addressed none of these experiences. It failed to deal with the limits of civil rights laws as written or with the judicial rulings that undermined enforcement of even those modest statutes. Law school education seemed oblivious to the causes and consequences of mass incarceration and appeared indecently complacent in the face of the substantial segment of the legal community that contended that securing constitutional rights for aggrieved racialized groups perpetrated "reverse discrimination" against white people.

Disappointed in the shortcomings of the law school curriculum, the students confronted and contested it. The legal realm had already been discredited in their eyes through the Supreme Court's decisions in school desegregation cases in San Antonio and Detroit in 1973 and 1974 that began a steady retreat from the commitment to integration that the Court had proclaimed in its 1954 *Brown v. Board of Education* decision. Actions by the Nixon, Ford, Carter, and especially Reagan administrations enacted what Crenshaw calls "the age of repudiation," a systemic reneging on the concessions granted to antiracist groups during the 1960s.[63] Decades of relentless white resistance to implementing school desegregation and the fair housing and fair employment practices articulated in civil rights laws provided members of aggrieved communities with expert knowledge about what they were up against and why they had to craft their own mechanisms for recognizing and resisting what at best were merely piecemeal forms of subordinate inclusion. The students came to draw on the kind of wisdom passed on to one young Black woman in Waco, Texas, as she prepared to attend a previously all-white public school. Her grandmother advised her to be respectful but not overly deferential to white teachers, to keep her head up and her back straight, and to honor obligations to the community that had raised and nurtured her by making sure that when she asked a question it was one that helped other people learn.[64] The student was counseled by her grandmother to not just enter into the system but to change it, to keep the door through which she was allowed to enter open to others, and to counter the individualist notion of education with an approach to learning as a shared social resource and practice. This kind of collective consciousness and drawing on community cultural wealth armed the law students with the dispositions and tools they needed to create CRT.

The law school students initially made modest requests to their teachers, first asking only for the appointment to the faculty of Black scholars whose presence would begin to desegregate what was then an almost all-white teaching staff. They asked for courses on civil rights–related issues in constitutional law. The school dean, one of the leading theorists of racial liberalism, dismissed their requests, telling the students that civil rights was of minor importance in the law and that there were no Black people qualified to teach law at Harvard. Had the dean acceded to the student requests, CRT might never have come into existence. The students' defeat set the stage for future victories because it showed them their needs could not be met within the institution as it then existed. The dean's resistance compelled them to confront the limits of racial liberalism and to construct a critique of it as a manifestation of the racial contract, just as it is the very campaign against CRT today that proves the need for its existence and an opportunity for its expansion.

The students responded by creating parallel institutions, initially in the form of collective study groups. They read widely in existing scholarship on civil rights and identified in that research key concepts that were absent from the law school curriculum. They discovered the existence of writings by scholars replete with original and insightful analyses about the limits of civil rights laws. The students used those writings to create an autonomous learning center that they named the Alternative Course, an unsanctioned noncredit class to which they invited Black legal theorists to give guest lectures. Those lectures and the book of readings the students assembled for it gave rise to key ideas that would eventually fuel CRT: (1) that civil rights laws did not meaningfully address how law itself constituted the racial structures that produce discrimination, (2) that law is fundamentally a political entity that needs to respond to struggles for social justice by aggrieved groups, and (3) that the principles of sameness/difference and single-axis injury in law distorted not only demands for racial justice but also struggles for justice on the basis of gender, sexuality, language, citizenship status, dis/ability, and many other modes of social differentiation.

The parallel institution that was named the Alternative Course, with its syllabus, course reader, and pedagogical successes, not only generated a wide range of courses at other law schools but also led to a wide array of *alternative courses of action* inside and outside the academy carried out by scholars, attorneys, advocates, activists, and artists in the years ahead.[65] Key concepts articulated by CRT scholars spread quickly across disciplines and social contexts. These include intersectionality, whiteness as property, interest convergence, looking to the bottom of society for the most perceptive critiques of it, and unconscious bias as a factor in racism. CRT thus provided tools that added new depth and breadth to scholarly studies of social identities and power while fueling activist interventions in a wide array of dispersed community settings, including fair housing councils, community land trusts, reproductive justice centers, prison abolition projects, labor union caucuses, mobilizations for environmental and disability justice, community gardens, and cultural artistic and performance collectives.[66]

These parallel institutions drew upon and expanded what Tara J. Yosso names "community cultural wealth." Aggrieved groups lacking material resources must cultivate a collective capacity to be resourceful.

They invent practices that nurture and sustain aspirations for success, that teach ways of navigating hostile social settings, that commit individuals to the well-being of the entire community, that rely on supporting and accompanying others, and that promote resistance to mistreatment.[67] In the process of meeting immediate needs, parallel institutions also function as *autonomous learning centers*—a concept to be addressed at length in chapter 3. As deployed here, *autonomy* does not denote full self-rule, complete independence from state power, or freedom from corporate domination. Instead, following Gustavo Esteva and the particular strains of Indigenous thought and action that he was educated by and that he endorsed, the term in this case refers to the willful reorganization of society from the bottom up on the basis of practices grounded in the things people do for themselves. Esteva stresses the importance of struggles that do not settle for merely improved access to state structures but instead demand "respect for styles and designs that surpass them."[68] Autonomous learning centers do not pretend that the racial contract does not exist, but they promote ways to interrupt its temporal, spatial, and social imperatives, while generating experiences that show participants that alternative courses of action are possible.

Autonomous learning centers and parallel institutions connect the work of ethnic studies to what musician and cultural theorist William Parker described as life's "many classrooms."[69] The forms of education that transpire in school settings shape and reflect lessons learned in household kitchens and houses of worship, on athletic fields and dance floors, during nature walks and storytelling sessions. The work performed in autonomous learning centers, parallel institutions, social movements, and ethnic studies centers cannot free participants fully from domination by the racial contract, but it can create temporal alternatives to the working day, the life course, and dominant narratives of historical time. When participants explore multiple temporalities in music, dance, and speech, they create crucibles for living outside the clocks and calendars of their oppressors and counter promises of future freedom with insistence on a semblance of liberation now.

THREATS COME FROM BOTH THE OUTSIDE AND THE INSIDE

Attacks on academic ethnic studies by privately funded think tank publicists, pundits, and politicians undermine the free exercise of academic inquiry, especially when institutions fearful of losing outside funding submit to these outside pressures. Institutions unwilling to explain and defend the necessity for affirmative action hiring and programs promoting diversity, equity, and inclusion relegate members of aggrieved groups and their advocates to second-class status within the academy and the wider world beyond it. Attacks on ethnic studies are intended to inflict harm on individuals, many of whose very identities are criminalized in the broader anti-Black, anti-Asian, anti-Latinx, anti-LGBTQ, antidisability, settler colonial society. They face implicit negative judgments about their worth as researchers, teachers, and public advocates because of their disrespected identities. This hostility damages individual careers and lives, while also meting out disastrous consequences for all of society. Refusing to fight back against these attacks deprives readers, listeners, and speakers of vital information and analyses. It impels educational institutions to substitute mandatory indoctrination for free inquiry. It kills curiosity, silences dissent, and turns public education into a locus of propaganda for the preservation of plutocratic privilege and the possessive investment in whiteness.

The campaign against CRT serves as part of a racist reaction against all race-conscious analyses of and remedies for race-bound subordination and exploitation. Its calculated cruelty and reliance on using perceived difference as justification for domination portends a future of endless aggression against aggrieved groups clamoring for justice. In the name of restoring an order that has never existed, it creates chaos. The powerful use it to protect their own interests while pitting relatively powerless people against each other in a perpetual carnival of misrule.

Participants in and supporters of the ethnic studies project have learned the necessity of standing up against all forms of dehumanization. Attacks on the project and the larger egalitarian, democratic, and inclusive social formation need to be recognized and resisted. At the same time, however, these attacks expose weaknesses and deep contradictions inside ethnic studies—within its core commitments, practices, processes, and affects inside the academy and in the field's relationships with aggrieved populations outside. As will be explained in greater detail in chapter 2, the same institutionalization that enables much of the good work performed under the aegis of ethnic studies to take place can also incorporate, co-opt, and contain its reach, scope, ambition, and impact.

2

Ethnic Studies as Incorporation

At the end of the academic year in June 2003, Joy de la Cruz, a Pilipinx ethnic studies major at the University of California San Diego, gave me a handwritten poem that she had composed. The poem she gave me reads:

> un means one
> ver means to see
> here this universidad
>   this university
> posits one way to see the truth
> with a big T, verdad?
> but Time out
> i became an ethnic studies major
> 'cuz I need to be
> able to articulately argue
> why skin hue should not determine
>   life chances
> how racialized experience does shape
>   political stances
> to build "identity based on politics
> not politics based on identity"
> imprisoned by isms
> racism sexism classism heterosexism
> capitalism
> solidarity means we understand
>   each other's struggles
> not because we fight for, but

>   because we stand with them
>   at the crossroads
>   at intersectionalities
>   together recognize realities
>   a contradiction: race is not real
>   yet racialized constructions have real
>   consequences
>   consequently teachers who eloquently
>   model ways to be activists
>   thinking critically empower & humble
>   students of struggle

Four months later, de la Cruz died in a car crash on a Nevada highway, eight weeks after her twenty-fifth birthday. Her poetry remains an enduring inspiration to me and to many of the other teachers and students who knew her.[1] Although Joy is gone, her poem signals the ways in which the ethnic studies project can fulfill the promise of its origins in grassroots demands for relevant, culturally sensitive, and useful education. Yet the partial incorporation of ethnic studies into higher education in the 1960s and 1970s immediately fueled a parallel project by the state and capital that was funded and controlled by powerful people and institutions. This counterproject sought to produce an ethnic studies far different from the one that de la Cruz experienced and envisioned; instead, it crafted one that would be safe for power. It funded initiatives designed to recognize difference but only so elites could contain and manage it successfully. It sought to cultivate a leadership group from aggrieved communities with interests separate from those of the grassroots, and to deradicalize opposition to racism—narrowing it into slightly *reforming* the demography of educational institutions rather than significantly *transforming* their mission. Incorporation of ethnic studies inside schools, research centers, philanthropic-funded initiatives, and businesses almost always entails promoting the idea that racial identity is a personal, embodied, private special interest competing with others for limited resources, that it is a kind of credential that under conditions of scarcity offers an alternative path to career success and individual upward mobility. Absent from this conceptualization of race are the processes of racist rule and critique of and contestation against normative whiteness and racial capitalism.

The ethnic studies project is a site of discursive contradiction that is riddled with social contradictions. Brought into existence initially through an alliance between diametrically opposed and innately antagonistic social forces, ethnic studies can function as both a mechanism for liberation and a tool of domination. This chapter explores the dilemmas of inclusion, the dynamics unleashed when antiracist, egalitarian, and democratic initiatives make their way into educational institutions that are structured in dominance and are set up to manage and maintain the existing social order. It begins with description of the perils of incorporation and consideration of the increasingly overt and direct political pressures on the university, and then presents a case study that demonstrates what is at stake in incorporation and the value of fighting back against it.

Ethnic studies came into existence as an educational project because egalitarian and democratic mobilizations against injustice on and off campuses created a crisis that posed very real threats to the privileged and powerful. Urban insurrections destroyed private property and challenged the legitimacy of the state and its police and military agencies. Opposition to the war in Vietnam potentially imperiled access to the overseas markets, raw materials, and low-wage labor on which the capitalist economy depends. Rising demands for participatory democracy made investors and bureaucrats fearful about future instability and unpredictability. Feminist organizing challenged the privileged status of the normative properly gendered patriarchal nuclear family, while environmental and health care activism exposed the harms perpetrated by fossil fuel extraction, tobacco and lead-based paint marketing, and medical racism and sexism. Attempts to promote the self-defense, self-definition, and self-determination of aggrieved racialized groups promoted visions of society antithetical to racial capitalism because they centered on the well-being of people rather than the protection of profits and property.

In the last half of the twentieth century, this complex conjuncture of circumstances led to some educational institutions becoming visible and viable sites for critical investigation of the racial order and for mobilization to change it. The growing need by capital for a workforce with advanced skills led to the expansion of higher education, while victories won by the social movements of the 1960s increased access to it by members of aggrieved social groups. Starting in the 1970s, however, a massive restructuring of society along neoliberal lines devastated entire communities, especially those with social, economic, and educational infrastructures that had been nurtured and sustained by the labor movement, the civil rights movement, and a wide range of activist and alternative learning spaces. Economic restructuring, political reorganization, automation, and capital flight led to massive job losses, declines in labor union membership and power, disinvestment in communities inhabited by aggrieved racialized groups, and devastating cuts in government funding for social services precisely at the moment when members of previously excluded racialized groups first won election to municipal offices.

In the 1930s, the demise of ethnic fraternal orders because of the economic devastation of the Great Depression led workers to join labor unions and build a pan-ethnic culture of unity inside it. In the 1960s the incorporation of the labor movement into labor-management partnerships and its resistance to civil rights helped fuel the rise of activist organizing in the Black freedom movement. By the 1980s, the weaknesses and diminished power among labor unions and civil rights groups encouraged some parts of their constituencies to seek homes inside academia.[2] People who in previous decades might have occupied posts in labor and civil rights organizations or the cultural and social institutions made possible by them wound up seeking positions available in the expanding world of school-based study and struggle. Many of the founders of ethnic studies drew on experiences inside community arts, education, and political institutions and used them as models for ways of working on campus.[3] The first stirrings of incorporation of ethnic studies in institutions of higher learning created a new home for ideas and perspectives from previous struggles and raised the possibility that campuses could become valuable resources for aggrieved communities.[4]

The democratic and egalitarian vision of early ethnic studies threatened the privileges and presumptions of power and wealth. This threat set the stage for a reactionary inversion of the field, one that attempted to imbue ethnic studies with a distinctly different mission. Racial justice initiatives were tolerated and even encouraged by some major philanthropic foundations, university administrators, and members of boards of trustees because they viewed them as potential safety valves for the system, as mechanisms likely to defuse explosive social tensions.[5] The hope was that granting entry into previously forbidden places to a few putatively exceptional individuals from aggrieved groups might entice potential critics and opponents of racial capitalism to become functionaries and bureaucrats helping administer it. The visibility of minority difference inside institutions of higher education held the potential to provide cosmetic cover for the system's relentless practices of exclusion and exploitation outside them.[6] Like similar projects of counterinsurgency and indirect rule all around the world, ethnic studies was seen by people in power as one way to recruit a comprador elite of accomplices from aggrieved communities of color who could be used to moderate, pacify, and perhaps suppress those who wished to rebel.

In its most fully established and most lavishly funded institutionalized forms, ethnic studies offered ruling elites potential social and spatial settlements to fix social problems (at least temporarily). The social fixes revolved around the promise of placing a few dark faces in high places and the promotion of research that made the *study of difference* rather than the *study of domination* the approved mission of the field. The spatial fixes concentrated the work of ethnic studies inside classrooms on campus rather than extending it to the quotidian spaces of aggrieved communities. Another spatial fix entailed privileging study of the racial order inside the United States over examination of the role of US racism and imperialism in the world.

Incorporation is a structural reality. It is not the product of the personal shortcomings of individual faculty members, students, or staff employees. While individuals still need to make the best available informed moral and political choices available to them, colleges and universities are controlled by corporate representatives on their boards of trustees. They supply research and development resources to business and the military. They make investments in companies that produce weapons of war, that put millions of housing units in the hands of private equity firms, and that promote fossil fuel–centered environmental destruction. Every division and discipline inculcates a managerial perspective in faculty members and students. Textbooks are produced and controlled by profit-seeking corporations, and they are vetted and censored by politicians and private stakeholders intent on preserving the existing racial order.

Yet meaningful work can still be carried out inside educational institutions. As chapters 3, 4, and 5 will explore more fully, participants in ethnic studies and attendant areas of inquiry, instruction, apprenticeship, and activism succeed best when they draw on the rich histories and survival strategies of aggrieved communities that have long lived with and negotiated vexing contradictions generated by attempts at incorporation and co-optation.

It would be a grave mistake to let the institutionalization and incorporation of ethnic studies obscure the important work it does. The good faith and hard work of participants has enabled ethnic studies units to do a lot with little financial support, to improvise new possibilities inside places and practices that school administrators reluctantly tolerate but rarely fully endorse. Despite chronic underfunding, marginalization, and tokenization, ethnic studies units make up one of the few sites in society where people discover how they are actually governed and where they can develop collective strategies for creating a more morally just world. Taking ethnic studies courses improves the attendance and graduation rates of K-12 and college students while preparing them with knowledge and skills needed to be responsible and successful community members, voters, workers, and parents in the multiracial, multilingual, multinational worlds in which they live. Ethnic studies research identifies serious social problems and suggests solutions to them. The project's classrooms, colloquia, conferences, and community events offer what in this society are rare opportunities for deliberative talk and democratic decision-making about social identities and power.

The infrastructure that enables and sustains the work of ethnic studies owes much to the opportunities, resources, and innovations made possible by arduous labor carried out inside institutions by teachers, faculty committees, support staff, and administrators. The actual commitment to ethnic studies by institutions, however, has been quite limited. Fewer than 10 percent of the 2,637 four-year colleges and universities in the US host stand-alone programs dedicated exclusively to ethnic studies. Over 20 percent of the students in these schools identify as Latinx, but Latinx studies majors are offered in only 3 percent of these institutions, in eighty-nine schools. Most of these units are underfunded and composed of faculty members with obligations in other departments. Adjunct and part-time instructors teach many of their classes, and these programs are often perceived by administrators and faculty governance decision makers as sources of service to the rest of the campus rather than significant sites for scholarly inquiry and instruction.[7]

Despite sparse resources, ethnic studies programs make significant contributions to higher education. Large lower-division courses provide schools with high enrollments that bring in revenues, while enabling students to gain credit hours, fulfill distribution requirements, and learn and refine skills for reading, writing, and analysis. These classes provide resources that make it possible for other disciplines to teach small, focused classes to students already trained for the work assigned. Original and generative research by ethnic studies scholars has influence and impact across the disciplines and interdisciplines. Faculty participation on thesis and dissertation committees introduces students and faculty colleagues in the disciplines to new perspectives, methods, and theories.

It would thus be a grave error to underestimate the achievements of institutionalized ethnic studies. Yet it would be equally inaccurate to underestimate the effects of incorporation inside institutions—an incorporation that generally amounts to little more than subordinate inclusion. Constantly expected to do more with less, perpetually judged by evaluators with little knowledge of or commitment to their areas of expertise, and contained within an educational system increasingly characterized by fiscalization, vocationalization, and privatization, classroom- and campus-based ethnic studies can lose its critical edge and emancipatory potential. As Stuart Hall argued a half century ago, people with even the best intentions can become tamed by the institutions they enter and hope to transform. Hall explains that entering the structures of exploitation and power can lead to internalizing "the beliefs, the rationalizations, the motivations of power and privilege" and beginning "to think of 'the dispossessed' as *them* and of those who take up the struggle alongside the dispossessed as—*the enemy.*"[8] Activists sometimes say that if you do not have a seat at the table you will be on the menu, but sometimes having a seat at the table only means someone else will be on the menu.[9] Ethnic studies today remains what it has long been: a crossroads for both bottom-up and top-down approaches to difference and domination.

ETHNIC STUDIES FROM THE BOTTOM UP AND FROM THE TOP DOWN

In the wake of the urban insurrections and mass mobilizations of the 1960s, members of aggrieved racialized groups and their allies in communities and classrooms launched ethnic studies initiatives in higher education in hopes that they might become crucibles for the development of new knowledges, new politics, and new polities.[10] The outbursts of energy that fueled the founding of ethnic studies programs drew upon the imagination and ingenuity of a wide range of alternative academies and autonomous learning communities off campus. These became generative sites for discussions, deliberations, and debates, as well as staging grounds for activism.[11] Ethnic studies courses responded to demands like the one articulated in the Black Panther Party's Ten Point Program calling for an "education that teaches us our true history and our role in the present day society." It was influenced by the formulation in El Plan de Santa Barbara that demanded community control over education, by the revised 13 Point Program of the New York chapter of the Young Lords that demanded "a true education of our Afro-Indio culture and Spanish language," and by the I Wor Kuen 12 Point Platform and Program demanding "an education which exposes the

FIGURE 1. Iris Morales leads New York Young Lords political education class. Photograph by Michael Abramson, reprinted with permission.

true history of western imperialism in Asia and around the world" and "teaches us the hardships and struggles of our ancestors in this land."[12]

High school students walking out of schools in the 1968 East Los Angeles "Blowouts" demanded better and more culturally sensitive education. Their action set the stage for the establishment of Chicano studies programs in the California State University system. A broad range of street actions, sit-ins, and building occupations by community members led to the establishment of what is now called Africana, Puerto Rican, and Latino studies at Hunter College/City University of New York and Latino and Caribbean studies at Rutgers University.[13] Women active in the American Indian Movement set up "survival schools" to educate Native young people in Minneapolis, Rapid City, and Pine Ridge. These schools refused to accept government funding in order to maintain control over pedagogy and curriculum.[14] Indigenous activists established Native studies programs on existing campuses and founded Indigenous-controlled colleges. The creators of D-Q University in California worked with community members to envision the emergence of a Native intelligentsia that would be independent of scholarly hierarchies in anthropology, literature, and history and free from domination by the Smithsonian Institution and the Newberry Library.[15] The New York Young Lords created their own parallel education institution by requiring members to read at least one political book a month and to always carry around a book or article to read, while the organization assembled reading lists and conducted weekly political education classes.[16]

Ethnic studies programs in turn contributed to the knowledge and commitments of people who became activists. El Plan de Santa Barbara emerged from a direct-action protest and strike at the University of California Santa Barbara staged by Chicano students working with Black and white allies. It presented a plan for the radical reorganization of higher education focused on community service and civic engagement that has informed the work of generations of activists. Work conducted inside ethnic studies initiatives rippled out to influence community activism. In 1969 when Indigenous activists calling themselves Indians of All Tribes took over the Alcatraz penitentiary on the basis of treaties allowing Native Americans to live on unoccupied settler lands, participants in the takeover and subsequent long occupation included students LaNada Means (Shoshone-Bannock), Richard Oakes (Mohawk), and Al Miller (Seminole) enrolled in the Native studies program in what was then San Francisco State College. Part of the project on Alcatraz entailed an intent to create "an all-Indian university."[17] The service organizations that proliferated inside Asian American communities in the San Francisco Bay area after 1968 drew a significant number of key staff personnel from individuals currently or formerly enrolled in Asian American studies courses in local colleges and universities.[18] A liberal, paternalistic, and tokenistic "college discovery" program designed to enroll underrepresented working-class students at the City University of New York produced critical spaces and infrastructures for dissent that helped direct key members to activism in the Young Lords Party. Central to the emergence of that organization was a study group among Nuyorican students at the State University of New York at Old Westbury that led them back to their communities and to organizing inside them.[19]

Despite the constraints imposed on them by subordinate inclusion and co-optive incorporation, participants in the earliest incarnations of ethnic studies discovered a treasure trove of source material in writings that previously had been marginalized, neglected, or excluded from college curricula. Works by Anna Julia Cooper, Americo Paredes, Amilcar Cabral, Audre Lorde, José Marti, Frantz Fanon, John Okada, John Rechy, and Pedro Albizu Campos, among others, began to appear on classroom syllabi and study group reading lists. Many of these works originated in the margins of academic research or from activist realms completely outside it, raising questions about how institutions determine which knowledge should be included and which knowledge should be excluded.

The bottom-up version of ethnic studies that emerged from struggle aspired to playing a role as parallel oppositional institutions inside dominant institutions. It sought to create a semiautonomous space in the university that could connect campus learning to community knowledges and needs. Its democratic vision called for more than merely desegregating the demographics of the faculty and the student body. It envisioned a knowledge project that would challenge the roles played by colleges and universities as places where white racial rule was learned and legitimated, where hierarchy, exploitation, and state violence were treated as natural, necessary, and inevitable.[20]

The quest for new kinds of *study* required new forms of *struggle*. Students and teachers on campuses joined with allies in communities to circulate petitions, stage strikes, occupy buildings, and pressure student and faculty governance bodies to make ethnic studies part of the curriculum. Responses ranged from outright refusals to modest gestures of inclusion. Hundreds of new Black studies and ethnic studies courses, programs, and departments started in the late 1960s and early 1970s, but often with mixed results.[21] On the one hand, incorporation enabled the establishment of a new public sphere inside classes that helped infuse succeeding generations with capacities to understand and take action against the many encounters they would subsequently have with discrimination and domination. On the other hand, incorporation always comes with a cost; everything that enables also inhibits. The inclusion achieved by ethnic studies started out and has remained a distinctly subordinate kind, centered in symbolic and cosmetic responses to deep structural and systematic problems. Incorporation follows the pattern pointed out by Malcolm X sixty years ago: When they cannot beat you they will join you, but when they join you, you will wind up traveling in a direction you never intended to go.

The reward structure of audit cultures on campus creates situations where ethnic studies departments and programs can be doing quite well while ethnic peoples fare quite poorly. The field's hopes for connecting campus knowledge to community concerns frequently become overshadowed by the demands of professionalization. Radical demands to transform the system are strategically misheard as requests for inclusion in it. Expressions of collective aspirations for dignity and freedom become translated into requests for individual visibility and upward mobility. Grassroots pressures to end racism lead to programs designed to manage difference. Analyses of Indigenous dispossession, coloniality, and slavery unwilling to die take a back seat to discussions of discrimination posited as a flaw in an otherwise fully functioning democracy.

Institutionalization involves an orientation toward order. Relentless pressures inside the academy promote forms of the ethnic studies project that focus on prejudice rather than power, that address difference but not domination, and that treat race as a biological reality rather than a political construct. This shrinkage and containment do not necessarily reflect personal failings of the individuals involved. They reflect circumstances structured by asymmetrical power. Cultural studies scholar Michael Denning observes astutely that "if we are incorporated in the university, it is because we are living in a corporation, not because conflicts and struggles have given way to guilt and alienation."[22] When people seek to share the resources and opportunities made possible by incorporation, they discover with discomfort the degree to which they have become obligated to it. As Sara Ahmed explains, even scholars who engage in "critique, complaint, and opposition" to the academy find that institutional imperatives occupy their center of attention and align them with their managerial commitments and ideological imperatives.[23]

Gary Okihiro argues that it is significant that *ethnic studies* became the umbrella term describing the field rather than *Third World studies, liberation studies, antiracist studies,* or *decolonial studies.*[24] The name *ethnic studies* stems from the managerial framework about social difference advanced by the Chicago School of Sociology in the first half of the twentieth century. This approach functioned to portray society and its institutions as sporadically and incidentally plagued by ethnic difference and viewed the mission of scholarship as giving society advice and instruction on how to deal with and manage those interruptions. Lorgia Garcia-Peña observes that the word *ethnic* has a long dehumanizing and colonizing history dating back to the eighteenth century.[25]

The ethnic framework promoted the myth of ethnic succession proclaimed in the Chicago School's assimilation cycle, positing that outsider groups always move from contact, competition, and conflict to accommodation, assimilation, and acceptance. This formulation counsels patience, telling aggrieved groups that if they are not yet free they soon will be. Based on a historically flawed and theoretically insupportable fable about the experiences of European ethnic groups, this paradigm obscures the ways in which forms of *ethnic inclusion* gained by whites have always entailed recruiting the newly included ethnics into policing the boundaries of *racial exclusion* against communities of color.[26] The assimilation cycle rests on a temporal illusion: It presumes that Black, Latinx, Indigenous, and Asian Americans are not really oppressed polities but simply groups still living in a previous period of human history, people who are not yet fully free but who eventually and inevitably are destined to be if they play by the rules and conform to the ideals of racial and gender normativity.

Tensions between top-down and bottom-up approaches continue to vex ethnic studies to this day. Neither side has been able to win a full victory. The field's most valuable impact on schooling and society has emerged precisely from its handling of contradictions that cannot be wished away or willed away. In keeping with the "both/and" rather than "either/or" approach to be outlined in the Bridge section that follows this chapter, the work of ethnic studies has been shaped by recognizing opportunities that accompany conflicts and forging solutions that turn problems into possibilities. Yet there is inevitably a degree of compromise and even complicity emanating from the location of ethnic studies inside higher education institutions designed and administered to make the existing property system and social order stronger and more efficient.

ETHNIC STUDIES AT THE CROSSROADS TODAY

In this moment of crisis, the uneasy coexistence of the top-down and bottom-up versions of ethnic studies is being replaced by an order where forces favoring the top-down version of the field seem no longer able to tolerate the version that views the world from the bottom up. The rise of revanchist racism and the relentless rule of neoliberal racial capitalism described in chapter 1 create a fundamentally new condition for ethnic studies today. Successful incorporation often leaves the project increasingly isolated on campuses and confined inside scholarly conversations, conferences, and publications—with a concomitant diminution of connection to the everyday lives of aggrieved communities.

The radical and emancipatory possibilities of early ethnic studies endeavors emerged inside a world that for the most part no longer exists. In an age of industrial production and Keynesian economics in the 1960s, capital was tethered to places where it was possible to use the state's power to regulate and tax corporations and advance modest reforms that could stoke more radical aspirations. Pursuit of concessions within capitalist nation-states and the building of alternative economic and social systems in newly independent Third World nations seemed plausible and even enjoyed a modicum of success. The creation of ethnic studies units was one of those projects that came about through limited concessions from those in power.

In part because of these modest successes, powerful people and institutions launched a massive counterrevolution that waged war against the Third World abroad and racialized working-class and poor people at home. They directed violence against revolutionary forces, managed the overthrow of radical governments, and imposed artificial austerity on the majority of the world's population through economic restructuring, free trade agreements, flexible accumulation production methods, privatization of public resources, and evisceration of the social wage. In the United States, during what Kimberlé Crenshaw calls "the age of repudiation"—enacted in response to the racial freedom movements of the mid-1960s—state agencies and vigilantes murdered leaders of antiracist groups, unleashed predatory policing and mass incarceration against aggrieved peoples, and blunted the radical edges of the labor and civil rights movements through a mixture of repression and co-optation. Ethnic studies spoke to the dangers and possibilities of the era of the cold war, its national liberation movements, and what the Black Panther Party named the "inter-communalism" of oppressed people. According to the Zapatista EZLN, this cold war era, the period of "Third World War" during which capital made some compromises and concessions, is now over. The new era that replaces it has reversed previous advances and enabled neoliberal profiteering and plunder. We are now, according to the Zapatista analysis, in the midst of the "Fourth World War."[27]

Patterns of incorporation take on new forms in the present-day academy where only 21 percent of faculty members have tenure. Part-time adjuncts and lecturers perform ever-increasing amounts of college instruction. They work without job security or meaningful academic freedom. If they are to be hired for the next quarter or semester they need to please their students, supervisors, and administrators and not offend donors. Online learning can provide meaningful outreach and instruction to students unable to attend classes because of financial pressures, illness, and disabilities, but colleges and universities increasingly turn to distance learning largely as a revenue generator designed to sell credentials rather than offer education.

The dangers of incorporation in colleges and universities may seem to pale in comparison to the challenges of providing K-12 instruction for the more than two million school-aged children (disproportionately from Black and Latinx backgrounds) who are houseless, locked in juvenile justice and child welfare systems, and part of families that need to migrate constantly to find employment.[28] Distinctions among different kinds of ethnic studies may mean little to the nearly fifty thousand youths under the age of eighteen, most of whom are Black or Latinx, who are in juvenile detention centers on any given day, or to the nearly eighteen thousand K-12 students in Chicago who reside in temporary living situations ranging from supervised shelters to subway stations.[29] One study estimated that across the nation some one and a half million students are houseless.[30] Students in rural schools live near sources of unregulated pollution, grow up in carceral communities, and live in overcrowded dwellings in under-resourced neighborhoods. Many K-12 teachers contend with students who cannot pay attention because they are hungry, cannot see blackboards because they have never been tested for glasses, and have no quiet place to read and study in their homes and neighborhoods. Many of these young people traverse streets dangerous for pedestrians. They live far from physicians' offices, fresh food sources, and pharmacies. It might seem that any education they secure would be better than none. Yet they may be the young people *most* in need of unincorporated ethnic studies, of curricula and pedagogies that provide them with the skills to see for themselves how and why they live as they do and that augment their capacities to be analysts, interpreters, and documentarians of the conditions that shape their lives. They need a different kind of ethnic studies than the one proposed for them by the opponents of CRT, who cry crocodile tears about the anxiety they think well-fed, safely housed, and healthy white children might experience from learning the facts about social differences. They need an ethnic studies different from the kind prescribed by racial liberals that treat race as a personal biological possession rather than a social construct. They are not alone in that need. All students need to be told the truth about their society and have the right to be equipped with the tools they will need to negotiate its injustices. One reason they do not receive the education they need, however, comes from the trickle-down effects of the ways in which elite institutions deploy incorporation and co-optation to isolate and marginalize scholars and scholarship critical of the prevailing racial order. Yet as demonstrated by the case study that follows, incorporation and co-optation can be resisted, opposed, and sometimes even overcome.

TWO CASES OF POLITICS IN THE UNIVERSITY

Granting or denying tenure to faculty members plays a central role in incorporation and co-optation. Unjustified denials of tenure to fully qualified scholars from aggrieved communities are not uncommon. Some of these cases evidence direct racial and/or gender prejudice by reviewers. Others occur because the scholars have taken political positions that offend people in power. Colleagues and community members opposed to these decisions have often mobilized in support of aggrieved scholars and have sometimes succeeded in getting adverse decisions reversed.

Institutions have every right and obligation to set strict standards for tenure. It is not unreasonable when granting security of employment to require evidence of successfully designing and executing original and generative research projects as indications of expected ongoing significant research and publications in the future. Along with requirements for successful teaching and positive service contributions, the tenure system encourages people entering the profession to master the skills they will need throughout their careers. The tenure process also protects the quality and integrity of academic inquiry and neutralizes the provincial prejudices and personal rivalries on any one campus by requiring outside letters of evaluation that demonstrate consensual approval for granting tenure from subject matter and field experts across the profession.

Despite its formal safeguards, however, the tenure process can also be a site where negative appraisals of candidates can disguise political disagreements. The confidentiality of tenure deliberations and the documents central to them in theory purports to protect candidates but in practice can shield institutions from scrutiny and accountability. Controversial tenure decisions about scholars in ethnic studies stem in part from the underrepresentation of women and people from aggrieved racial groups in the ranks of the senior faculty members and administrators whose decisions determine the outcome of such cases. Ethnic studies scholars are more likely than others to be challenging conventional wisdom, to be producing research that champions the powerless and threatens the powerful. What seem like decisions solely about the worth of individual scholars are also registers of how the institution sees itself and its mission in society.

The problems yet residual possibilities of incorporation came into sharp relief in 2019 when a confidential ad hoc committee at Harvard University denied tenure to Professor Lorgia Garcia-Peña. This case involved familiar elements but in important ways also signaled a new conjuncture of forces with oddly both foreboding and encouraging implications for the future of ethnic studies. I argue that Garcia-Peña's case marked a defining moment in part because the decision revolved around issues of what kinds of knowledge would be acceptable in the academy. It concerned more than one person's employment and career. Denying tenure to a scholar with Garcia-Peña's record of distinction made it clear that while scholars of color can be marginally included in elite institutions, their inclusion depends upon their not seeming to disturb the racial contract, not bringing with them into the academy the archives, imaginaries, epistemologies, and ontologies of the aggrieved communities from which they come and whom they seek to serve.

Prior to the decision denying her tenure, Garcia-Peña did not experience the benefits of an atmosphere of professionalism or recognition of achievement that one might expect for a professor at Harvard. She recounts instances of overt hateful racism like the incidents on the campus when two men doused her with hot coffee while shouting "Build the wall," when a note replete with racist and misogynist slurs affixed to her office door warned, "You don't belong here," and when a live online lecture during the COVID-19 pandemic was Zoom-bombed and punctuated by threats to lynch her. Security guards and other college personnel constantly challenged her right to be on campus, to use the library, and to hold class outside with her students on warm days. These expressions of direct racism took place in the midst of indirect and yet perhaps more insidious exercises in othering enacted through the routine practices of the university. It was made clear to Garcia-Peña that the purpose of the presence on campus of faculty members from aggrieved racialized groups was representational, that once one of them was hired others would not be, that their work would always be vetted by colleagues unfamiliar with their research objects and research questions, and that their appearance, speech, clothing, and personal mannerisms would be held against them if they did not display gratitude for the self-celebrated generosity of the people that allowed them entry into the academy. In *Community as Rebellion: A Syllabus for Surviving Academia as a Woman of Color*,[31] published after she left Harvard, Garcia-Peña presents a picture of how inclusion in higher education for those traditionally excluded from it inflicts injury after injury. These injuries cumulatively make it clear that inclusion for them is subordinate, provisional, and contingent on conforming to the phobic fantasies and racist resentments determined by the racial contract.

Tenure decisions are said to be based largely on evaluation of the quality of a faculty member's research and, to a lesser degree, their contributions to teaching and service. Garcia-Peña's case for tenure was backed by the unanimous vote of her department colleagues and was endorsed enthusiastically by a considerable number of outside peer reviewers, experts in her field. She is widely recognized as an original, generative, and award-winning scholar with an exemplary record of consistent peer validation from prestigious venues. In her work as a teacher and mentor, she created and directed the Latinx Secondary concentration, an innovative graduate student certification program that has trained some two dozen students across the disciplines at Harvard. The decision to deny tenure was made at later stages of her evaluation, particularly by the traditionally confidential membership of the ad hoc review committee. But subsequent events demonstrate that the committee's judgment of the work was not shared by distinguished scholar-experts in her fields of study.

As soon as Harvard's decision became public, undergraduate and graduate students launched vigorous protests. They were joined by distinguished members of the university's faculty including Evelyn Brooks Higginbotham, Walter Johnson, Khalil Gibran Muhammad, and Cornel West. Outside Harvard, petitions condemning the denial of tenure to Garcia-Peña drew support from many of the most distinguished researchers in her fields of study: for example, from Robin D. G. Kelley, Pedro Noguera, Ana Ramos-Zyas, Kelly Lytle-Hernandez, Nelson Maldonado-Torres, and Barbara Ransby. A symposium organized at Harvard in the wake of her being denied tenure featured presentations lauding her research by distinguished scholars including Laura Briggs, Cornel West, Nicole M. Guidotti-Hernandez, Robin D. G. Kelley, Lourdes Torres, Elizabeth Manley, Silvio Torres-Saillant, and Ramona Hernandez.[32]

The mobilization in support of Garcia-Peña generated increased attention to the quality of her research from scholars across the disciplines. In the immediate aftermath of the tenure denial, it secured extraordinary recognition and distinction. Her second and third books, *Translating Blackness* and *Community as Rebellion*, won major awards from the Caribbean Studies Association, the Latin American Studies Association, and the National Women's Studies Association. She was named one of six 2021 Freedom Scholars by the Marguerite Casey Foundation and received the 2022 Angela Y. Davis Award for Public Scholarship from the American Studies Association. Four years after being denied promotion to the rank of full professor at Harvard, Garcia-Peña secured appointment as a full professor at Princeton.

Appointment at Princeton, of course, comes with its own contradictions and difficulties. On the positive side, it enables Garcia-Peña to continue to publish and teach ideas that counter the racial contract, to produce more of her innovative research, and to mentor graduate students. The victory won because of popular support allows Garcia-Peña to add to official archives and help build parallel institutions within and beyond it. Her survival inside the academy serves as an invitation to others to do similarly important work. Moreover, the collective campaign of support for Garcia-Peña enacted embodied repertoires of struggle that participants can learn from and deploy in the future. Garcia-Peña has moved from one elite institution structured in dominance to another equally vexed venue where incorporation and co-optation also reign. But her case demonstrates clearly the value of fighting back and the potential for making ethnic studies a parallel institution inside the academy and a resource for parallel institutions outside it.

AN EVENT THAT MARKS A NEW MOMENT

The battle over Harvard's decision to deny tenure to Garcia-Peña marks a moment when the processes of incorporation and co-optation are diminishing and processes of outright repression and exclusion are ascendant. The degree to which the corporate university can tolerate and wishes to incorporate oppositional ethnic studies changes over time. Garcia-Peña's case is significant, not simply because a brilliant original and generative working-class immigrant Afro-Latinx scholar was denied the tenure she deserved, but because the reasons for that denial expose so much about the terms and limits of ethnic studies under current conditions.[33] It was not just her embodied identity but her ideas that made Garcia-Peña's file unacceptable to Harvard—although as noted earlier she in fact had many experiences that indicated that her race, gender, and class were held against her. I argue that the key factors for Harvard in deciding her fate and the key factors for her supporters in intervening against Harvard were that her teaching, research, and service were too closely connected to the needs, desires, and aspirations of aggrieved communities and that she took an intellectual stance in firm opposition to the racial contract and the ways of knowing complementary to it. I have described at length the contours of Garcia-Peña's scholarship and its importance elsewhere.[34] Here I provide a brief glimpse of what makes her research so threatening to her enemies and so inspiring to her allies.

Dominant scholarly conventions have long been prescriptions masquerading as descriptions. They divide the people of the world along lines of binary oppositions that privilege the definers over the defined, the modern over the premodern, the propertied over the property-less, the normative over the non-normative, and the presumed to be human over the presumed to be not fully human. Garcia-Peña shows how the existence of the Afro-Latinx subject challenges the epistemological and ontological foundations of this system by being an identity that cannot be confined within the narratives or norms of any one nation and cannot be measured by the metrics of identity, autonomy, and individuality privileged by reigning Western conceptions of the "human." Her research recognizes, but does not valorize, the discursive and physical sites traditionally treated as central to national projects and to the ideals of the humanities. Instead, she gives special attention to places in the interstices, at the margins, and on the borders and edges. These are places where currents of power intersect, where one identity bleeds into another, and where the seams of the fabric of social construction begin to show. Garcia-Peña does not seek to celebrate Afro-Latinx individuals as worthy candidates for admission to the category of the human but rather shows how the very category of the human is premised on their subordination and domination and on the erasure of their experiences, aspirations, ontologies, and epistemologies. She demonstrates that the bodies of Black Dominicans and Haitians—in their nations of origin as well as in the many different nations to which they migrate—contain archives of knowledge that refute and resist dominant conventions of research and attendant mechanisms of social categorization and control. Instead of viewing Afro-Latinx people as atypical, marginal, or socially peripheral, Garcia-Peña recognizes the importance of their situated knowledges as eyewitnesses to—and insightful critics of—the dramatic transformations taking place in the world in relation to race and representation, language and law, citizenship and social membership, nationalism and knowledge production, patriotism and patriarchy, and criminalization and capitalism.

As a research object, Afro-Latinidad has enabled Garcia-Peña to do more than merely fill in gaps in what was previously an incomplete historical record. Afro-Latinx identity has been most important in her work as a provocation for asking new research questions and developing new research methods. She demonstrates again and again how seemingly private, personal, parochial, and microsocial experiences and expressions can be read as alternative archives of macro- and microsocial systems and structures, as evidence of the collective, cumulative, and continuing effects of conquest, colonialism, Indigenous dispossession, slavery, migration, and exploitation. Her research is empirically deep, theoretically broad, and punctuated by original and infinitely generative new terms and word inflections of her own invention such as *vaivénes* (crossings to and fro), *dictions* (speech acts, sources, and narratives), and *contradictions* (the speaking back that exposes occlusions and omissions).

Denying tenure to Professor Garcia-Peña revealed that the racial liberalism that dominates institutions like Harvard is grounded in *recognizing* discrimination but not *resisting* it. The corporate university is willing to offer some people from aggrieved communities of color a measure of symbolic inclusion in places of power as long as they support the racial order upon which that power depends. Racial liberals at Harvard and elsewhere seek to solidify their influence and secure their power by posing as managers of the crisis, as protagonists with sufficient political legitimacy to protect the system from radical alternatives. They position themselves as capable controllers of the resistance that has been mounted in the streets, in schools, and in workplaces by movements that have emerged against war, environmental destruction, and economic inequality and on behalf of Black lives, gender justice, sexual democracy, and the right to health care and housing. Just as the actions by the liberal dean of the law school at Harvard described in chapter 1 demonstrated that he viewed his mission to be crushing the demands by Black students for teachers and classes attentive to racial injustice, liberal faculty members and administrators today secure their positions as representatives of "diversity" by suppressing and repressing demands on the institution to address and redress its historical allegiance to the racial contract.

In the past both the bottom-up and the top-down versions of ethnic studies have been represented on the Harvard faculty: the radical democratic tradition evidenced in the work of (among others) Cornel West, Walter Johnson, and Elizabeth Hinton, and the managerial and entrepreneurial complicit-with-power and structured-in-dominance version of racial liberalism emblematized by (among others) Orlando Patterson, Henry Louis Gates, Jennifer Hochschild, and Roland Fryer. The denial of tenure to Garcia-Peña signals that the crisis confronting dominant groups is now leading them to abandon the compromise built into the ethnic studies project, to decide that only the system-supporting and power-justifying version of it will be acceptable.

The racial liberals secure their status within the institution by working to police the boundaries of respectability, to provide versions of an ethnic and racial presence that will be perpetually safe for power. The system treats them as exceptional on the condition that they refuse solidarity with the vast masses of people demonized and deemed disposable. The willingness of racial liberals to control and limit the research and speech of other faculty members and students opens the door to even more obvious repressive control and limitations.

Claudine Gay became promoted to the presidency of Harvard in part because as dean she oversaw and supported the denial of tenure to Garcia-Peña. Yet when the hedge fund investors who dominated Harvard's Board of Trustees collaborated with the Republican Party to demand that Harvard ban protests and even suppress statements opposing Israel's collective punishment and ethnic cleansing of Gaza, Gay became their scapegoat and was forced to resign. Student groups protesting Israel's brutality issued statements that forthrightly condemned the Hamas attacks of October 7 but at the same time called for peaceful nonviolent protests against Israel's use of collective punishment of an entire population as its response. The protesters insisted on placing the events in Gaza in the context of Israel's long military suppression of Palestinian freedom. Gay and her fellow racial liberals at Harvard responded to the attacks on them orchestrated by the political right and emboldened by the silence of liberals in Congress and the White House as liberals almost always do in these situations. They caved. They declared fundamental agreement with the goals of their attackers, citing only differences about methods to achieve them. They proposed concessions and compromises as evidence of their deference.[35] A succession of statements by President Gay about the crisis and Harvard's response to it emanated from pressure from wealthy donors insisting on ever more fervent allegiance to Israel's actions and ever more draconian repression of students protesting against them. The campaign at Harvard to suppress dissent entailed trucks circling the campus with photographs of individual student protesters declaring them antisemitic. Pressure was put on businesses and law firms to blacklist any students involved in the protests. Online doxing was used to pinpoint those suspected of being part of demonstrations on campus. Conducted in concert with a campaign by the Diaspora and Foreign Affairs Ministries of the Israeli government to target what they alleged were "antisemitic students" (significant numbers of whom were Jewish), these campaigns relied on the claim that Jewish students who were Zionists had been made to feel uncomfortable and unsafe because of the protests. College administrators and trustees, and the politicians defaming the protests as antisemitism, made no mention of the Jewish students and faculty members in the demonstrations who felt compelled to protest precisely because of what they had learned about acting honorably in the world from their Hebrew school classes, bar mitzvah and bat mitzvah lessons, rabbis' sermons, and Torah and haftarah readings in their synagogues. Moreover, focus on the discomfort of Jewish students who might be offended by criticism of Israel obscured the agony of Palestinian students whose loved ones were being killed by Israeli forces and violent settler vigilantes. These students risked expulsion from college, deportation, and incarceration because of opinion pieces they wrote for newspapers. The US secretary of state justified the arrest, incarceration, and proposed deportation of legal green card holder Mahmoud Khalil on the grounds that while he had done nothing wrong, he might in the future do something that the Trump administration judged to be detrimental to the interests of the US.

None of the concessions made by Harvard to outside pressure sufficed. They only signaled weakness and led to new demands. Republicans in Congress, prominent Democratic Party donors, a former cabinet officer in the Clinton presidency, and ultimately the Trump administration applied increasing pressure to make Harvard conform to their politics and interests. Former secretary of the Treasury Lawrence Summers and hedge fund billionaire Bill Ackman joined with Manhattan Institute propagandist Christopher Rufo to claim that Harvard's problems in failing to suppress protests in support of the people of Gaza stemmed from the school's stated commitments to diversity, equity, and inclusion, a position that paved the way for the Trump administration's taking away all federal funds allocated to Harvard and promising their return only if the university disavowed DEI policies and configured all of its research and teaching to conform to the goals of the current president. Harvard's leaders then made a public show of refusing to cede complete control of the university to the Trump administration while working behind the scenes to cave in to nearly every order from Washington, D.C.[36] As Ricardo Levins Morales notes, liberals can secure power inside the corporate university mainly by throwing others under the bus, but this often backfires, leaving them powerless when the system no longer finds their servility useful.[37] Liberals who throw others under the bus are almost always surprised when that bus later runs over them.

The attack on the semiautonomy of universities has not come about because white supremacy is so strong that it can now wipe out its enemies. Quite the contrary, it has happened because the system of racial capitalism has now been exposed and opposed by masses in motion in the United States and around the world. The attempt to silence and suppress the Gaza protests and the ideas that Garcia-Peña emblematizes reveals the panic that people in power experience when confronted with crises they cannot solve. They seek something that they cannot achieve: to make people who have been eyewitnesses to the calculated callousness and cruelty of racial capitalism remain silent about what they know and remain meekly submissive within the confines of what institutions permit them to be.

When the ad hoc committee at Harvard voted to deny tenure to Garcia-Peña in 2019, it did so despite widespread protests inside and beyond the institution. University administrators adamantly refused to reverse the decision. These actions were designed to discredit Garcia-Peña and her scholarship. As it turned out, however, it was the university that discredited itself in the eyes of aggrieved populations while setting itself up for being attacked by the very powerful outside forces the administrators imagined they were placating. The ideal of meritocracy so central to the self-image and public legitimacy of institutions like Harvard was exposed in this case as a self-serving lie. The injustice perpetrated against Garcia-Peña mobilized her supporters inside and outside the academy and brought public attention to the lack of integrity in Harvard's personnel review process. The attempt to shame and silence her backfired. The dismissal of her work by Harvard unwittingly set in motion a process that gave her work much more recognition, reward, influence, and impact than it would have had if that institution had granted her tenure.

ETHNIC STUDIES TODAY

The scholarship produced by Garcia-Peña and the resistance to it at Harvard provide an opportunity to evaluate the current state of ethnic studies. Her case illustrates how innovations in humanities and social science research that ethnic studies has provoked have now started to become visible (and threatening) even inside top-ranked institutions because they have succeeded in producing new knowledge that equips scholars with tools for asking and answering vitally important questions. They have changed the course of research across the disciplines. Their impact underscores how even the infinitesimally small desegregation of faculty demographics that has taken place as a result of fair hiring laws and modest affirmative action programs has led to large results in helping to bring rich new currents of research into the academy. Successful scholarship depends upon drawing interlocutors from the broadest possible pools of qualified participants, but structural racism, coloniality, and other forms of exploitation and exclusion lead to artificial, arbitrary, and irrational exclusions that maximize the perspectives of the privileged and powerful while minimizing the interests of the dispossessed and displaced. The narrow range of experiences typically represented among faculty members and students who come from a small sample of racial, class, linguistic, and citizenship positions render dominant research parochial and provincial. The resulting distortion of academic research and teaching impedes analysis of some of the most important questions facing society about the tragic and enduring effects in the modern world of Euro-American conquest, colonization, enslavement, and exploitation.

The rise of the generative research exemplified by Garcia-Peña and other similarly situated talented scholars has proceeded at a rapid pace in the past decades. New knowledge paradigms are being pursued with a sense of great urgency in the midst of the pervasive crises that continuously confront the economy, the environment, the electoral process, and the educational system. The unraveling of social cohesion and the shrinking of civil society impel scholars to ask and answer new kinds of questions. Ethnic studies scholarship offers meaningful alternatives to the donor-driven and state-supported expertise that has been wrong about nearly everything. Well-funded "experts" predicted and promised that wonderful things would result from economic austerity, mass incarceration, and broken windows policing, from wars on crime, drugs, and terrorism, from economic deregulation and privatization, and from the fiscalization and vocationalization of education. They celebrated public-private partnerships as cures for urban inequality, promoted cap-and-trade investment credits as an effective response to climate change, and claimed that the election to the presidency of one Black man would usher in an era of post-racialism and color blindness. This abysmal record of error after error has discredited and delegitimized much of what has traditionally passed itself off as expertise. Widespread recognition of the catastrophic failures of dominant scholarship has led to projects inside and outside the academy that turn to new ways of knowing and new ways of being. This emerging scholarship, like that of Garcia-Peña, exposes flaws in the dominant knowledge systems that remain in place at Harvard and at other highly ranked institutions despite their manifest record of shortcomings and failures. Perhaps this is what Harvard found unacceptable.

The denial of tenure to a Harvard University professor of Romance languages and literatures takes place on a very different scale, and with very different stakes, than the injuries endured by the targets of police brutality, the people of Puerto Rico abandoned in the wake of hurricane devastation, the caged children and separated families in border detention camps, and the deaths, illnesses, and injuries caused by the deliberate mishandling of COVID-19. Yet the dismissal of Professor Garcia-Peña was a symptom of the same systemic and structural breakdowns of social institutions and social relations that caused these other crises. For the ethnic studies constituency, this tenure denial offers yet another indication that the compromises created to sustain the property system and the power structure through the temporary social fixes of the twentieth century are no longer in effect. The temporary toeholds that aggrieved groups have established inside institutions in the wake of the democratic and egalitarian upheavals of the past half century may now be seen as concessions that cost the system more than it gains from them. The system of racial capitalism that once sustained itself by covering up its practices of differentiated exclusion with promises of universal inclusion now may need to show its craven cruelty by embracing exclusion openly.

The contradictions that can kill can also cure if used creatively. They can enable people to make their enemies unwitting accomplices in their liberation. As Cedric Robinson often observed, acts of subordination and exclusion do not necessarily determine *who we are*. They are merely *conditions of our existence*.[38] The ultimate political import of the denial of tenure to Professor Garcia-Peña depends upon what forces it sets in motion. It hinges on whether dictions of the powerful will be countered by the contradictions of the people. Ethnic studies scholarship and activism can play a part in identifying, analyzing, and amplifying the voices of contradiction and refining the people's ability to turn hegemony on its head.

The calculated callousness and cruelty of racial capitalism leave the majority of the people in the world with no viable option other than to refuse unlivable destinies and to build a new and better world. The existing and emerging research conducted by Garcia-Peña and others of her generational cohort teaches us that some of the people who are most oppressed by the new social and spatial fixes of racial capitalism are its most original, generative, and insightful critics. The displaced, the dispossessed, and the disinherited can teach the world how to understand, appreciate, and oppose the ways in which dominant systems and stories have sustained violence in the past and perpetrate it in the present. Garcia-Peña proposes reading the rhetorics and realities of our world in contradiction in order to shatter the silences that sustain state violence, exclusion, and oppression. This can be difficult and painful work. It may, as she warns, open old wounds and compel us to reexperience individual and collective defeats, injuries, fears, and discomforts. But it holds the potential as well to bring us closer to justice. Armed with the concepts of diction, and contradiction, aware of the possibilities of *vaivén,* this dark moment of our despair may yet be the first moment of our victory.

The denial of tenure to Professor Garcia-Peña enacted a defeat for academic excellence and for social justice. Yet the mechanisms deployed to implement that denial have been so transparently illegitimate that the decision holds the potential to be the kind of short-term defeat that points the way toward long-term victory. The tenure denial is an insult and an injury that demands a collective response from antiracist and decolonial scholars. Turning indignation into action requires receiving the message sent by Harvard not as it was intended—as a warning to other scholars against following the trail blazed by Garcia-Peña—but as a stimulus to draw the opposite conclusion and choose to follow in her footsteps. The dismissal of Professor Garcia-Peña from Harvard can be one of those moments in history when repression goes too far, becomes too transparent, compromises its own credibility, and comes back to haunt its perpetrators. This can become a watershed moment for the field of ethnic studies and the constituencies to which it is accountable if teachers and students analyze, interpret, and build on it in the right ways.

Some clear lessons emerge from the battle over Garcia-Peña's case:

1. Tenure decisions concern more than the fate of individuals; they affect the entire ethnic studies project and antiracist social formation. They influence the dissemination of knowledge about the ideas, experiences, aspirations, and epistemologies of aggrieved groups.

2. Mobilizing a community of support inside the academy can highlight the nature and value of work by scholars denied tenure. It can bring their ideas to new audiences and encourage graduate students and emerging scholars to invent and embrace new paradigms.

3. The corporate university's rejection of research does not mean that research is bad, and institutional approval does not make it good. Connection to community concerns and struggles enables research and writing to be vetted by people who are not recognized as intellectuals but whose creative responses to their life experiences with the use of difference as an excuse for domination make them expert interlocutors. Whether academia accepts or rejects the research that emerges from that dialogue, it nonetheless advances knowledge and the possibilities for a more just world.

4. Unjust tenure denials harm individual scholars and their communities while depriving educational institutions of greatly needed knowledge. But securing tenure and promotion, as Garcia-Peña eventually did at Princeton, is not automatically a victory. The value of tenured positions rests in what is done with them. They enable recipients to make the classroom a forum for producing and evaluating new knowledge, to bring into research the wisdom of a wider world, and to train graduate student researchers to venture out and discover new research objects and new research methods.

5. Fights to desegregate the classroom, the curriculum, and the demography of campuses are important. It is worthy work to challenge the knowledge regimes that excuse and justify domination based on difference. Finding ways to share the resources of the academy with communities historically excluded from them, however, can produce important new projects and social formations.

6. If every ethnic studies program and department disappeared tomorrow, antiracist learning, teaching, imagining, and inventing would still continue among people refusing unlivable destinies in different places and different ways.

The Bridge section of this book that follows shows how dispositions, stances, tools, and commitments necessary for ethnic studies work inside life's many classrooms can be augmented and enriched through the frameworks of the crossroads, the caduceus, the archive, and the repertoire. How to apply those frameworks in ways that connect campus learning and teaching to the important work carried out inside autonomous learning circles forms the focus of the chapters that follow the Bridge.

A Bridge for This Book

Ethnic Studies: The Crossroads, the Caduceus, the Archive, and the Repertoire

The metaphor of the crossroads looms large in ways of knowing and ways of being in Africa and its diaspora. Robert Farris Thompson notes that for the Yoruba people of West Africa it is thought necessary to "cultivate the art of recognizing significant communications, knowing what is truth and what is falsehood, or else the lesson of the crossroads—the point where doors open or close, where persons have to make decisions that may forever affect their lives—will be lost."[1] In Haiti, Moris Moriset, president of the Rara aggregation Rara Ti-Malis Kache, declares, "To get anywhere in life you have to follow a road. To make things happen you have to move through a crossroads."[2]

The ways of knowing illuminated by Thompson and Moriset embody one of the aims of this book: to cultivate the capacity to make informed and generative decisions at the crossroads. This section introduces the key terms *crossroads, caduceus, archive,* and *repertoire* as conceptual tools for moving from the focus on opposition and incorporation in chapters 1 and 2 to discussions of accompaniment in chapter 3, intersectional justice in chapter 4, and inquiry and instruction in chapter 5. This section serves as bridge between what has come before and what is to follow.

WHAT IS A BRIDGE?

Composers working within the four-line, thirty-two-bar format of popular song make a statement in the first eight bars, repeat it in the next eight, craft the third eight as a place of rhythmic or harmonic contrast, then return to the original statement. The third section is known as "the bridge" because it interrupts a pattern, causes a moment of pause, and connects the past to the present and the future.

The crossroads and the caduceus have long histories as metaphors and symbols inside many different cultures. Their deployment here reflects a particular understanding of them that is concerned not so much with their essence or ultimate identity in general terms but rather with what they can do for ethnic studies and related struggles against domination. In my interpretation, they provide particular ways of knowing, being, and acting. At crossroads, decisions must be made and new paths can be followed. In chapter 1, liberal law school professors and administrators belittling the importance of racism provoked students to discover and develop the oppositional potential of critical race theory. In chapter 2, the contradictions of incorporation confronted by Lorgia Garcia-Peña and her allies led to a battle against corporate control inside the academy and to the discovery and mobilization of parallel community institutions outside it. In both of these cases, seemingly crushing defeats set the stage for major victories.

This chapter argues for the importance of recognizing that while ethnic studies specifically—and liberation study and struggle more generally—have not soared from victory to victory, they have survived and thrived by recognizing problems and obstacles as provocations for developing for new ways of knowing and acting. The seeds of solutions have often resided inside what seem like insurmountable problems. Improvisation, invention, and inversion have enabled ethnic studies and its allies to turn fetters into tools for liberation. The work of ethnic studies requires reading dominant archives against the grain but also creating new repositories of collective knowledge. Antiracist knowledge gets transmitted across generations through events, actions, rituals, and performances that create and sustain repertoires of embodied memory. Inside struggles for dignity and democracy, the crossroads, the caduceus, the archive, and the repertoire have functioned as central tools and terrains of study and struggle.

THE CROSSROADS

The Haitian metaphor of the crossroads has guided my participation in ethnic studies in many ways. Inspired by the scholarship of Patrick Bellegarde-Smith, Claudine Michel, Elizabeth McAlister, and the musical ensemble Boukman Eksperyans, I titled one of my books *Dangerous Crossroads* and picked the name *Kalfou* (the Haitian Kreyol word for crossroads) for the comparative and relational ethnic studies journal that I helped start and coedit. This book appears in the American Crossroads series, which I coedit at the University of California Press.

Other cultures use the symbol of the crossroads as well. The Persian word for crossroads, *chehareah,* evokes the four cardinal directions as symbols of tension, orientation, and choice. The Arabic word *taqaato* stands for an intersection, a place where paths cut or sever.[3] Key works in the inventory of ethnic studies authored in diverse contexts come back to the crossroads again and again as a generative metaphor. Gloria Anzaldúa's poem "To Live in the Borderlands Means You" ends with the affirmation that survival in the borderlands requires living without borders and being a crossroads.[4] Houston Baker introduces his landmark study of Afro-American literary consciousness with lyrics from the song "Crossroad Blues" and concludes by identifying crossing signs at railroad junctions as symbols that signify change, process, motion, and transience.[5] In what is perhaps the quintessential intersectional ethnic studies poem, "Child of the Americas," Puerto Rican, Jewish, feminist, bisexual, antiracist, environmentalist, sexual exploitation survivor, and disability justice activist Aurora Levins Morales delineates the many different currents of identity flowing through her as "a child of many diasporas" and a "child of many mothers" who was "born at a crossroads."[6] Singer, dancer, composer, environmentalist, and Asian American activist Nobuko Miyamoto expressed admiration for her friend and fellow freedom fighter Yuri Kochiyama's connections to Black and Puerto Rican artists and their social justice struggles. "Her house was a crossroads," Miyamoto observes, and "she was a crossroads."[7]

In West African traditions, the crossroads designates a place, time, or circumstance where paths come together and decisions need to be made. Crossroads are sacred but dangerous sites. Collisions can occur where roads come together, where strangers meet, where the way ahead is not predetermined. Travelers can go down the wrong path and become lost. Yet the same crossroads that can inhibit can also enable. At the crossroads, it is neither easy nor desirable to determine too quickly what is right and what is wrong, what is good and what is bad, what will work and what will fail. At the crossroads it is possible and often necessary to look in more than one direction, to make choices about which paths to follow, to exercise discernment, judgment, and agency. Negotiating crossroads requires seeing beyond surface appearances and recognizing deeper truths. At the crossroads the right thing can look like the wrong thing and the wrong thing can look like the right thing. Its challenges require active engagement, not passive contemplation.

At the crossroads the insignificant can become significant, what seems small can loom large. Toni Cade Bambara describes her writing as an exercise in finding profound significance in what others might perceive as insignificant. She tells ordinary truths about everyday people's lives, celebrating their struggles, and bringing to center stage "all those characters, just ordinary folks on the block, who've been waiting in the wings, characters we thought we had to ignore because they weren't pimp-flashy or hustler-slick or because they didn't fit easily into previously acceptable modes or stock types."[8] At different crossroads Bambara cultivated capacities for discerning the meaning and value of a wide array of signs, symbols, messages, and communications. That ability holds great potential import for research. Scholarly studies that focus on grand personalities, major events, and loci of institutional power can seem self-evidently significant, but they may in fact be less important than they appear. The seemingly small everyday, ordinary, and quotidian world might be suffused with large generative implications when discerned and interpreted correctly. Standing at the crossroads requires an advanced disposition to see through surface appearances, to welcome surprises, and to improvise in response to them.

The ways of knowing that predominate in Western thought encourage taking the straight road and avoiding the crossroads. Managing risk, avoiding surprises, and remaining on the narrow path mapped out by the market, the church, the school, the state, and the disciplines and favored by political ideologies, self-help advisers, and the conventions of scholarship promise safety and reward. Physical places are configured to promote order, while stories with predictable beginnings, middles, and ends introduce surprises largely only to signify either temporary danger or refuge before getting back on the right path. In this dominant epistemology, contradictions are to be resolved once and for all.

The epistemology of the crossroads promotes a different way of knowing and being. It entails recognizing and exploring unities of opposites, perceiving the mutually constitutive nature of the tonic and the toxic. Interruptions serve as welcome challenges to the pitfalls and shortcomings of the normative path. For example, traditional textile artists in Senegambia favor irregular angular patterns because their cosmology dictates that only evil travels in straight lines.[9] Resisting linear patterns encourages people to expect surprises, disruptions, and detours, to enjoy their ability to invent and improvise. For practitioners of vodou in Haiti, serving the spirits at the crossroads requires both *konesans* and *balans*. The knowledge signified by *konesans* blends discernment with empathy and judgment as capacities gained with age and respect for those who have lived previously. *Balans* cultivates moral consciousness and strategic acumen by reconciling opposites, recognizing their mutually constitutive qualities, and taking their negative elements and channeling them toward positive results.[10]

The epistemology of the crossroads eschews "either/or" binaries to pursue instead the promises of "both/and" frameworks. Some binaries, of course, are useful and necessary. Intellectual and political responsibilities make it necessary to distinguish labor from capital, settler coloniality from Indigenous survivance, democracy from dictatorship, and domination from resistance. Yet polarities and binary oppositions that divide the world into good and bad can obscure more than they reveal. Solutions can become problems and problems can become solutions. Things that enact harm can also be used to help heal; things that can kill can also be used to cure. Michel Foucault argues that the same powers that oppress and repress also provoke opposition. Working with this concept, Indigenous scholar Chris Andersen (Métis) describes statistics as a tool the state and capital use to individualize disorder and find deficits in individuals rather than in structures and systems. For that very reason, however, Andersen and other academics and activists find it necessary to master statistical methods, to challenge their base assumptions, and to fight over ownership of collected information through projects that include the Indigenous Data Sovereignty initiative.[11]

Tales told in the Afro-diasporic world relate the presence at the crossroads of a mischievous trickster who poses riddles, problems, insults, jokes, diversions, and evasions. This challenging but (ultimately) benign spirit—named Eshu Elegba by the Yoruba people—is neither devil nor angel, but an embodied contradiction, an intermediary between the human and the divine who prods those he meets to use intellect and imagination to recognize problems and take action to solve them. His presence is to be welcomed rather than feared. Robert Farris Thompson explains that the trickster at the crossroads can be "the master of possibility," provoking action that imbues the world with augmented potential to make right and just things come to pass.[12] Exercising discernment and judgment at the crossroads requires what Walter Benjamin calls "presence of mind," the practice of being fully aware of the present and its possibilities for the future. The goal of presence of mind for Benjamin is "to turn the threatening future into a fulfilled 'now.'"[13] This entails interpreting the "omens, presentiments, and signals" that appear subtly, like wave impulses, and acting upon them. The vexations inherent in standing at the crossroads create discomfort, but that discomfort can serve a stimulus to set out on new and better paths.

THE CADUCEUS

At this crossroads in history, the ethnic studies project specifically and the broader antiracist formation from which it emerges face circumstances as horrifying as our worst fears might conjure. For that reason, learning how to turn poison into medicine is an obligation of the greatest urgency. The metaphor of the caduceus can help people to fend off despair, resist surrender, and deploy the tools they have in the arenas open to them to help themselves and others. The caduceus is an ancient symbol depicting two snakes with wings entwined around a stick. It symbolizes the recognition by the physicians of antiquity that substances that can kill—like the venom of snakes—can also cure if deployed as medicine in the right ways and in the right doses. Its close relative, the rod of Asclepius (which displays one snake with no wings curled around a stick), appears on bottles of medicine, in pharmacy windows, on insignias of health agencies, and sometimes on the medical school rings and license plates of physicians.[14] In Greek mythology the caduceus represents the staff of Hermes, the messenger of the gods. His wand can induce sleep in those who are awake and awaken those who are asleep; the wand can provide the dying with a peaceful death but also bring the dead back to life.[15]

The caduceus thus symbolizes both poison and medicine, both evil and the potential to overcome evil. According to Ricardo Levins Morales, the Ojibwemowin word *maskhiki* connotes that which is medicinal but can also refer to poison because harm can come from the same materials that heal depending on how they are deployed and in what context.[16] Western ways of knowing associate the snake with evil and danger, with the temptation of Eve in the Garden of Eden and the threat that knowledge poses to innocence. The Catholic Church venerates St. Patrick for ridding Ireland of evil by driving out the snakes that pagans worshipped. Yet in that pagan tradition, and in assorted Indigenous cosmologies around the world, the snake also serves as a symbol of awakening, purification, renewal, and transformation. The Lakota Black Snake prophecy inspired Indigenous water protectors in 2016 protesting pipeline construction in North Dakota—by serving as a doubly accented sign, portending both impending doom and resurgent resistance.[17] Even inside the major religions of the world, snakes shedding their skins sometimes signify getting rid of old identities and their impediments. Chicana Indigena queer feminist Gloria Anzaldúa perceives the snake to be a symbol "of awareness and intelligence not grasped by logical thought."[18]

Turning poison into medicine and using the appearance of evil as an opportunity to oppose and overcome it characterizes the work described in chapters 1 and 2. In those cases, oppositional groups maneuvered their oppressors into becoming unwitting accomplices in their liberation. The very discomfort and appearance of defeat felt by the minoritized and racialized law students who invented critical race theory and by Lorgia Garcia-Peña and her supporters led them to initiate the forms of convivial cocreation that gave them comfort, courage, clarity, and conviction. Negative descriptions of them by their oppressors became the basis for positive affirmation by themselves. As Judith Butler argues, being subjected entails subordination to power but also can create a subjectivity that becomes the basis for emancipatory knowledge and action.[19] This is a central dynamic within ethnic studies. The terms used to describe aggrieved groups and the broader project that brings them together are all structured in dominance, originated by the oppressors, and inaccurate about the identities and activities they describe. Butler notes, however, that even though "the terms by which we are hailed are rarely the ones we choose (and even when we try to impose protocols on how we are to be named, they usually fail)" nonetheless "these terms we never really choose are the occasion for something we might still call agency, the repetition of an imaginary subordination for another purpose, one whose future is partly open."[20] By reclaiming and repurposing the tools of their subjection, aggrieved peoples can create new pathways and possibilities.

The caduceus makes its presence felt inside many different contradictions. A knife grabbed by the handle can carve wood and cut food, but a knife grabbed by the blade injures the bearer. Fire can destroy forests, but strategic burning can help ecosystems survive and thrive. Heavy rains can be a boon for farmers but a torment to tourists. Cosmopolitan cities function as places that people move to in order to secure safety from rural poverty and oppression and to experience personal freedom, while at the same time they also become loci of new forms of alienation, anxiety, and anomie. Indigenous harvesters warn against taking too much from the fields and forests, thereby exceeding the capacity of the plants to regenerate. But they also know that taking too little makes traditions die and relationships fade in ways that cause damage to the land.[21]

Embracing contradictions and working through them has shaped much of the history of liberation struggles. Throughout the Afrodiasporic world the Christian Bible was used to justify conquest, slavery, and segregation, to teach meekness and submission, and to tell the oppressed their deliverance would only come in the next world after their deaths. The targets of these messages turned them upside down, focusing on biblical accounts of imperfect heroes whose actions freed them in this world, interpreting references to deliverance as coded messages meant for them, and using the portrayal of a divine power in the universe as a heavenly boss more powerful than their earthly boss and as eternal justification for resisting submission to temporal social structures and hierarchies.[22] The theology of the Catholic Church has been deployed to administer and justify European conquest, coloniality, Indigenous dispossession, and slavery, but workers around the world have also embraced the Church as a global institution whose imperatives supersede the authority of nation-states and whose teachings can be used for liberation. The very forms of narrative, spectacle, and drama deployed by the Church to induce passivity about the injustices of this world formed the basis of tactics by social movement mobilizations against dictatorships in Argentina and El Salvador and on behalf of farmworkers' rights in the US.[23]

Activist groups illustrate and contest their conditions by turning hegemony on its head, turning the very terms and tools used to oppress them into mechanisms for liberation. When police officers beat former Black Panther Michael Zinzun so badly that he lost his sight in one eye, he used the monetary settlement he secured in court because of that beating to set up the Coalition Against Police Abuse, an organization established to keep an eye on the police—offering a different meaning to the phrase "an eye for an eye."[24] Similarly, the People's Paper Co-Op (PPC) of the Village of Arts and Humanities in Philadelphia works with legal professionals to force the police department to release records of arrests and charges that did not lead to convictions because that "bad paper" often serves to prevent innocent people from obtaining employment, housing, education, and other necessities. The project invites people to tear up their criminal records, put them in blenders, and pulp and press the scraps into new blank sheets of paper. Participants then decorate these blank sheets with Polaroid portraits of themselves (a reverse mugshot) and respond to an invitation to write an end to the sentence

"Without my record I am free to be . . . ." Some of the "bad paper" is preserved and installed as hanging sheets in a space designed to resemble a prison cell. Other pieces are recycled into writing paper and mailing envelopes to be used to correspond with currently incarcerated people. Another project has women who are undergoing reentry from incarceration to author messages screen-printed on handmade paper to be sold as posters—with the proceeds going for bail to free mothers awaiting trial to be home for Mother's Day.[25]

The peril and promise of the caduceus also appear in the creation and deployment of scholarly concepts. Michel Foucault demonstrates repeatedly how discourse functions as an instrument of coercive power but also can serve as the starting point for opponents of unjust domination.[26] The word *black* became used by post-Enlightenment thinkers to signify evil, ignorance, immorality, and epistemological deficiency. In the 1960s, however, activists in the US and elsewhere embraced Blackness as an emblem of linked fates, collective pride, and a political orientation toward liberation.[27] Leigh Ann Duck explains the enduring contradiction: "While blackness is mobilized by governments as a technology for dividing a population and disenfranchising a labor force, it also serves to assemble people with experiences and memories that attune them to local and global injustice."[28]

Militarized agents on the Mexico-US border direct migrants toward desert lands where heat, thirst, and predatory animals exert violent retribution against those who try to cross them. Government agents at the border deploy the desert and its flora and fauna as instruments of the state that contribute to the deaths of people attempting to cross borders. Yet Indigenous farmers and goat herders help border crossers by using that same desert as a provider of hidden water sources, edible plants, and navigable trails. They point to trees that provide shelter and medicinal plants to be tapped for antioxidant and anti-inflammatory remedies for bites and cuts incurred in the wilderness.[29]

The inversions symbolized by the potential of the caduceus can be tactically effective, yet they entail compromises that never fully erase the traces of poison in their origins. Embracing *Blackness* as a unifying term can promote solidarity and recognition of a linked fate, but it runs the risk of endorsing a narrow racialism that reifies rather than resists conceptions of race as biological rather than political. Trans activists confront the caduceus in contradictory ways. They resent the legal categories, social practices, and institutions that oppress them, while nonetheless working within them and trying to overcome them by using the tools they offer to gain measures of rights, respect, resources, and recognition. Trans authors and activists Jules Joanne Gleeson and Elle O'Rourke maintain, "We resent the society that birthed us, just as we refuse to set aside the tools it has offered us," and add that "we find ourselves at once immersed and resistant."[30]

The contradictions of the crossroads appear vividly in conservative conceptualizations of idealized motherhood, child protection, and familial privatism. These formulations have been used to legitimate fascist dictatorships in Argentina and Germany. In the US they propel movements to keep schools segregated, ban books, and harass and fire gay and trans teachers. They are frames that perpetuate enormous harm. Yet invocations of idealized motherhood and child protection have also been appropriated and inverted by rebellious groups protesting immigration authorities who separate families and incarcerate children in cages. Mothers' love for daughters appears prominently in campaigns protesting murdered and missing Indigenous women and girls in Canada and the US and against feminicides in Mexico. While tremendously valuable in exposing the unstated racialized assumptions that support the tropes of idealized motherhood and child protection, these inversions also run the risk of naturalizing the nuclear family and ignoring the vulnerability of children and women outside it. Yet they can also serve emancipatory purposes. The organization Southerners on New Ground frames its feminist, antiracist, queer, and class struggle politics through appeals to a kind of kinship and familial solidarity. They offer membership in a chosen family not confined to blood ties or nuclear households, instead imagining kinship as composed by many different forms of connection.[31]

In analyzing liberal scholarship, Michel-Rolph Trouillot remarks that the word *culture* emerged originally as a term deployed by anthropologists to ease fears of difference, promote pluralism, and rein in racialist explanations for social hierarchies. Yet that very term has been used as a concept deployed for racist ends by scholars and policymakers who blame the plight of the oppressed on their allegedly deficient cultural practices instead of on the forces that dominate and exploit them.[32] Chicana and Indigenous feminists have established the physical places of *borderlands* as metaphors for understanding the generative possibilities of complex and contradictory social identities. These concepts have been embraced widely and deployed productively by scholars across the disciplines. Yet as T. Jackie Cuevas observes, the concept of the borderlands has also been appropriated by scholars out of context as an abstract and uncritical "default way of seeing" that stands for any in-between state, ignoring the concept's emergence and grounding in specific regional struggles by queer women against specific "subjugated identities, normative sexualities, and gender variances."[33]

The crossroads and the caduceus offer tools for contending with and confronting the contradictory aspects of study and struggle. In *Strength to Love,* a collection of his sermons, Martin Luther King Jr. presents the Christian cross as at one and the same time a symbol of the greatness of God and the lowness of man. He calls for uniting a tough mind with a tender heart, for embracing both religion and science, for acknowledging the presence of some good in the worst of us and some bad in the best of us. King references the Book of Psalms as a guide in moments of despair, noting its promise that the weeping that lasts for a night heralds the coming of joy in the morning. King argues that the darkest moments of our despair can be the first moments of our victory.[34]

In "The Drum Major Instinct," a sermon delivered two months to the day before his assassination in 1968, King deployed the dual qualities of the caduceus. Describing at length many of the harms perpetuated by ego-oriented selfishness, by desires to stand out from the crowd and be viewed as better than others, King's sermon initially seems to be calling for lessened investment in the self. In a deft turn, however, he argues that this desire to be first, to surpass others, and to have an augmented sense of personhood can be a positive force if used in the right ways. King counsels his listeners to want to be first, not in wealth, power, or prestige, but rather in love, generosity, and moral excellence. If everyone is trying to be first in recognition and reward, only one person can be first. But if being first entails finding shelter for the houseless, feeding the hungry, clothing the naked, welcoming the stranger, visiting those in prison, and making peace, then everyone can be first, because everyone can serve.

For practitioners of vodou, the cross has a connotation slightly different from (although related to) the one it has in Christianity. In vodou it signals the crossroads of the four cardinal directions of the universe, and the locus of conversations between humans and the spirits, the living and their ancestors, and the sacred and the profane. In this context, the trickster Legba serves as an interlocutor and interpreter embodying the possibilities and the perils of transformation and change. Words spoken and songs performed at the crossroads contain conflicting and contradictory meanings conveyed through double, triple, and quadruple entendres. Disruptions at the crossroads can bring both chaos and calm. They require forging harmony out of disharmony and keeping opposing entities in balance through synthesis and recombination.[35] Similarly, throughout the African diaspora, burial grounds serve to connect the past with the present and the living with departed ancestors. Plants, flowers, and used cups, saucers, and plates decorate grave sites to simulate conversations with the dead. Water in jars and rivers symbolizes the flow of history across generations. These items symbolize rupture and continuity, sorrow and joy simultaneously by marking the grief of separations caused by death while at the same time honoring the ancestors as welcomed actors and accompaniers in the present.

Members of aggrieved communities and the scholars who study about, with, and for them are well acquainted with the crossroads and the caduceus. In struggles against the calculated cruelties of domination, nearly everything that can cure can also kill. There is no demand that cannot be co-opted, no pure or unproblematic mode of struggle. Working for social justice requires a judicious blend of the opposites of urgency and patience. Being excluded from institutions can cause suffering, but being incorporated inside them can be as bad. The solidarities of sameness necessary for group self-defense, self-definition, and self-determination can come at the expense of the dynamics of difference within a group, imposing uniformity rather than unity and disavowing the experiences, aspirations, and interests of the group's least normative or most complex members. The establishment of a community of struggle that enables resistance can become its own self-interested and self-serving bureaucracy or dictatorship.

These vexing contradictions, however, can be confronted and creatively reconfigured. Displaced, dispossessed, disregarded, and disrespected peoples inhabit spaces structured by their oppressors to control, constrain, and contain them. Ugly, unjust, indecent, and inhuman realities are intended to produce resignation and despair, and they often achieve that end. Choices made at the crossroads, however, can subvert and invert asymmetrical power relations. The survival strategies of oppressed people often revolve around finding and cultivating value in undervalued people and places. The epistemology of the caduceus leads them to respond to condescension and dismissal by deploying what Robert Stam describes as "the strategic redemption of the low, the despised, the imperfect, and the trash as part of a social overturning."[36] Through subversion and inversion they use subordination as an impetus for solidarity, discern segregation as an opportunity for congregation, and respond to intended individual social death with insistent affirmation on a rich collective social life.

Inner-city mural artists transform blank building walls into art galleries. Yard art sculptures crafted from discarded items transform dilapidated ghetto and barrio neighborhoods into spectacular sites of display. Uncredentialed art makers turn discarded empty milk containers into works of art.[37] Undocumented immigrants transform strip mall and big box store parking lots into labor hiring halls and pop-up markets where vendors can sell homemade tamales from the trunks of their cars. Swap meet stalls can become music libraries, while jazz album covers can function as introductory catalogues to works of modern art. Ethnic studies scholar Rick Bonus notes how alienated first-generation Pacific Islander students at the University of Washington, unfamiliar with college conventions, transform their school by thinking of the institution as being like the living ocean environments they know well. Bonus observes that precisely because the students have limited knowledge of college life, they craft "fresh, bold, and serious ideas for transforming schooling."[38] They invent ways of making the school fulfill the functions their communities derived from the ocean, viewing it as a home connected to many diverse locations, a repository of meaningful knowledge, and a shared space and ecosystem that demands respect and caretaking.

The crossroads and the caduceus do not make subordination disappear. As Jennifer L. Morgan, Cherríe Moraga, and others have argued, scholars who study the suffering of subaltern groups find themselves perpetually on the brink of both an intellectual breakthrough and an emotional breakdown. There is nothing to be gained by romanticizing realities that offer precious little justification for romance. Celebrating the persistence and resistance of oppressed people can run the risk of naturalizing and excusing the indecent conditions that force them to persist and resist. It can be a matter of the greatest importance and urgency, however, to recognize the value of the crossroads and the caduceus as knowledge tools that compel thinking that is relational and intersectional, that goes beyond surface appearances and conventional categories, that privileges thinking critically over merely reciting rules, and that recognizes the need to find balance between competing impulses and forces.

Being left out can entail excruciating pain and suffering. Activism can emerge from harsh circumstances such as those to be discussed in chapter 4 facing queer cofounders of antiracist gay liberation movements, disability justice activists, bridge builders inside aggrieved racialized groups, people whose lives are shaped by borderlands, displacement, exile, and migration, and people attempting to provide sanctuary for criminalized migrants. Their triumphs should not be used to minimize the misery and mistreatment they face. Yet their deft deployments of the epistemologies of the crossroads and the caduceus, their ability to make a way in worlds not made for them, and their ability to use their suffering to diagnose the ills of the entire society stand as important pillars of the ethnic studies project and the broader antiracist social formation that it both reflects and shapes.

While international agreements and transnational financial institutions facilitate capital's free movement around the world, workers face the barriers of border enforcement through militarized policing, walls, passports, technological surveillance, and policies that force people onto dangerous seas and perilous desert terrains. Yet many of them recognize the necessity of living transnational lives and as a response develop forms of cognitive mapping that transcend state-centric notions. Mary Pat Brady's *Scales of Captivity* exposes how thinking about social stratification has been constrained by conventional approaches to geographic scale.[39] Mobile migrant communities around the world develop forms of cognitive mapping that challenge the conventions of scale in dominant scholarship and civic life and offer powerful alternatives to state-centric identity projects. Martha Gonzalez elucidates a Chicana identity located neither solely in Mexico nor solely in the US, one that uses what is known by living in the US while looking at life in Mexico to forge a transborder consciousness. Gonzalez led the way in organizing Entre Mujeres, a translocal musical project made possible by in-person and technologically mediated music making that documented the varied ways in which fifteen women from five different countries negotiate their lives as women, wage earners, caretakers, and mothers in the age of neoliberal austerity.[40] Jessica Bissett Perea (Dena'ina) connects the local roots of Alaska Native music to the crossroads created by cultural interactions resulting from incursions onto Yupik land by explorers, missionaries, oil field workers, and conduits of commercial entertainment. She reveals how juridical connections to the US and other Indigenous Peoples in the lower forty-eight states affect Alaskan Natives, but also how they also envision themselves as part of an Indigenous Arctic world with organic connections to Indigenous Peoples in Greenland, Norway, and Sweden.[41] Part of this cognitive mapping appears inside Bissett Perea's analysis of the utility of Indigenous performance as a form of "world making without stateness."[42]

Even at its best, ethnic studies cannot resolve or shut down contradictions encountered at the crossroads. It can, however, use them as provocations to create a conscious counterculture of restorative justice and social healing through acts of improvisation and accompaniment. Thinking in terms of the crossroads and the caduceus enables recognition of ethnic studies as explained in chapter 2: as *both* a liberating repository of radical thought *and* also a mechanism for containing and co-opting it. The hypervisibility of ethnic studies intellectuals in public life runs the risk of bring rewards to individuals while occluding the conditions, causes, claims, injuries, and aspirations of the communities they are purported to represent. Yet attending to the grassroots in communities with which ethnic studies scholars identify—from which they come and for whom they often speak—has its own pitfalls. Claims made on *behalf of*—rather than *by*—the masses can position the grassroots as yet another exotic "other" in need of sympathy, pity, and protection, a group to be taught and trained rather than learned from and accompanied.[43]

Every racist injury enacts lasting harm that cannot be ignored or fully suppressed. Yet as Homi Bhabha quips, in every emergency there can also be an emergence.[44] The antiracist social formation composed of race-based liberation movements that set the stage for ethnic studies proceeded steadily by creating tactical and consensual unity out of felt disunity, finding medicinal potential hidden inside poison, and turning the fetters of exploitation into tools for liberation. The prophetic tradition of Black religion requires discerning *what can be* hidden beneath the surface appearances of *what is* and acting on that knowledge through improvisation, invention, and often inversion. José Esteban Muñoz shows how what he calls "disidentification" enables queers of color locked out of representation completely or included in it only in caricatured form to appropriate, subvert, and invert dominant images as ways of imagining and inhabiting "spaces of productivity where identity's fragmentary nature is accepted and negotiated."[45] Enacting the key lesson of the crossroads, Muñoz argues that disidentification neither rejects nor completely accepts the dominant heterosexist ideology but rather finds way to work within, on, and against it.[46] Queers of color in Muñoz's analysis can neither fully submit to the dominant race and gender order nor separate fully from it. But at the crossroads they can balance competing forces and formulate paths toward liberation built on "both/and" rather than "either/or" formulations. The dynamism of the "both/and" stance appears vividly in the logo that Chicano artist Rupert Garcia designed for the prison abolition organization Critical Resistance. The image consists of a large eye superimposed on an orange background, one that can be seen as either a sunrise or a sunset. The eye represents the surveillance of targeted populations by systems of policing and incarceration, but also the optics of those able to see new possibilities emerging on the horizon.[47]

The caduceus involves situations that are neither purely oppositional nor purely submissive to power. The hurts of history need to be acknowledged, yet still resisted. Attempting to turn hegemony on its head always entails the possibility that counterhegemony can also be co-opted and turned back into hegemony. Jack Halberstam argues, for example, that transgenderism's valorization of gender fluidity and transgression can fulfill the hopes of decades of gender activism, yet can also be evidence of "the reincorporation of a radical subculture back into the flexible economy of postmodern culture."[48] Argentinian artist and activist Claudia Bernardi observes that some wounds are so deep they cannot be healed and there is no escape from them. The challenge, she argues, is to find ways to live with the hurt and not cause future harm, to embrace the uneasy balance of the caduceus in a space composed of a "delicate membrane between horror and hope."[49]

The epistemologies of the crossroads and the caduceus entail embracing contradictions and complexities, finding hidden potential in threatening appearances, forging unexpected tactical and temporary unities among differently situated peoples, and using improvisation, invention, and inversion to understand the world and make it better. Many of the key concepts developed within and around ethnic studies have built upon the generative potential of contradiction, ambivalence, and discomfort. Chicana feminist and queer formulations of *nepantla* and borderlands, Black feminist intersectionality, and queer of color disidentification all revolve around rejecting single-axis solutions to problems generally posed as binaries. They forge new temporary unities out of historically constructed opposites. Rather than seeking to impose solidarities of sameness on differently situated people, they point toward the generative potentials of the dynamics of difference.

THE ARCHIVE AND THE REPERTOIRE

The qualities that make the ethnic studies project both similar to and different from the broader antiracist social formation's autonomous learning circles can come into clear relief through performance theorist Diana Taylor's distinction between the archive and the repertoire.[50] In her formulation, the archive is an official written record, an identity consistent with the origin of the term as the Greek word for a public building in which important documents are kept. The archive is an especially privileged site for scholars, especially for historians who think (often incorrectly) that it is objective, unmediated, and reliably accurate. Yet every word in an archive has been transmitted by someone to someone else under specific conditions and circumstances. What appears in the archive has been selected for inclusion by interested parties who judge other evidence as unworthy of entry.

Scholarly research in ethnic studies often attempts to expand the archive. It produces reports, articles, and books, and collects documents and images in order to make them part of a permanent authoritative record available to others. It is no small task to make visible what archives structured in dominance have hidden: histories of conquest, coloniality, dispossession, displacement, looting, and labor exploitation responsible for the wealth and power of empires, nation-states, and corporations. Attempts to expand the archive can identify and transmit the insistence by subordinated, silenced, suppressed, shunned, and segregated groups to be recognized and represented, to be seen as something other than forever foreign, strange, inferior, or unknowable.

Archives can be valuable and even indispensable sources of ethnic studies and antidomination knowledge. Mia Mingus views her blog *Leaving Evidence* as an archive of the love, pain, and survival of disabled queer people of color. "We must leave evidence," she affirms. "Evidence of the wholeness we never felt and the immense sense of fullness we gave to each other. Evidence of who we were, who we thought we were, who we never should have been. Evidence for each other that there are other ways to live—past survival; past isolation."[51] In similar fashion, recognizing how privatization of public education in New Orleans threatened the innovative Students at the Center project (to be discussed more fully in the next chapter) and the community that nurtured and sustained it, Kalamu ya Salaam points to the books published by the students as an alternative archive. "I don't believe we're gonna win this one . . . but I do believe the story is important. We have to tell our story."[52] The privatizers eventually succeeded in terminating Students at the Center, but the books it produced make it clear that the students, teachers, and parents working with it wanted a kind of education directly at odds with the neoliberal audit system. The books show how they created—and for nearly two decades sustained—a community-based, participatory, student-centered curriculum and pedagogy.

Consulting archives increases the likelihood that research will reflect more than one point of view. Even archives structured in dominance can be read against the grain to reveal much about the lives of subordinated peoples.⁵³ Because the archive is always structured in dominance, however, the inclusion it offers to those previously excluded is limited and conditional. While the professional and personal papers, correspondence, and press releases of powerful people fill the archives, the records of subordinated and oppositional individuals and groups are often scattered in alternative archives found in scrapbooks, boxes, and file cabinets in activists' garages, basements, and living rooms. The history of Chicanx and Latinx art is sparsely represented in museum and archival collections, but thanks to the efforts of grassroots collectors whose purchases of art are motivated by commitment to cultural preservation rather than economic speculation, it survives on the walls of dwellings inhabited by artists' families, friends, and community admirers.⁵⁴ Diligent and determined scholars sometimes collect materials from these alternative repositories and place them online or inside institutions, as is the case with the Flint Water Crisis Archives, the Hemispheric Institute's Ecologies of Migrant Care digital repository, and the Lesbian Herstory Archives and the Stonewall Archives.⁵⁵ Yet even when the archive expands its purview to include those it deems marginal, it rarely displays recognition of how the margins challenge the legitimacy of the center. Taylor explains that when dominant scholarship encounters those designated as "other," it almost always presumes an active white male subject examining a passive nonwhite object.⁵⁶ The archive perpetuates domination through valorization of a unidirectional gaze that precludes reciprocal communication and presents aggrieved populations as static research objects rather than as active and knowing historical subjects.⁵⁷

Alessandro Portelli punctures the myth of the archive's authority and credibility by pointing to the ways it often treats as true what are actually errors of fact and interpretation made by powerful people.⁵⁸ Michel-Rolph Trouillot exposes the ideological policing performed by the archive, demonstrating that events that contradict the premises and presumptions of the powerful—like the Haitian revolution—get minimized and marginalized in the official record, not because they have not happened, but because their existence refutes the assumptions about the world and how people act in it held by the gatekeepers of the archive. He explains that "when reality does not coincide with deeply held beliefs, human beings tend to phrase interpretations that force reality within the scope of those beliefs. They devise formulas to repress the unthinkable and to bring it back within the realm of accepted discourse."⁵⁹ The archive purports to be an objective and unmediated window into the workings of society, but when it comes to portraying the experiences of the majority of the world's population it offers not a window but what Ernst Bloch acerbically describes as "a beautifying mirror which often only reflects how the ruling class wishes the wishes of the weak to be."[60]

The repertoire, from Taylor's perspective, has different qualities than the archive. It gets played out in performance. Gestures, movements, songs, dances, and words that persist in embodied memory and action but are usually not written down make up the repertoire. Here again, etymological roots are instructive. The word *repertoire* connotes an inventory or treasury but also evokes the existence of a finder or discoverer. Taylor views the repertoire as something that involves personal presence. It connotes "being there" and initiates a process of becoming. The repertoire consists of more than an inventory of expressive cultural practices; it also involves how people come together to find common ground, to recognize and solve the problems they share, to lift up flagging spirits by sharing food, jokes, and stories, and to take steps to defuse potentially explosive conflicts.

Much of the work carried out by aggrieved racialized communities rarely appears in the archive but appears in rich relief in the repertoire. Experiences of collective cocreation and expression that might seem too ephemeral and transitory for the archive permeate repertoires that serve important purposes as embodied memories and practices influencing future instincts, impulses, aspirations, and expressions. Taylor argues that performance exposes, if only briefly, things that have always been there but have not been acknowledged, such as "the ghosts, the tropes, the scenarios that structure our individual and collective life."[61] Repertoires of embodied memory can provide intuitions and dispositions for action and resources for improvisation that aggrieved communities need in order to be prepared to face unexpected crises. The performances that build on embodied repertoires of memory do so by activating generally repressed aspirations, desires, and fantasies in ways that are not soon forgotten, leaving traces that influence future behavior. The components of the repertoire only rarely appear in the archive and in fact survive and thrive largely because they escape the disciplinary and punitive purview of those who control institutional knowledge. The repertoire exceeds the power of the archive to capture and contain it. Yet like the archive, the repertoire's embodied actions produce, register, and disseminate knowledge.[62] The traditions of the oppressed appear vividly, for example, in the Chicanx performance practices of mariachi, Danza Azteca, and ballet folklórico ensembles.

The archive and the repertoire not only collect and transmit knowledge but produce it. As Antonio Gramsci argues, ideas and opinions do not arise on their own inside each individual mind but rather emerge in centers of formation, irradiation, dissemination, and persuasion.[63] The work carried out by the repertoire is aimed not so much at persuading already existing publics but at using the mechanisms of performance to bring into being publics that might coalesce by finding their appeals legible and desirable. Participants in the ethnic studies project face the daunting twin challenges of (1) transforming the archive to lessen its privileging of writing and language and widening its scope to include the repertoire, and (2) enhancing the repertoire by expanding its access to the knowledge of the archive but also treating it as an indispensable repository on its own of how aggrieved peoples have survived and can thrive.

While the distinctions between the archive and the repertoire produce valuable frames of interpretation, the two do not function as incommensurable spheres. Taylor argues that the archive and the repertoire often work together and that knowledge production requires both. The people who help build the archive and those who construct the repertoire come to a crossroads where they experience the caduceus. The Nuyorican youths who came together to found the New York chapter of the Young Lords organization had no accessible archives to draw on in formulating their policies and programs because of the repressive dimensions in educational and cultural institutions of colonialism, racism, and countersubversion. The very absence of the archives, however, propelled them to develop oppositional repertoires that entailed occupying churches and hospitals, blocking streets, and creating "serve the people" projects providing food, clothing, health care, day care, education, reproductive services, and campaigns against rape and gender violence in their community.[64] Memories of those actions persisted as embodied repertoires long after they were completed.

The archive, even when modestly desegregated, contains only small slivers and threads that purport to represent the infinitely diverse, plural, and intersecting dimensions of collective social life. The valuable pieces of evidence that exist in archives remain inaccessible to most people because they lack the credentials, connections, and codes of conduct that access to them requires and enables. Material from the archives generally reaches a broader public through the modes of relational address conveyed through the repertoire. Yet the very forms of presence that the repertoire requires always threaten to render it provincial and parochial, unaware of connections to the broader structures of power and resistance that can be found in the archive.

Repertoires can't overcome all political obstacles, but political action often proceeds powerfully through the preservation and repositioning of them. Noisy mass gatherings and silent vigils, sit-ins, marches, walkouts, and strikes are all kinds of performances. Political activism pursues specific goals—higher wages and better working conditions, preservation of reproductive rights, an end to predatory, punitive, and violent policing, recognition of and respect for Indigenous sovereignty, protections against hate crimes and sexual violence, an end to wars, and the addressing of climate change. These aims are important, but whether they are won or lost, political campaigns also change those who participate in them by reinforcing existing embodied repertoires and enacting new ones. Collective action enhances awareness of other people. It turns private worries into public issues and counters loneliness, isolation, and depression. Collective ability to act can be informed by previous participation in political mobilizations, but it also emerges from repertoires learned and legitimated inside autonomous learning and artistic circles.

Political participants do not travel down one single path to arrive at activism. Any activist movement draws on repertoires learned in places and practices rarely represented in the archive. In the 1980s, St. Louis Black activist Ivory Perry "celebrated" Easter by inviting children to hunt for the seventy-five dozen dyed eggs that he and his friends placed in different places on a football field amid photographs and mounted newspaper stories about the Black freedom movement. Members of Khmer Girls in Action in Long Beach, California, today create a Halloween haunted house where the "horrors" of the house include anti-immigrant nativism, poverty, sexism, and structural violence.[65] The mural *Women Hold Up Half the Sky,* painted in the 1970s by women from the Royal Chicano Air Force (RCAF) arts collective from Sacramento, adorns a concrete pylon holding up the Coronado Bridge in Chicano Park in San Diego. It uses a slogan from the Chinese Revolution as the title for painted images celebrating Chicana activism and militancy, as one might expect in the heart of the Latinx Barrio Logan neighborhood. On the side of a pylon next to the main mural, however, the women of RCAF painted an image of Joan Little, a Black woman on trial for murder in North Carolina, charged with defending herself from a guard who was in the process of raping her. Daniel HoSang explains Little's presence on the pylon as evidence of "a shared understanding of the ways race structures sex- and gender-based violence, and a vision of the body's freedom, autonomy, and interdependence produced in response."[66] The Easter egg hunt in St. Louis, the haunted house in Long Beach, and the mural in San Diego all originated in politically conscious performance practices honed and refined inside alternative academies. They cultivate repertoires of embodied memory and evidence the potential of alternative archives rooted in contact with the egg hunt, ongoing engagements with the haunted house every year, and the existence in public of an image of homage to a long-ago struggle that serves as an informal public archive.

Taylor's contrast between the archive and the repertoire has great value for interpreting the different imperatives that shape relationships between academic ethnic studies and the autonomous learning circles to be discussed in chapter 3. To be sure, the epistemologies of the crossroads and the caduceus should make us wary of "either/or" contrasts that obscure the "both/and" qualities that make seeming opposites mutually constitutive. Repertoires can function as informal archives, while archives are constructed through learned repertoires of academic instruction, investigation, and exposition. Scholars who have made major contributions to the archives have often done so equipped with dispositions and determinations drawn from their participation in social movement mobilizations, their training as artists and performers, and their choices as consumers of commercial cultures and creators of oppositional subcultures.

The transmission goes in both directions, however. Creators of the repertoire are rarely completely cut off from the archive. Mobilizations by the Okinawa Women Act Against Military Violence draw upon writings by peace studies scholar Betty Reardon as well as on her work with that organization to formulate their core political position that what creates security for nations, armies, and corporations produces insecurity for women, the elderly, and the environment.[67] Project Row Houses, an arts-based community development and residential program for young mothers in the Third Ward in Houston, came into being largely as an effort by artist Rick Lowe to put into practice what he had learned in college art classes about the paintings of John Biggers and the practice of social sculpture associated with German artist and activist Joseph Beuys.[68] In recounting her path to leadership of the Frente Indigena de Organizaciones Binacionales (FIOB) in Los Angeles, Odilia Romero Hernández points to a literature class she took at a community college. She explains how the teacher—a white feminist of Irish descent—displayed commitments to women's rights and critiques of anti-Black racism that resonated with Romero Hernández. Although the experiences and aspirations of the white feminists and Black activists discussed in the class were not exactly the same as those of Romero Hernández, they were close enough to provoke comparisons that enabled her to perceive affinities. The class helped Romero Hernández interpret her own experiences with discrimination and subordination by juxtaposing them against those of the groups highlighted in classroom sessions. She recalls that in that community college classroom, "I learned how to name the positive and negative things that were going on, especially when you experience discrimination, racism, and inequality in your own flesh. You know it's not right, but you don't know how to call it. Imagine what a simple literature class gives."[69]

Repertoires of embodied memory are not written down or housed in one location, but they can serve as fugitive archives that preserve collective memory, fuel a sense of linked fate, and offer an inventory of tools useful for self-defense, self-definition, and self-determination. Indigenous Guatemalan migrants to the US bring with them what Floridalma Boj Lopez calls "a mobile archive of indigeneity" made up of weavings, stories, clothes, food, children's coloring books, and other things that link their places of arrival to places of origin through objects steeped in Maya epistemologies. They view these objects through a perspective similar to the one that led the National Movement of Weavers in Guatemala to title a book about their art *Our Weavings Are Books the Colonizers Could Not Burn*.[70] Archives can be ephemeral as well as mobile. In the early 2010s, Los Angeles artist Jay Lynn Gomez documented and honored low-wage Latinx laborers by spray-painting images of them on large pieces of discarded cardboard that she found outside big box stores that sold appliances. Gomez placed her images of gardeners, pool cleaners, nannies, and maids on hedges, lamp posts, and bus stop facades in wealthy neighborhoods. When low-wage service workers left for their homes at the end of the day, their images remained in affluent neighborhoods, testifying to the crucial role played by low-wage laborers in creating and maintaining the environments enjoyed by the wealthy. Gomez's images rarely stayed up for more than a day; they shared the transient ephemerality of the deportable workers they depicted. Even in their short lifespans, however, they were seen and remembered by both the workers and their employers as visible archival traces of labor and laborers routinely treated as invisible.[71]

José Esteban Muñoz identifies anecdotal, performative, and ephemeral queer practices as components of an important immaterial archive, one that is valuable because of—rather than in spite of—its transitory enactment of the repertoire. Largely excluded from the archives of official culture, the achievements, insurgences, inventions, experiences, and aspirations of queer people become available to succeeding generations through repetition and remembrance of overt and covert expressions of queer identity in music, dance, style, speech, affect, and affiliation. Jack Halberstam writes articles and books that enter traditional archives, but they do something more. They also contribute to queer archives and queer memory by forging alliances between minority subcultural producers and minority academics. In the process of recording, recoding, circulating, and interpreting queer subcultural practices, Halberstam keeps them available for admiration and emulation, expanding repertoires of embodied memory and action. The archive for Halberstam is not a static repository controlled by gatekeepers but rather a popular, democratic, and active site built on structures of thinking in a discursive field that does not need an institutional home to survive and thrive.[72]

Documentary films and family scrapbooks, photographs, diaries, and collections of letters may seem to function as archives—as static repositories of images, ideas, affiliations, and experiences. Yet they also entail and encourage performances. Angela Aguayo highlights the ways in which documentary filmmaking is often a participatory process steeped in communication, conversation, and collaboration. Aguayo argues that the processes of collective scripting, acting, editing, showing, and sharing documentary films produce a participatory media culture and commons.[73] This quality appears boldly in the films made about exiles, refugees, immigrants, low-wage workers, and the incarcerated elderly made by Yehuda Sharim. Each film of his emerges from convivial cocreation with the people depicted in it. Film showings often involve talk-backs by film participants and audience members, turning the film—which never changes—into a series of unpredictable events.[74] Sharim's films have the permanence of an object in an archive, but their processes of creation, distribution, and reception create mobile repertoires of embodied action and engagement.

Su'ad Abdul Khabeer explains how for Black people perusing the family photo album, displaying treasured mementos, and rereading letters from long ago promote conversations and ruminations about the enormous grief that Black people suffer from discrimination, displacement, and premature death. These objects register painful memories of lost loved ones but also awaken respect for and celebration of how the ancestors carried life's burdens.[75] K. T. Ewing argues that these quotidian items inside Black homes are fugitive family archives that ground the present in images, documents, and artifacts from the past. These serve as a defense against the perpetual displacement, uprooting, rupture, and discontinuity that Black people experience because of housing insecurity, urban renewal, and redevelopment.[76]

Attention to repertoires and archives can save ethnic studies advocates from the trap articulated by Roderick Ferguson. He warns against being beguiled by the idea that ethnic studies work is most effective when it is most visible, when it wins the attention and approval of prominent celebrities, political power brokers, mainstream media, or wealthy donors. Ferguson concedes that those spheres can be beneficial but insists that building relations with everyday people inside aggrieved communities is the most important thing scholars can do. "Building social relations means developing a relationship with students over ten to fifteen weeks in a classroom. It means showing up in a community over and over again. It means getting to know this or that person or organization over a long period of time. It means talking to people about what is happening in the world and strategizing about what can be done."[77] Building social relations also entails learning from and with autonomous learning circles such as the ones to be described in chapter 3.

WHERE DO WE GO FROM HERE?

Both bottom-up and top-down initiatives establish the contours of institutionalized ethnic studies and the broader antiracist social formation that it both shapes and reflects. A compromise that allowed for limited incorporation of previously excluded groups coupled with systematic counterinsurgency temporarily settled the crises caused by the conflicts of the mid-twentieth century. Oppositional antiracist initiatives did not always win, but neither were they always defeated. Ethnic studies remains shaped by the contradictions of that settlement, by the crossroads and the caduceus that leave its strengths and weaknesses closely related. In that way, the field has functioned in the academy much as the War on Poverty did in aggrieved inner-city communities in the 1960s. The antipoverty program created spaces for new democratic and egalitarian processes, practices, and institutions, yet at the same time it also worked to turn many activists into bureaucratic functionaries and administrators. Because of the War on Poverty, however, a wide range of activists, artists, and academics gained important skills, experience, and expertise that later proved valuable in subsequent egalitarian antiracist mobilizations. The reach and scope of their achievements permeate progressive social movement organizations and activism to this day. At the same time, however, the War on Poverty recruited and rewarded a cohort of professionals whose upward mobility hinged on their acting as token representatives of excluded groups, as administrators of institutions structured in dominance, and as people charged with disavowing and controlling the most radical and oppositional currents in communities of color. Their legacy explains much of the alienation that young antiracist activists feel today in relation to the established civil rights organizations and their leaders, and the resulting efforts by the 2020 uprisings in the streets on behalf of Black lives to create new forms of collective identity and struggle. Ethnic studies scholars, teachers, classes, programs, and departments, which have their own vexed histories with incorporation, can play constructive roles in theorizing and activating these new forms of accompaniment, improvisation, contestation, and struggles for liberation.

The solutions of yesterday can cause part of the problems of today. The concessions that provided temporary resolutions of the problems of the 1960s through the 1990s no longer satisfy either side in the 2020s. Economic restructuring, deindustrialization, war without end, mass incarceration, environmental destruction, and the ever-increasing privatization of public resources portend the end of ethnic studies as it was originally conceived and instituted. Powerful groups are repudiating and reversing many of the concessions made in previous decades, while aggrieved groups can no longer see meaningful possibilities for progress in a society whose main institutions are unraveling. The privatization, fiscalization, vocationalization, and virtualization of education undermine schooling's traditional goals of equipping students with the judgment and discernment necessary for democratic citizenship and convivial social membership. Fiscal imperatives drive reductions in tenure-track faculty positions, reducing needed research on important social issues and leaving more and more courses taught by adjuncts and part-time online instructors. The hedge fund investors and tech profiteers who pervade university boards of directors demand an end to scholars and scholarship that might challenge the prejudices and privileges of the wealthy, while corporate ownership of scholarly journals leads them to fire editors who publish oppositional research.

The ever-increasing fiscalization of education leads to institutions attempting to spend as little as possible to produce as many credentialed graduates as possible. Overburdened instructors with heavy course loads cannot meet the needs of students whose financial circumstances often make it necessary for them to work long hours outside of school and to cram as many courses into as short a time as possible to avoid paying high tuition fees. The result is fewer and shorter reading and writing assignments, less time for student interaction and group discussion, and intense competition for grades and places in the most sought-after majors that induce more than a few students to see cheating as their best option. Under these circumstances, without interventions by instructors in ethnic studies and attendant fields, far too few students will experience higher education as a place where they learn to learn, where they come to see things for themselves rather than being told the right answers, where they recognize that we know more together than we know separately and that it is better to be contributive than competitive. The fiscal forces that control education make it likely that most ethnic studies classes will be conducted via large lectures, impersonal encounters, and high-stakes testing. This circumstance makes the experimental exceptions all that much more important. For some students, these may be the only times in their educational journeys that their instructors and fellow students care what they think, or even if they think.

Colleges and universities in thrall to their funders no longer feel the need to pretend to be sites where conclusions are based on their intellectual validity rather than their utility to vested interests. In the communities that students and teachers come from and return to, struggles for social justice take place today in a social world suffused with sadistic and self-destructive impulses. Mass shootings, substance abuse, and suicide register the disillusionment and despair of wide swaths of the population. Many distract themselves through the meteoric rise and profitability of gambling, gun play, and pornography. Much of the entertainment they consume serves as a shop window displaying sadism for sale in many incarnations that contribute in no small measure to increased antisocial actions expressed through cyberstalking, cyber-stealing, and cyber-swatting. Both political and commercial culture outlets offer a curriculum of cruelty that incites and encourages a particular personality structure. Rita Laura Segato astutely observes that this personality needs ever increasing stimuli to experience emotion. It cultivates insensitivity to the feelings and pain of other people. It revels in dehumanization and deploys unlimited desires and capacities to prey upon bodies and plunder territories.[78] It falls to ethnic studies to be one of the sites where this pedagogy and culture of cruelty can be countered and supplanted.

Even those who imagine themselves opposed to neoliberal individualism are influenced by it and infused with it. As Kalamu ya Salaam observes, it is easier to change our minds than to change our ways.[79] The ethnic studies project is no more immune than any other social site to the enticements and rewards of branding, bragging, bullying, and backstabbing. Without a strong and self-consciously created counterculture committed to connecting with the broader antiracist formation, the ranks of ethnic studies will be no different from those of its enemies with respect to its proportion of clout chasers, exhibitionists, finger-pointers, parasites, mountebanks, misogynists, opportunists, and ego-trippers. Raised in this society, hailed by its entertainment and advertising apparatuses, and trained to treat segregation and stratification as natural, necessary, and inevitable, those who embrace the ethnic studies vision are not yet the people they will need to be to change this world. It is incumbent for the field to create the social practices, processes, and relations that bring forth new ways of thinking and acting differently.

At the crossroads it is vital to be cognizant of both danger and opportunity. It would be a terrible mistake to underestimate the gravity of the systemic breakdown of major institutions and their import for racial justice education. Yet it would be equally dangerous to succumb to resignation and despair. As Avery Gordon argues, "There is something terribly wrong with the picture of hopelessness and total social control by remote powers that so characterizes intellectual discourse today."[80] Ricardo Levins Morales argues that preparing for the future requires imagination, speculation, prediction, and planning, but also an expectation of being surprised and being forced to improvise in response.[81] What comes next will be shaped by the clash already under way between historical blocs determined to preserve the profits and privileges of racial capitalism and those committed to creating fundamentally new democratic practices, processes, institutions, ideas, structures, and systems. Both the successes and failures of ethnic studies leave its advocates and allies at another crossroads where paths come together, interests collide, and decisions need to be made. The next chapter explores the importance for ethnic studies of autonomous learning circles and art-based community-making projects in building a mutually supportive, respectful, accountable, and effective counterculture.

3

Ethnic Studies as Accompaniment

Autonomous Learning Circles

In her memoir recounting her life experiences in music, dance, and political struggle, Nobuko Miyamoto describes the exhilaration of dancing in a circle during the intercultural FandangObon celebration in Los Angeles that she helped to invent. With words that apply to circles of learning as well as dance, Nobuko states,

> In this circle we reclaim our power, our creativity. We make music with our own hands, our own voices. We circle the Earth with our feet and remember we belong to it. In this circle everyone is equal, everyone is seen, everyone has a place. In this circle there are no borders, no us and them. There is plenty of room for more circles. In this circle we weave our many roots, knowing our diversity is our strength. In this circle, we are enacting the world we want to live in. In this circle, in this circle . . .[1]

This chapter explores the importance to ethnic studies of autonomous learning circles like the FandangObon dance circle as described by Miyamoto. Social justice cannot simply be proclaimed; it must be performed in real-life situations that help people enact the morally and socially just futures they envision. Operating both on and off campuses, these circles become crossroads where academics, artists, and activists convene and cocreate. They expand the possibilities of study and struggle through the cultures of opposition they draw on, create, and sustain. Connections to arts-based community-making collectives propel ethnic studies participants to develop new pedagogies and politics.

In our book *Insubordinate Spaces,* Barbara Tomlinson and I pointed to the importance of the practice of *accompaniment* as developed in El Salvador through the liberation theology articulated in the 1970s by the martyred archbishop Oscar Romero (subsequently canonized by the Catholic Church). We described accompaniment as "a disposition, a sensibility and a pattern of behavior" and as "a commitment based on a cultivated capacity for making connections with others, identifying with them, and helping them."[2] Accompaniment assigns first priority to those in greatest need and those most likely to be left out of dignified and decent treatment. It requires constant presence of mind and awareness of other people's circumstances as guidelines for working with them.

Many efforts to link the campus and the community fail because they do not embrace the spirit of accompaniment. Campus projects often take place under the names of "outreach" and "service learning" as if everything the campus contains is good and as if the community has no resources or knowledge. These initiatives often amount to little more than poverty tourism and condescending meddling. Academic institutions are imbued with unstated but powerful managerial impulses that train people to speak rather than listen, to give orders before learning what needs to be done, to assume they know what is needed without consulting those in need. Combating this managerial mentality requires a conscious counterculture with a radically different understanding of knowledge, culture, pedagogy, and purpose. That understanding can often be found inside community-based autonomous learning circles such as the ones described below.

The audit culture and the professional ethos of higher education work together to inhibit capacities for accompaniment, but accompaniment plays a central role in the ideas, discourses, and practices of autonomous learning circles. Of course, all principled inquiry deserves respect. Autonomous learning circles are not being presented here to belittle the importance of original discovery scholarship—quite the contrary. The argument here is that knowledge production can be advanced most fully when the campus and communities are connected.

The practices that link campus knowledges to community needs and collective ways of knowing are omnipresent but rarely acknowledged. Community art and activist projects resonate with ideas brought to these sites by student interns, with the insights that activists and artists have gleaned from their enrollment in K-12 and college classes, and with references to books and articles originating in ethnic studies that activists and artists read. These influences permeate internal education sessions, strategic conversations, and public pronouncements. In turn, because some ethnic studies scholars have worked as allies, interlocutors, interns, and fundraisers with these groups, those experiences inform the scholars' subsequent academic endeavors. Profound ideas and powerful political projects emanate from these connections.

SUNNI PATTERSON, "MY CITY AIN'T FOR SALE"

Participants in the ethnic studies project can learn a lot by recognizing and accompanying the knowledge generated within the broader antiracist social formation's autonomous learning circles. The critique of neoliberal racial capitalism articulated by New Orleans spoken-word artist, political activist, and educator Sunni Patterson exemplifies what scholars, teachers, and students can learn from the grassroots theories and practices nurtured and sustained inside autonomous learning circles. In her remarkable poem "My City Ain't for Sale," Patterson offers an incisive critique of neoliberal racial capitalism seen from the perspective of the Black resistance tradition of New Orleans. She shows how neoliberalism profits by exploiting racial difference while declaring itself innocent of racism. In this poem, Patterson decries the ways in which promoters, developers, and boosters use the appeal and allure of a romanticized and exoticized depiction of the local Black culture in New Orleans as a weapon against the actual Black people who live there.

Promotional materials designed to encourage and justify redevelopment, gentrification, and tourism in New Orleans present evocations and images of the very things that development will destroy—carnival celebrations, street parades, brass bands, jazz ensembles, funeral processions, decorated mausoleums, and Afro-diasporic traditions of cooking and conjuring. These images are marketed in ways that reduce the rich and dynamic Black culture of New Orleans to a series of small, static, and superficial signs, symbols, and spectacles that convey an appealing "otherness" in order to attract attention and entice outside investment. A vicarious and symbolic enjoyment of Black culture is used to promote a regime of gentrification that entails invasion and occupation of Black neighborhoods and expulsions of their current residents. Patterson protests that these plans purport to build the city "up" but work to "keep me down."[3] She warns those "who gentrify and plot" and "calculate and allot" that her people's "dignity, legacy and pride" are not for sale.[4]

Patterson's lyrical recitation in rhyme builds in intensity as she identifies the Black origins of the practices used to market New Orleans by city boosters who know nothing of "me or my kind, my heritage, my history, my line." Insisting that "some things just ain't up for buying," Patterson presents an evocative and alliterative list of the Black cultural creations that redevelopers deploy as local color: crawfish and crabs, dessert cups and confections, magic spells and cemeteries, stories of sinners and saints, and even the Black community's "could's and can'ts."[5]

"My City Ain't for Sale" is a present-day manifestation of the poetic vision that Patterson has crafted for decades inside a wide range of autonomous learning circles, alternative academies, and community conservatories. Her art resonates with the pulse of the people. It emerges from and speaks to the conditions, commitments, and creative impulses of Black people in New Orleans. At the same time it contains significance for people all around the world struggling to resist the newest iterations of neoliberal racial capitalism's relentless practices of cooptation, commodification, displacement, and dispossession. In her 2005 piece "We Know This Place," Patterson chronicles the calculated cruelty of the local, state, and federal officials as evidenced by their abandonment of the Black working class in the wake of the devastation and mass death caused by responses to Hurricane Katrina in that year. As she exposes the evils of white supremacy in this poem, Patterson also points proudly to the long, honorable, and enduring legacies of resistance, mutuality, and solidarity that sustain the Black community in times of crisis. Patterson salutes Black people's resolve not "to break or bow" and "to push on for freedom" in the here and now.[6] In her art, Patterson identifies the crimes of the perverse nexus of racism and commodification, its production of a society that values things more than people, and the determined resistance that oppression provokes among people insistent on refusing unlivable destinies.

To claim that "some things just ain't for sale" today flies in the face of the logic and values of neoliberalism: the conjuncture of interrelated economic policies, political projects, and social pedagogies that place buying and selling at the center of the social world. Neoliberalism coalesces around the insistence that all people are, and must be, acquisitive and avaricious. It demands that all institutions serve as generators of rich returns on investments. It promises that unbridled pursuit of self-interest will "free" people from the "burdens" of accountability, responsibility, and obligation to others.[7] Patterson's poem gestures to the potential to think otherwise, to create a world built on mutuality and conviviality, on respect for people rather than for property and profit.

It should not be surprising that some of the most perceptive criticisms of the elevation of property rights over human well-being should come from people whose ancestors were defined by the law to be merely property and not people, and who in the afterlife of slavery have seen their labor cruelly exploited and their wealth systematically expropriated.[8] Patterson's resistance to seeing her culture and her people placed up for sale expresses more than a personal point of view; it exemplifies impulses, ideas, and ideals that permeate the art and politics of Afro-diasporic artists and activists around the world. In a dialogue with African American bass-playing virtuoso and educator William Parker, novelist Patrick Chamoiseau from Martinique critiques contemporary society as captured by "a religion of markets." The present time, he maintains, is an era when capital and commodities rule the earth.[9] Yet the victory of materialism is not complete. Chamoiseau explains that "in the wake of those slave ships," people abused and shackled nonetheless gave birth to another world, to "our world," a world he describes as one waiting to be enjoyed, experienced, and pondered over, a world shaped "by all our creativities gathered in unison."[10] Creativity is honored by Parker and Chamoiseau not as a way of ornamenting social life or escaping from it but as a force provoking people to work together to build new forms of enjoyment and experience that cultivate collective capacity for caretaking relations.[11] Patterson, Parker, and Chamoiseau do not focus on shedding the marginal status of oppressed people by seeking entry into the rewards and benefits of the mainstream. Instead, they describe the margin as a privileged vantage point for critique of the dominant society and as an impetus for rejecting its priorities and values.

Patterson graduated from Tuskegee University with a major in English and has been a high school teacher in the New Orleans public school system. While deriving much from her engagements with these formal educational institutions, Patterson's art and activism also draw upon the profound wisdom she gained from participation in autonomous learning centers inside family and community circles, from exposure to the survival strategies of oppressed people, and from what Cedric Robinson defines as the Black Radical Tradition—composed of "an accretion, over generations, of collective intelligence gathered from the struggle."[12] Within the Black Radical Tradition, being creatively misaligned with the affective appeals of the dominant society requires alignment with ideals and aspirations oppositional to it, especially replacing individual self-interest and competition with convivial collaborations and relations.

Patterson's artistic creations emerge in part from her labors as resident artist in the Afro-diasporic performance group Junebug Productions, from her position as cofounder of an art, music, and spoken-word project known as "Breath Is Lyfe" that is designed to promote awareness of the prevalence of asthma in Black communities, and from her experiences working with the improvisational story circle pedagogy of Students at the Center in New Orleans high schools, a project discussed later in this chapter.

Direct engagement with the everyday frustrations of her community and accompaniment with masses mobilized in emancipatory struggle enable Patterson to extend a lifeline to people in danger of drowning in despair. She encourages readers and listeners to understand, accompany, emulate, and embrace freedom struggles. Through her poems and politics Patterson identifies neoliberalism not just as an economic and political project but as a conjuncture of policies, practices, and pedagogies that seek to structure interior aspirations and external actions. Patterson identifies the determined resolve and unwavering commitments that the struggle demands when in "We Know This Place" she advises, "Hold onto the prize, never put it down, Be firm in the stance, no break, no bow, got to forward on, Mama, make your move now. Forward on Papa, okay make your move now, Forward, dear children, freedom is now."[13]

The intellect and artistry that Patterson has honed and refined in community spaces has been an important influence on scholars who critique neoliberal racial capitalism. She has presented spoken-word pieces and delivered keynote addresses at conferences at Brown, Vanderbilt, Dartmouth, and the University of California, Merced. Clyde Woods invited Patterson to appear on a panel with fellow New Orleans poets Kalamu ya Salaam and Brenda Osbey at the American Studies Association annual meeting in 2007. The piece she delivered on that occasion appeared in a special issue of the *American Quarterly* that addressed the abandonment of Black New Orleans in the aftermath of Hurricane Katrina and was subsequently issued by Johns Hopkins University Press as a book. Jordan T. Camp and Laura Pulido placed Patterson's poem "We Made It" at the beginning of Woods's posthumous book *Development Drowned and Reborn,* which they coedited.[14]

Patterson's influence on ethnic studies research, writing, and teaching demonstrates the importance of autonomous learning circles as crucibles of people-centered realms of mutual respect and accompaniment. These circles provide spaces where participants learn to be the kinds of individuals they need to become to survive the unlivable destinies designed for them by the individualist and competitive profit-centered world of neoliberal institutions and affects. They are oppositional to the individualism, materialism, belligerence, and brutality of the world, yet also propositional in envisioning and enacting how a people-centered rather than profit-centered world might come into being.[15]

The people of the world today are faced nearly everywhere with the conditions that Patterson protests against in "My City Ain't For Sale." These conditions entail a way of thinking and a way of being that have been increasingly dominant in the US over the past fifty years. Today, however, this worship of the market has reached a point where it shows its true colors, where the disguises are dropped, where the diversions no longer divert. The eloquence, artistry, and intelligence that Patterson displays archive past struggles and provide repertoires attuned to the creation of new ones. They evidence the dynamics that Frantz Fanon observed when he noted that manifestations of radical change often appear in culture before they appear in politics. In times of crisis and impending social upheaval, Fanon argues, a new vigor appears in works of expressive culture that are "fresh and imbued with power," that summon people to come together in struggle, and that "make unreal and unacceptable the contemplative attitude or the acceptance of defeat."[16]

Patterson stimulates her audiences to resist the contemplative attitude and to reject the acceptance of defeat. This requires love for the people who are suffering, who are shunned, segregated, and suppressed. It means accompanying them, fighting beside them and for them, taking the same kinds of risks they do, and working with them to create a decent, dignified, and democratic shared social existence. This is the work that takes place in the autonomous learning circles that are highlighted in the next part of this chapter.[17]

LEARNING HOW TO ARRIVE IN EAST LOS ANGELES

In East Los Angeles, mother and daughter Ofelia Esparza and Rosanna Esparza Ahrens assemble altars that they construct with everyday life objects, flowers, and plants in order to remember and honor the dead. Esparza and Esparza Ahrens say everyone can eventually experience three deaths—the first when the heart stops beating, the second when the body is buried in the ground, and the third when the one who has passed on is forgotten. People are powerless against the first two deaths, but the third can be dealt with in one way by the creation of altars that promote remembrance and respect, convey gratitude, and acknowledge honor. The practice of making altars and the ways of knowing and ways of being that the practice promotes help make East Los Angeles an exemplary and generative locus of autonomous learning circles.

Drawing on long spiritually infused artistic traditions, Esparza and Esparza Ahrens not only make works of art but create artistic ways of working together. They begin gatherings with the practice of "learning how to arrive." This practice promotes full presence of mind at the crossroads. They contend that coming together with mutual recognition and respect requires deep thought and full feeling about what each person brings to the convening. Thinking of "arriving" as something *we need to learn how to do* rather than something *we have already done* prevents slipping back into old and often deeply programmed habits. People who have been socialized to compete for attention and reward and have been made to feel small and powerless in many areas of their lives may arrive at meetings, classrooms, and discussions with intentions and attitudes that harm the entire group. Learning how to arrive asks people to pause, to not perform who they think they are but to welcome the ways the meeting can help move them closer toward who they need to be. Esparza and Esparza Ahrens enact this process through practices they name ACCA, an acronym constructed by the first letter of the first word in each step. These steps are (1) *Arriving* with full awareness of ourselves, our ancestors, and the powers of what we call the natural world; (2) *Connecting* fully with humans and the natural world we inhabit; (3) *Convening* based on agreements for collective conduct; and (4) *Affirming* and appreciating our collective practice. When spoken, the word ACCA evokes the Spanish language word *aca*, which means "here" as "in the here and now," but that utterance also evokes the English language homonym "to hear" as in the "hear and now."

Arriving entails taking a moment to breathe deeply, to be aware of relations with the earth, to take cognizance of the natural world, to remember, honor, and invite ancestors to be present in the gathering, to open hearts, and to welcome the work to be done. The world does not begin when we enter it, it does not end when we pass on. We have obligations to be accountable to both our ancestors and our descendants but also to live every moment fully aware of and accountable to others.

Connecting is achieved by talking, listening, and looking, by being in community, and by feeling fully engaged in it. Connecting promotes an ethos of conversation rather than conversion, competition, or conquest. It elevates the convivial quality of cocreation over the cruelty of envy, avarice, rancor, and resentment.

Convening is based on agreements (known as *acuerdos*) rather than on rules or regulations. These spell out in advance the principles of community to govern what is to take place. They encourage participants to think of the well-being of the entire group, to take pride in helping everybody be better rather than trying to appear better to others.

Affirmations are statements at the end of the meeting that express appreciation for what has been learned and from whom it has been learned. Affirmations can also point to the ways in which particular ideas and insights taken from the meeting can guide individual and collective action in the future.

Acuerdos that guide learning how to arrive as defined by Esparza and Esparza Ahrens have been developed, amplified, and elaborated on by them and other *artivistas* (art activists) working with the Alliance for California Traditional Arts and the Building Healthy Communities in Boyle Heights. These change with each encounter, but in general they entail these steps:

1. Our first responsibility is respond-ability. Each speaker should recognize and build on the words of the previous one. Speak from the heart. Feel the pulse of the people and contribute to it.

2. Withhold judgment. Learning to listen and to look requires patience. Our first task is to hear and to see, to absorb fully what is in front of us. Moving too quickly to decide what we like or dislike or what we agree with or oppose in the things we hear from others can inhibit our ability to recognize that we are at a crossroads and to recognize clearly the paths that are in front of us and why they are there.

3. Find common ground. Rather than focusing first on other people's difficulties and deficiencies, start with what connects, what is generative, productive, and life-affirming. Finding out what we can build on together is more difficult but ultimately more rewarding than moving too quickly to address the things that divide us.

4. Don't overinvest in—or overidentify with—positions, opinions, and conclusions. Collaboration is a process that requires the cultivation of patient deep listening and a willingness to adapt and change because of the ideas and words of others. We are all works in progress, unfinished entities capable of being on our way to something more and better.

5. Leave room for others to speak, listen carefully to their speech, and respond to it. Build together by being together.
6. Listen carefully and look closely for the "I" that speaks and recognize its struggles.
7. Notice and address the things that silence voices, suppress feelings, harm relationships, and perpetrate violence and exclusion.
8. Don't plan what you are going to say next while someone else is speaking. Think about how you can help someone else solve their problems rather than how what you say might make you look to others.
9. Throw glitter, not shade. Learn to appreciate, acknowledge, and amplify the value in other people.
10. Be a croissant, not a donut. A donut is closed in on itself. A crescent-shaped croissant is at least part-way open.
11. Avoid STDs—sidetrack discussions.
12. Reclaim history and rethink our places in it; reimagine the future and our roles in it.

Learning to arrive and the practices it promotes have infused a wide range of collective community projects of cocreation. High school students created and published a book of interviews, poems, biographies, and narratives mapping the cultural assets of the Boyle Heights neighborhood and celebrating the many acts of kindness that undergird its solidarity.[18] The Alliance for California Traditional Arts (ACTA) organizes collective songwriting sessions, mural-painting projects, youth radio programs, and quilting and embroidering workshops while providing Arts in Corrections classes in eighteen state prisons. The Community Power Collective and the Building Healthy Communities in Boyle Heights initiatives stage cultural events grounded in the practice of *convivencia,* which scholar *artivista* Martha Gonzalez defines as "being present and engaging together in mind, body, and spirit via participatory music and art practice."[19] *Convivencia* establishes a new kind of democratic public sphere, a locus of voluntary association and cocreation among differently situated people.

Activist groups in East Los Angeles utilize the Restorative Cultural Arts Practice/Praxis (RCAP) model developed by Chicano artist Omar G. Ramirez in dialogue with many others. This model permeates the

118 | Chapter 3

FIGURE 2. *El Arbol del Pueblo*, mural in the cafeteria of Roosevelt High School in Boyle Heights in East Los Angeles. The mural was created by Roosevelt students and Omar G. Ramirez, in collaboration with the Mural Workforce Academy and the Mexican American Legal Defense Fund. Photograph by Omar G. Ramirez, used by permission.

work of autonomous learning circles and is designed to change people as they change society. RCAP rests on specific principles: (1) **reclaiming** histories of collective struggle and survival, (2) **resisting** unjust conditions, (3) **restoring** social connections, (4) **re-storying** the past and present, (5) **respecting** differences but **rejecting** domination, (6) **relating** in new ways, (7) **responding** to problems responsibly, (8) **redefining** people's places in the world, and (9) **reimagining** the future.[20] Ramirez teaches and mentors students at barrio high schools, in the College of Ethnic Studies at California State University, Los Angeles, and in the Intercollegiate Department of Chicana/o Latino/a Studies at Scripps College, and works with the Mexican American Legal Defense Fund.

In one of his art and education projects, high school students explored the contrasts between the healthy food production and consumption practices of their Indigenous ancestors and the diets laced with processed sugar and saturated fats marketed by contemporary agribusiness conglomerates. They learned how to grow cacao and to use it as a pigment in works of art portraying past and present health food ways based on Indigenous knowledge. They created a mural displayed in a school cafeteria as well as mobile murals that illustrated the presentations they made in school and community sites about the politics of food.[21]

Learning to arrive, *convivencia,* and Restorative Culture Arts Practice/Praxis perform educational and cultural work that has important political ramifications. Their repertoires of embodied memory served as guides for social movement struggles. They have helped fuel campaigns by parents and students to replace punishment with restorative justice in East Los Angeles schools, mobilizations by community residents working with street vendors to repeal the city's ordinances that criminalize vending, and efforts by people mobilized by the Community Power Collective to create a community land trust designed to provide permanently affordable housing, promote culturally sensitive development, and resist gentrification. The principles of RCAP appear inside college ethnic studies and feminist studies courses taught by the *artivistas* associated with it. They provide the framework for the campus-community collaborations at San Jose State University that will be described in chapter 5, and they form key parts of research publications by several scholars.[22]

THE STORY CIRCLE PEDAGOGY IN NEW ORLEANS

Autonomous learning circles invent pedagogies attuned to the specific histories of the communities from which they emerge. These pedagogies are not just spurs to innovative learning but often express and enact *complex theories of how social change can and should take place.* Like the "Learning to Arrive" and RCAP methods deployed in East Los Angeles, the story circle pedagogy of Free-Dem Foundations in New Orleans and the Community Transformational Organizing Strategy deployed by Asian Immigrant Women Advocates in Oakland exemplify the generative potential of pedagogy as social theory.

From 1995 to 2020, teachers, students, and community members in New Orleans—working under the aegis of Students at the Center (SAC) classes in local high schools—invented and implemented an exemplary approach to reading, writing, and discussion. They created an interactive, collective, and improvisational pedagogy derived from the story circles of the 1960s Free Southern Theater. These classes enabled students to grapple with challenging readings, to connect them to their own lives, to write essays, to collaboratively critique writings, reflections, and ruminations authored by other students, and then to test their ideas in practice through engagement inside activist movements for social justice.

The pedagogy of Students at the Center required students to read challenging works by (among others) Edwidge Danticat, Mark Twain, Michelle Alexander, and Virginia Woolf, to write responses that connected the readings to their own lives, and to engage in activism that addressed big issues like segregation, imperialism, and mass incarceration. Most of the students in these classes did not own personal computers, so they composed their essays on cell phones, sending their work to their instructors as e-mail and text messages. They read out loud to the other students from their phone screens during class. Listening and providing criticism to others turned out to be as important as one's own writing in this curriculum. The instructors began each session by asking one student to read the current draft of their essay. After doing so, the student picked two classmates to offer comments. The "pick two" process enabled both predictability and rupture. Some responders were chosen by the student author on a particular day for their expertise about writing techniques. Others were invited to speak because their life experiences compared closely to those of the writer. Some were prized because they were gentle with their critiques; others were valued because they were blunt, forthright, and thorough. But sometimes a writer would select what might seem an unlikely respondent—the class clown, someone who had not spoken for a while, or a participant seemingly disconnected from the group on that day. These choices sometimes turned out to produce the best results: a burst of seriousness from someone who had previously seemed frivolous, a thoughtful statement from someone who had long been silent or an unexpected insight from someone who had been listening carefully all along while not speaking.

Choosing a critic might depend on how the writer felt on that particular day or on the focal point of any particular piece of writing. According to the teachers and teachers' aides, eventually nearly everyone was asked to respond to everyone else. The process allowed for individual differentiation, yet located authority in the abilities and traits that the group possessed as a collective. Through their individual writings and their shared conversations the students transformed the space of the classroom into a site of mutuality and solidarity, a forum for deepening their collective capacity for mutual recognition and respect, and a place for working together to engage in democratic deliberation and decision-making.

Before it was canceled by school system administrators—a victim of the privatization and vocationalization of education—Students at the

Center published four books of student writing, produced student-written, -directed, and -acted films, presented and performed their work before adult audiences, and left lasting imprints on the lives of participants, several of whom later went on to become teachers and community leaders. Their books attracted approval, support, and written contributions from distinguished scholars including Robin D. G. Kelley, Lydia Pelot-Hobbs, Bill Quigley, Adrienne Dixon, Kristin Buras, and Zeus Leonardo.[23] The books became part of a community archive of struggle located on shelves in the homes of the student authors, on coffee tables in grandmothers' parlors, and situated next to magazines and newspapers in a local barbershop. The story circle pedagogy described in these books has also made its way into the academy as a practice used by ethnic studies teachers and students seeking to develop transformative pedagogies for a decolonial world.[24]

The story circle pedagogy originated outside of school settings. It was created initially by the Free Southern Theater (FST) associated with the Student Nonviolent Coordinating Committee in the midst of the 1960s Black freedom movement in Mississippi and Louisiana. At a time when it was dangerous for Black people living under the oppression of Jim Crow white supremacy to pass out or even possess a political leaflet, theater students from Jackson State University sought to use dramatic performances in barns, fields, churches, and stores as a way of conducting outreach to the rural working class. They quickly realized, however, that the plays their audiences needed had not yet been written: The repertoire prized in drama classes had little relevance to the lives of Black farmworkers, sharecroppers, equipment operators, and domestics. The theater activists also chafed at the limits of conceptions of theater that revolved around rigid divisions separating active playwrights and performers from passive spectators and audiences. They developed a method of collective playwriting that entailed having people sit in a circle and speak in sequence about their daily lives and concerns. Those conversations provided the raw materials for collectively creating ethnographic plays written and performed by the college students and their community contacts. Story circle conversations in the process of composing the plays and community talk-backs assessing them after performance promoted an ethos of conversation to the degree that audience members often called out advice or uttered responses to what was being said on stage. As mentioned in the introduction to this book, what the FST organizers called "theater" or "plays" were described by the audiences as "meetings."[25]

John O'Neal, Tom Dent, and other activists brought this pattern of cocreation to New Orleans, where Kalamu ya Salaam found a way to make it the focal practice of the Students at the Center high school classes that he cotaught with teachers' union leader Jim Randels.[26] They did so out of recognition of what Elizabeth Rodriguez Fielder describes as the dynamic through which "cultural activists asked the same questions as progressive educators: how to teach without being didactic, and how to enter into nonhierarchical dialogue in the process of social justice."[27]

Moving to the classroom did not sever the story circle from its community roots. Assignments directed students to recruit a community elder as a mentor, to develop their writing through an intergenerational dialogue, and to present their work before their mentors and community audiences in a local Black-owned and -themed book store. One assignment encouraged students to become pen pals with people from their neighborhoods who were incarcerated. Their city, New Orleans, locks up a greater percentage of its population than any city in Louisiana—the state that incarcerates a greater proportion of its citizens than any other state in the US—the nation that sends a greater percentage of its citizens to jails and prisons than any other country in the world. Through correspondence, two of the students connected with Jerome Morgan, a man locked up in the Angola Penitentiary for a crime he did not commit. Letters from the students introduced Morgan to books that he subsequently read, while his letters alerted them to his unjust incarceration. The SAC students played a key role in the successful campaign to free Morgan from prison. Upon his release, he began coming to their classes, which inspired his long-planned work with fellow formerly incarcerated Black New Orleans residents Robert Jones and Daniel Rideau—forming the Free-Dem Foundations project, which mentors and provides job training for young men through a curriculum based on the story circle method.[28]

The story circle pedagogy made it possible for students to correspond with Jerome Morgan and to work with him as coauthors of the book *Go to Jail*, about the impact of mass incarceration on Black people in New Orleans. It introduced Morgan to allies who helped free him from prison and to a pedagogy that he made a centerpiece of the mentoring program for young people that he established with Jones and Rideau after release. The pedagogy also helped provoke direct political action. The students joined with Morgan in campaigns to repeal the Louisiana law that stipulated that juries do not need to render unanimous verdicts, and they joined in campaigns to help elect prosecutors and city council members sensitive to community needs. They helped educate elders about the damage done to education by privatization of the public school system and participated in campaigns against closing neighborhood schools.

SAC alumni continue to work today as teacher leaders of aggrieved communities, carrying on the practices of the story circle even without the support or approval of the school system. Current United Teachers of New Orleans union president Dave Cash works with Kalamu ya Salaam to participate in the Black Is Brilliant Study Group organized by the BE NOLA educational initiative headed by Adrinda Kelly, who was part of SAC classes in high school. BE NOLA builds on the practices created by Students at the Center to explore and advance the role of Black education in shaping the future of learning in New Orleans.

THE COMMUNITY TRANSFORMATIVE ORGANIZING STRATEGY IN OAKLAND

For nearly half a century the Asian Immigrant Women's Advocates (AIWA) organization has mobilized low-wage limited-English-speaking Asian immigrant women workers who labor in garment assembly sweatshops and electronics assembly lines in Oakland and San Jose in California. AIWA developed and practiced new ways of producing and applying knowledge through what the organization names the Community Transformational Organizing Strategy (CTOS).[29] This involves a curriculum that blends organizational governance with political education, skill building, personal development, and participation in fights for improvements in workplaces and communities. AIWA presents a nonhierarchical way of learning and working together that has enabled the organization to make alliances with people from different races and classes who accompany them in their struggle against the many layers of marginality and discrimination that shape immigrant women workers' lives. The CTOS method enables group members to initiate elaborate processes of collective self-reflection and growth through discussion, deliberation, and decision-making. Meeting in AIWA's offices in Oakland's Chinatown neighborhood, the group invented the CTOS paradigm as a way of cultivating the development of grassroots leaders and creating new understandings of how leadership should be defined.

FIGURE 3. Asian Immigrant Women Advocates discussion. Photograph courtesy of and with permission from Asian Immigrant Women Advocates.

CTOS participants move through a series of steps. They attend events and workshops that explain AIWA's mission and activities. They receive instruction in workplace and computer literacy. They develop skills for self-education and leadership in peer-led sessions, practice documenting the organization's work, facilitate meetings, and learn public speaking. Experience on committees carrying out different tasks makes women eligible to serve for a two-year period on the board overseeing the organization. These experiences open the door to the Peer Leader program, which positions women to conduct training sessions for new members and to represent the organization in public venues. Over the course of these steps, AIWA provides its members with practical skills like computer literacy, employment rights, and English language proficiency. It cultivates their knowledge about the labor and civil rights movements and explores the ramifications of language discrimination, imperialism, and sexism in their lives. Several classes are team taught by English-speaking staff members and volunteers from local colleges and universities along with non-English- or limited-English-speaking members who have completed leadership training. Being heard and being spoken to in one's native language is embraced by the organization as a fundamental human right.

The CTOS method is communicated and orchestrated by AIWA's executive director and a board of twenty rank-and-file members who rotate on and off it in order to give leadership experience to as many women as possible. The CTOS conception of leadership is not about elevating individuals to positions of power; rather, it is aimed at developing collective leadership of the organization as a collaborative endeavor, preparing AIWA members to take the lead in changing society, and enabling the women to be more effective agents in "leading" their own lives.[30]

CTOS revolves around an organizational chart that delineates the steps participants take to move from devaluation and silencing to empowered positions of self-representation and self-activity. The chart articulates the aims, activities, and expectations that come with successive stages of leadership development. Women who have reached the higher steps are paired with those entering the process so that each learner becomes a teacher and every teacher remembers being a learner. Because the key goal of CTOS concerns developing the long-term capacity for political and personal leadership among low-wage limited-English-speaking immigrant women workers, the effects of this training do not stay within AIWA but migrate out to other sites as women move on to new jobs, participate in political mobilizations, start businesses, and develop new egalitarian relations inside their families.[31]

Grassroots community organizers recognize that mobilizing Asian immigrant women for social change necessitates attending to intersectional issues of health, housing, and political disempowerment but also to the problems the women confront because of sexism at the workplace and in the home, due to language discrimination on the job and in the public sphere, and stemming from the denigration that they and their children experience because of anti-Asian racism. Engaging in the organizational and political work of AIWA often leads women to contest the devaluation they experience in other aspects of their lives shaped by gender hierarchies. When women gain experience training their peers through classroom instruction, researching health and safety issues, and mobilizing politically and speaking out in public demonstrations and meetings, they begin to renegotiate the terms of their identities as wives, mothers, sisters, and daughters in ways that reflect their evolving capacities for self-activity as people engaged in deliberative talk, democratic decision-making, and dignified self-representation.

Collective self-education has stood at the center of many AIWA projects designed to cultivate capacities for identifying the structural forces that shape the conditions of the members' lives. Field trips to department stores and boutiques revealed that dresses for which they were paid five dollars sold for as much as $175 to the public. When city officials denied the organization access to classrooms in a civic cultural center, AIWA developed an economic literacy curriculum that examined the municipal budget and how its lavish subsidies to developers and sports arenas contrasted with the austerity guiding the provision of public services and accessible public venues. The Community Equity Campaign studied the city budget and proposed ways of providing low-income groups access to meeting rooms in city-owned properties.[32]

The CTOS model helped make possible one of AIWA's great victories in the early 2000s: its Ergonomic Chair Campaign. Work in the garment industry for women entails neck, back, and shoulder strains and sprains from laboring as much ten hours per day for six or seven days a week, hunched over sewing machines while sitting on rickety crates, stools, or folding chairs. Living in the racialized Oakland Chinatown ghetto, largely in dilapidated and poorly maintained rental housing units, and limited in job opportunities because of race and gender discrimination, language barriers, uneven citizenship status, and inadequate access to transportation, these women can feel trapped in their onerous and poorly paid jobs, under-resourced neighborhoods, and patriarchal families. Only one in five of them at the turn of the century had any health insurance at all, while only one in eight had access to paid sick leave. The concentration of health hazards at work and the lack of medical providers where they lived left them feeling perpetually fatigued and ill. Seemingly always at work, they had little time left to spend with their friends and relatives and grew increasingly alienated from their children, whose experiences in English-language schools and exposure to mass media and advertising promoted consumer-centered desires that their parents' wages could not satisfy and peer-driven prestige hierarchies and values often hostile to family traditions.[33]

CTOS conversations that focused on occupational injuries led the women to conduct research on their own about their workplaces. That led them to contact specialists in ergonomic health and safety. The workers learned that ergonomic chairs at their work sites would help curtail the back, neck, and shoulder injuries that caused them much misery, so they asked their employers to provide that equipment. Their demands were rebuffed immediately by sweatshop managers who claimed that small profit margins prevented them from making such expenditures. In response, the women decided to launch a political campaign on several fronts to secure this improvement at their worksites. They reached out to sympathetic doctors, nurses, and occupational therapists to learn about repetitive motion injuries. They made connections with health care professionals from the University of California San Francisco Medical Center and the California Wellness Foundation, which led to the establishment of the Asian Immigrant Women Workers Clinic to attend to their medical needs. They distributed leaflets in Chinatown inviting other women to come to the clinic where AIWA activists collaborated with specialists to design an ergonomically sound model garment workstation with rotating chairs replacing stationary ones.

AIWA activists recognized that the same forces that saddled their neighborhood with racial segregation provided opportunities for congregation and mobilization, so they organized their neighbors to pressure the city council to allocate funds to create a "library" of ergonomic chairs that workers and employers could check out for limited periods of time. The city council authorized funds to provide 135 chairs. Women mobilized by AIWA helped the chair library reach its intended constituency by leading trainings on ergonomic health and safety for some 120 women in twenty-two different worksites.[34]

The Ergonomic Chair Campaign succeeded in reducing workplace injuries but also helped heal generational ruptures between immigrant mothers and daughters who joined AIWA's Youth Build Immigrant Power initiative. Opportunities to work together intersectionally—across generations, different Asian languages and national histories, and different levels of job skill and English language facility—enabled AIWA to counter the political powerlessness of immigrant women's lives through convivial and collaborative deliberation and mobilization. The organization offered women a political life suffused with degrees of agency the women had rarely experienced before on the job as workers or at home as wives, mothers, daughters, and sisters.

For members of AIWA, studying is not an abstract endeavor, nor is it ruled by competition among individuals for higher grades. It is a collective project of struggle. Solving immediate problems for them requires evaluating knowledge through many different disciplinary frameworks. The process produced new institutions in the form of a medical clinic and a chair library, but also new social relations among low-wage workers and scientific researchers in a university medical center, Chinatown neighbors, city council members, and mothers and their daughters.

The autonomous learning circles created by AIWA drew from and contributed to academic ethnic studies. The organization was founded by distinguished Asian American Studies literary critic Elaine Kim and educator Pat Lee. The Ergonomic Chair Campaign and other initiatives by AIWA drew on volunteer assistance from students majoring in ethnic studies at nearby colleges and universities. That experience equipped these students with understandings of learning and leadership they would not have discovered on campus alone.

AIWA's founding director Young Shin has taught courses on community organizing through the auspices of the Ethnic Studies Department at the University of California Berkeley. In 2016 two AIWA peer advocates spoke about how participation in the organization enriched their lives on a panel at the American Studies Association annual meeting in Denver, a panel that included spoken-word performer Sunni Patterson and visual artist Jay Lynn Gomez. When AIWA worked with organizer and activist Gary Delgado to create the documentary film *Becoming Ourselves: How Immigrant Women Transformed Their World*, scholars inspired by the film developed a teacher's guidebook to shape the film's use in college classroom settings.[35]

WHY AUTONOMOUS LEARNING CIRCLES MATTER

The participatory, convivial, and creative work inside autonomous learning circles makes them places where new social relations develop, new economic, social, and political practices emerge, and people encounter difference without dominance. They open the door to thinking about how to use time without being trapped in teleology, to inhabit what Avery Gordon calls "abolitionist time," which she describes as "a way of being in the ongoing work of emancipation, a work whose success is not measured by legalistic pronouncements, a work which perforce must take place while you're still enslaved."[36]

Autonomous learning circles provide participants with embodied repertoires that resist the countersubversive campaigns and racial nationalist repressions mobilized to maintain neoliberal economics, politics, and culture. These spaces cultivate empathy, discernment, and judgment, promote suspicion of simple solutions to shared social problems, and deepen collective capacities for imagining and inventing new kinds of caretaking relations. Convivial and collaborative acts of cocreation and arts-based community making help to create change from the bottom up by deepening the social cohesion, collective efficacy, and capacity for democratic deliberation and decision-making within aggrieved communities. Their ways of working are part of a dispersed but powerful network of grassroots initiatives around the world mobilized against the logics, cultures, and politics of neoliberalism.[37] Although scarcely legible in electoral politics or in online and mass-mediated communications, they provoke people at the grassroots to participate in processes that change themselves as they work to change society.

Mobilizations on the right like the campaigns against critical race theory and antiracist practices, ideas, and institutions described in chapter 1 can rely on lavish funding, favorable media coverage, and fervent support from elected officials. Mobilizations against racial capitalism have none of these advantages. What others will not do for the majority of the world's population they will have to do for themselves. They need to deepen the capacity for democratic deliberation and decision-making among people without property or power. They need to create spaces of collaboration and exchange dedicated to envisioning and implementing radical alternatives to the structure and culture of neoliberalism. Autonomous learning circles can play an essential role in those struggles.

RIPPLE EFFECTS IN AND OUT

K-12 and higher education make up important institutions in society. There is important work to be done inside one of the few public spheres not yet completely controlled by profit-making imperatives. Yet the opposition to the academy delineated in chapter 1 and the ever-increasing incorporation of colleges and universities described in chapter 2 make it more important than ever to connect formal schooling to the archives, imaginaries, epistemologies, and ontologies generated within alternative academies and autonomous learning centers. Folklorist, sociolinguist, and medical anthropologist Charles Briggs states, "Many of the people who have affected my thinking the most are not scholars, never published, and in some cases never had access to formal schooling." Briggs found that wood carvers in northern New Mexico and Indigenous healers in the Delta Amacuro rainforest in eastern Venezuela turned out to be "some of the most profound, abstract, subtle, and creative thinkers I have ever known."[38] The ideas, analyses, concepts, and categories that these grassroots mentors deployed emerged out of dire necessity. They were forged as tools for survival in the face of colonial domination, displacement, dispossession, and denigration. While maintaining deep respect for academic inquiry and mentors, and while achieving exceptional success as a scholar himself, Briggs discerns that unique and profound insights emerged as he engaged in the practical work of social struggle, trying to help people confronting corporations and governments stealing their land and destroying the environments in which they lived, and strategizing along with people seeking to keep their family members from dying in epidemics. "These engagements," he asserts, "forced me to identify the commonsense frameworks and practices that produced and normalized these profound inequalities and ally with others in imagining alternative futures."[39]

Many scholars have received important early life lessons about discipline, perseverance, and teamwork from seemingly unexpected sources as members of sports teams, music, theater, and dance ensembles, and through arts and crafts and martial arts practice. Some of these experiences have led directly to new scholarly paradigms and practices. Participation in the work of the Free Southern Theater helped Richard Schechner discover and develop concepts that played a central role in the creation of the field of performance studies.[40] Johari Jabir's work off campus as a choir director leads him to deploy what he calls "gospel music pedagogy" in his University of Illinois-Chicago African American studies classrooms, through exercises based on the presumption that choirs are only as strong as their weakest links. Just as choirs need to sing together, students in Jabir's classes learn to learn together. John-Carlos Perea (Mescalero Apache) draws on traditional Indigenous pow-wow and fish camp science pedagogies in creating forms of collective learning for students enrolled in the music and American Indian studies classes he taught first at San Francisco State University and now teaches at the University of Washington.[41]

George Sanchez credits his experiences mixing, scratching, and playing records as a disc jockey at multiracial parties as one inspiration for the concepts and practices of comparative and relational ethnic studies that later fueled his scholarship and program building.[42] Charles Briggs points to his training in ballet and modern dance and his stint as host of a radio music program as endowing him with skills that later proved productive in conducting friendly, respectful, and convivial forms of ethnographic research.[43] Deborah Wong draws on her experiences playing music inside taiko drum ensembles as the source of her contributions to the field of ethnomusicology. Participating in music and analyzing it forms a routine feature of ethnomusicology, but Wong expanded the reach, scope, focus, and relevance of her discipline by demonstrating how taiko has become a site where Asian and Asian American women recognize and rehearse physical actions that reject gendered stereotypes and create an "embodied feminism of performative sound and movement."[44] José Esteban Muñoz cites the disco dance floor and the punk rock mosh pit as key parts of his formation as a queer of color theorist.[45] He recalls how seeing queer performance artist Marga Gomez on a television show—recycling damaging stereotypes into "powerful and seductive sites of self-creation"—spoke to his then closeted queer identity and aspirations.[46] There would have been no queer theory in the academy, he maintains, had it not been for the cultural performances of Gomez and others like her.[47] Muñoz notes that in his youth the punk band X "was the only avant-garde I knew. It was the only cultural critique of normative aesthetics available to me."[48] Similarly, Jack Halberstam remembers embracing punk music because "it gave me a language with which to reject not only the high-cultural texts in the classroom but also the homophobia, gender normativity, and sexism outside it."[49]

COMMERCIAL CULTURE'S AUTONOMOUS LEARNING CIRCLES

Not everyone has direct access to art-based community practices. For many participants inside the project of ethnic studies and the broader antiracist social formation, commercial culture functions as an alternative although hardly ever autonomous learning circle. One of the most important missions of ethnic studies revolves around teaching critical media literacy to help students decipher how social ideologies can be encoded and decoded in YouTube, TikTok, Instagram, Facebook, Threads, Bluesky, and other social media conduits. Although often filled with morally and politically poisonous content and organized by ideologically inflected search engines, social media conduits also enable young people to speak with each other about experiences, like being young parents, feeling isolated from their peers, and securing reproductive health services denied them in their own communities. Indigenous activists in the Idle No More movement in Canada in 2012 found their dispersal across vast territories an impediment to meeting in person, making online communications a preferred option.[50] Trans people on YouTube videos document their transitions and provide advice that might not be available by other means for others contemplating or undergoing transition.[51]

College students not exposed to ethnic studies in high school may nonetheless know about Black Lives Matter because of hip-hop music lyrics or because a football player takes a knee during the national anthem to protest predatory policing. They access archives of the oppressed in graphic novels about the Holocaust in Europe, theocracy in Iran, apartheid in South Africa, and the occupation and attempted destruction of Palestine. Their knowledge of the assassination of Martin Luther King Jr. may start with listening to U2 sing "In the Name of Love" or the Old Crow Medicine Show's "Motel in Memphis." A film like *The Revenant* may be a first point of entry into knowledge about the ways in which the military and the fur trade devastated Indigenous communities in the nineteenth century, while *Stonewall* may serve as an introduction into the gay liberation movement. They may have learned about the crisis in Puerto Rico after Hurricane Maria in 2017 from the song "Afilando los Cuchillos" (Sharpening the Knives) by Bad Bunny, Residente, and iLe, which became a powerful force for mobilizations against the corrupt, incompetent, homophobic, and ableist administration of Puerto Rican governor Ricardo Rosselló.[52] Campaigns by the African American Policy Forum calling attention to police killings of Black women became amplified and disseminated to a broad audience through Janelle Monae's song "Hell You Taimbout," which featured a chorus of women calling out the names of Black women killed by police officers.[53]

Commercial artists evidence traces of influence from ethnic studies through the reading lists that KRS-ONE provided with his hip-hop albums, Tish Hinojosa's tribute song to Americo Paredes "Con Su Pluma en Su Mano: With His Pen in His Hand," and Michael Franti and Spearhead's shout-out to Angela Davis in their song "Dream Team." Martha Gonzalez of the Chicano band Quetzal locates the origins and inspiration for the group's song "Imaginaries" in scholarly research and theorizing by Emma Perez about the decolonial imaginary. In her multidisciplinary music and theater performance piece "Breaking the Thermometer to Hide the Fever," singer, composer, banjo player, and cellist Leyla McCalla draws on personal and family histories of involvement in social movements, archival research, and conversations with Haitian studies scholar Laurent Dubois. McCalla describes her album *Vari-Colored Songs* as a tribute to the poet Langston Hughes and his influence on her and other musicians.

AUTONOMOUS LEARNING CIRCLES AND THE ETHNIC STUDIES PROJECT

Autonomous learning circles only rarely identify themselves as part of ethnic studies, yet they play an important role in both the academic project and the broader antiracist social formation that it reflects and shapes. The pedagogical innovations crafted inside autonomous learning circles such as Learning How to Arrive, Restorative Cultural Arts Practice/Praxis, Story Circle Pedagogy, and the Community Transformational Organizing Strategy reveal possibilities for new pedagogical practices on and off campuses. Their work is not without complications and contradictions. Like all experiments, they involve failures as well as successes. The local circumstances and particular constituencies that shape them may not be easily transferrable to academic settings that have different race, class, and gender demographics. But taking them seriously can help ethnic studies participants move beyond treating aggrieved groups as passive objects rather than active subjects and past seeing oppressed communities as sources of only fascination or fear.

Not everyone in ethnic studies settings will be able to work directly with the artists and activists inside autonomous learning circles. But nearly everyone in the academy can read about them, learn from them, teach and write about their ideas, chronicle their achievements, criticize their shortcomings, and invite them to give paid presentations on campus. Ethnic studies instructors teaching in carceral institutions, workers centers, and public libraries have found it valuable and necessary to develop new forms of pedagogy and new kinds of publications that they have subsequently incorporated back into their K-12 and college classrooms.[54]

The pedagogies of autonomous learning circles on and off campuses express and enact theories of social change honed and refined in social movement struggles. Chapter 4, which follows, explores how struggles for social intersectional justice have played key roles in defining the work of ethnic studies on campus and the broader antiracist social formation beyond it.

4

Ethnic Studies and Intersectional Justice

Nearly all forms of discrimination entail using difference as an excuse for domination. Small differences in appearance or condition are used to justify large differences in treatment in ways that impose unfair and unjust impediments to living decent and dignified lives. The presidential election of 2024 revolved around the demonization of difference: around attacks on immigrants perceived as not white, on children and adults portrayed as not properly gendered and sexed, on the Black woman running for president demeaned as a diversity, equity, and inclusion hire, and on unmarried and childless women as people not to be respected by the political system. After decades of condemning desegregation and affirmative action as social engineering, the people guiding the campaign proposed their own mechanisms of social engineering, such as giving extra voting representation and directing government spending toward people in heterosexual marriages raising children. During the election season, the Republican candidates aired a story that even they admitted was made up about legal immigrants from Haiti eating white people's pets in Springfield, Ohio. Before and after the election, politicians and pundits fabricated false claims that diversity, equity, and inclusion policies were responsible for barges crashing into bridges, plane crashes, wildfires, and inadequate government responses to hurricane damage. No accountability rested on the shoulders of normative heterosexual propertied white male citizens who disproportionately held positions of power and authority; all problems were blamed on non-normative others.

The ethnic studies project and the broader social formation it reflects and shapes expose these unquestioned allegiances to normativity as destructive to all of society, not just to their targeted allegedly non-normative victims. This chapter delineates how people designated as non-normative have deployed the powers of the caduceus at the crossroads to use their socially degraded status as an impetus for treating difference as a source of strength rather than weakness. In the process they formulate newer, truer, and better understandings of how society does work and should work. They invent, enact, develop, and deploy forms of creative non-normativity, recognizing that their non-normativity can enable a caduceus-inspired practice that inverts power and promotes possibility.

Normativity is a subjective perception based on value judgments used as standards for behavior and identity. It distinguishes what is good and desirable from what is not. Deeming people as non-normative because of their race, gender, sexuality, disability, national origin, or language justifies and excuses their mistreatment. It hides the flaws in the actions, beliefs, and standards of those who understand themselves as normative while obscuring how those deemed non-normative can have what Glenn Coulthard (Dene) in the context of the knowledges and place-based practices of Indigenous people calls "grounded normativity." In similar but not identical fashion, those deemed non-normative because of race, gender, sexuality, and disability create forms of grounded normativity based on the actions, behaviors, and values they choose.[1] This chapter explores and evaluates the situated knowledges of people designated as non-normative and different because of their race, gender, sexuality, disability, and citizenship status, and others' perception of them as being out of place.

INTERSECTIONAL RACE AND SEXUALITY JUSTICE

Roderick Ferguson demonstrates in his book *One-Dimensional Queer* how queer liberation movements neither preceded nor followed the racial freedom struggles of the mid-twentieth century but emerged inside and alongside them. Although early ethnic studies all but ignored the links to these movements, it is now well known that leaders of the Black freedom struggle included LGBTQ individuals such as Angela Davis, James Baldwin, Pauli Murray, and Lorraine Hansberry, while pioneers in the gay, queer, and trans liberation movements such as Sylvia Rivera, Marsha P. Johnson, Miss Major Griffin-Gracy, and Stormé

De Laverie came from communities of color. Rivera and Johnson (and many other queer antiracist activists) derived part of their politics from being trauma surviving and/or chronically ill. Racism, homophobia, transphobia, and ableism all have common roots in eugenics, in its concepts of assigning value to bodies based on expectations of productivity and fantasies of fitness and normativity. These links help explain why disabled queer of color activists took the lead in creating the disability justice movement described later in this chapter.[2]

Ferguson calls attention to the long history of interlocking struggles against domination led by queers of color in a wide range of progressive struggles against racism, misogyny, homophobia, transphobia, and disability injustice. He salutes the intersectional activism in which "gay liberationists were putting to use the political discourses that were being crafted by various progressive struggles, discourses that took the relational nature of progressive struggles as the basis of political interventions." He adds, "Part of the relational politics involved an interest in disrupting the liberal notion that forms of difference are inherently antagonistic to each other, that difference was a source of separation and antagonism."[3]

Ferguson's argument about the vital presence of queer people of color in many different progressive struggles entails more than the mention of the embodied identities of individuals involved in antiracist, gay liberation, and disability justice struggles. He presents evidence that these activists developed their understandings of the significance of their social identities through their politics, rather than assuming that their politics flowed inexorably from their ascribed identities. Ferguson shows that many different progressive struggles of the twentieth century reached similar conclusions about the ways in which difference serves as the rationale, justification, and excuse for domination. In opposition to liberal thought that treats difference as a problem and posits sameness, equality, and interchangeability as its solution, radical movements for racial, gender, and sexual justice have viewed the dynamics of difference as generative of new ways of knowing and being, as registers of the ways many different currents of power flow through individuals and groups, and as provocations for envisioning and enacting new and better social identities and social relations.

Sylvia Rivera, who had a Puerto Rican father and Venezuelan mother, left her home in New York shortly before the age of eleven because of relentlessly cruel treatment from her family when she refused to accept normative gender roles.[4] Like many LGBTQ young people, she lived on the streets, hustled to make enough money to survive, and became connected to other youths and adults in similar conditions. Rivera's activism included participation in the Stonewall Rebellion's famous resistance to a police raid on a gay bar in 1969 that many credit with starting a new phase of the gay liberation struggle. In 1970 she attended the Black Panther Party (BPP) Revolutionary People's Constitutional Convention in Philadelphia, where she had the opportunity to speak with party leader Huey P. Newton, who offered encouragement for her organizing. Newton drew on his contact with gay men while in prison, conversations with James Baldwin and Jean Genet, and his admiration for the Stonewall uprising and for all people who took risks and lived outside of normative categories. He delivered a talk and wrote a letter calling for solidarity among Black, gay, and women's social movements. He also called for Panthers to no longer use antigay epithets in their writing and speech.[5]

In New York Rivera threw herself into work with activists in the Young Lords Party and their campaigns for health and housing justice, reproductive freedom, and childcare. While committed resolutely to Puerto Rican freedom, the group numbered among its members people of Cuban, Dominican, Mexican, Panamanian, Filipinx, and South Asian ancestry, imbuing the organization with a proclivity to treat difference as productive rather than destructive.[6] Rivera was not a member of the Young Lords but proved to be a reliable and welcome ally. "Any time they needed help," she recalled, "I was always there for the Young Lords. It was just the respect they gave us as human beings. They gave us a lot of respect. It was a fabulous feeling for me to be myself—being part of the Young Lords as a drag queen—and my organization STAR being part of the Young Lords."[7] When her lawsuit charging a prison guard with beating an inmate made Rivera the target of death threats, the Young Lords assigned members to do security and protect her.[8]

Rivera established queer homeless encampments, defended sex work as legitimate labor necessitated by the employment system's exclusion of gender-nonconforming people, and developed an intersectional radical critique of gender coercion, incarceration, and forced psychiatric institutionalization.[9] Along with Marsha P. Johnson, she created the Street Transvestite Action Revolutionaries organization that eventually became known as the Street Trans Action Revolutionaries (STAR) on the Lower East Side of New York. STAR offered support and shelter to houseless trans women and queer young people from aggrieved racialized groups. It provided a place where people could mobilize in response

FIGURE 4. Entrance to the Marsha P. Johnson State Park in Williamsburg, Brooklyn, New York City. Photo by Randy Duchaine/Alamy Stock Photo.

to the intersectional ways gay and trans people were injured by racist, sexist, classist, and ableist police harassment, jail and prison conditions, and policies in mental institutions. STAR functioned as a parallel institution that provided services unavailable elsewhere, such as meeting immediate needs for food, shelter, and childcare.[10] Rivera viewed the issues facing trans people as directly connected to racism, class oppression, and imperialism. "Part of our mission statement," she proclaimed, "is to be out there for all oppressed people."[11]

Rivera's life has been honored by having a New York street named after her and through the name of the Sylvia Rivera Law Project that provides legal assistance to low-income, poor, and racialized transgender, intersex, and/or gender-nonconforming clients. In 2020 the State of New York changed the name of East River State Park in Brooklyn to Marsha P. Johnson State Park, making the site the first state park to honor the name of an LGBTQ person, activist, and drag queen. Yet while Rivera and Johnson are now hailed in retrospect as heroes, they are often remembered by different constituencies as primarily queer or transgender or Latinx or Black, or chronically ill or drag queens, rather than all of those identities (and more) at once. As Jessi Gan observes about the life of Rivera, even non-normative groups can create their own kinds of single-axis normativity that fail to encompass multiple, intersecting, and overlapping identities.[12]

Queer of color activism organized by (among others) Rivera and STAR, by Proyecto ContraSIDA por Vida in San Francisco, and by the Combahee River Collective in Boston recognized differences inside their own ranks as sources of strength. Rather than seeking to overcome divisions and enforce unity through uniformity, they pursued solidarities that thrived on difference, incorporating and building upon their diverse social experiences, identities, aspirations, and ideologies.[13] Instead of striving to make liberalism more inclusive, these formations exposed and questioned the terms of inclusion and exclusion to show the democratic possibilities they precluded. As Sara Ahmed observes, "What is astray does not lead us back to the straight line, but shows what is lost by following that line."[14]

In *Aberrations in Black*, Ferguson reveals how the unjust racial order derives legitimacy and justification from association with gender and sexual normativity.[15] The systems that subordinate putatively non-normative racial, gendered, and sexual identities do not exist separately but work together in concert to produce normativity as a crucial component of what C. Wright Mills called "the centralized say-so," and what other scholars, following Antonio Gramsci, name "ideological hegemony."[16] Ferguson delineates in detail the unjust suffering that this nexus of exclusion and denigration produces. Yet he applies the epistemologies of the crossroads and the caduceus to point to the potential of the people presumed to be failing and dysfunctional as uniquely positioned to critique and correct the evils perpetrated by the state and capital.[17] Ferguson notes that some of the most powerful and perceptive critiques of normativity have come from transgender people whose perceived non-normativity causes their very identities to be policed and persecuted.[18] As this chapter will demonstrate, similar critiques of normativity and its narrowness permeate struggles for disability justice, pan-ethnic and pan-racial antiracism, queer and woman of color feminism, and immigrant sanctuary.

Sara Ahmed views gay liberation as linked inextricably to antiracism through her assertion that "race can be a queer matter." This is not simply because racialized populations include people who have same-sex romantic and erotic attachments or are gender nonconforming. For Ahmed (following Mandy Merck), queerness entails broad opposition to what is expected or accepted.[19] She embraces the term *queer* as a word signifying specific sexual practices and identities but also as a term that calls attention to what is oblique or off line. Jodi Byrd (Chickasaw) finds that Lauren Berlant's framing of sexuality as a set of patterns that align people with the world in particular ways illuminates what Byrd calls "the conjunctive intimacies produced within the ongoing US colonization of people and lands," which work in ways to position both queer and Indigenous politics as disruptions of liberal notions of rights grounded in categories of "inclusions, recognitions, and tolerance."[20] Similarly, José Esteban Muñoz explains that performing queerness entails "thriving on sites where meaning does not properly 'line up.'"[21] He sees white racial normativity and sexual heteronormativity as mutually constitutive ideological formations.[22] Ahmed identifies one of the missions of compulsory heterosexuality to be the reproduction of whiteness as a possession and an investment that is passed down along the family line of inheritance.[23]

DISABILITY JUSTICE

The critique of normativity that emerges at the crossroads of race and sex has affinities with the affirmation of the value and possibilities of difference central to campaigns for disability justice, a cause and movement that is innately intersectional.[24] Assumptions of normative able-bodiedness create artificial, arbitrary, irrational, and unnecessary exclusions that narrow the spheres of social interaction, squander talents and abilities, misallocate resources, and obstruct invention and innovation. Everyone is harmed by these exclusions and they need to be countered. Yet like abolition democracy's opposition to racism, disability justice concerns more than eliminating particular barriers to inclusion in the unjust society that exists—instead it seeks to create a society that understands difference as an asset rather than a liability.[25]

Like queer of color antiracist activists and intellectuals, disability justice advocates including Patty Berne, Mia Mingus, Leroy Moore, Aurora Levins Morales, Eli Clare, and Stacey Park Milbern demand more than removal of barriers to inclusion. They insist that all bodies deserve to have their needs met, a stance that requires rejection of the shared social structures and beliefs that use ascribed disability and impairment as ways of diminishing people's dignity, worth, and well-being.[26] These structures and beliefs do not exist in isolation but flow logically and inexorably from the rationales needed to create and protect colonial conquest, capitalist domination, and white supremacy.

Disability is not an objective factual identity: It is a relational social construct created by reserving privileged access to social spaces and interactions to those with mobility, sight, hearing, and other capacities deemed normative. Just as homosexuality was once defined as mental illness and the brains of people of color were deemed inferior to those of whites, disability is posed as a matter of biological or physical lack on the part of the disabled rather than the product of the limitations of a world designed for those considered able-bodied. For many disabled people, however, disability entails valued identities, communities, politics, actions, analyses, and commitments. Moreover, in ways similar to—but also different from—racism and homophobia, disability never exists alone.

The disability justice movement emerges from queer disabled people of color for both demographic and political reasons. Nearly one in five Black people in the US experience disability. The populations with the highest numbers of disabled people are women, people with low incomes, Native Americans, and Indigenous Alaskans. Unemployment and employment discrimination against disabled people lead to poverty, while poverty exposes people disproportionally to disabling conditions.[27] Capitalism's excessive valorization of labor productivity and profits contributes to defining and devaluing disabled people, a dynamic that makes disability justice innately anticapitalist and antiracist.[28] Residential racial segregation and labor exploitation are disabling processes that produce disproportionate incidences of debilitating asthma, diabetes, and valley fever in places inhabited by members of aggrieved communities of color. Mass incarceration disproportionately targets the disabled and generates disability by packing people into small unventilated spaces with poor water quality and rife with infectious diseases and compelling them to perform hard labor without adequate nutrition and medical care.[29]

Antiracist struggles confront the dominant culture's treatment of whiteness as the unmarked norm against which difference is measured. Queer liberationists similarly recognize that their marginalization and mistreatment stems from enshrining heterosexuality as a universal norm that renders queer sexuality deviant and deficient. A similar inversion makes it possible for people also minoritized because of their sexuality and race to perceive affinities with the ways in which the norm of able-bodiedness produces the category of disability and perpetuates discrimination.[30]

Queer of color and disability justice advocates alike face the consequences of the deeply rooted ways of knowing that they work to contest.

Their labors have significant import for ethnic studies. The category of disability emerged historically as a consequence of the emergence of methods of calculation, quantification, and evaluation produced in the nineteenth century that rested on distinguishing the standard from the nonstandard and the normal from the putatively abnormal. These methods led researchers, clinicians, and political authorities to portray impairment and disability as objective conditions rather than socially constructed judgments. This division of the world into binaries between normal/abnormal and standard/nonstandard echoes the domination rationalized by the distinction between *humanitas* and *anthropos* and the concept of the savage slot to be discussed in chapter 5. Just as dominant practices labeled gender-nonconforming identities as evidence of individual mental illness rather than as a consequence of the narrow, punitive, and cruel exclusions built into normative heterosexuality, disability became defined as the unfortunate physical condition of individuals rather than as an unjust socially constructed set of obstacles formed by ableist assumptions about how to configure the physical and social worlds.

Like queer of color activists, campaigners for disability justice participated in a wide range of progressive struggles that generated relational politics grounded in opposition to the liberal idea that forms of difference are inherently antagonistic to one another. Virtually every progressive struggle has entailed actions by people with disabilities, even though these movements may not have been accessible and sensitive to disability issues. As Talila A. Lewis observes, "Since we live under racial capitalism, settler colonialism and white supremacy, ableism in the united states has *never* solely been about disability."[31]

Sami Schalk recounts important incidents in the past and present when movements for disability justice and racial justice have intersected. In 1977, members of the Black Panther Party (BPP) joined and supported a twenty-six-day disability rights sit-in occupation of the federal building in San Francisco, demanding passage of a bill outlawing disability discrimination by any recipient of federal funds. For nearly one month, the Panthers supplied some 150 demonstrators with hot food dinners, set up showers for them, provided security, and publicized the cause in the party newspaper. The demonstration identified the challenges posed at crossroads of racism, poverty, inadequate social provision, and disability.[32]

Party member Brad Lomax was a wheelchair user with multiple sclerosis and was also legally blind. His experiences with the BPP included working with the party's George Jackson Clinic that offered free medical care to the community and helping to plan a Center for Independent Living in East Oakland that for a brief time offered attendant referrals and peer counseling.[33] He participated in the sit-in and brought it to the attention of the Panthers as an issue of intersectional justice, a commitment parallel to the disability justice principle of centering the experiences of multiply marginalized communities whose situatedness may enable them to discern connections that other may not see. The 1977 action at the federal building attracted and relied on a diverse constituency. The range of participants encompassed well-off suburban mothers with disabled children, drug addicts living on the streets, militant Chicanos from the Mission District, and the Butterfly Brigade—an organized group of gay men who patrolled the streets to protect queer men from violent attacks.[34]

Schalk delineates how Lomax worked to make disability politics part of the BPP agenda, leading to the group's decisions to support the sit-in at the federal building, to supply food to the demonstrators, to create wheelchair ramp access to party offices, and to install grab bars in the bathrooms of buildings that party members used. In its coverage of the demonstration, the *Black Panther* newspaper published a quote from a demonstrator explaining that the "handicaps" medical and political authorities discerned among the protesters were not features of their bodies but consequences of ableist configurations of space. These might have included favoring stairs over ramps and elevators, making doorways too narrow for people in wheelchairs to pass through, establishing sidewalks without curb cuts, and making communication dependent on sight and hearing with no audio or visual accommodations for people who needed them. Schalk attributes this sophisticated and accurate understanding of disability to the Panthers' recognition that the injuries experienced because of race and class oppression stemmed from the failures and biases of social institutions rather than deficiencies in people targeted for discrimination and exploitation.[35]

The crossroads where the Black Panther Party and a wide range of allies participated in a struggle waged by disability activists demonstrates how a critique of allegiance to normativity as an exclusionary and destructive practice contains significance for ethnic studies, not only as an object of study, but also as a sensibility needed in political practice inside the academy. Universities that can afford nuclear research reactors, particle accelerators, and flight simulators claim they cannot afford to provide sign language interpreters or closed-captioning technologies.

Courses teaching students to stage music, dance, and theater productions rarely acknowledge even the possibility that audience members, performers, lighting and sound technicians, or directors might be disabled.[36] Most educational institutions proceed through ableist norms that confuse normative identity with merit. The social definition of merit that looms large in academic evaluation and reward is suffused with outmoded and unquestioned baseline norms that work to the disadvantage of people with cognitive conditions considered disabled. Time-limited multiple-choice standardized tests and exams presume to judge ability objectively. Yet that format measures only the speed of information retrieval, not the depth of students' knowledge or their ability to apply what they know to the actual tasks required in academic and professional life. The standardized timed test disadvantages neurodivergent applicants, while it measures skills irrelevant to the academic tasks the test takers will be asked to tackle. It evidences impairments in the tests rather than deficiencies in the test takers. This practice resonates with the same logics used to disadvantage people by race and class. Standardized tests with origins in eugenics still play a major role in deciding who is admitted to undergraduate and graduate study. Giving extra weight in admissions decisions to advanced placement courses not available to students of all classes and races, rewarding test takers who pay for courses that coach them to improve their scores, and using tests that privilege questions geared more toward measuring privilege than merit limit the range of interlocutors in academic ethnic studies and make the field and campuses unnecessarily more parochial and provincial.[37]

Dominant notions of disability as a category can obscure the failures of social institutions to welcome different kinds of bodily and mental ability. Disability is a mixed ability category that is innately diverse. Disabled people often have more exposure to difference because of this and as a result have frequently learned to see beyond binary oppositions. There are clear parallels with ways critical race theory argues that racial subordination is a product of systemic structures of exclusion rather than of the alleged unfitness of racialized subjects. Disability justice helps everyone realize new possibilities, inhabit new identities, and envision and enact new social relations.

Struggles by racialized queer, trans, and disabled people emerge from and contribute to equally important forms of study. Their relevance rests not simply on their identities—on who they are, what has been done to them, and what they have done—but also in what they know as a result of their social positions. Their day-to-day existence requires identifying, understanding, analyzing, and countering dominant categories of normativity and social inclusion. Lessons learned in one modality of study have positive ramifications for others. Chronically ill and disabled people find themselves compelled to conduct research on many different hazards to their health and to devise and share homemade remedies. When the COVID-19 pandemic posed health hazards that were novel to many people, chronically ill and disabled persons had advanced knowledge about calculating risks, wearing masks, and practicing sanitation. Disability circles of care function as collectively created autonomous learning circles. Naomi Ortiz describes what she calls "crip ecologies" as "living, breathing spaces of conflict and creativity" that arise in response to "having to plan for everything. And then having a backup plan for each plan." People in these circles live with contradictions that facilitate what Ortiz describes as "a kind of problem-solving that is inclusive, a means of tackling problems in which diversity and an expectation of difference is valued."[38]

Collective learning leads to collective teaching. The mission statement of Sins Invalid declares, "As queer brown disabled people, we are forced to teach the basics—asserting that we, too, are humans deserving of human rights; that we have a collective history and future; and that we are not deviant or aberrant but an essential part of humanity."[39] Some of the blend of study and struggle central to the disability justice movement takes place in classrooms, but it also spreads through a rhizomatic public sphere that includes graphic zines, online communications, visual arts, music performances with adaptive use instruments, graffiti, and wheat-posted messages.

Like disability, transgender identity also generates important practices of study and struggle. Nathaniel Dickson argues that being transgender "draws attention to, and estranges, the social relations that produce shared oppression—while simultaneously providing an opportunity for resocialization, and thus a potentially better model for relating to others."[40] Angela Davis notes how prison abolitionists learned important lessons from transgender activism, not just because trans identity is so often criminalized, but also because challenges to the normativity of the gender binary provide a model for challenging society's seemingly normal and inevitable reliance on jails and prisons as forms of social control.[41] The artificial, arbitrary, irrational, and unnecessary impediments to full social membership enacted by homophobia, transphobia, and ableism harm everyone, while the movements for justice that emerge in response produce new and important ways of knowing and being that are beneficial to all. The diverse ways of knowing and being that emerge within and because of these movements coalesce around the stated mission of the disability justice group Sins Invalid—to move together with no one left behind.

ETHNIC AND RACIAL CROSSROADS

Dealing with difference poses enduring challenges within ethnic studies. Study and struggle offer occasions for groups to work together but also to remain apart when situations require it. Some ethnic studies projects serve one group at a time while others entail comparative, relational, and intersubjective work. Experiences with racialization and resistance have similarities across group lines but are not experienced identically. The work of the caduceus at crossroads inside ethnic studies requires acknowledging and honoring the things that flow from being in difference, while remaining cognizant of the value of each group's density, hybridity, and affiliations with other similarly but not identically positioned groups. The presence of difference, which can often be seen as a liability, can be a powerful asset when negotiated intersectionally. Ethnic studies can also, however, succumb to creating new arbitrary norms and boundaries by insisting dogmatically either on organizing initiatives that deal with only one racial group at a time (Black studies, Chicanx studies. etc.) or on privileging fused projects built on interactions among groups (ethnic studies, Third World studies, etc.). Either formulation can be destructive, but each can also be situationally valuable as long as its norms are acknowledged as tactical, contingent, provisional, and constructed.

The common method of organization in universities that creates separate departments of Black studies, Latinx studies, Asian American studies, and Indigenous studies runs the risk of cultivating narrow nationalisms and group-based competition for recognition and resources. It can focus so much attention on the particular identities of specific oppressed groups that it impedes recognition of the general dynamics of oppression. Dividing study and struggle into discrete units defined by their exclusion from a putatively white center can also erase the important polylateral, intersectional, and mutually constative aspects of antiracist formations.[42] Taking an opposite path, however, does not make danger disappear. Some ethnic studies academic units entail expansive and open-ended confederations of ethnic groups. Others place diverse racial groups within overarching units of feminist studies, justice studies, disability studies, migration studies, or social analysis. These confederations risk homogenizing disparate experiences and flattening out differences. In both struggle and study there are times when it makes perfect sense to be together and others times when it makes perfect sense to work apart. It will always be difficult to theorize and negotiate tensions between partiality and totality in a world suffused with contradictions. But these tensions can be managed productively by recognizing the generative power of what can emerge at the crossroads, where "both/and" might be much more useful than "either/or."

Identity-based one-group-at-a-time ethnic studies units have not been nearly as narrow nor comparative and relational units as capacious as their signifiers suggest. Even the most fully institutionalized, incorporated, and seemingly ethnically and racially isolated ethnic studies has never lost touch completely with broader antiracist and liberation-seeking social formations. Centered in antiracism, it has also accompanied and promoted powerful forms of anti-imperialism, anti-capitalism, feminism, and critical queer, trans, and disability studies. Many of the broad liberation studies and practices that we might attribute to comparative and relational units emerged originally as intersectional initiatives inside units organized to foreground racial specificity. Rather than dead ends, group-specific organizations facilitated paths to making affiliations, alliances, coalitions, and coalescences across social barriers. Whether groups join together or work separately is a tactical and strategic question rather than a moral or theoretical choice.

Exploration of the particular histories of single aggrieved groups can quickly lead to discovery of structural frames that shape the experiences of other groups. Indigenous Peoples in the Americas have very different histories from people in Palestine, yet both suffer from settler colonialism, as do Indigenous peoples in Australia, New Zealand, and Canada. The constituencies central to the ethnic studies project make its scholars, departments, and professional associations especially aware of the links between racism in the US and imperialism and settler colonial violence overseas. Currents of thought and activism in Arab studies, Asian American studies, Indigenous studies, and Chicanx studies highlight the families of resemblance that link each of these groups' histories to the suppression of self-determination in Palestine and the mass slaughters and ethnic cleansings that Palestinians face. At the K-12 and college levels, ethnic studies scholars have stood firm against campaigns pressuring them to exclude even the mere mention—much less sustained study—of Palestine from their courses and research.[43]

Ethnic- and race-based mobilizations that coalesce around the specific histories and conditions of a single group often lead to or already include recognition of families of resemblance with other groups. Diane Fujino's richly generative history and analysis of the origins and evolution of the Asian American Political Alliance (AAPA) reveals that organization's deft suturing of education with social movement mobilization as well as its participants' commitments both to their own communities and to cross-racial solidarity.[44] College students fashioned political stances and pedagogical projects rooted in the specificities of Asian American life that they witnessed firsthand as children of laborers in restaurants, garment workshops, agricultural fields, canneries, care facilities, and the hotels and private homes they were hired to clean. Organizing as Asian Americans enabled AAPA members to burrow into community spaces and build them up, but it also underscored the necessity of—and provided opportunities for—branching out through alliances with similarly situated groups.[45] The lessons learned about racial capitalism in the community as well as in the classroom led them to reject narrow nationalisms and embrace broader frames of solidarity. Some of them had already done so inside activism that transcended group separations.

Vicci Wong, who became involved in AAPA as a University of California Berkeley undergraduate, started her forays in activism as a twelve-year-old working in the fields of Salinas alongside Mexican laborers. She cofounded a union local of the National Farm Workers Association made up largely of Chicanos, set up a junior chapter of the Student Nonviolent Coordinating Committee to advance Black Power work in Monterey County, and joined with people of different races to stage antidraft protests at Fort Ord.[46] Labor exploitation, racial discrimination, and militarization placed Wong in dialogue with members of similarly but not identically situated racial groups.

Intersectional cross-ethnic solidarity came freely and easily to many Asian American activists because of its long history in their communities. In the 1960s, Filipinx labor activists Larry Itliong and Philip Vera Cruz used the success of the largely Filipinx Agricultural Workers Organizing Committee (AWOC) to prod Cesar Chavez and Dolores Huerta to organize the United Farm Workers (UFW) union. One of the first martyrs in the farmworker struggles was Yemeni Arab worker Nagi Daifallah, who was killed by a Kern County sheriff's deputy in 1973. The Student Nonviolent Coordinating Committee delegated African American Dickie Flowers to take a leave of absence from the southern Black freedom movement to work with fellow Black farmworker

Mack Lyons to build support for the UFW in the California cities of Bakersfield and Arvin among Black, white, and Puerto Rican workers.[47] Japanese Americans Masaru Edmund Nakawatase and Pamela Egashira, born in World War II concentration camps, joined the Black freedom movement of the 1960s as college students: Nakawatase as an organizer with SNCC in Mississippi and Egashira as a member of the Black Student Union at the University of Washington. Chinese American Grace Lee Boggs worked closely with her Black husband James Boggs and expatriate Trinidadian activist intellectual C. L. R. James in organizing Black workers in Detroit. Intersectional antiracism did not have to be made up in libraries or lecture halls—it was already an ongoing organic reality inside social movement struggles for liberation.

Nobuko Miyamoto's life of artistry and activism presents a perfect blend of intersectional ideas about multiracial relational expressive culture, education, and political mobilization. Mass incarceration displaced her as a child, along with other Japanese Americans, on lands in Utah stolen from Shoshone-Banock people. Racially restrictive housing covenants compelled Miyamoto to grow up in neighborhoods populated by Black, Latinx, and Chinese as well as Japanese people. Employment as a professional dancer had her performing Orientalism on Broadway in *Flower Drum Song* and Tropicalism in *West Side Story*, while nightclub engagements as a jazz singer led her to spaces inside Black expressive culture. Attending a Japanese American Citizens League meeting in Chicago, she engaged in conversations and formed coalitions with the Black Panther Party, while also joining a protest for safe and affordable housing by Indigenous activists. Through marriages to Black men, Miyamoto acquired African American relatives and became mother to a Black-Japanese son. As part of the trio that recorded the album *A Grain of Sand*, Miyamoto sang songs emblematic of the Asian American movement but also sang the Republic of New Afrika's song "Free the Land" and a song in tribute to seventeen-year-old Black militant Jonathan Jackson, who was killed outside a courthouse in 1970 while trying to free his imprisoned brother George. Miyamoto's 2021 album *120,000 Stories* includes old songs, a new composition "Black Lives Matter," and, most importantly in the context of this chapter, "Bam Butsu—no Tsungari (10,000 Things, All Connected)," a composition featured in the FandangObon ceremonies that Miyamoto co-invented and that she performs with *son jarocho* Chicanx musicians Martha Gonzalez and Quetzal Flores. The FandangObon blends traditional music and dance performances from Japan, Mexico, West Africa, and the Middle East.[48]

The comparative and relational dimensions of the Asian American movement exemplify the intersectional qualities of what may at first seem like a discrete and homogenous group identity. Just as intersectionality shows that every individual is a crowd, every aggrieved social group is a coalition formed through interactions internally and externally. The Asian American movement and Asian American studies stand as exemplars of intersectionality. While never neglecting the particular, distinct, and unique nature of the diverse national groups inside it, and by necessity opposing anti-Asian exclusion, exploitation, and demonization, Asian American identity has never been formed in isolation or only in response to the racial contract. Instead it has emerged from affiliation, alliance, and cooperation among people with different national ancestries, languages, religions, and phenotypes as well as coalitions with other aggrieved racialized groups, representing the best possibilities of ethnic studies intersectionality.

While Asian American study and struggle fit neatly into the paradigm of comparative, relational, and intersectional antiracist ethnic studies, Indigenous mobilizations and studies have a more uneasy relationship with it. As the original inhabitants of the land, as sovereign nations recognized by strong although not enforced treaties and federal laws, as people with powerful connections to lands stolen from them, as the original "others" against whom Euro-American concepts of difference were deployed, and as frequent victims of the successful assimilation of other aggrieved groups into the settler colonial nation, Indigenous Peoples have features they do not share with Black, Latinx, and Asian American participants in the ethnic studies project.

Aileen Moreton Robinson's *The White Possessive* makes a powerful case for Indigenous dispossession and domination as the root of what Mills calls the racial contract. Even the term *dispossession* gets called into question by Moreton Robinson, who shows that the Western concept of possession does not describe accurately relations between Indigenous peoples and the land and the lives sustained by it. Moreover, she argues that terms like *conquest* and *dispossession* deflect attention away from what were in reality campaigns of mass murder. Only recently in the midst of revised Indigenous activism around the world and in the US have ethnic studies participants come to appreciate the unique importance of the role of indigeneity (and what Lyz Jaakola calls "indigenuity") in social justice work.[49]

Nick Estes (Lower Brule Sioux) notes that Indigenous resistance requires not just the absence of settler colonialism but also "the amplified presence of Indigenous life and just relations with human and non-human relatives and with the earth."[50] Confronting the long fetch of coloniality calls attention to the ways in which settler domination works relentlessly to destroy traditional fluid gender and sexual identities among Indigenous Peoples and to replace them with a male-female binary. Settler gender categories have led generations of white occupiers to feel free to violate Indigenous women's bodies just as they ravaged the land and killed the animals inhabiting it. The deeds perpetrated by trappers and traders in the past continue today with attacks on Native women by oil field and pipeline workers among others.[51]

The confluence of Indigenous dispossession in perpetuity and slavery unwilling to die leaves Indigenous and Afro-diasporic peoples facing similar but not identical consequences of the White Possessive. Intersectionality has aided the emergence and continuation of both struggles. The same dynamics that have led to antagonisms between the two groups have also led to alliances. W. E. B. Du Bois served as the only non-Indigenous voting member of the Society for American Indians. Vine Deloria Jr. admired the sense of peoplehood articulated in Kwame Ture and Charles Hamilton's book *Black Power*.[52] Arthur Manuel of the Neskonlith Indian Band of the Secwepemec Nation remembers how Native Alliance for Red Power traveling organizer Wayne Bobb directed him to read writings by Malcolm X and the Black Panthers as essential parts of his political education.[53] Dennis Banks formulated part of the critique that led him into the American Indian Movement (AIM) when reading about the Black Panther Party while incarcerated in Stillwater Prison. Estes recalls seeing in Robin D. G. Kelley's arguments about Black freedom dreams powerful resonances with parallel traditions of Indigenous thought and action.[54] The patrols that AIM set up to monitor police misconduct in Minneapolis and St. Paul were modeled on the ways in which the Panthers sought to protect their community in Oakland.[55] The campaigns by water protectors against oil pipeline construction on Indigenous lands drew participants from diverse racial groups and from people with a wide range of religious, gender, and sexual identities.[56] Black people have also been influenced and inspired by Indigenous struggles. New Orleans musician and activist Cyril Neville constructed a religious altar in his home that featured images of Crazy Horse, Sitting Bull, Bob Marley, and Malcolm X.[57] Black Panther leader Fred Hampton recruited representatives of AIM to be part of his Rainbow Coalition.[58] A Native American delegation participated in Dr. King's 1968 Poor People's Campaign and March.

Drawing on ideas about Black people and Black culture expressed by Kelley, Indigenous scholars Chris Andersen (Métis) and Jessica Bissett Perea (Dena'ina) point to the two-sided qualities of Indigenous identity. On the one hand, Indigenous difference serves as an excuse for the oppressors to enact displacement, dispossession, resource extraction, rape, kidnapping, and violent aggression. On the other hand, however, Indigenous difference is the source of ways of knowing, ways of being, ways of relating, and ways of claiming sovereignty that have been essential for the survival of Indigenous Peoples, their cultures, and the more-than-human world around them. Yet while difference is necessary, it may not be sufficient. Exercising treaty rights and protecting sovereignty serve as indispensable tools for Native survivance. Rights guaranteed by treaties have high status in the law (in theory if not in practice) because they stem from agreements between nations, not the procedures of domestic lawmaking. In addition, treaty rights offer one of the few places in US law where group rights are expressly acknowledged. Yet treaty provisions can also serve as instruments of exclusion and impediments to reciprocity and solidarity with other groups. For Bissett Perea, sovereignty is *both* a juridical category recognized by the state *and* a personal and collective responsibility that requires an expansive range of intellectual curiosity, commitments, and cross-cultural connections.[59]

Andersen and Bissett Perea contend that exclusive focus on difference obscures the density of Indigenous being. Density involves complex relations with lands, lifeways, and waters. It entails advanced knowledge gleaned from bitter experience about whiteness and its central role in perpetuating and justifying imperialism, capitalism, and sexism. The multiplicities of Indigenous life extend beyond unique difference to involve polylateral relations with other aggrieved groups, cultural coalescences and fusions with a wide range of interlocutors to author and authorize right relations. Density encompasses interactions and affiliations with Black Americans descended from Indigenous Peoples of Africa, recognition of a linked fate similar to but not identical to that of Indigenous Peoples in Canada, Mexico, New Zealand, Australia, and Scandinavia, as well as a long and honorable history of solidarity work with many different non-Indigenous-centered campaigns for social justice.

The density of Indigenous existence includes nations recognized by the Bureau of Indian Affairs as having centralized political governance and ethnic homogeneity as well as communities with ancestors from several different Native nations whose people might have blond hair or Black skin.[60] Indigenous density encompasses people who speak Spanish,

French, and Triqui. It includes the 1960s activism of the Indigenous contingent in the Poor People's March and movement and that of John Salter (later known as Hunter Gray) in the Black freedom movement in Mississippi. Indigenous density can be found in the Afro-Indigenous fusions found in the sculptures of Edmonia Lewis, the music of Mildred Bailey, and the complicated cultures of Black Seminoles and Black Cherokees. Indigenous density includes Leanne Betasamosake Simpson (Nishmaabeg) being introduced to the Black Radical Tradition in classes at Guelph University taught by Dr. Clarence Munford that helped her formulate an Indigenous internationalism to be built alongside "the brilliance of Black theorists, artists, activists, revolutionaries, and radical imaginaries and their communities both within my territory and beyond in the hope that we can become mutual co-resistors in our flight to freedom."[61]

The Inuit Soul music group Pamyua, led by brothers Phillip Kill'aq and Stephen Qacung Blanchett, who have a Yup'ik mother and Black father, traces its musical origins to the wide range of sounds the brothers heard growing up in southwest Alaska. These include Russian Orthodox Christmas songs and church hymns, Ukrainian folk carols, and Yupiit drum-dance music. When their parents divorced, their mother took them to Seattle, where they had easy access to hip-hop and top-forty songs. After four years in Seattle they moved back to Alaska to live with their father and his new family, a situation that enabled them to sing doo-wop songs with the family and participate in Black church gospel choirs. Over the years they experimented by inflecting Yup'ik songs and dances with African American vocal styles. They recruited fluent Yup'ik speaker drummer-dancer Aasanaaq Philip "Ossie" Kairaiuak to join them and welcomed Inuk singer Karina Moeller from Greenland to join the group after she encountered them at a festival for Northern Peoples. Pamyua's range of musical forms and diverse membership exemplifies a density in Native life that cannot be reduced to uniform difference.[62]

Perhaps the scholar working in the Black Radical Tradition who was most closely attuned to Moreton-Robinson's contention that Native dispossession produces the whiteness that shapes Black slavery and immigrant exclusion was Vincent Harding. Harding rejected assimilation and inclusion as the ultimate goals of the Black freedom struggle. He condemned the presumption that freedom entails securing "equal opportunity employment with the pain deliverers" of this world.[63] Harding developed this view at the very moment when his life trajectory led him to take seriously his relationships with the Indigenous and Chicanx people of the Southwest.

FIGURE 5. Yup'ik musician, dancer, and artist Aassanaaq (Phillip) "Ossie" Kairaiuak leading a dance workshop at University of California Davis, November 2021. Photo by Jim Coulter, used by permission.

Harding moved with his family to Denver in 1981 to take a position as professor of religion and social transformation at the Illif School of Theology. Born in Harlem to immigrants from Barbados in 1931, he secured a PhD in history from the University of Chicago. Rather than embarking on a purely academic career, however, Harding journeyed to Atlanta in 1960 as a representative of the Mennonite Church, where (along with his partner, activist and theologian Rosemary Freeny Harding) he set up a social justice center. He became a frontline participant in freedom struggles throughout the South and an adviser and speech writer for Dr. King. Harding played a key role in establishing the Institute of the Black World in Atlanta, a research center located in a house once occupied by Du Bois.

Harding explained that his move to Denver came from his conviction that Black people like himself had to take on a major responsibility for revisioning and reshaping US society. To pursue that path, he maintained, it was necessary for him and his family "to participate more deeply in the life of Native American and Chicano communities." He argued that a decent and democratic future for the nation depended on "taking to heart the wisdom, the insight, the history, and the vision" of the peoples he described as the "children of Mexico" and the "children of the earth."[64] Harding pointed to what he believed was a Hopi prophecy predicting the presence of Africans on Indigenous lands long before the actual slave trade began. As he understood it, the Hopi vision concerned a dark people from the land of morning—the east where the sun rises—whom they described as "the people of the light." Harding understood the prophecy to say that the land on which the Hopis lived could not be healed without the coming of the people of the light.[65]

Harding interpreted this prophecy as a moral challenge to himself and all Black people. He argued that they needed to oppose the nation-state, not just request inclusion in it. He declared, "When black scholars hear the call to equal opportunity in darkness, they must remember that they do not belong in the darkness of an American culture that refuses to move toward the light. They are not meant be pliant captives and agents of institutions that deny light all over the world."[66] Consistent with his Christian theology, Harding elevated responsibilities to a world-transcending citizenship over allegiances to any temporal nation-state. He affiliated himself with the stance that Dr. King took in a speech opposing the Vietnam War on April 4, 1967, when King identified himself as "a child of God and brother to the suffering poor of Vietnam."[67] In Harding's description of what he hoped to learn from the children of Mexico and the children of the earth, he described Blacks, Native Americans, and Chicanx, not as national minorities seeking full citizenship rights, but rather as "children of God who seek a new beginning" for a society that badly needs one.[68]

Harding also spoke from the decolonial perspective he had helped forge at the Institute for the Black World in dialogue with Walter Rodney, who located the origins of the slave trade in the dispossession and enslavement of Indigenous Africans.[69] In a 1974 essay emanating from their work together at the Institute of the Black World, Harding wrote that "a major part of the truth of our community resides in its present colonized condition."[70] For Harding, recognition of the colonized condition required critiquing and contesting colonial whiteness. The study of colonized peoples needs to shed light on the colonizers, he argued, on "white America and its deepest intentions and actions towards us."[71] Although it is difficult for Black people "enmeshed as we are in the machinery of white American systems of life and thought" to face evil and confront it, Harding explains they have no choice. As long as the mass of Black people "live as unmistakably colonized victims (yet courageously more than victims) of white America, there is no escape from the knowledge that white America and its systems of domination are the enemy. Nor is there any escape from acting on that truth."[72]

Harding's emphasis on action helps explain his desire to connect with the Indigenous inhabitants of the Southwest. He suspected that their ways of knowing could be indispensable for the Black freedom struggle. Equally important to him, however, were the ways of being that generate new knowledge projects. We are called, Harding contends, "to remember our selves, to recollect our beings, to know that our deepest origins have little to do with American style, but are to be found in a series of cultures in which much emphasis is often placed on the living, acting, dancing, performing of the truth."[73]

The parallel struggles against the White Possessive by Indigenous and Black people should not be allowed to occlude important differences. The discourses of antiracism can lead to reductionist frames that portray Indigenous people as simply another community of color disadvantaged in the same ways and to the same degrees as African Americans, Asian Americans, and Latinx Americans. Moreover, as Jodi Byrd (Chickasaw) explains, portraying hundreds of individual Indigenous nations as a single racial minority in the US depicts as relations between *races* matters that are in fact often relations between *nations*.[74] Moreover, gestures of affiliation and alliance with Indigenous people in ethnic studies have succumbed too often to what Kim TallBear (Sisseton-Whapeton Oyate) astutely critiques as yearning for an ideal, inclusive, and multicultural settler state, a state that simply distributes more evenly the privileges and benefits that flow from Indigenous suppression, displacement, and dispossession, from relentless resource extraction and violations of treaty-protected rights, from unprosecuted hate crimes and criminalization of Native religious practices. For TallBear, dreams of a multiracial America impede the cultivation of caretaking relations among humans and between humans and the other-than-human world while implicitly supporting the dispossession and elimination of Indigenous Peoples.[75] Audra Simpson (Mohawk) demonstrates the incommensurable antagonisms between inclusive racial liberalism and Indigenous sovereignty and survivance by noting how the words *town destroyer* or *town eater* have been used in the Haudenosaunee language to describe every US president since George Washington (who ordered the destruction of Haudenosaunee villages in 1779, decades after his great-grandfather John Washington orchestrated the massacre of Susquehannock and Piscataway settlements).[76] Michael Yellow Bird (Mandan, Hidatsa, and Arikara) observes that Abraham Lincoln, known as "the Great Emancipator" because of the Emancipation Proclamation, gave the order for the greatest mass execution in US history: the hanging of thirty Dakota people who resisted being pushed off their lands by the US Army.[77] Like the Black community in the Sunni Patterson poem presented in chapter 3, Indigenous people "know this place," largely in response to their displacement, dispossession, and denial of treaty rights.

INTERSECTIONALITY AND FEELING OUT OF PLACE

The work of ethnic studies often entails grappling with the discomforts of feeling displaced, out of place, or in between places. The places designated as "home" are attached to feelings of safety and refuge, but these serve very different functions for people with ancestral and current histories that involve conquest, colonization, migration, exile, refuge, enslavement, and exploitation. A large body of scholarship in queer theory, disability studies, postcolonial studies, and Black studies identifies how discomfort, dislocation, and disidentification can become surprisingly and counterintuitively generative. The things that make displaced people feel different and discomforted inflict injuries upon them, but they also generate insights about the provincialisms and parochialisms produced by uncritical valorization of safety, security, home, and homogeneity. Sara Ahmed, Stuart Hall, José Esteban Muñoz, and Julietta Singh (among others) reveal how being deemed different can enhance critical capacities, how living with dislocation can provide alternatives to the heteronormative home and the state-centric subject, how acknowledging vulnerability can be a key mechanism for building convivial cocreation, and how the valorization of mastery in academic work echoes, legitimizes, and reinforces cruel and unjust forms of mastery in social life.

Gloria Anzaldúa and other similarly situated Chicana/indigena queer feminists shaped by life in the Mexico-US borderlands use the in-between nature of the binational and bilingual physical places of the border as a stimulus for formulating discursive spaces shaped by contradiction, conflict, and creative transformation. They use the Náhuatl word *nepantla* to describe a space in the middle, a space that Anzaldúa describes as unstable, precarious, unpredictable, uncomfortable, and always in transition.[78] Barbara Andrea Sostaita interprets *nepantla* to signify a site of psychic rupture, "a crack between worlds," a place where turbulence prohibits stasis or resolution.[79] Confusion and conflict cause great pain at many crossroads where nations, languages, cultures, genders, and sexualities intersect. Yet when negotiated by conscious and determined *nepantleras*, this middle ground can also become a locus of creative transformation, a zone of possibility that Anzaldúa describes as a place "where the outer boundaries of the mind's inner life meet the outer world of reality" and "the place where different perspectives come into conflict, and where you question the basic ideas, tenets, and identities inherited from your family, your education, and your different cultures."[80]

Living in the physical and psychological spaces of *nepantla* places people at many different crossroads, in sites where identities, perceptions, and belief systems clash and coalesce. They become aware of the constructed nature of categories that others take for granted and benefit from the necessity of making choices. *Nepantleras* resist the "either/or" binary oppositions and choices that the dominant culture deploys to frame individual and collective lives. They embrace "both/and" relationships to place and displacement. Their ways of being and ways of knowing can open doors for everyone, but especially for migrants, refugees, and exiles that move back and forth and in between borders.

Stuart Hall recalls the out-of-placeness he felt as a Jamaican immigrant in England. "Nothing was ever codified as having its correct place and time" as "displacement moved to the center of things."[81] At that crossroads, Hall and his fellow émigrés found themselves forced to fuse "contraries into new formations."[82] He states that he came to understand that no history exists free from disorder and that a diasporic existence counters expectations of whole, integral, and unchanging identities by placing the displacements and dysfunctions of lived experience in the forefront.[83]

Discursive spaces can offer reparation and repair in response to lack of agency in physical places. Mexican Indigenous Nahua activist María de Jesús Patricio argues that struggle is a homeland from which one cannot be evicted and one that the people collectively control. In the face of forces that disrupt traditional Indigenous views of necessary relations linking land to human and more-than-human life and dignity, she identifies struggle as a source of compensation, relocation, and reparation. She writes,

> The capitalists want to make us believe that our territory is the miles of oil wells, dozens of mining concessions, assassinated women, and the disappeared. But we know this is not our territory, just like violence, deforestation, high tariffs on water and light, water controlled by regional caciques, and extractive megaprojects are not part of the Indigenous territory of Veracruz. Our territories are the original languages, ancestral cultures, our resistances, community organization that invites us not to sell out, to never give up, to not forget what we've inherited from our ancestors to be protected, that invites us to organize and govern ourselves, exercising that which we decide collectively.[84]

INTERSECTIONALITY, CITIZENSHIP, AND SANCTUARY

State-centric notions of identity make forceful distinctions between citizens and aliens. People are presumed to belong to their places of birth unless they gain a new place of belonging by naturalization as citizens elsewhere. Migrants without citizenship or proper documentation are judged to be out of place and therefore criminal interlopers in their nations of arrival. These ideas about citizenship, subjectivity, place, and displacement originated in a previous era when people and capital seemed more rooted and place bound than they are today. Over the past half century, however, massive movements of people and production around the globe have been provoked by new forms of dispersed production and flexible accumulation, rapid movement of capital across the world, and the huge displacements of people caused by consolidation of land ownership, economic austerity, political repression, climate change, famine, and war. Millions of people now reside outside the nations where they were born. Many live existences of perpetual back-and-forth movement, discussed in chapter 2 as what Garcia-Peña calls the *vaivén* precluding simple distinctions between nations of origin and nations of arrival.[85]

The globalization of investment, production, labor, and culture does not eliminate the nation-state but on the contrary makes it more important as a disciplinary force protecting the mobility of capital while regulating, constraining, and sometimes completely preventing the mobility of workers. International agreements and the influence of transnational corporations greatly limit the nation-state's ability to attend to injustices or shape internal cultures and politics. Policing borders, however, plays a key role in creating the unequal relations that make migrants move from low-wage to high-wage places and that destroy small farms and replace them with agribusiness. These practices direct the worst effects of resource extraction, climate change, and perpetual war toward those nations that people find themselves forced to leave. Migration becomes one of the few vehicles for individual improvement for people, especially in places suffering from imposed austerity orchestrated to augment the profits that flow to investors in wealthy countries.

Michel-Rolph Trouillot identifies the policing of borders as a key mechanism for creating and sustaining global inequalities, but perhaps even more important, as a means of promoting moral panics that obscure who profits from the new global order. He notes how "the protection of borders becomes an easy political fiction with which to enlist support from a confused citizenry."[86] By blaming migrants—

rather than the processes that make people migrate—for the diminution of the social wage and the disintegration of the social fabric in postindustrial nations, the very people who implement and profit from globalization shift blame for its consequences away from themselves and toward the migrants whom they have victimized.

Moral panics about borders and phobic fantasies about the imagined criminality of migrants (often manufactured artificially by state categorization) obscure how the overwhelming majority of migrants are hardworking and positive contributors to society, very few of whom have as many criminal felony convictions as the forty-seventh president of the United States. These panics fuel massive regimes of asylum denial, incarceration, and deportation embraced by both major political parties in the US. Repressive measures do not diminish the numbers of migrants but only make their lives more precarious, their labor more exploitable, and their political voices more muted. These measures do not restore the social wage that anti-immigrant advocates have promised but offer permanent scapegoats and targets of hatred and violence to those whose hopes have been disappointed.

By portraying both the noncitizen with documentation and the undocumented migrant as non-normative, the incarceration-deportation regime encourages citizens to view themselves as normative and therefore entitled. Rather than directing criticism upwards against the haves, they direct anger, resentment, and hatred toward the have-nots. People opposed to the inhumane treatment of migrants and to policies that violate international law by refusing to process requests for asylum find themselves forced to defend those deemed non-normative and to create intersectional identities and alliances in support of them. In the process, many of them have to question and disavow the normativity they enjoy as citizens and craft a basis for finding affinities and connections despite the citizen-noncitizen difference, a process on clear display in attempts to provide sanctuary for migrants.

The sanctuary movement flowers in houses of worship among congregations whose theology guides them to welcome the stranger and extend mercy to those who suffer. Willingness to break the law and defy the state often comes from deeply held religious commitments. Congregations offering sanctuary insist that noncitizen and undocumented migrants are children of God whom they are obligated to help and that no act of government can make it otherwise. A white Presbyterian minister in Ohio whose church offered sanctuary to an immigrant mother targeted for deportation made this argument: "Separating a mother from her children is not what we do as people of faith. It is not what Americans should do either. Rather, giving women shelter is what we do. Showing hospitality to those in need is what defines us. Standing with all of God's children everywhere is who we are. Being the beloved community is what we'll be."[87] This invoking the beloved community ideal of the Black freedom movement in the context of contemporary sanctuary work evidences how repertoires of embodied memory sustain social justice struggles across generations.[88]

Research by Gina M. Pérez and Barbara Andrea Sostaita, scholars with close connections to ethnic studies, reveals how a process of organizational learning through activism has led sanctuary supporters to develop intersectional identities and alliances grounded in critiques of the veneration of the category of the normative citizen. What started as an effort to provide temporary refuge to individuals evolved into campaigns to eliminate the forces that make people migrate and thereby become targeted for incarceration, family separation, and deportation. Sanctuary supporters view the deportation regime as less a single offensive state of exception aimed at migrants than a part of the same system of subordination that makes all aggrieved racialized communities susceptible to police violence, mass incarceration, and labor subordination. Offering temporary sanctuary to migrants targeted for deportation reveals families of resemblance that connect their situation to the problems facing Puerto Ricans displaced to the US mainland because of Hurricane Maria and Black drivers plagued by police traffic stops designed as pretexts to make arrests. Intersectional connections between differently situated aggrieved groups become evident when sanctuary activists realize that the monitors placed on the ankles of noncitizens in sanctuary by immigration officials first came into widespread use because of predatory policing of Black and Latinx citizens. Amber Evans, a young activist from Columbus, Ohio, asked a sanctuary support teleconference to consider what it would mean to think about sanctuary for all. She argued that Black, Brown, poor, and working-class people needed to come together to resist the criminalization of their families and communities.[89]

Intersectional identifications emerged organically within the sanctuary movement as it drew upon social justice traditions and commitments of diverse communities. It is a movement that out of necessity and choice has become multiethnic and cross-racial, attached to a wide range of issues. Indigenous peoples in Arizona and New Mexico offer sanctuary to strangers in need as a traditional and sacred obligation rather than a new political tactic. They note that their commitment to sanctuary predates the nation-state that presumes to deny it.⁹⁰ Repression of migrants harms them directly when border patrol agents prevent people on the Tohono O'odham Reservation on the US-Mexico border from transporting bird feathers, pine leaves, sweetgrass, and other materials needed for sacred ceremonies from the Mexican side of the reservation to the US side. Yet more than resistance to their own mistreatment motivates them. Tohono O'odham traditions view the criminalization of hospitality as a violation of the values that elders pass on to children about the importance of sharing water, food, and shelter with all, but especially those in greatest need.⁹¹

A Puerto Rican police chief in Ohio attributes his openness to and support of the sanctuary movement to his experiences growing up in a Black neighborhood reading his friends' copies of *Jet* magazine and learning about the civil rights movement from Black soldiers he served with during the Vietnam War. Reverend Deborah Lee, an Asian American ordained as a minister in the United Church of Christ, traces her involvement in the sanctuary movement to fights against anti-immigrant legislation in California and to examples set by people of faith working for social justice in Brazil and the Philippines. White clergypersons Quaker Jim Corbett and Presbyterian John Fife have long energized sanctuary networks in Arizona. Baja California native Francisco Olachea provides food shelter and access to medical care for people near the US-Mexico border in Arizona. The intersectional influences that guide his practices appear in the Rod of Asclepius embroidered on his polo shirt, the Buddhist ceremonial scarf that covers his coffee table, the Tibetan prayer flags on his walls, the Buddha and Ganesha in a wooden box, and the Christian cross, conch shells, and earrings that his partner makes out of discarded tin cans she finds in the desert to honor the dead of the migrant trail. "We pray to everything and anything," he explains.⁹²

Sanctuary challenges the normative ideal of the national citizen-subject through what Sostaita calls "mobile practices of care and mutuality."⁹³ It sets in motion processes that enable participants to discover seemingly unlikely affinities across social and geographic divisions. The technologies that monitor migrant movements in Arizona originated with the towers deployed to surveil Palestinians on the West Bank in Israel. People in sanctuary and their Dreamer children chose to "come out" in the open in part because of the example set by acts of coming out of the closet by gay activists. Sanctuary started as a political tactic designed to help individuals in specific situations, but it has become understood as what Sostaita describes as a "fugitive crossing of worlds, a relentless activity," as "a search for relation and not as the desire for settlement elsewhere," and what Pérez calls "a gift that transforms the immediate communities involved and has the power to transform and radicalize others."[94]

Because of the power and malevolence of the state, people in charge of houses of worship, schools, and clinics cannot effectively guarantee sanctuary to people fleeing oppression, war, and poverty. But the people who run and go to clinics, schools, and houses of worship can become *sanctuary people*. They can remember what religious leaders enamored with power seem to have forgotten—traditional religious commitments to welcoming the stranger, feeding the hungry, housing the houseless, and protecting the persecuted. Sanctuary people can refuse pressures to call the authorities to come to arrest and deport their neighbors. They can create "Know Your Rights" training sessions to inform people of their constitutional rights and resist illegal apprehensions. They can mobilize community watch groups to discover and expose illegal acts by government officials. As Aurora Levins Morales states, speaking in a different but related context: "This is the work. To turn ourselves into the people we don't yet know how to be."[95]

INTERSECTIONALITY AT THE CROSSROADS

The affinities across difference discovered and developed by queers of color, disability justice activists, pan-ethnic and pan-racial ethnic studies, people seemingly out of place, and sanctuary people resonate powerfully with scholarship grounded in intersectionality. Participants in the ethnic studies project face unrelenting internal and external pressure to identify a single axis of power or a single racialized group as the locus of domination and oppression that can be deemed fundamental and foundational. Some models of radical critique and contestation hold that liberation can come only by giving priority to class, race, or gender as the oppression from which all others flow. Dominant currents in public policy, law, and medicine treat racism as an aberrant interruption in an otherwise just world, as a producer of stand-alone injuries to be attended to in isolation, unconnected to racism's intersectional affinities with social identities rooted in class, gender, sexuality, language, disability, citizenship status, and more.

Intersectional inquiries illuminate the limitations of taken-for-granted single-axis approaches that presume normative understandings of race, sexuality, ethnic group identity, able-bodiedness, and place. Inside the ethnic studies project, some wish for a one-size-fits-all institutional configuration for departments and programs that will be immune to co-optation. This envisions a unity based on compulsory uniformity. It presumes that there should be only one kind of political project, student, teacher, curriculum, or pedagogy. These impulses can seem radical, but they are merely dogmatic. They only delay days of reckoning with the dynamics of difference, with the provisional and contingent imperatives of all antisubordination struggles.

Because single-axis identity categories have been so privileged in dominant epistemologies, even critical scholars can come to believe that differences are destructive and that sameness is a precondition of solidarity. This disposition may fall prey to the foundationalism at the heart of post-Enlightenment thought depending upon binary oppositions that view the "different from" as necessarily "better than" or "worse than." It promotes a search for epistemological and moral absolutes that lead some scholars to either uncritically embrace or completely condemn ethnic studies. This "either/or" approach can generate an aura of certainty and self-satisfaction, yet be strategically paralyzing. People in struggle cannot afford the luxury of purism. They must fight with the tools they have in the arenas that are open to them. They need to keep alive possibilities that will give them a chance to live to fight another day.

The radical ethnic studies tradition views difference not as debilitating and destructive but as dynamic and generative, as evidence of questions unasked, archives unexplored, and problems yet to be solved. There is no nonconflicted or uncomplicated way to do this work, no practice that does not entail difficult choices, and no tactic capable of solving problems once and for all. When people are fighting for dignity and self-determination, there is no such thing as an automatically bad or good device. In actual social struggle, the task is to discover which differences make a difference and when. Contradictions cannot be avoided, but they can be worked through to create new and better conditions for struggle. Yesterday's solutions can become today's problems, but today's problems can be the basis for tomorrow's solutions.

Ethnic studies does more than merely add on previously unknown extraneous information about aggrieved groups; it uses the experiences of those groups as points of entry into developing new theories and concepts that explain how difference became used to excuse and justify domination. Intersectionality has emerged as one of the most important and generative tools for understanding social relations by demonstrating the importance of recognizing the limits of single-axis one-at-a-time approaches to discrimination and domination and replacing them with multiple-axis approaches cognizant of how multiple currents of power intersect. The manipulation of social identities for purposes of social control works in uneven ways, creating and exaggerating differences across groups and within groups.[96]

Coalescing around a shared identity through group politics is often necessary because in many instances the common injuries that are experienced collectively are more important than the differences that exist within a group. Harm enacted on all members of a group requires a common response. Misogyny harms all women, homophobia injures all who are gender nonconforming, and racial profiling affects every member of the targeted group. Yet there is never only one way to be a woman, queer, or racialized. Solidarity among Black people might not recognize the particular circumstances that confront Black women. Uniting all Black women in a common cause might obscure the special conditions faced by Black women who are queer, disabled, or denied citizenship status. Attending to the places where identities intersect can provide a more accurate diagnosis of what power is and how it works.

People who belong to more than one aggrieved group—who are women *and* Black, lesbians *and* working class, immigrants *and* members of mistreated religious minorities—can have unique and generative understandings of how power works on many levels. Lorena Garcia relates how women of color feminists bring to the academy awareness of complex interactions and social locations that they learned long before being introduced to the concept of intersectionality. This awareness promoted and sustained commitments to rejecting "the exclusion of diverse perspectives" and disrupting "misinformed assumptions about our communities."[97] Philosopher Kristie Dotson and critical race theorist Mari Matsuda argue that intersectional thinking and activism promote vigilance about the ways in which the experiences, aspirations, and identities of multiply marginalized groups disappear when injustice is viewed through single-axis lenses.[98] This concern about *what* and *who* get disappeared has affinities with the practice of accompaniment articulated in the 1970s by then-archbishop and now-canonized Catholic saint Oscar Romero that commands special attention to those most likely to be forgotten inside group-based mobilizations and cross-group coalitions. It exudes the sensibility that the great freedom fighter Fannie Lou Hamer invoked when asked if her politics put her "on the left." Mrs. Hamer declared that she did represent the left—"the left out."[99] The next chapter explores how the dynamics of difference have been utilized by researchers, teachers, students, and community educators.

5

Ethnic Studies as Inquiry and Instruction

What does it mean to carry out the work of ethnic studies in this dangerous moment when the planet and its people are in peril? What is at stake in the books and articles that scholars read and write, in the classrooms where they learn and teach, in the statements they make, and in the silences they wittingly and unwittingly sustain? What is the proper role for ethnic studies inside the academy at a moment when ethnic peoples outside it face increasingly unlivable destinies?

Participation in the ethnic studies project and the broader antiracist social formation often entails working within enemy-centered spaces that generate provocations and temptations to embrace the tools and terms of the oppressors in order to combat them. While this is sometimes tactically valuable in the short run, in the long run it risks reinforcing rather than resisting the acts, affects, and actions of domination. As Robin Wall Kimmerer advises, it is important to "see the dark" and "recognize its power" without feeding it.[1]

Chapters 1 and 2 describe how the critical work of ethnic studies attracts opposition, yet risks the dangers of incorporation. Chapters 3 and 4 delineate the importance of connecting ethnic studies to the work of autonomous learning circles and intersectional struggles against narrow notions of normativity. This chapter addresses the obligations of ethnic studies to perform the difficult and dangerous work of challenging the racial contract and its effects inside research, teaching, and public discourse. At many different crossroads, deploying the power of the caduceus can transform the power-knowledge nexus that undergirds domination into an inventory of tools for liberation.

ETHNIC STUDIES AT THE SCENE OF ARGUMENT

Important aspects of the ethnic studies project take place at what Barbara Tomlinson calls *the scene of argument*, which she defines as "a discursive site, a textual stage, a platform for social contestation, and a location for the rhetorical enactment of power."[2] She argues that much of the identity, influence, and impact of feminism and antiracism results from what takes place at scenes of argument: inside papers, articles, books, presentations, and classroom lectures and lessons. Reading, writing, and arguing are material social practices and socializing pedagogies that make up the meanings of feminism, antiracism, and ethnic studies.

Scenes are bounded entities defined by display. They present and contain what occurs in them. They are places where significant things can take place.[3] Ethnic studies publications and pronouncements play an important role in creating a public; they carry out valuable, significant, and worthy work. The properties of the caduceus, however, can make things that can help into things that can harm. Tomlinson argues that choices made at scenes of academic argument can unwittingly inflect challenges to domination with affects that reinforce rather than resist injustice, that poison the well from which we all must drink. The *ways* in which we write and speak can undermine the intended effects of *what* we say. Band leader Sun Ra routinely told the musicians in his orchestra, "Be careful what you play. . . . Every note, every beat, be aware, it comes back to you."[4]

POLITICS AT THE SCENE OF ACADEMIC ARGUMENT

When ethnic studies researchers succeed in presenting principled, true, and useful claims about the importance of the knowledge of aggrieved communities, organic intellectuals, and autonomous learning circles, they can expect some—and maybe even most—reviewers to be hostile. Gatekeepers who feel that their core beliefs and social positions are threatened by such work will respond with defensiveness, dismissal, condescension, and contempt. It is easier for reviewers to belittle research with which they disagree than to diagnose it and present principled helpful responses and recommendations. Reviewers often view that course of action as necessary to defend themselves and their social positions against premises they do not share and arguments they cannot refute. Sometimes a hostile review can be helpful because it shows that the author has got something wrong, but a negative response can also mean that the piece being vetted has struck a nerve and provoked the reviewer to lash out in self-defense. This produces reviews that demean the authors whose work is being reviewed—that try to make them feel small, inadequate, and ashamed. The fervor of these reviews seems designed more to punish authors than to assist them in seeing how their work can be better. These attacks can be demoralizing and paralyzing.

Whether their submissions get accepted or rejected by reviewers, ethnic studies scholars often experience extreme levels of vituperation and hostility, especially when their research contends that the collective intelligence honed in struggle inside aggrieved communities has enormous generative significance for everyone. Potawatomi botanist Robin Wall Kimmerer has secured more than six thousand citations in scholarly research, has been awarded a MacArthur "genius" fellowship, and has authored the book *Braiding Sweetgrass,* which has sold more than two million copies. Yet she recalls the pain of encountering time and time again "the condescension, the verbal smack-down from academic authorities, especially if you had the audacity to ground your work in the observations of old women who had probably not finished high school, and talked to plants to boot."[5] The editors of the *Ethnic Studies Pedagogies* journal observe that nearly all of the scholars in their orbit recall getting reviews that were scarring and damaging. The editors try to counter this way of working by deploying a review process designed to nurture writings not yet ready for publication. One of their tactics entails having a special-issue editor bring all the authors together in advance to share ideas and discuss writing strategies as they develop their pieces. Another involves providing extensive feedback on pieces, viewing them as developmental and improved by convivial dialogue. Collaborating authors and reviewers do not shy away from what might be unproductive in a piece but focus on what is generative in it and work with the author to have the article reach its full potential.[6]

Attacks from outside ethnic studies can be debilitating, but mistreatment from within can be even more devastating. At the scene of ethnic studies argument, editors, reviewers, and readers regularly approve writing that is cruelly competitive rather than convivially contributive. Finding fault with others can give readers the impression that authors are more selective, smarter, and less easily fooled than the writers they criticize. Antagonism and aggression in civic and scholarly discourse can function to titillate readers and reviewers. Conflict and controversy produce dramas laden with cruelty and contempt similar to those that pervade popular and political culture. Ethnic studies scholars who have been unfairly attacked, dismissed, and ridiculed themselves understandably may wish to inhabit the superior position so often used against them by turning others into objects of scorn and derision.

At the scene of argument, performances of moral indignation that rely on degrading others, engaging in sectarian sniping, and confining criticism to negative judgments rather than balanced evaluation can feel good in the short run. In the long run, however, they serve as exercises in submission to domination masquerading as critiques of it. Writers can try to elevate themselves by lowering others, to misrepresent and minimize the complexity of research they critique, to tear down rather than build on previous studies. In order to make themselves seem like heroes, they need to depict others as villains. They may attribute small tactical disagreements to the personal moral failings of others without considering why different truths become compelling to differently situated people.[7]

Destructive patterns of argument do not obviate the need for argument itself. Although argument gets perceived popularly as innately involving antagonism, a more useful interpretation of argument conceives of it as a mechanism for reasoning and explaining, a way of presenting premises and following them to their conclusions. Argument when presented as principled communication and conversation can augment and improve collective abilities to diagnose problems and formulate solutions to them. When reduced to invidious competition and laced with contempt and cruelty, however, argument impedes rather than advances knowledge. Like many things at many different crossroads, argument can be a caduceus with potential to be both destructive and constructive.

Robin Wall Kimmerer describes writing as "an act of reciprocity with the world," as something she can give back in gratitude for all that has been given to her.[8] At the scene of argument, however, gratitude, reciprocity, generosity, and admiration are often not seen as strengths. They routinely get suppressed and dismissed as weaknesses. Critics blame canonical works for not knowing in the past what the critic knows today—knowledge often developed only as a result of the dialogue set in motion by that original work. Reviews become pretexts for foregrounding the reviewers' favored (or current) object of study by scolding authors for not anticipating what the reviewer wished they had explored.

Tactics that Tomlinson calls rejection, replacement, rectification, regulation, and reduction pervade academic arguments. They turn other scholars into straw person opponents, often engaging only with the weakest rather than the strongest parts of the concepts being critiqued.[9]

As Foucault argues, criticism that wallows in negative evaluation and dismissal squanders the generative potential of critique, its ability to expose how unchallenged and unconsidered assumptions constrain inquiry, to show that things may not be as self-evident as they appear, and to avoid diminishing the quality of scholarship by taking the path of least resistance that comes from making facile gestures.[10] Part of the work of changing society entails changing ourselves. We are not yet the kinds of people capable of bringing a new society into being. As Martin Luther King warned us decades ago, advancing social justice requires a radical revolution in values and the creation of a powerful and inclusive counterculture steeped in mutual recognition and respect that can initiate meaningful change.

DEALING WITH THE DISCIPLINES

One of the most frequent forms of rejection that readers, reviewers, editors, and editorial boards deploy in response to equity-oriented collaborative community-based scholarship is to deem it deficient for failing to adhere to narrow traditional disciplinary conventions. These gatekeepers do not treat the disciplines as tools to better understand the world but instead view the world's events, people, and structures as objects suited primarily for providing occasions to demonstrate intellectual mastery of the complexity of disciplinary paradigms. Solving serious social problems, however, often requires raising concerns that cut across disciplines and go beyond them. Community thinkers and the scholars who work most closely with them frequently produce writing that is interdisciplinary. Dismissing that work because its methods do not fit within narrow disciplinary frameworks and because its claims and conclusions do not advance disciplinary conversations is the easiest way for reviewers to repress and hide their fear of confronting new archives, imaginaries, epistemologies, and ontologies.

At the scene of argument, deploying conventional disciplinary categories, methodologies, and rhetorical frames can do much good. These conventions often help make research findings legible and credible to reviewers, editors, readers, and listeners. Yet they often contain ideological premises and presumptions inimical to understanding that fail to challenge the forces that make domination seem natural, necessary, and inevitable. The disciplines demand particular ways of knowing that too often disaggregate intersectional social realities into discrete and often incommensurable realms. The *manner* in which research is conducted can distort, obscure, and even erase the *matter* it purports to illuminate. Conventional disciplinary categories, research methods, and rhetorical frames are not neutral technologies that convey already existing ideas to a passive audience.[11] They help construct the world they claim only to describe and analyze.

Scholars versed in community ways of knowing can expose the parochial and provincial nature of their disciplines. For example, musicologist Jessica Bissett Perea (Dena'ina) demonstrates that for Native Alaskans singing, drumming, dancing, and storytelling do not exist in isolation from all other aspects of life; rather, "Songs and subsistence are deeply interconnected ways of respecting reciprocity and the responsibility one has to all human and more-than-human entities." In these communities, Bissett Perea observes, it is "common knowledge that if there are no songs, there are no animals and vice versa."[12]

Imperatives to produce original discovery research take on greater urgency in four-year colleges and universities than they do in community colleges, technical schools, and K-12 classrooms. Yet the creation of new knowledge capable of exerting influence and impact on society ultimately affects teachers and students at all levels. College and universities are important institutions in society. They serve as places where publics are created, educated, and inspired, but sometimes they also function as crucibles of misinformation and demoralization. The knowledge produced and disseminated in classrooms, colloquia, and conferences helps inform what policymakers do, what courts decide, how communities see themselves, and what choices adults make in raising children. The imperatives of academic life that so often compel scholars only to build careers can also be incentives instead to build communities, to engage in convivial cocreation rather than inhabit isolated self-absorption. Realizing the best possibilities of ethnic studies requires recognizing how the disciplines, methods, and rhetorical frames in the academy that are presented as medicine can also be poison. It requires the epistemologies of the crossroads and the caduceus to decide when to use dominant ways of knowing, when to avoid them, and when to turn them on their heads to produce oppositional knowledges, affects, and actions.

Traditional forms of inquiry that focus on separate groups and separate aspects of human experience through case studies, experiments, analyses of variables, surveys, and critical interpretations are not useless; they can produce valuable findings. All methods and objects of study deserve respect, and nearly all have proved to be useful in particular instances. Education researchers using empirical methods have documented how ethnic studies has salutary effects on students of all races.[13] A conventional survey sample study by the National Latina Institute for Reproductive Health enabled activists in the reproductive justice movement to forge strategies infused with more complex and useful understandings of the ways in which Latinas throughout the nation view reproductive issues.[14] Many of the studies cited and praised previously in this book follow the traditional methods of the disciplines. The question of the disciplines is not whether to use them but rather when deploying them is valuable and how and when their limits impede understanding.

An "either/or" approach to the disciplines overlooks the possibilities of the "both/and" option. One of the most important effects of ethnic studies has been how its premises and practices have in fact helped move the disciplines in new directions. This movement appears in the influence and impact of Evelyn Nakano Glenn and Patricia Hill Collins on the sociology of race and gender, of Ruth Wilson Gilmore and Clyde Woods on the geography of racism and place, of Michel-Rolph Trouillot and Arlene Davila on anthropology and coloniality, of Robin Kelley and Vicki Ruiz on race and class in history, of Philip Ewell and Loren Kajikawa on the uninterrogated whiteness of musicology, of Glenn Adams and Mary Watkins on individual versus liberation psychology, and of Kimberlé Crenshaw and Cheryl Harris on the limits of racial liberalism. Important challenges to uninterrogated disciplinary assumptions appear in Robin Wall Kimmerer's engagements with botany, in Dorothy Roberts's critiques of racial science, and in Nancy Krieger's challenges to epidemiology. While there are times when the disciplines need to be utilized, times also exist when they need to be questioned, engaged and contested internally, and, when possible, transcended.

Ethnic studies scholarship has blazed new paths for interdisciplinary scholarship as well. Research by Indigenous intersectional feminist Sarah Deer (Muscogee Creek) and others has directed feminist studies, global studies, and decolonial studies toward recognition of the ways in which rapes of Native women play a central role in historical settler-colonial conquest and domination and how sexual domination remains a crucial component of colonial oppression to this day.[15] Ethnic studies researchers have played a leading role in moving the American Studies Association away from its foundations in American exceptionalism and toward recognition and reflection on the existence and consequences of empire.[16]

Interdisciplinary ethnic studies scholarship enables discovery of seemingly unlikely parallels and families of resemblance among groups generally studied separately. Potawatomi basket maker John Pigeon and Haitian vodou healers alike declare establishing balance among competing forces as the great challenge of life.[17] The Mayan concept *In Lak' ech* (interpreted by Chicanx and Indigenous activists as *Tu eres mi otro yo*, "You are my other me") expresses interdependence in ways similar to that encapsulated in the Southern African Nguni people's concept of *ubuntu*, a term that describes openness, availability, and affirmation of others as well as feeling diminished when others are mistreated.[18] *In Lak' ech* and *ubuntu* have affinities with the Tagalog word *kapwa*, which in Filipinx culture conveys the ethical principle that the inner self is shared with others.[19]

The concept of intercommunalism forged by the Black Panther Party contains resemblances to Indigenous radical internationalism.[20] Mixed-race identities described as "hybridity" in India and the African diaspora appear as *mestizaje* in Latin America.[21] The liberation theology that leads martyred and canonized Salvadoran archbishop Oscar Romero to criticize capitalism for encouraging people to want "have more" but not to "be more" resonates with Potawatami biologist Robin Wall Kimmerer's contention that it is trickery that leads us to believe that *belongings* will satisfy us when what we really crave is *belonging*.[22]

José Esteban Muñoz derives part of his queer of color formulation positioning utopia as a future that resides immanently inside the present from Black Marxist C.L.R. James's analysis of worker solidarity on the shop floor as a prefiguration of the future world that workers wish to inhabit.[23] Both Indigenous jingle dress round dancers in Minnesota and Asian immigrant women worker activists in California define leadership as a collective rather than individual act that needs to be honed through a process of "leading" lives committed to accompanying and following others, to learning from them and teaching them at the same time.[24] Mesoamerican languages steeped in concepts of unity and interconnectedness have no word for "I," while Jamaican Rastafarian argot never allows the "I" to appear alone but instead insists on the phrasing "I and I."[25] In their discussions of creative artists in West Africa and the US, Robert Farris Thompson and Kalamu ya Salaam—writing thirty years apart and from different vantage points—observe Afro-diasporic fondness for the asymmetrical and resistance to the straight line. Sara Ahmed makes a similar observation about queer identity, which she portrays as not just a matter of sexual desires and practices but also a locus of *creative disorientation,* a way of seeing and acting in the world that is off-center, bent, and oblique, that disturbs the order of things by refusing to travel down a single path, and that instead twists and turns to create new social registers. Ahmed argues that like being queer, being racialized can produce opposition to what is expected and demanded.[26] These affinities and families of resemblance do not collapse the distinctions between and among different groups; they do not erase their particular histories and independent needs. They do, however, illuminate patterns of power and resistance as systemic and structural rather than as aberrant and episodic. Across communities seemingly separated by time, space, social positions, traditions, and belief systems there are similar and parallel ways of being, seeing, imagining, and acting.

As explicated in chapter 2, it is difficult to work inside educational institutions and not become co-opted by and incorporated into their managerial impulses and imperatives. The epistemologies of the crossroads and the caduceus, however, promote recognition of the two-sidedness of everything and encourage balancing opposites in ways that open rather than close doors. Area studies of Latin America, Africa, Asia, and the Middle East often work to deprovincialize ethnic studies and bring previously unheard voices into US academic life. These fields can also function, however, as parts of the national security state's efforts to provide stability, predictability, and security for the empire's economic and military aspirations. American studies started as an uncomfortable crossroads created by mutually antagonistic groups— adherents of popular front communism on the one hand and agents of cold war anticommunism on the other.[27] Balancing complex and competing forces requires the caduceus with its capacity to accept living with uncomfortable contradictions. Ethnic studies participants can feel guilt and shame when they learn that their work participates in projects antithetical to their ideals, but that same recognition can also impel them to assume greater accountability and responsibility.[28]

Michel-Rolph Trouillot reveals how the disciplines contain assumptions and premises suffused with uninterrogated allegiances to the power and logic of the state. Scholarly traditions inherited from the nineteenth century enshrine the hegemony of the nation and promote state-centric thinking. Areas of scholarly expertise often revolve around studies of particular national politics, economies, languages, geographies, institutions, and local works of literature, music, and visual art. While there is value in learning how the geographic and juridical boundaries of nations inflect social relations and social practices, this focus on the nation marginalizes processes that traverse national boundaries and shape the lives of people who cross them. It obscures how economic and political elites inside nations often have direct ties, affinities, and affiliations with elites in other countries, connections that provide them with very different views and interests than the nonelite populations inside the nations they rule. The cognitive mapping and physical boundedness of the nation-state often obscure the actual constant transnational interactions that emanate from fragmented and segmented processes of migration, manufacturing, and marketing, from religions that aspire to universal reach, and from families of resemblance that for example give cultures created in port cities and urban slums around the world similar qualities. Imagining the geography of the world as a series of entities bounded by state institutions facilitates administration but inhibits other kinds of cognitive mapping.[29]

Trouillot argues that categories as well as lands are divvied up by the state-centric thinking that deploys words, concepts, and frames to aggregate diverse peoples artificially into collectivities in order to classify and regulate them. State-centric practices work insidiously, leading scholars to embrace taken-for-granted assumptions and premises that should be examined carefully and countered creatively. The seeming naturalness of the rights-bearing citizen-subject of the law, the market actor of capitalism, and the psychic self of psychoanalysis leads researchers, writers, and teachers to interpellate listeners and readers as primarily isolated individuals brought together as a public by state and nonstate institutions of governance.

The state-centric and binary oppositions and practices of boundary protection that pervade academic research originated in Europe's conquests of the peoples of the Americas, Africa, and Asia. Presenting Europeans as creators and defenders of civilization—rather than merely as conquerors and plunderers—entailed creating what Trouillot calls "the savage slot." The savage in this portrayal could sometimes be associated with premodern innocence and virtue but most often appeared as a phobic fantasy of Europeans' previous existence, a frightening specter of life shaped by a world without technical mastery and not ruled by human masters. The racial capitalism that emerged and flowered in the age of empire required the discursive construction of dangerous "others" that need to be conquered and contained, sometimes allegedly for their own good.

The symbolic order of the West continues today to rely on the binary between "us and them" and "here and there." This requires physical, cultural, and intellectual borders to be policed and protected. Scholars are welcome to debate who rightly belongs in the savage slot but not to question the slot itself. They can argue for the worthiness of various aggrieved groups for inclusion into the liberal order, but they are chastised when they call into question the necessity for state-centric forms of identity and social organization. The savage slot initially most often referenced the Indigenous people whom Europeans encountered as "other" in the course of their conquests, but "savage" became a floating signifier applied to any demonized enemy identified by its difference.[30] The racial contract remains a central mechanism for making constructed social differences seem rooted in fundamental and immutable biological facts.

The same impulses that divide the globe into administered territories govern the division of knowledge into discrete disciplines. Drawing on the research of Thomas Gieryn, Charles Briggs argues that a central function of the disciplines is "boundary work"—the demarcation of intellectual activities that builds individual reputations and solidifies disciplinary commitments by giving symbolic and material resources to what is considered science by rendering all else pseudoscience or nonscience. It keeps members of a discipline "in" by keeping others "out."[31]

As might be expected, influence on the disciplines by ethnic studies scholars has been paralleled by influence on the interdisciplines of feminist studies, American studies, cultural studies, and environmental studies. This influence has sometimes sadly gone unacknowledged when the interdisciplines engage in their own forms of boundary work. A prime example appears in Leslie McCall's widely cited *Signs* article identifying intersectionality as the most important theoretical achievement of feminist studies. As Barbara Tomlinson observes, the footnote that accompanies this claim credits eleven "feminist" scholars without mentioning that ten of the eleven are women of color and that all eleven proceed from expressly antiracist and ethnic studies stances.[32]

Interdisciplinary ethnic studies scholars often find themselves charged with inadequate allegiance to the disciplines and their canonical grand theories. Following Mary Poovey, Charles Briggs notes that the elevation of abstract theory over nuanced description proceeds from the premises in Western thought that general propositions must refuse intimacy with the world and that grounded opinions, interests, and ways of knowing need to be expunged from knowledge in order for it to be universally valid. Yet positions that presume to be *universal* almost always in practice express only the ideas and interests of *some dominant particular*. Trouillot contends that grand metanarratives and theories hide precisely what autonomous learning circles and intersectional social movement mobilizations bring into clear view: the voices, ideas, aspirations, and analyses of people deemed marginal by those in power.[33] In *Unlearning: Rethinking Poetics, Pandemics, and the Politics of Knowledge*, Charles Briggs points out that canonized works of grand theory consistently treat processes of subordination and exclusion as given, taken for granted, and natural, while they render opposition to unjust social relations as disruptive, deviant, and in need of correction.

Ethnic studies work is often profoundly theoretical. Previous chapters of this book document broad theoretical claims by scholars in the field that emerge in works organized around the concepts (among others) of intersectionality, *nepantla, conocimiento,* decoloniality, hybridity, *mestizaje,* abolition, density, and non-normativity. Yet the applied dimensions of these theoretical interventions and their connections to the political, economic, cultural, and social goals of social justice struggles lead ethnic studies scholars most often to use theory provisionally, to see it as tactically useful and often politically necessary, but in ways that resist the one-size-fits-all and once-and-for-all mandates of normative grand theory. In their most useful iterations, these theories contribute to quests for decolonial options and pluriversality rather than universal solutions. Stuart Hall explains how engagement with the lives and struggles of insurgent people led him away from the ways Marxism had taught him to search for all-embracing totalities and had directed him toward acknowledging and thinking about the power of contingency in social life—contingencies that make it clear that no single axis of power such as class, race, or gender can account for or explain the social totality.[34]

Laura Briggs reveals how original, generative, and influential scholarly arguments can contribute to and emerge from intersectional struggles against normative social and scholarly categories.[35] In her paradigm-changing research, she argues that neoliberal racial capitalism lowers wages, increases hours at work, and channels tax dollars away from funding social services in order to subsidize the excess profits of wealthy individuals and corporations. These dynamics lead to a crisis in social reproduction, in the ability or inability to give birth to and raise healthy children. The administrators and orchestrators of neoliberalism deflect attention away from the pain produced by their policies by blaming and shaming their victims. They foment moral panics that attribute the crisis of the family to immigration, gay marriage, welfare, feminism, the existence of trans people, and movements for racial justice as smokescreens to insulate them from responsibility for the crises they create.

Instead of protecting reproductive rights, funding prenatal and postnatal care, providing affordable day care, raising wages, reducing hours at work, providing affordable housing and health care, and keeping children and adults safe from gun violence and environmental racism (among other measures), the neoliberal establishment stokes the flames of fear and hatred. It presents the people with the most serious problems as problems themselves.

Laura Briggs reveals how reproduction gets framed within what Mills calls a "contrapuntal ensemble." This reveals some of the limits of disciplinary frameworks and their separate silos. At the same time, it is useful for the groups she studies because it shows that their crises cannot be solved separately. Part of this analysis comes from her distinction as an empirical researcher and feminist theorist, but these achievements have been shaped in part by her participation in and observations about social movement mobilizations. She calls for the creation of reproductive rights and labor movements that can in concert recognize and address how these diverse crises all have connections to the structural changes that have altered the nature of work, reward, health, childbearing, and child-rearing.

The intersectional critique that enables Laura Briggs to expose the links between crises that scholars and civic leaders most often treat separately emanates in part from the critiques of normativity forged by the social movement mobilizations described in chapter 4. She notes how early efforts to secure legal rights for gay and lesbian parents to gain custody of their children, to gain guardianship of same-sex partners with disabilities, and to hold common property all emanated from activists with strong ties to movements for welfare rights, civil rights, and reproductive rights. They also had experience inside mobilizations against forced sterilizations of women of color and in protests against the Vietnam War.[36] In turn, a broad range of social movement activists affirmed the importance of recognizing, respecting, and supporting gay and lesbian causes. Black Panther Party leader Huey P. Newton articulated in a 1970 speech the party's support for the principle that all people should have the freedom to choose how to use their own bodies. Newton declared that gay people might be the most oppressed people in society and therefore should be welcomed at revolutionary conferences, rallies, and demonstrations.[37] United Farm Workers' leader Cesar Chavez mobilized opposition to California's 1978 homophobic ballot initiative that tried to ban gay and lesbian people from employment in schools. In 1987 Chavez served as grand marshal of the Second March on Washington for Lesbian and Gay Rights.[38]

The epistemology of the caduceus at the crossroads often takes the form of intersectionality. Intersectionality is not merely an intellectual conceit. It is a disposition toward solving problems that recognizes the presence of multiple currents of power and multiple possibilities for resistance in any site of injustice. Research conducted by Patricia Zavella reveals how Latinx reproductive justice activists create new ways of knowing and new ways of being at crossroads where racism, sexism, poverty, addiction, and criminalization inflict intersectional injuries. These activists develop and deepen a collective capacity to analyze their circumstances and act upon them through workshops grounded in the concept of *conocimiento*, which Zavella defines as "a process of gaining knowledge, awareness, and political consciousness based on storytelling."[39] Like the story circle pedagogy of the Free Southern Theater and Students at the Center described in chapter 3, the act of narrating personal experiences and then locating them within broader social processes brings to the surface repressed pain and grief but also hope for change. "Storytelling is a methodology that comes from our community," explains Tannia Esparza of Young Women United in Albuquerque. Rather than viewing the telling of stories as simple diversion or escapist entertainment, Latinx reproductive justice advocates recognize stories as repositories of collective memory and expertise, performances that position the people living with injustice as uniquely suited to shape strategies that contest it. Hearing the testimonies of other women shows how what seem like personal and private issues have public and political causes and consequences. Zavella argues that *conocimiento* "connects the inner life of the mind and spirit to the outer worlds of action."[40]

The reproductive justice movement creates an inventory of tools for change that are both old and new. It draws on what Anzaldúa identifies her book *Borderlands/La Frontera* as *la facultad*, the ability that border dwellers develop to confront uncertain and ever-shifting power differentials and to draw on the diverse aspects of their identities in response. The movement coalesces around the ideal and goal of healing justice as a tool that enables participants to address their own personal wounds, ailments, and injuries while at the same time working to cure the body politic of misogyny, sexism, homophobia, transphobia, racism, and class domination. Healing justice acknowledges and builds on the wisdom of community healers while challenging the for-profit model of medicine dominant among physicians, hospitals, pharmaceutical companies, and public health officials.[41] Healing justice recognizes and seeks to rectify trauma and violence inflicted across generations. Loretta Pyles describes it as a process of *attention and intention* "that can impact and transform the consequences of oppression of our bodies, hearts, and minds."[42]

Ethnic studies research like that done by Laura Briggs and Patricia Zavella emerges from long histories of feminist and antiracist activism and scholarship. But it is also constructed with and speaks for the autonomous learning circles explored in chapter 3 and the intersectional mobilizations in chapter 4. It poses particular threats to dominant scholarship because it seeks to advance theories grounded in what Walter Mignolo names "decolonial options."[43] These contain an aversion to premature universality. In the language formulated by Mexican Zapatista activists, decolonial options envision a world in which there is room for many worlds.[44] The Zapatista concern is not about which abstractions should rule the earth but rather about how all existing forms of rule portend unlivable and unjust destinies. Mignolo explains that decolonial options advance an ethic of *conversation* rather than *conversion*. They seek, not to build *alternative modernities,* but instead to forge *alternatives to modernity*. Inspired primarily by the politics and pedagogies of Indigenous peoples in the Andes and in Mexico, Mignolo finds decolonial options emerging from communal identities and practices with no pretensions to become universal—at least not yet—but instead trying to speak to local needs, aspirations, and struggles. They propose changing the world from the bottom up: using the tools people have in the arenas open to them in order to create practices, processes, and institutions that nurture new politics, new polities, and new kinds of people. From this perspective neoliberalism is less a matter of a specific dominant political or economic order and more a symptom of modernity's systemic poisoning of souls and suppression of caretaking relations. In ethnic studies scholarship such a stance does not propose another universal political and economic order to replace neoliberal racial capitalism but serves to build infrastructures where many new ways of knowing, being, and relation can be envisioned and enacted.[45] Rather than trying to wish that racial capitalism can be quickly overturned or will somehow suddenly develop a good heart, decolonial options proceed by insisting that "the *regeneration* of life shall prevail over the primacy of *production* and *reproduction* of goods at the cost of life."[46]

METHODS STRUCTURED IN DOMINANCE

Conducting research on, with, and for activists and artists from aggrieved racialized communities is an innately difficult task. It entails crossing social borders, moving outside the comfort zones and conventions of academic life, and creating new social relations of research by learning to listen and listening to learn from people who engage in thinking but are generally not recognized or respected as thinkers. Alessandro Portelli describes this kind of research as an experiment in equality, an attempt to challenge the social, structural, and systemic forces that divide researchers from those about whom they conduct research. It aims at producing equity-oriented collaborative research that speaks both with and for aggrieved subjects. Yet this equality can never actually be achieved fully. Differences of class, race, gender, sexuality, language, and levels of education do not disappear simply because participants have good intentions.

As he attempted to collect oral histories among workers in Italy, Portelli used the methods in which he had been trained. He presented himself as a neutral observer, never mentioning his ideas, opinions, class position, and background, believing that doing so would compromise the objectivity of his interviews. His interlocutors, however, perceived these silences to be indications of class privilege. Along with his forms of speech, body language, and dress, they marked him as part of the apparatus of interviewing and questioning carried out by employers, police officers, and government employees. Their experiences with surveillance led them to view the scholar as an agent of an administrative and disciplinary apparatus they knew well. They did all they could to avoid answering his questions and consistently obfuscated their experiences and beliefs. Portelli thus discovered that his attempt to perform objectivity produced biased data.

When he dropped the mask of neutrality, however, and spoke openly about his intentions, commitments, and beliefs, Portelli's interlocutors abandoned their performances of evasion and servility. The new liveliness of their testimony did not presume that differences had been erased. The workers in fact valued the difference embodied in his status as a professor, as someone who could convey their experiences and aspirations to a wider audience. In the misguided process of attempting to find sameness with the workers, Portelli found that it was exposure and appreciation of his differences that enabled a temporary moment of equality within the research conversations. This fleeting moment enabled both interviewer and interviewee to experience difference without subordination or hierarchy. Instead of pretending they were the same, they used their differences to craft a moment of equality in which difference did not become domination. Tensions between researchers and those they research can never be eliminated completely, but when they are constructively worked through they can produce new relations of research that promote new ways of knowing and new ways of being for all involved.[47]

Equity-oriented collaborative community-based engaged scholars cannot assume that their work will be welcomed in the communities they study. They have learned to ask permission to accompany their subjects, to derive their research questions from community concerns, and to produce knowledge that helps rather than harms those they study. Their work entails crafting friendly, respectful, and reciprocal relationships. Their obligations are never fulfilled completely, but each attempt can be a step along the path of a long process of accompaniment. Much of what scholars contribute toward those ends will take the form of behind-the-scenes work through actions such as conversing with interlocutors, helping them organize and mobilize, participating in vetting, editing, and distributing their writing, and assisting with the logistics of their public appearances. For example, scholars working with Indigenous migrant organizations provide services by authoring press releases, documenting community events, producing flyers, and helping with the creation and delivery of speeches and other oral presentations.[48]

Researchers who have succeeded in producing publications and political projects that have helped create social change from the bottom up have developed an inventory of tools of enormous value to ethnic studies and to all people battling domination. These include staging cross-sector conversations among organic intellectuals and traditional intellectuals through collaborations that bring together both campus and community knowledges. At their best, these projects discover how new research objects produce new research questions and new relations of research. They discover and mine archives, imaginaries, epistemologies, and ontologies that loom large inside social struggles but that have often remained all but invisible in the academy. These projects explore how the expressive cultures, customs, and politics of aggrieved groups inhabit temporalities and spaces that confound the categories of Enlightenment history, traditional cognitive mapping, and narrow definitions of rationality. They demonstrate how self-reflexive openness about the positionality and subjectivity of scholars and commitments to vetting research among the direct participants in the processes analyzed can actually augment objectivity because it draws on a wider range of expert knowledges than scholarly vetting alone can provide.

This research requires commitments to long-term projects, affiliations, and collaborations rooted in creating, preserving, and altering social relations, rather than submitting to the seductions of excessive attention to short-term processes that begin with a research design and end with a scholarly publication. Academic research has been transformed meaningfully through writings authored by scholars working *with*, *by*, and *for* rather than merely *on* or *about* social movement mobilizations. This writing carries the ideas and actions of social movement mobilizations to a wider audience, helps community activists assess and diagnose the strengths and weaknesses of their work, and serves as a warning to the forces of repression that the aggrieved have allies who can be mobilized against attempts to crush their movements.[49]

The influences of the Zapatista uprising and the 2020 movement against anti-Black racism, the spread of prison abolition activism, recognition of the urgency of the climate crisis, refusals of gender normativity, and the creation of coalitions of housed and unhoused people affirming the public's right to the city have given rise to a plethora of autonomous learning circles and intersectional mobilizations. These bring the eyewitnesses to the worst depredations of racial capitalism into dialogue with academics and artists. These circles have produced their own books blending artistic, activist, and academic knowledge. *Freedom Now! for the Human Right to Housing In LA and Beyond* stages a conversation in print among scholars and houseless activists who present different perspectives on the criminalization of poverty, mass incarceration, and housing insecurity.[50] *Collective Creative Actions: Project Row Houses at 25* places art museum education directors, art critics, and academic experts on urban design and social relations in dialogue with artists, activist administrators, and alumni of Project Row Houses, an arts-based community-building and housing provision project in Houston's Third Ward.[51] *Saludarte: Building Health Equity on the Bedrock of Traditional Arts and Culture,* by the Alliance for California Traditional Arts and Building Healthy Communities in Boyle Heights, presents politics and pedagogies that activists have invented to educate about and agitate for community health and well-being.[52] *Life Sentences: Writings from Inside an American Prison,* by the Elsinore Bennu Think Tank for Restorative Justice in Pittsburgh (2019), and *Go to Jail,* by Students at the Center in New Orleans (2021), document collaborations between high school and college students and teachers with currently and formerly incarcerated people in order to assist community reentry and reconciliation as they rebuild the ties severed by mass incarceration.[53]

ETHNIC STUDIES CAN BE ITS OWN WORST ENEMY

Ethnic studies scholars are not immune to the allure of the recognitions and rewards that come from demonstrating subject matter mastery and becoming fixated on formal complexity. Their jobs compel them to spend most of their time inside enemy-centered spaces that privilege the prevailing distributions of power. They contend with demands on their time and labor that leave them few opportunities to interact with the most aggrieved members of the communities they are asked to understand and represent in academia. The audit cultures of the institutions that employ them routinely treat engagement with off-campus social movements as either activism or service but almost never as an important part of research. Even worse, the reward system often welcomes warmly and provides ample support for scholarship that condemns the shortcomings of ethnic peoples or other ethnic studies scholars while giving a free pass to the calculated cruelty and systematic subordination of white supremacist institutions. People credentialed as experts can come to treat those they study and those they study with as easily fooled dopes and dupes. They can become enamored of conflict and view their main task as cutting others down to size. Gloria Anzaldúa observes how being engaged perpetually in conflict can dissolve the sense of connectedness needed for constructive convivial work. She remembers being "in gatherings where people luxuriate in their power to prevent change instead of using it to cause transformation, where they spew verbal abuse in a war of words and do not leave space for others to save face, where feelings are easily bruised or too intense to be controlled by will alone."[54]

Ethnic studies participants engage in boundary work by imposing an "either/or" approach to past ideas and theories rather than "both/and." As the work of Mikhail Bakhtin insists, nothing from the past ever goes away completely, yet nothing from the past remains completely applicable to the present in its original form. The acclaim and prestige that accrue to claims of newness and innovation in academic life can promote an excessively antagonistic relationship with past research findings and claims. This becomes exacerbated in ethnic studies because disillusionment with the emergency-in-perpetuity continues to plague the lives of racialized individuals and groups. What Trouillot calls the "fetish of newness" can lead scholars to attack rather than build on previous paradigms, to assail their own field's history with more vigor than they direct against the institutions of racial capitalism and its academic architects and defenders. This impulse does not necessarily emanate solely from the scholars themselves: It may be imposed on them by promotion reviewers and search committees that insist on evidence of innovation. Yet claims of newness often unwittingly serve to reproduce the past. Trouillot observes that loud rejections of previous scholars and scholarship often appear prominently in work that quietly reproduces the very research techniques and methodological assumptions being critiqued. Performing newness can create great careers, but by itself it does little to solve serious social problems.[55]

As Barbara Tomlinson and I have argued elsewhere, the cultures of academic reward and recognition encourage scholars to assert they have either the first word or the last word.[56] When scholars present themselves as the creators of the one new term, method, theory, or social identity that will transcend past mistakes, they inhabit the persona of the articulator of the first word. They confuse branding with building. When they attempt to tear down the work of other scholars by asserting it is not really new but rather has been said before by a previously unknown or undervalued past author—often a member of their group—they preserve the idea that the goal of scholarship is to be first, to surpass others, to build a present that is bearable by tearing down its links to the past. They forget that all flourishing is mutual.[57]

At the other extreme, ethnic studies scholars can succumb to the lure of the last word by claiming to have found some master narrative or frame of analysis that settles things once and for all and shuts down competing visions of the situation. Attempts to have the last word often deploy the tropes that Charles Briggs calls "magic nominalism" and that Toni Cade Bambara described as "abstractionism."[58] During the necessary process of building on previous scholarship, some researchers, teachers, and students will decide that a change in words is sufficient to effect a change in conditions. Charles Briggs notes that valid critiques of the vexed histories of terms like *tradition, authenticity,* and *folklore* lead some scholars to try to ban the use of those terms instead of investigating and altering the representational practices and institutional positionalities they signify. It can be valuable to apply new names to familiar objects, to attend to the gender politics that expose the use of *Latina* or *Latino* instead of *Latinx* as an imposition of gender binaries, to embrace the terms *Black* or *Chicanx* as ways of turning terms of scorn into badges of pride, to use uppercase letters at the start of *Indigenous* and *Black* as a way of presenting collective identities as political projects rather than merely embodied associations. Inventing new areas of study with names that shed the historical limits associated with ethnic studies and related studies fields can perform important work. Each new name that enables, however, also inhibits. Adding the adjective *critical* before an area of study can express a commitment to and an invitation for fully aware kinds of work attentive to new circumstances. It can, however, also be an exercise in branding, novelty, and product differentiation that disrespects previous paradigms and coasts on claims of newness instead of actually being new. As Judith Butler argues, the names applied to us never fully describe our positionalities or our identities, yet the tension between external ascription and internal aspiration creates momentum that coalesces around ever-changing forms of agency.[59] It is healthy and necessary to break with the past and to create innovative new tools appropriate for new circumstances. It is however, an illusion and a delusion to believe that any participant in scholarly and civic conversations has the first or the last word. Each interlocutor speaks the middle word grounded in what has been learned in the past and aimed at open-ended dialogue with others in the future.

CONNECTING CLASSROOMS AND COMMUNITIES

Scenes of argument emerge in the classrooms where students learn and in the projects they pursue outside them. Roderick Ferguson calls attention to the importance of the seemingly small actions that take place through teaching, training, accompanying, encouraging, conversing, and counseling. These promote the creation of what he calls "critical forms of community, forms in which minoritized subjects become the agents rather than the silent objects of knowledge formations and institutional practices."[60] Ferguson cautions that inordinate attention to achieving herculean feats—like writing books of monumental influence and giving rousing keynote speeches—can lead ethnic studies participants to underestimate the importance of attending to what seem like minor details that can have profound effects in the long run. Activities, exercises, and assignments in ethnic studies college and K-12 classrooms enable students to research conditions in their communities and create pamphlets, zines, and books reporting their findings.[61] People of all backgrounds who have taken ethnic studies courses will be in rooms when decisions are made about employment, medical care, and legal interpretation. Their beliefs, actions, and ideas can help shape how individuals, communities, and institutions perceive sexuality, disability, citizenship status, and language use. Ferguson's observation amounts to more than a guide to good pedagogy; it references an increasingly important interpretation of the nature of social change. Even dramatic moments of insurrection at the barricades draw their power from the accretion of many small acts. Diana Taylor notes how the Zapatistas point to the steady and slow pace of the snail to convey how meaningful work requires patient effort. Snails carry their homes on their backs and stay close to the ground with the humility and tenacity needed for long journeys.[62]

The work of ethnic studies takes place in widely dispersed sites where improvisations and experiments expand the sphere of inquiry and connect classroom instruction to community concerns. Teachers, parents, and students in a midsized upper Midwest city work together to implement a sociocultural approach to learning that enhances literacy skills for African-descent students in K-8 grades.[63] Twenty-nine students in a ninth-grade ethnic studies class in San Diego collectively produce a graphic zine/comic chronicling (and archiving) the activism of the Environmental Health Coalition, a group that mobilizes community members to fight the effects of polluted air, water, and land caused by pesticides, toxic waste, smoke, auto and truck emissions, and harmful chemicals.[64] The Public Scholarship Team and Alumni at the University of California Irvine publish a booklet making available contents of letters written decades ago by relatives and caretakers to students enrolled in El Sol Science and Arts Academy in Santa Ana during the 2002–3 academic year. In the sixty letters to students in this archive, the writers praise bilingual education as an aid to communication across generations and as preparation for a time when the student may be asked to help someone in trouble. One father writes to his child that being in a school with many different kinds of people representing diverse cultures and languages offers good training to help build a better world.[65] These letters stand as an archive ready to be consulted as defense against future assaults on bilingual schooling and demographic diversity.

An innovative pedagogical project at the University of California Davis traversed disciplinary and social boundaries through a class that focused on studying Inuit fermented foods such as seal blubber and flippers, caribou, and walrus. The instructors shaped that inquiry to be a point of entry into teaching fundamental principles of microbiology and the nature of the scientific method, but also the ways in which microbiology affects social life through explorations of Indigenous people's rights and food sovereignty. Class activities included lectures on microbiology and fermentation, laboratory work experimenting with fermenting food, a workshop on Inuit dance and drum making, a visit to a Native American contemplative garden, and a performance by the multiracial Inuit Soul music ensemble Pamyua (described in chapter 4). The course came into existence through collective efforts by faculty at UC Davis from the Department of Food Science and Technology and the Imaging America: Artists and Scholars in Public Life unit, in accompaniment with a scholar from the program Scientific and Indigenous Teachings on Life in the Arctic at the University of Greenland. The course identified microorganisms as entities that affect diverse facets of human and planetary life while locating science as an activity carried out by humans and influenced by their subjective perceptions, premises, and assumptions. Open to enrollment by students from any major, the small honors class exposed nonscience students to scientific principles while helping microbiologists perceive the connections that require science to take into account human rights, Indigenous and feminist studies, creative arts, and performance. The class paired the study of dominant scientific methods with Stó:lō scholar Jo-ann Archibald's Indigenous Storywork methodology grounded in principles of respect, reverence, responsibility, and reciprocity.

One exercise required students to create a Tribalography—an infographic displaying a tree or plant from their home lands or waters. That project asked students to name the people and places that made up their anchoring roots and shaped their journey to the present. It then asked them to name places and people whose projects the students felt aligned with and inspired by. The course helped students see how some forms of knowledge get valued over others, especially how colonialism has shaped scientific inquiry. A special feature of the project entailed a concert and three-day residency by Pamyua that enabled students to participate in a drum-making workshop and read about and discuss Inuit relations with and respect for the environment. The music and dance at these events offered more than entertainment. In keeping with the worldviews of Alaska Native Peoples, they highlighted how making relations with environmental, human, and more-than-human entities produces self-active ways of being and becoming. The learning circle enacted through this class ended with a physical talking circle positioned around a *quelleg* (traditional Inuit oil lamp) to review and ruminate about the importance of cultivating holistic approaches to knowledge, study, and struggle.[66] Like the autonomous learning circles described in chapter 3, this class deployed radically innovative and relational research practices that originated in the collective experiences of aggrieved communities.[67]

Innovative projects initiated at Yale, New York, San Jose State, and Brown Universities link campus and community knowledge and concerns in innovative ways. The Anti-Eugenics Collective at Yale (AECY) that Daniel HoSang organized and advises engages students in collective research about the long history of that institution's culpability in the creation and dissemination of racist, classist, ableist, and sexist ideas and public policies. The project exposes the eugenic roots of long-accepted but fraudulent and destructive practices in medicine, biology, law, statistics, psychology, and other disciplines. The Yale group works with colleagues at institutions around the world conducting similar inquiries. The initiative also connects college students and faculty members to diverse publics that include K-12 teachers and people locked up in carceral institutions. One project entailed having incarcerated students write about their memories of schooling, about the ways in which what they now recognize as eugenics shaped their experiences in K-12 classrooms. They then used those memories to advise the K-12 teachers associated with the project about how they could build curriculum units that would not reproduce eugenics thinking.[68] While instigating these innovative cross-sector conversations off campus, the AECY initiative also enables ethnic studies activists on campus to waste less time lobbying for the necessary but always inadequate resources hoarded by college administrators and to devote more time using the semiautonomy that faculty members possess in relation to teaching, student mentorship, and obtaining resources for convening campus-community conversations and campaigns.

Like the Anti-Eugenics initiative at Yale, the Latinx Project (TLP) organized and administered at New York University by Arlene Davila creates a new active, engaged, and convivial public sphere that connects campus knowledge with community art and activism. Vexed by systematic underfunding and marginalization of Latinx studies in a university located in one of the most populous, creative, and politically significant Latinx cities in the world, TLP came into being initially to stage original art exhibitions and to host poetry readings, lectures, and film showings. These were intended to augment official and alternative research archives on campus while cultivating repertoires of embodied memory and struggle among a diverse cross-sectoral population. Frustrated by the university's lack of support for Latina/o/x studies research and teaching, TLP activists envision and enact what the corporate university will not and perhaps cannot be—an academic, artistic, activist, cultural, pedagogical, and political space grounded in accompaniment with New York City's large but all too often marginalized and aggrieved Latinx people struggling for social transformation and social justice.

TLP activities documented on its website and Instagram page call a community into being that develops new models of artistic, intellectual, and political engagement. While exposing a broad public to already-existing academic and artistic work that has been produced over decades, the TLP also generates new knowledge and new imaginaries through in-depth conversations about critical Indigeneity, Afro-Latinx studies, queer and trans studies, and media and publishing opportunities and impediments. Artistic creation, reception, and analysis emanating from group art exhibitions function as portals of entry into meaningful discussions about collective responses to gentrification, environmental racism, the coloniality of museum practices, and the social impact of dominant digital technologies. The TLP draws on and contributes to university research and teaching, but it also generates publications and public events that involve a broad array of participants with widely varying social positions and educational histories. Born out of frustration with the shortcomings of the corporate university, TLP deploys the resources of that very institution to imagine ways to go beyond it.

Challenging the norms of academia opens the door for TLP to contest pernicious practices in the art world. Emerging artists outside the social circles frequented by gallery owners and curators have few opportunities to show their work. TLP provides a venue for them as well as for novice curators who get to curate original exhibitions in institutional settings. Students from aggrieved racialized groups meet artists who look like them and who work on themes that resonate with their shared concerns. Artists get the opportunity to overcome obstacles of the art world—such as having to donate their work to be put up for auction but then finding that auction prices are generally lower than gallery prices. Tax laws also prevent artists from claiming the full price of their artworks as donations. TLP counters this by having artists sell their work during its annual spring celebration, fundraiser, and online auction. At this event artists set the price for their work and determine what part of the sale they wish to share with the auction. Davila argues that the ultimate success or failure of TLP will be measured, not by the degree to which it does or does not grow or endure as a single institutional entity, but by its role in fostering new imaginations and innovations that advance antiracist futures within and beyond academia.[69]

In the Chicano Studies Department at San Jose State University, Jonathan Gomez leads three projects that connect campus learning to community concerns: the Culture Counts Reading Series (CCRS), the Cultural Work of Poetry Project (TCWP), and the Restorative Healing and Justice Mentorship Program (RHJMP). The Culture Counts Reading Series organizes current students and alumni on the San Jose State campus to read prose and poetry together and to write and perform works of their own. One part of their activities has entailed inviting distinguished writers to visit the group, read their work, and lead discussions about it. The group hosted a discussion led by poet and author Luis J. Rodriguez with students, faculty, and staff as the centerpiece of an afternoon of collaborative and convivial spoken-word presentations. They prepared for his visit by reading and discussing an essay by Rodriguez on applying Indigenous ways of knowing to classroom instruction in order to combine thinking with feeling, creativity with caretaking relations, and critical learning with committed social action. Another event involved reading and discussing the poems of Lorna Dee Cervantes collected in her book *Emplumada* and then welcoming her to come to campus for a day of dialogue and poetry, to do a public reading in a community venue, and to have her conduct a guided tour of the Barrio Horseshoe in East San Jose where she was raised.

Community members from off campus attended CCRS events but initially were reluctant to lead discussions or present their own poetry in the campus setting. At the same time, students complained of the campus's distance and detachment from the places in San Jose where many of them were raised and still live. CCRS members responded to these concerns by creating the Cultural Work of Poetry project (TCWP). They set up events in community meeting rooms in branches of the San Jose Public Library scattered throughout the city. That move expanded the conversations and creative work to include wage laborers, elders, houseless people, and K-12 students. The CCRS and TCWP projects also gave rise to the creation of the Healing Youth Justice Platica and Poetry initiative led by high school teacher Alberto Camacho. This project is open to all students in a high school attended primarily by disregarded and disrespected young working-class, Chicanx, Latinx, and Indigenous youths. In these sessions, university students and faculty members establish horizontal and mutually respectful relationships with the high school students as they work together to write, hear, and critique poems that speak to the many contradictions of their lives.

In addition to these initiatives, Gomez works with attorneys and social workers associated with the Santa Clara County Public Defender's Office Post Conviction Unit in the Restorative Healing and Justice Mentorship Program. This project uses the story circle method and the *acuerdos* described in chapter 3 to stimulate writing exercises designed to cultivate augmented capacities for reentry into society among people returning from incarceration. Participants share stories of attempting to reconnect with loved ones and reintegrate into society in the face of barriers to employment, collateral consequences of criminal convictions, health problems developed behind bars, and fragile support networks due to the family fragmentation that poverty and its criminalization create. Sharing stories reveals how seemingly individual and personal problems are connected to public policies and practices, while the search for coping and enabling devices becomes enhanced by thinking about them through convivial conversations and collective creativity among similarly situated people.

A routine feature of Gomez's advanced graduate class on comparative and relational ethnic studies entails a community *convivio* that brings off-campus activists, artists, organizers, teachers, and students to the campus for a story circle discussion. Sitting inside a circle where everyone is equal and committed to listen and learn from each other, participants speak about the kinds of worlds they wish to inhabit and talk about how they imagine arriving there. They read and discuss poems by Mari Evans and Luis J. Rodriguez. The story circle method enables participants to escape their designated social roles, to let down their defenses, and to express respect and support for each other. The *convivio* connects the campus to the community in novel ways and encourages differently situated people to commit to accompanying one another.[70]

Tricia Rose holds the Chancellor's Professorship of Africana Studies and serves as associate dean of the Faculty for Special Initiatives at Brown University. As a researcher she has blazed new trails for the study of racism, gender, and expressive culture. Rose's Systemic Racism and Resilience Project blends advanced scholarship with engaging and accessible forms of public outreach and community building. Her 2024 book *Metaracism* presents a carefully constructed demonstration of the causes, consequences, and contours of systemic racism.[71] She has now collaborated with a team of digital design experts to create and make available the web project *Way Outta No Way*, an initiative whose name embodies the caduceus described throughout this book. The website that Rose and her coworkers have created presents many of the key ideas and concepts delineated in *Metaracism* and Rose's many other books and articles. It offers a dynamic, engaging, accessible, interactive experience.[72] Visitors to the site learn through character-driven stories grounded in rigorous research that shine the light of truth on the harms perpetrated by systemic racism. At the same time the site highlights the power of antiracism and demonstrates the many things that can be done to counter the indecent and unjust world that racism engenders. The site invites viewers to join the *Way Outta No Way* learning community and participate in its efforts to build social justice in their locality.

These projects address diverse aspects of racism and antiracism. The Anti-Eugenics Collective at Yale focuses on science. The Latinx Project at NYU identifies art as its unifying concern. The Cultural Work of Poetry Project and attendant innovations at San Jose State use poetic and first-person writing to explore displacement, dispossession, and incarceration. The *Way Outta No Way* web project started at Brown creates public education in the new public sphere that it calls into existence. Each of these initiatives connects the research, teaching, learning, and resources of college campuses to community concerns. As they facilitate these community conservatories and alternative academies, HoSang, Davila, Gomez, and Rose continue to produce excellent original discovery scholarship that exerts significant influence and impact on research. The enormous amounts of time and energy they expend on these projects extends the reach and scope of ethnic studies beyond the campus but also infuses classroom instruction and research projects with the collective intelligence honed in struggles by aggrieved groups. These projects evidence a broader emergence of new curricular initiatives and projects creating new public spheres connected to or emerging from ethnic studies.

ETHNIC STUDIES IN A MOMENT OF DANGER

The current attacks on ethnic studies and all people deemed nonnormative—and therefore susceptible to domination—can produce sorrow, sadness, despair, and resignation. That is the result intended by the forces attacking critical race theory and diversity, equity, and inclusion initiatives; suppressing Indigenous sovereignty, survivance, and refusal; denying disability justice; punishing immigration and denying asylum; outlawing gender and reproductive justice; and fighting against fair housing, fair hiring, school desegregation, affirmative action, queer and trans rights. This evil turn comes as more of a shock to many ethnic studies teachers and students, however, than it does to members of aggrieved communities, who, as Sunni Patterson's poem described in chapter 3 states, already "know this place." As Trouillot explains, perceiving acts of destruction as shock and revelation implies previous complacency about forces that have been there all along but only now are reaching new victims.[73] Similarly, Arlene Davila observes that the pessimism that anthropologists routinely display in response to accounts of liberation and resistance exposes the discipline's enduring although often disavowed "compromised liberal impulses and its existence as the handmaiden of colonialism."[74]

Events that seem like momentous departures from past practice to people who are relatively privileged provoke memories that—as Walter Benjamin observed—flash up in a moment of danger among the oppressed.[75] The abandonment of the Black poor and working class in New Orleans in the wake of Hurricane Katrina in 2005 came as a shock to many outside observers, but the victims of post-Katrina racism noted that it took place nearly fifty years to the day after the lynching of Emmett Till in Mississippi in 1955. Community mobilizations protesting the killing of Michael Brown by Officer Darren Wilson in Ferguson in 2014 included demonstrators who had taken to the streets in 1966 in a direct-action protest against the killing of Russell Hayes by St. Louis police officers. When Officer Derek Chauvin choked George Floyd to death on a Minneapolis street in 2020, residents of North Tulsa in Oklahoma noted that the killing took place shortly before the ninety-ninth anniversary of the white vigilante violence known as the Tulsa massacre. That episode of racist violence and ethnic cleansing destroyed the city's prosperous Black business district, incarcerated some six thousand residents, sent six hundred people to hospitals, and ended up with an estimated seventy-five to three hundred people dead. The COVID-19 syndemic of 2020 struck many people as a fundamentally new and frightening breakdown of public health and interpersonal interaction. Jessica Bissett Perea explains that for Indigenous People, however, it manifested only the latest iteration of a long-standing pattern of death by epidemic disease reaching back to the smallpox carried to the region by Russian traders and missionaries in the nineteenth century, the "great death" that killed up to two-thirds of the Yup'ik population during the flu epidemic at the turn of the twentieth century, and the spread of tuberculosis in the 1930s and 1940s that decimated Native villages. For the most vulnerable members of aggrieved groups, every president has been Trump; every illness has been COVID-19; every natural and unnatural disaster has been Katrina; every police officer has been Derek Chauvin; every Supreme Court decision has been *Dobbs*.

Most academic ethnic studies researchers and teachers have advantages and resources that are unavailable to the most deeply aggrieved members of the communities with which they identify. Those advantages can cloud their vision and deprive them of intellectual and political tools honed and refined through struggle. Differently situated people perceive the current moment of danger differently. Those who hold professional positions, who own property and have pensions, who have housing and health care, whose citizenship status is secure, whose identity has not yet been criminalized, may see the past two decades as a nightmarish decline from what they believed previously to be a vexed yet acceptable norm. It may seem to them that the Trump presidencies, the attack on the US capitol aimed at negating the results of the 2020 election, the flaunting and celebration of gun violence, the attacks on reproductive rights and on LGBTQ people, the mass slaughter of civilians in Gaza and the attendant criminalization of opposition to the state of Israel's illegal and immoral actions, the efforts to expunge race from K-12 and college curricula, and the massive attack on social justice enacted by the second Trump administration's Project 2025 evidence a decidedly new and dangerous political reality. They may long for a return to what they previously perceived as normal and what they expected to continue to be reality—a multicultural and pluralist society adhering to democratic values with adequate social insurance for themselves and a sound social safety net for those in greatest need. They may look back longingly at the era of the emancipatory race and gender justice movements of the 1960s and 1970s, to the sunrise they perceived at the start of institutionalized ethnic studies. In relation to public issues, their politics may coalesce around desires for restoration of trade union bargaining power, living wages, and safe working conditions; for a return to respect for disregarded reproductive and civil rights; for needed policies such as debt relief and paid leave for parenting and illness. These are worthy aspirations and goals. Yet they are desires that speak from and for a certain social position that is incomplete. They act as if the cruel and oppressive policies enacted by Trump and Trumpistas destroyed something that in fact has not existed for wide swaths of the population, who have long lived with economic, legal, and political precarity.

People who see themselves as deserving to inhabit prominent places in the center of powerful social institutions view the world differently from those whose lives are lived on the margins. The dangers that appear novel and disturbing to people who have been relatively privileged are all too familiar to the oppressed. As Clyde Woods consistently argued in calling attention to the predatory machinations of racial capitalism in New Orleans and Haiti, the extreme punishments and naked plunder enacted first in places where power imbalances are greatest merely rehearse what the powerful seek to do everywhere.[76] The contempt and cruelty initially directed against the colonized, the criminalized and incarcerated, the poor, the houseless, immigrants, and sexual, religious, and linguistic minorities rehearses what will soon be directed against public and private pension holders, government employees, women in need of health care, people in debt because of predatory loans, working librarians, and school teachers merely doing their jobs. The violence, suffering, and misery that US tax dollars have produced and sustained around the world is now being experienced harshly by residents within the geographic and juridical boundaries of the US nation-state.

These circumstances can generate pessimism, even despair. Yet they also offer an opportunity to examine and draw on the enduring relevance of the survival strategies, knowledge repositories, and acts of convivial cocreation among aggrieved groups. These rich resources have been preserved and augmented inside autonomous learning circles, intersectional activist mobilizations, alternative archives, and repertoires of embodied memory. In this moment of danger, large portions of the population need to find ways to replace divisive competitive individualism with convivial collaboration and cocreation, and to create forms of mutual aid and self-defense that are not merely reactive or simply *oppositional* to the social relations that now exist but are instead *propositional* in envisioning and enacting new and better ones. They desire to find ways to reject the affective and ideological enticements of the dominant culture and to replace them with practices and processes that nurture and sustain caretaking relations among humans and between humans and the more-than-human world.

The colleges and universities where ethnic studies work has traditionally been nurtured and sustained may not be ideal sites for that work. They are exclusionary class-based institutions, funded by the state and private philanthropy in order to produce managers who can make the existing system more efficient and more effective. Parochial exclusions by class, race, sex-gender, language, citizenship status, and disability constrain who participates in the academy. The audit system of professional promotion and reward fuels a competitive and entrepreneurial ethos of individualism. Life in academia segregates scholarly critics of social suffering from the direct eyewitnesses and primary resisters against the worst injustices of the system. This means that even well-intentioned critics can unwittingly produce, preserve, and protect the conditions they purport to critique. Producing an ever-expanding list of eloquent and indignant works condemning suffering does not necessarily help those who suffer. Without engaging in the difficult work of connecting with and learning from aggrieved communities in struggle, scholars may resort to a self-serving stance of superior intellectual distance, learning to present themselves as potentially better managers of the system that exists rather than questioning the unjust and undemocratic foundations of that system.

Oppositional intellectuals lacking direct contact with aggrieved social groups have all too often used their alienations as a kind of personal absolution and abdication of responsibility. Melancholy and sadness about society's ills can become a perverse source of aesthetic pleasure grounded in the conviction that social problems are "out there" rather than "in here," that expressing pity for those who suffer suffices as a moral stance. Acclimated to savor writing that displays mastery and formal complexity, these intellectuals may find direct descriptions and expressions of the problems faced by ordinary people to be crude, simplistic, inelegant, and beneath them. They may be bored by fights that take place outside their direct spheres of affiliation, association, and aspiration. As a result, the ingenuity and inventiveness of social movement mobilizations may escape them. As C. L. R. James observed about the politics of knowledge, art, and social action in another era, "Intellectuals are bored. The masses are not. They have no freedom and they resent it."[77]

The academy is not an innocent victim of neoliberal racial capitalism. It is a key crucible in which the system's values are learned and legitimated, proclaimed and practiced. In his assessment of the early twentieth-century British intellectuals known as the Bloomsbury group, Raymond Williams argued that their awareness of many important things did not include self-reflexivity about their own formation and class position. Enjoying being friends, they saw themselves as independent, free, and civilized individuals, not as people whose platforms depended on class privileges. In an observation replete with significance for ethnic studies departments and networks, Williams proclaimed that "friendship is not innocent."[78]

Criticizing unjust power is not the same thing as *diminishing* it. As Paula Ioanide argues, inhabiting the radical negativity of critique can make people "feel good about feeling bad," cultivating an interior oppositional identity that requires no exterior social action.[79] Declaiming against the increasingly unjust and indecent social relations of our time is valuable and worthy work, but left to itself it does too little to change the conditions it decries. Being reflexively *oppositional* without being *propositional*, being *denunciatory* without being *annunciatory*, grievously underestimates what is at stake in this moment of danger. Finding new ways of working requires moving beyond the boundaries of academic inquiry and instruction, connecting with and learning from the survival strategies of excluded, disregarded, and disrespected social groups.

Not everyone inside academia will be able to travel to and participate in direct-action protests and mass mobilizations, but not everyone needs to do so. Publications reporting findings by scholars whose work centers on consulting archives, conducting experiments, critiquing expressive culture, and theorizing social relations remain as important as ever. But scholars who choose to write about past, present, and emerging struggles can connect scholarly findings to the needs and knowledge of aggrieved groups. They can also act as academic citizens to connect campuses to communities. People with stable incomes can donate money to activist groups. Teachers can assign readings that introduce students to the world beyond the campus. Students, staff, administrators, and faculty members can invite social justice–minded activists and artists to receive compensation for campus presentations about their work. The semiautonomous dimensions of university employment make it possible for scholars to make bold statements about injustices in the criminal justice system, the art world, and public health that are unlikely to be raised by professionals in those fields because their livelihoods and reputations depend on approval by bureaucrats, funders, politicians, and professional gatekeepers.[80]

Moments at the barricades when decisive confrontations with power take place are important; they can clarify and crystallize long-held aspirations. As Ella Baker noted, however, too much attention to dramatic spectacles of protest can obscure the importance of what she called the "arduous work of collective development."[81] People who participate in direct action as well as people who do not can promote an ethos of caretaking relations, accompaniment, and solidarity with those who suffer most. They can become sanctuary people. In this moment of danger, at this particular historical crossroads, nobody can do everything. But everybody can do something.

6

Ethnic Studies and the Current Crisis

Ethnic studies as an institution is not an end in itself; its worthiness depends upon its ability to understand and advance emancipatory struggles. It is a vehicle to promote social justice more generally. Its institutional survival is desirable but far less important than its long-term effects. As a character in Toni Cade Bambara's novel *The Salt Eaters* advises a Black community embattled in a struggle against racism, "Keep the focus on the action, not the institution; don't confuse the vehicle with the objective; all cocoons are temporary and disappear."[1]

In an episode in a novel by another author named Toni—Toni Morrison's *Song of Solomon*—two Black teenagers complain to their elders that a local merchant has refused to sell them a beer. Their complaint provokes one of the listeners to rebuke the young men, belittling their complaint by giving voice to a long series of grievances based on his life of demeaning work as a Pullman porter. His job required him to shine shoes, fetch cigars, serve meals and drinks, carry luggage, make beds, and witness passengers sitting on luxurious chairs and sofas wearing clothes that he knew he would never be able to afford to buy. Declaring that not being able to buy a beer pales in comparison to the frustrations of the elder's life and labor, the old man proceeds to present a list of all the things the young men will also *not get* in life, things that he watched white people on the trains enjoy routinely. He lists them in rapid succession: a private coach graced with red velvet chairs, a private toilet, a custom-made bed, money in the bank, a valet, a cook, a traveling secretary, a tray with red roses, hot croissants and coffee delivered to bed in the morning, pheasant under glass, and baked Alaska.² Recoiling from the volume and vehemence of the elder's inventory of all the things the young men would have to go without, one of them replies sarcastically, "No Baked Alaska. You're breaking my heart!" His interlocutor pauses for a beat and says, "Well now. That's something you will have. A broken heart. A broken heart and a whole lot of folly." As his face falls and the merriment leaves his eyes, the old man repeats, "And folly. A whole lot of folly. You can count on it."³

In the years ahead, participants in ethnic studies projects and the communities designated as different and deficient that they come from and speak to can expect to have broken hearts and face a whole lot of folly. There will be many rivers to cross, many crossroads to negotiate. Catastrophes come quickly and repeatedly. Even those that have not yet occurred loom forebodingly because the policies that cause them, the structures that enable them, and the logics that excuse and justify them are already in place. In a society driven mad by its contradictions, there will be no personal escape from suffering, sadness, and sorrow, but there will always be possibilities for study and struggle.

Obstacles, challenges, and defeats have destructive effects. But they can also alert us to things that have been here all along but unnoticed—questions unasked and unanswered, tasks neglected, responsibilities evaded, problems unsolved. The suffering will not stop unless we stop it. Doing so requires knowing the work we want our work to do: mobilizing mass social movements in the face of the forces working relentlessly to make the market the center of the social world—forces that incite relatively powerless people to channel their frustrations and anger into orgies of vituperation and acts of violence against even less powerful racialized and otherwise demonized "others."

Under these conditions, many will wish to make ethnic studies a locus of safety, sanctuary, and security. They envision spaces made pleasant, predictable, and problem free through trigger warnings, bans on offensive words, and recognition of and remediation for individual and collective trauma. Practices of self-care and self-love will be appealing responses to wounds and injuries. Some will seek solace in private worlds walled off (at least temporarily) from the crises outside. These are understandable desires and they can achieve some short-run successes. The depths and dimensions of the current crises, however, ultimately allow for no private and personal escapes from collective problems. As Gloria Anzaldúa reminds us, there are no safe spaces.

"Staying 'home' and not venturing out from our own group comes from woundedness, and stagnates our growth," she explains.[4] Of course, home can sometimes be a base for action and connection. Bedridden people and others with limited ability to venture outside the home can do care work for themselves and others without having to leave their dwellings. Whatever levels of mobility people possess, activism can be a great equalizer. But things that are terribly messed up outside the home cannot be made right solely by actions inside it.

The forces arrayed against social justice have emerged from the systemic breakdown of central social institutions, from problems that those in power will not and cannot solve. A process has been set in motion that portends a future filled with a whole lot of folly that will break many hearts. While it would be a grave error to underestimate the magnitude of the hate, hurt, fear, contempt, and cruelty that lies ahead, it would be equally wrong to minimize the significance of the mass mobilizations, collective organizations, and personal transformations that have taken place over the past two decades that evidence strong desires for profound changes. The defenders of white supremacy's power and privileges are correct to see these mobilizations and their connections to ethnic studies and autonomous learning circles as threats to the practices that use difference as an excuse for domination. White supremacists worry that students taught the true history and current contours of the racial order might become disloyal to racial capitalism. They fear that expressions of gender and sexual nonconformity threaten patriarchal power and its policing of identity and desire. They turn to calculated cruelty to protect their privileges and intimidate those who might challenge them. They direct ridicule and contempt toward disabled people. They punish and persecute hardworking immigrants whose labor augments the wealth of those who hate them. They deny reproductive rights to women, endangering their health in order to make them dependent, deferential, and homebound. They stoke rage and violence against despised others at home and abroad to provide affective reparations for all that has been lost economically and socially by the plunder perpetuated by neoliberal racial capitalism.

The ethnic studies project and larger antiracist social formations have not soared from victory to victory. But neither have they suffered a simple succession of irretrievable losses. Some victories have been illusory and transitory. Some defeats have provoked responses that in the long run led to victories. As documented throughout this book, the battle under way is far from over. Both what Walter Benjamin calls the "tradition of the oppressed" and what Cedric Robinson names as "the collective consciousness informed by the historical struggles for liberation" teach us that the survival strategies of aggrieved groups contain powerful and generative repertoires of embodied memory and repositories and archives of effective study and struggle.[5] These can serve as sources of moral and political instruction and provide ways of calling communities into being through performance and oppositional activism. They teach skills for mining and expanding archives, imaginaries, epistemologies, and ontologies that enhance the present, revisit the past, and enable the fight for fulfilled futures.

Because we will be perpetually attacked, it will be necessary to be ready always to fight back. But knowing whom to fight, how to fight, when to fight, where to fight, and why to fight are not simple matters. Kalamu ya Salaam describes fighting the oppressors and the exploiters as a necessary but insufficient practice. "The real battle," he maintains, "is to improve ourselves and to make the world a better place." He warns against falling in love with fighting, because that hinders recognizing that actualizing love for one another should be "the ultimate goal, the organizing principle, and the guide for when and how to fight."[6] Similarly, Irene Lara concedes that healing the wounds of oppression requires being engaged in perpetual struggle against the hauntings of the past, battling what she calls the "shadow beasts": the spirits, forces, memories, and injuries that induce anxiety, shame, and depression. Lara explains, however, that while "standing in rigid opposition" can be a strategy for survival, it has also been a stance "that has killed us and will continue to sever our souls and assail our hearts."[7]

Negotiating contradictions requires a "both/and" rather than an "either/or" perspective. Profound tactical, moral, and intellectual challenges arise when people try to envision how to engage in battle constantly without falling in love with fighting, how to stand in rigid opposition but not become defined by their enemies' actions. Avery Gordon proposes that people who face domination because they are perceived as different need to live "in difference," to inhabit *partially* the dominant culture's social systems and negative ascriptions. This means understanding that the institutions, structures, and systems we encounter were not designed for us, not intended to serve our needs. Gordon asserts that being *in difference* also entails *becoming indifferent* to the psychic and material incentives that ask us to fit in and succeed by standards that are not our own. She declares, "To be in-difference is to refuse to be intoxicated with the deathly, to stop loving that which you claim to despise."[8] Living in difference and becoming tactically indifferent to power (albeit without losing sight of its destructive effects) helps cultivate what Gordon calls the necessity to "practice freedom in preparation for collective self-governance."[9] This practice of freedom is difficult, Gordon concedes, but she describes it as also joyous, "for it is, in short, the process by which we do the work of making revolution irresistible, making it something we cannot live without."[10]

THE CURRENT CRISIS

I have been making public presentations at professional conferences, campus colloquia, and community forums for more than fifty years. Since the killing of Trayvon Martin in 2012, every single session has been punctuated by the need to respond to a new atrocity perpetrated against aggrieved communities. One unprosecuted police murder follows another. Each court decision voiding civil rights and reproductive rights sets the stage for the next one. Every deployment of drone strikes, bombings, and armed occupations leads to another. The rise to prominence of one expressly and vulgarly racist politician or celebrity becomes only a rehearsal for even worse ascendancies in the future. Depictions of asylum seekers fleeing violence and poverty as an invading army lead to unleashing thuggery against people who look foreign by masked Border Patrol and ICE agents who refuse to identify themselves and claim they do not need warrants to detain, brutalize, kidnap, and deport immigrants, even those with legal status and no hint of a criminal record. Emergencies no longer qualify as states of exception when they become the norm. As Brian D. Lozenski observes, the very word *crisis* connotes a temporary problem rather than a long-term structural imbalance.

The crossroads we face at the present moment resembles the one that motivated James Russell Lowell in 1845 to write his poem "The Present Crisis." Written at a time when the slaveocracy controlled all three branches of government (Congress, the courts, and the presidency) and in response to the war against Mexico designed to expand both the slave system and the empire, the poem portrays a world with "truth forever on the scaffold" and "wrong forever on the throne." The scaffold is where executions take place and lives are snuffed out. The throne is the place that symbolizes state power and enables it to exercise its will and whims unhampered. The "forevers" in Lowell's opus evoke the permanence rather than the transience of states of exception and emergency. The lines of the poem that follow, however, express radical hope: "Yet that scaffold sways the future," Lowell writes, adding, "Behind the dim unknown stands God, Within the shadow keeping watch above his own."[11]

Fourteen years later, the slave system seemed stronger than ever. In October 1859, US marines led by Colonel Robert E. Lee captured John Brown at Harper's Ferry, where Brown had raided a federal arsenal as part of an attempt to foment an armed uprising against slavery. In December, John Brown's body swayed from the scaffold. His execution was widely celebrated. Nearly all prominent politicians, journalists, preachers, and teachers condemned him as a traitor while hailing Lee as a hero. Just four years later, however, in 1863, when white people in the North and South were at war against each other with neither side winning, President Lincoln issued the Emancipation Proclamation in a desperate attempt to cripple the Confederacy and aid the failing fortunes of the Union Army. At that moment, Black people knew what to do. Nearly two hundred thousand of them joined the military forces of the Union, which sorely needed their services, and another one million staged a general strike in the fields, crippling the slaveholders' economy. Their self-activity transformed a war effort designed to preserve the Union into a war for the abolition of slavery.[12]

White people in 1863 went into battle singing songs that changed John Brown from a traitor to a martyred hero, while Robert E. Lee became depicted as the traitor. The tide of history turned because some of what had not yet been seen in 1845 and 1859 became visible through collective actions of Black people and their impact on the wider society. Beneath the surface, behind the scenes, and beyond the disciplinary purview of white supremacy, enslaved Africans over centuries nurtured and sustained an infrastructure that would one day bring them freedom. Despite their darkest moments of despair they forged solidarity and mutual recognition and respect through resisting labor exploitation, offering assistance to those fleeing to freedom, asserting their rights to be free through covert lyrics in hymns, affirming their love of life and each other in midnight revels in brush arbors, and blending African cosmologies with particular interpretations of Christianity's claim of Jesus coming into the world to make one blood of all nations.[13] The scaffold where John Brown's body swayed also swayed the future because of actions, events, intentions, and inventions that came before and continued afterwards. Those actions resonated with another passage in Lowell's poem, the part that reads, "When a deed is done for Freedom, through the broad earth's aching breast, Runs a thrill of joy prophetic, trembling on from east to west."

Just because in one instance a dark moment of despair turned out to be a first moment of victory does not mean that it will happen again. But it does show that it is possible. Injuries that portended unlivable destinies and required radical responses have shaped other turning points in history, such as the general strike of 1934 that launched the CIO culture of unity, the Montgomery Bus Boycott of 1955–1956 that marked a key stage in the emergence of a modern civil rights movement, and the mass mobilization on behalf of Black lives in 2020. When the moment was propitious, long-suppressed and subordinated people were ready to act. In our present moment of "truth forever on the scaffold" and "wrong forever on the throne," we need to do what we can to make ourselves and others ready. If you can be ready, Stokely Carmichael used to say, you don't have to get ready. There was something before the current crises and there will be something after it.

In an era when hearts are broken and folly runs rampant, principled people can succumb to despair. Michel-Rolph Trouillot describes the academy's propensity to embrace intellectual moods of malaise and shock as evidence of the destructive practice of viewing preexisting power relations and their regulations as immutable and taken for granted.[14] Yet if freed from the delusions that come from subordinate inclusion, participants in ethnic studies can create, embrace, and offer lessons about living *within* but also *against* systems of domination, which despite all their power, as Gordon argues, "never quite overtake or become us."[15]

The malaise is not a mirage. It is a response to decidedly dire conditions. The systemic crises confronting the economy and the environment, the demise of putatively democratic norms and institutions, and the warfare that creates ever-increasing numbers of migrants, exiles, and refugees evidence a world unraveling at the seams. Yet the traditions of the oppressed teach us that what relatively privileged people see as a state of emergency has been the normal condition of life for the global majority.

THE CROSSROADS AND THE CADUCEUS

The social formation that exists today differs markedly from the one during the years when ethnic studies began. Deindustrialization, automation, privatization, outsourcing, and economic restructuring make production, products, people, and capital move rapidly around the world. Climate change, environmental destruction, wars without end, and artificially imposed austerity make vast numbers of people become migrants, refugees, and exiles. Revanchist racism and right-wing authoritarianism in the US and around the world increase state investments in policing, incarceration, and warfare while also fueling state cutbacks in support of the social wage. In the US context where so many ethnic studies initiatives have been launched, the age of repudiation produces fewer concessions to—but more constraints on—aggrieved social groups.

As delineated in chapter 2, colleges and universities are increasingly surrendering decision-making to wealthy funders and members of their boards of directors on a wide range of issues. Rashid Khalidi captures accurately the relationship between the changing nature of higher education institutions and the diminishing conditions of possibility for academic studies of race and other social identities. He finds himself both "disgusted and horrified by the way higher education has developed into a cash register—essentially a money making, MBA, lawyer-run, hedge fund-cum-real estate operation, with a minor sideline in education, where money has determined everything, where respect for pedagogy is at a minimum."[16] University leaders, with sparse exceptions, comply meekly to demands by legislators and pressure groups to repress dissent forcibly, to criminalize ideas about structural racism, to outlaw actions such as the encampments protesting the mass slaughter of civilians in Gaza, and even to turn over key decisions about admissions, curriculum, and research to government officials and outside pressure groups. Prodded by politicians and members of their boards of trustees, educational administrators now deem it "antisemitism" to protest in public or even speak out against the illegal and immoral policies of the Israeli government.

Like the corporations whose representatives dominate higher education boards of directors and regents, colleges and universities will still need to give at least the appearance of not being overtly racist in this multicultural, multinational, and multiracial world. They will announce themselves as allies in the struggle for social justice and present a plethora of press releases proclaiming that position as proof. Yet what they *practice* speaks louder than what they *preach*. Ethnic studies will not disappear, but powerful forces will seek to ensure that it is watered down, its critiques muted, its incorporation more carefully monitored and managed. Higher education will remain what it has long been: an exclusionary managerial institution set up to produce research and researchers who can administer the existing social order efficiently and profitably. The funding that will flow relatively freely for ethnic studies will go to initiatives that promise more pleasant race relations, but not for those that pursue racial justice. Under those conditions, ethnic studies departments, programs, teachers, students, and student affairs counselors and advisers will find themselves increasingly pressured to embrace the individualist racial interest model, to focus on difference but not domination, to talk about prejudice but not about power. The unraveling of the ethnic studies compromise marks the present moment as a time of radical conjuncture suffused with both peril and promise.

Attempts to demonize and destroy the worthy work carried out inside and attendant to ethnic studies and related projects inside K-12 and college education do not occur in isolation. They emanate from the broader social agenda of what the Ejército Zapatista de Liberación de Nacional (EZLN) in Mexico calls the Fourth World War, from policies that portend and produce endless war, economic austerity, environmental destruction, and perpetual displacement. This agenda seeks to reverse the gains secured by past social movements—to make the courts, the schools, the professions, the political process, and the patterns of everyday life conform to the market-centered imperatives of neoliberalism. The people with the most wealth and power seek to make the least powerful and most vulnerable populations bear the harshest burdens of these changes.

Questions about how or even whether ethnic studies will survive need to asked and answered in the context of how or even whether all the people designated as other and therefore targeted for domination will survive. Toni Cade Bambara advises paying attention to the action and not the institution, not confusing the vehicle with the objective, and recognizing that all cocoons are temporary. Ethnic studies is *an institution*, not *the action*. It is *the vehicle*, not *the objective*. Its success or failure does not rest on its place within the corporate academy, the corporate media, or the corporate political system. It needs to be judged by the work it does in the world, by the things it enables, by its identity as a cocoon that nurtures practices augmenting the potential for building a morally just world.

In a snapshot, a sunrise and a sunset can look exactly the same. It is possible to view the current state of ethnic studies as *either* a sunrise *or* a sunset. This book documents emergent and ascendant practices filled with promise. The educators teaching the true history and enduring presence of racism in US society discussed in chapter 1 and the faculty members, students, and staff personnel described in chapter 2 are fighting back against the incorporation of education, offering convivial cocreation of communities of solidarity as an antidote to the poisonous divisions forged by forces seeking to use difference as an excuse for domination. The autonomous learning circles described in chapter 3 and the social movement and scholarly challenges to normative policing of race, sexuality, gender, disability, and place discussed in chapter 4 cultivate new social relations, archives, and repertoires, develop new imaginaries and actions, and offer alternatives to the calculated cruelty and callous competition fomented by neoliberal racial capitalism. The scholars described in chapter 5 challenge the centrality of the savage slot to Western knowledge regimes and forge new, true, and useful critiques of the ways in which the disciplines disaggregate knowledge and assign aggrieved groups to separate slots.

The ethnic studies project and the broader antiracist formation to which it is attached stand as primary targets for the folly that is fascism. That means a future filled with broken hearts, but it also means that there are many sites where important work can be done and needs to be done. At the crossroads, poison can become medicine, broken hearts can be mended, and folly can be foiled. It may well be that ethnic studies will not survive in its present form, that the forces of incorporation, co-optation, and overt repression and suppression will make it part of the system it was formed to contest.

This pattern of a temporary settlement dissolving into incorporation and co-optation has plagued oppositional social movement formations in the past. During the 1930s the labor movement became an unexpected crucible for the creation of new democratic practices, processes, and institutions. Forged in response to the suffering caused by business domination of government, a decade of violence and repression aimed at immigrants and their children, and the conservatism and complicity of leaders of the American Federation of Labor, workers mobilized by the Congress of Industrial Organizations launched organizing drives, staged sit-ins in factories, and waged general strikes in society. They expanded the sphere of politics by using the shop floor as a locus for the kinds of democratic deliberation and decision-making denied to them in electoral politics.[17] They fused together a culture of unity that repositioned immigrants and their children from being seen as unwanted aliens into claiming rights as redemptive saviors of the American dream.

Some of the victories won by the 1930s culture of unity persist to this day, but others were contained and reversed by a mixture of co-optation and repression. Leaders of business and government became willing to let labor leaders act as junior partners in managing the economy as long as they became incorporated into the goals of management, limiting their demands to pay raises and augmented health care benefits for already-employed workers, not fighting for workers' control at the point of production or for universal government health care and pensions. In order to secure concessions they had to abandon much of what had supplied them with bargaining leverage in the first place: resisting management practices at the point of production, enacting solidarity across job sites and industries through sympathy strikes and general strikes, and demanding gains not just for company employees but for the whole working class by tying wage increases to reductions in the prices of the goods produced and spreading benefits through universal reforms like the eight-hour day.

The labor movement has not disappeared. Fights to raise the minimum wage and to organize the unorganized continue to this day, but the labor movement is no longer the key locus of democratic aspirations that it was in the 1930s and 1940s. The union movement still largely refuses to organize the unorganized, offer political education to its membership, fight for universal social benefits, or help mobilize an active and engaged public sphere constituency for justice. The police officers who gun down and brutalize Black people and the firefighters who deny membership and harass their Black colleagues are union members. Pipeline workers belonging to unions crossed the picket lines set up by Indigenous water protectors in North Dakota in 2016 and took no action when police officers and National Guard troops used military-grade weapons to punish, humiliate, and torture defenders of treaty rights.

The civil rights movement of the 1960s followed a similar trajectory. Trade unions' abandonment of fights for social justice and the general social wage set the stage for the Black freedom movement and attendant mobilizations on behalf of new democratic practices, processes, and institutions. Displacements of rural workers to cities because of government subsidies to mechanize farm labor on plantations, US opposition to land reform in the global South, urban renewal policies that destroyed hundreds of Black neighborhoods, massive resistance to implementing the desegregation mandates of the *Brown v. Board of Education* decision, and the early impacts of disinvestment, capital flight, and automation on assembly-line workers created the preconditions for the racial justice movements of the mid-twentieth century. In the course of fighting for fair access to education, jobs, and schooling and seeking to win self-governance and economic self-sufficiency, Black people and members of other racialized groups established themselves as an aggrieved and insurgent polity. They developed new forms of participatory democracy inside activist and community organizations, relying on the participation of the entire population rather than delegating change to elected officials and social movement organization leaders. Much as the labor movement instigated what Michael Denning calls "the laboring of American culture"—a transformation of national values and norms rooted in valuing the labor of common people, asserting their dignity and worth, and expanding opportunity for those previously excluded from full social membership—the antiracist activists of the 1960s initiated a radical revolution in values grounded in the ideal that the Mississippi Black freedom movement called "a beloved community"—one characterized by mutual respect, recognition, responsibility, and accountability.[18]

As with the labor movement of the 1930s and 1940s, victories won by the racial freedom struggles of the 1950s and 1960s persist to this day. What the labor movement achieved in transforming understanding and institutional accommodation to ethnic difference and the dignity of labor, the civil rights and freedom movements succeeded in winning for the roles of race and popular participation. Yet once again, co-optation, repression, and economic restructuring combined to moderate and water down the most oppositional elements of the movement. Racial liberalism's responses to the antiracist challenges posed by mass mobilizations revolved around allowing a few dark faces in high places, primarily through election to political positions in gerrymandered districts and cities with disintegrating infrastructures, appointment of individuals to highly visible but often powerless bureaucratic offices, and celebrations of famous firsts—the first Black astronaut, the first Black chairman of the Joint Chiefs of Staff, the first Black golf or tennis champion, or the first Black president—as evidence of the generosity of the system rather than proof of long histories of shameful exclusion. Entry of members of racialized groups into long-denied positions on assembly lines occurred at the precise moment when automation and capital flight made those jobs less remunerative and less stable. Election to municipal political offices coincided with termination of federal aid to cities and tax "reforms" that drained localities of previously secure sources of revenue. Limited entry into opportunities for housing took place in the midst of predatory and fraudulent mortgage lending, followed by takeover of large numbers of housing units by private equity firms. Reductions in government spending targeted the programs most important to aggrieved racialized communities, while reductions in taxes on income, capital gains, and property for the wealthy led to onerous increases in sales taxes and user fees for workers.

Direct repression and co-optation also shaped the influence and impact of the antiracist movements of the mid-twentieth century. Leaders seen as too bold in their condemnations of white supremacy—Medgar Evers, Malcolm X, Martin Luther King, Fred Hampton, and dozens of others—were assassinated. Pressured by donors, government agencies, and elected officials, civil rights organizations abandoned their mass bases and tactics of direct action and embraced lobbying and deal making behind closed doors. Like the labor movement, these organizations continue to have visibility, impact, and influence, but they no longer serve as crucibles for the radical revolution in values that Dr. King identified as the key goal of the movement. The major civil rights organizations did little to mobilize the masses into social movements but used their institutional positions to support politicians including Bill Clinton, Barack Obama, and Joe Biden, who ended welfare and public housing, supported the deregulation responsible for the largest loss in history of assets in Black and Brown households, and enthusiastically promoted the militarization of the police.

The void left in society by the co-optation and incorporation of the labor and civil rights movements helps explain the founding of ethnic studies and the dramatic momentum it achieved in the first decades of the twenty-first century. Many participants in ethnic studies and in education and autonomous learning circles maintained membership in or ties to the labor and civil rights movements, but these were no longer their primary sites for action. One of the seeming disadvantages of ethnic studies—its identity as more of an ungainly force field than a centrally located institution or universally agreed-upon doctrine—provided the advantages of being able to generate constantly new improvisations and inventions honed from local circumstances yet applicable elsewhere. The sobering lesson to be learned from the labor and civil rights movements is that projects and formations are vulnerable to incorporation and co-optation and capable of being crushed by repression. The encouraging lesson generated by the history of those movements, however, is that, as William Cullen Bryant proclaimed, "truth crushed to earth will rise again."[19] The suppression of the institution does not mean the end of the action. Destruction of the vehicle need not obliterate the objective. Cocoons offer protection, but eventually life depends on leaving them behind.

At the crossroads the right thing can look like the wrong thing and the right thing can look like the wrong thing. This society conditions people to view victories and defeats as clear and evident incommensurable opposites, to glory in victory and be ashamed by defeat. Yet apparent victories can be ephemeral, transitory, and limited in their actual impact, while defeats can produce responses that lead to eventual victories. Actions intended to suppress dissent and revolt can become the sparks that ignite them. Radical oppositional conjunctures offer opportunities for the oppressed to turn hegemony on its head.[20] In 1927 the State of Massachusetts executed Italian migrants Nicola Sacco and Bartolomeo Vanzetti, who were convicted of robbery and murder on the basis of questionable and flimsy evidence. The criminal charges, convictions, and punishments appeared to many as an orchestrated spectacle aimed at Sacco and Vanzetti because they were radical anarchist immigrants whose ideas and actions threatened both capital and the state. The prosecution and executions of Sacco and Vanzetti were intended to promote public panic about dangerous aliens. Their deaths were designed to intimidate and silence all those who might agree with the radicals.

The questionable nature of the evidence brought against the defendants, however, and the vicious anti-immigrant prejudice driving their prosecution made the proceedings appear illegitimate, even to many who opposed anarchist politics. The nativism that characterized the prosecution of the case and publicity about it made it seem like part of an Anglo-Protestant crusade against all immigrants and their children. The injustice perpetrated against Sacco and Vanzetti encapsulated, distilled, and crystallized a wide range of prior injuries inflicted on migrants. These included the histories of attacks on "hyphenated Americans" and foreign-language use during World War I, the prison sentences and deportations emanating from the Palmer raids and repression directed against the Industrial Workers of the World and the Socialist Party, the anti-Catholicism and antisemitism of the Ku Klux Klan, and the provisions designed to end legal migration from southern and eastern Europe written into the 1924 Johnson-Reed Act. The resentments and anger generated by this history simmered beneath the surface until August 23, 1927, when the execution of Sacco and Vanzetti moved millions to protest in the streets and mobilize in what evolved into the labor movement's culture of unity in the 1930s.

The spectacle of the execution of Sacco and Vanzetti was designed as a public pedagogy, as an intimidating action that would produce docile and tractable subjects with no choice but to knuckle under to Anglo-Protestant domination. Instead of producing submission, however, the executions provoked people of diverse ethnicities into new forms of action. People who had been bystanders decided to act as upstanders.

They built an oppositional culture of unity grounded in celebrating the multilingual and multinational character of the nation. They portrayed migrants and their children, not as undeserving and unwanted outsiders, but as redemptive insiders, people who had become American by choice and therefore were ideally suited to represent, reform, and redeem the nation's democratic promises. Their work in labor unions, cultural institutions, and political parties set in motion dynamics in the national culture that lasted for decades. They made it legitimate and desirable to celebrate ethnic diversity, to honor the labor of workers, and to institute egalitarian and democratic reforms in the property system.[21]

Another moment of radical oppositional conjuncture appeared in June 1963 in Winona, Mississippi, when five white law enforcement officers ordered two black inmates in the local jail to beat Black activist Fannie Lou Hamer savagely and repeatedly. At one point, one of the excited and sexually aroused white overseers directly joined in the violence as well. Mrs. Hamer was returning to her home from a voter registration conference in South Carolina. The members of the group with which she was traveling were all arrested when their bus stopped outside Staley's cafe in Winona. The brutality that followed in the jailhouse against Mrs. Hamer and the other members of her group was orchestrated to silence the voices of people like her fighting for their freedom.

This project of silencing continued even after the beating. Six months after the incident the Department of Justice brought five white officers to trial, charging them with violating the civil rights of those they had brutalized in the jail. Despite Mrs. Hamer's eloquent testimony, an all-white jury declared all of the defendants to be not guilty after deliberating for only a little more than an hour. Yet rather than accept being silenced, Mrs. Hamer used the incident and the exculpation of its perpetrators as a platform from which to speak out again and again for the rest of her life. She spoke about the Winona beating in her nationally televised testimony before the Democratic Party Presidential Nominating Convention in 1964, at many civil rights rallies and mass meetings, in an appearance with Malcolm X at a church in Harlem, in testimony at congressional committee hearings, and in speeches before college audiences and community groups all across the nation. Hamer turned the humiliating experience of the beating into a badge of honor, transforming the mechanism designed to make her shut up once and for all into an impetus to speak out loudly, boldly, and repeatedly. Mrs. Hamer's speeches made Winona famous as the site of the beating. Those who intended to disgrace her only wound up disgracing their city and themselves. The people who were supposed to be intimidated into silent acceptance of injustice by the beating and others like it used the event as a way to amplify their voices, turning their oppressors into unwitting accomplices in their mobilization for liberation.[22]

Like the executions of Sacco and Vanzetti, the beating of Fannie Lou Hamer in Winona encapsulated, distilled, and crystallized a long history. Her status as a plantation timekeeper with little formal education, and her identity as a heavyset dark-skinned woman who sang gospel songs and spoke eloquently and powerfully with a southern accent, made her seem like a perfect representative of other silenced, shunned, segregated, and suffering people. As Chana Kai Lee delineates in her biography of Hamer, the life of the activist had long been marred by acts of white violence, sexist abuse, disability, poverty, and reproductive injustice. Yet Mrs. Hamer's willingness to speak out was political as well as personal, a manifestation of collective resentment among Black people against the racial dictatorship that had injured them again and again, most prominently and visibly perhaps in the gang rape of Recy Taylor, the lynching of Emmet Till, and the murder of Medgar Evers. Operating in a context where legal remedies were not available and armed insurrection would most likely have been futile, Hamer turned hegemony on its head, using the attempt to silence her voice as an invitation and impetus to use that voice as her prime vehicle for inciting opposition.

The executions of Sacco and Vanzetti and the beating of Fannie Lou Hamer marked moments of radical oppositional conjuncture. They evidence how the seeming success of repression unwittingly can set the stage for new forms of resistance and opposition, how the caduceus at the crossroads enables people to turn defeat into victory. The CIA coups in Guatemala and Iran in 1954 ushered in a new era of imperial dominance by the US but at the same time convinced a generation of young Latin Americans (including Che Guevara) to become revolutionaries. The passage of the anti-immigrant Proposition 187 in California fueled the reelection of Republican governor Pete Wilson and the election of a wave of anti-immigrant candidates but set in motion the forces that marginalized the state's Republican Party for decades and led to legislation that helped protect immigrants and promote declarations of sanctuary.[23]

Moments like these appear in clear relief today. In the US during the past decade, seemingly isolated incidents have repeatedly encapsulated, distilled, and crystallized long histories. The killings of George Floyd and Breonna Taylor in 2020 evoked the recent histories of anti-Black violence embodied in the impunity granted to the killers of Trayvon Martin, Rekia Boyd, Michael Brown, Eric Garner, and Sandra Bland, among others. The Floyd killing also took place in the context of other highly public acts of disregard for the lives of people of color, from the caging of children and the separating of families seeking asylum at the southern US border to the cruel and callous disregard of mass sufferings caused by hurricane damage in Puerto Rico and the COVID-19 pandemic nationwide. Each of these incidents enacted collective injuries too severe to be evaded or excused. They served as symbols of seemingly unsolvable crises and exposed vividly the meanness, mendacity, calculation, and cruelty of the rich and powerful. They discredited the legitimacy of the academic, political, and journalistic "experts" who championed the status quo.

The future of ethnic studies will be shaped in part by decisions made at the crossroads. Decisions that can promote opposition can also lead to incorporation, co-optation, and repression. Seeming defeats may set the stage for future victories. The fate of the ethnic studies project and the broader liberation formation does not lie solely—or even primarily—with its enemies. We do not have to resign ourselves to being passive spectators to or victims of the predations of power. As the lyrics of a Bobby Womack–authored song recorded in 1966 by Wilson Pickett assert, the world we live in is made by people. It is shaped by many things beyond our control, but also by the ways we live and the things we give, the cries we hear and those we ignore, the people we help and the ones we hurt.

The ongoing racist apocalypse that we have faced—and can expect to face for the foreseeable future—has affinities with the description of the climate crisis formulated by artist Lisa Hirmer. In the text accompanying her installation and performance work *Weather Watcher,* Hirmer writes that climate change feels like something in the atmosphere beyond our control, not yet fully here but still signaling that something is deeply and troublingly wrong. We are not mere spectators to—or victims of—climate change, Hirmer argues. The atmosphere is a partly a register of the consequences of centuries of human action and inaction. We help create the atmosphere through the choices we make about production, consumption, extraction, and investment.[24] Similarly the racial order is not an immutable external force but something we help shape through our deeds of commission and omission. Participation in social movements does more than *react* to the way the world is: It helps *shape* that world. As Robin Kelley explains, "If we are ever going to defeat fascism—entirely—we need more than sound scholarship; we have to be aligned with a strong and united movement that thinks beyond nation. We need to embrace decolonization and the principles of caretaking and creating just relations between human and other-than-human worlds on a planet devastated by capitalism."[25]

The current crisis is both new and old. The epistemologies of the crossroads and the caduceus illuminate how each of the inspiring practices and hopeful signs described in chapters 1 through 5 came about in response to detestable practices and conditions. The beauty of ethnic studies rests in its responses to—and transformations of—harsh and ugly intersectional realities: mass murder and Indigenous displacement and dispossession, slavery unwilling to die, coloniality in perpetuity, religious bigotry, labor exploitation, predatory policing, environmental racism, misogyny, homophobia, transphobia, disability designation and discrimination, and many other forms of using difference to institute and justify domination. The epistemologies of the crossroads and the caduceus teach us that evil cannot be avoided but can be inverted, subverted, and countered. We cannot purge ourselves of our contradictions, but we can use them creatively to pave a path to different worlds.

There may come a time when ethnic studies is no longer the appropriate vehicle for the objective of creating a morally just world. It may happen that the institution gets in the way of the action. The cocoon that has protected many may no longer protect any. But not everything is ephemeral. In their 1957 version of "Love Is Here to Stay," a song composed in 1938 by George and Ira Gershwin, Ella Fitzgerald and Louis Armstrong sing about the relationship between stasis and change. With their unique and incomparable artistry, the singers present a list of things central to their present lives but not guaranteed to be eternal. They sing that the movies, the radio, the telephone, and other things they know might just be passing fancies that at one point will have had their day. Fitzgerald and Armstrong play with the Gershwin brothers' rhyme of the possibility that one day the Rocky Mountains may crumble and the Rock of Gibraltar may tumble because they are just made of clay. For all this susceptibility to change, however, the song insists that love is here to stay. Ethnic studies and related projects and formations are expressions of love—love of the people and love for the people. There is no way to gauge accurately its prospects for longevity. But come what may, our love is here to stay.

Acknowledgments

I am deeply grateful to all the people whose comments, criticisms, questions, and conversations helped me in writing this book. It began with a suggestion by Niels Hooper of the University of California Press that a volume like this might speak honorably to the crises and opportunities of our time. Working with Niels and my coeditors of the American Crossroads series—George Sanchez, Laura Briggs, and Nikhil Pal Singh—has kept me in touch with many different versions of antiracist study and struggle. Once again I am grateful for the sharp eyes, astute critical judgments, and mastery of language that copyeditor Elisabeth Magnus applied to this volume, I am grateful as well for the helpful critiques contained in the anonymous readers' reports.

In preparing this book, I learned a great deal from workshops hosted by Jonathan Gomez, Jordan T. Camp, and Christina Heatherton that placed me in conversation with Jessica Bissett Perea, Arlene Davila, J. V. Decemvirale, Nan Enstad, Roderick A. Ferguson, Diane Fujino, Lorgia Garcia-Peña, Alexandra Gessesse, Jennifer Hamer, Annie Hikido, Johari Jabir, Jasmine Kelekay, Clarence Lang, Jorge Lopez-Ramirez, Neda Maghbouleh, John-Carlos Perea, Gina Pérez, Sarah Rios, Ana Rosas, Marisa Salinas, Yehuda Sharim, and Julie Sze.

Correspondence about specific sections of the book offered me the gift of drawing on the expertise of Rosanna Esparza Ahrens, Rick Bonus, Manolo Callahan, Ofelia Esparza, Quetzal Flores, May Fu, Martha Gonzalez, Lisa Hirmer, Daniel HoSang, Talila A. Lewis, Elizabeth McAlister, Jerome Morgan, Sunni Patterson, Juliana Hu Pegues, Omar G. Ramirez, Jim Randels, Chandra Russo, Susan Schweik, Young Shin, Lawrence LaFountain Stokes, Diana Taylor, and Sherrie Tucker.

The mutually constitutive and reinforcing qualities of study and struggle have been brought home to me through participation in social movement mobilizations by the African American Policy Forum, the National Fair Housing

Alliance, Asian Immigrant Women Advocates, Building Healthy Communities in Boyle Heights, the Cultural Work of Poetry Project, and the International Institute for Critical Studies in Improvisation.

Many thanks to Ricardo Levins Morales for his artistry and activism and for letting me use the poster *Volcano* as cover art. Parts of the chapters in this book appeared previously in "FandangObon: Amplification, Counter-publics, and Fugitive Spaces of Belonging in Los Angeles," *American Anthropologist* 126, no. 2 (June 2024): 260–70; "Rejecting the Racial Contract: Charles Mills and Critical Race Theory," *Race Ethnicity and Education* 26, no. 4 (May 2023): 533–52; "Shattering Silences: Dictions, Contradictions, and Ethnic Studies at the Crossroads," *Kalfou* 7, no. 2 (Fall 2020): 222–48; "*The White Possessive* and Whiteness Studies," *Kalfou* 6, no. 1 (Spring 2019): 42–51; "No Ordinary Time: Indigenous Dispossession and Slavery Unwilling to Die," *Kalfou* 5, no. 2 (Fall 2018): 223-31; and "Theorizing Liberation and Liberating Theory: Learning from Gary Okihiro," *Journal of Asian American Studies* 28, no. 1 (February 2025): 11–26. They appear here by permission of the journals in which they were published.

The work that I do has been guided at every step for decades by the accompaniment, inspiration, intelligence, and integrity of Robin D. G. Kelley and Tricia Rose. This book is dedicated to them in honor of the trails they have blazed, the battles they have fought and won, and the love of the people that informs all of their writing, teaching, and activism.

Everything I write, say, and do is enhanced by the presence in my life of Barbara Tomlinson, by her wisdom, discernment, and encouragement. Learning from her and with her continues to a source of great joy and inspiration.

George Lipsitz
August 2025

Notes

INTRODUCTION: ETHNIC STUDIES AT THE CROSSROADS

1. Eduardo Galeano, *Upside Down: A Primer for the Looking Glass World* (Henry Holt, 2000), 8.

2. Daniel Martinez HoSang, *A Wider Type of Freedom: How Struggles for Racial Justice Liberate Everyone* (University of California Press, 2021), 13.

3. Destin Jenkins, *The Bonds of Inequality: Debt and the Making of the American City* (University of Chicago Press, 2021); Andrew Kahrl, *The Black Tax: 150 Years of Theft, Exploitation, and Dispossession in America* (University of Chicago Press, 2024); Louise Seamster, *The Flint Water Coup: Debt at the End of Democracy* (Columbia University Press, forthcoming).

4. My mention of coloniality evokes Anibal Quijano's concept of "the coloniality of power" which argues that conquest and colonialism are both past and ongoing events, and that knowledge formations and social relations around the world remain shaped by a powerful and pervasive matrix of colonial power. See Anibal Quijano, "Coloniality of Power, Eurocentrism and Latin America," *Nepantla: Views from the South* 1, no. 3 (2000): 215–32. The term is not meant to supplant "settler colonialism" or "settler capitalism." In *Incarcerated Stories: Indigenous Women Migrants and Violence in the Settler-Capitalist State* (University of North Carolina Press, 2019), especially 23–24, Shannon Speed emphasizes the importance of recognizing settler logics as the key forces structuring colonial exploitation of Indigenous people in the Western Hemisphere.

5. Gloria E. Anzaldúa, "Now Let Us Shift . . . the Path of Conocimiento . . . Inner Work, Public Acts," in *This Bridge We Call Home: Radical Visions for Transformation*, ed. Gloria E. Anzaldúa and AnaLouise Keating (Routledge, 2002), 541.

6. Racial categories can hide as well as reveal. The Black/Latinx dichotomy leaves out Latinx people who are Black and suppresses understanding of the

multiracial composition of the Latinx population, which includes people who are (among other origins) Asian, Indigenous, and Middle Eastern.

7. Walter Benjamin, "Theses on the Philosophy of History," in *Illuminations: Essays and Reflections* (Shocken Books, 1968), 257.

8. George Lipsitz, *The Danger Zone Is Everywhere: How Housing Discrimination Harms Health and Steals Wealth* (University of California Press, 2024).

9. Robin D.G. Kelley, "Black Study, Black Struggle," *Boston Review*, March 1, 2016, 8.

10. Eduardo Galeano, *The Open Veins of Latin America*, 25th Anniversary Ed. (Monthly Review Press, 1997), 265.

11. Stokely Carmichael (Kwame Ture), "Toward Black Liberation," *Massachusetts Review* 7, no. 4 (1966): 639.

12. Aurora Levins Morales, *The Story of What Is Broken Is Whole: An Aurora Levins Morales Reader* (Duke University Press, 2024), 60.

13. Charles L. Briggs, *Incommunicable: Toward Justice in Health and Medicine* (Duke University Press, 2024); Kimberlé Crenshaw et al., eds., *Critical Race Theory: The Key Writings That Made the Movement* (New Press, 1995); Lipsitz, *Danger Zone Is Everywhere*; Ruth Wilson Gilmore, *Golden Gulag: Prisons, Surplus, Crisis, and Opposition in Globalizing California* (University of California Press, 2007); Michel-Rolph Trouillot, *Global Transformations: Anthropology and the Modern World* (Palgrave Macmillan, 2003); Robin Wall Kimmerer, *Braiding Sweetgrass: Indigenous Wisdom, Scientific Knowledge, and the Teachings of Plants* (Milkweed, 2013); Jessica Bissett Perea, *Sound Relations: Native Ways of Doing Music in Alaska* (Oxford University Press, 2021).

14. Ricardo Levins Morales, *Tending the Soil: Lessons for Organizing*, zine/pamphlet (RLM Art Studio, 2020), 10–11. Thanks to Yarden Katz for alerting me to this source.

15. Gary Y. Okihiro, *Third World Studies: Theorizing Liberation*, 2nd ed., rev. and expanded (Duke University Press, 2024); Charles P. Henry, *Black Studies and the Democratization of American Higher Education* (Palgrave Macmillan, 2017); Roderick A. Ferguson, *The Reorder of Things: The University and Its Pedagogies of Minority Difference* (University of Minnesota Press, 2012); Roderick A. Ferguson, *We Demand: The University and Student Protests* (University of California Press, 2017); Christina G. Mora et al., "How Many Latino Studies Programs Are There? Tracking Departmental Growth, Stagnation, and Invisibility, 1960–2020," *Latino Studies* 21, no. 3 (2023): 388–410; Marc Arsell Robinson, "Black Student Unions to the Gang of Four: Interracial Alliances and Community Organizing from San Francisco to Seattle," *California History* 98, no. 2 (2021): 24–49; Lara Kiswani et al., "Palestine Is Ethnic Studies: The Struggle for Arab American Studies in K-12 Ethnic Studies Curriculum," *Journal of Asian American Studies* 26, no. 2 (June 2023): 221–31.

16. Patricia Zavella, *The Movement for Reproductive Justice: Empowering Women of Color Through Social Activism* (New York University Press, 2020); Tamara Kuennen, "Uncharted Violence: Reclaiming Structural Causes in the Power and Control Wheel," *Arizona State Law Journal* 55, no. 561 (2023): 560–607; Kayla Vasilko, "Dr. Kim Scipes: Building a Network of Compassion in a World Waiting to Be United," *Purdue Journal of Service-Learning and*

International Engagement 9, no. 1 (2022): article 8; Lipsitz, *Danger Zone Is Everywhere*; Angela Steusse, *Scratching Out a Living: Latinos, Race, and Work in the Deep South* (University of California Press, 2016); Emma Shaw Crane, "Lush Aftermath: Race, Labor, and Landscape in the Suburb," *Society and Space* 41, no. 2 (2023): 210–30.

17. Diana Taylor, *!Presente! The Politics of Presence* (Duke University Press, 2020), 143.

18. For links connecting antiracism to parallel and intersecting projects for liberation, see HoSang, *Wider Type of Freedom*; Gary Y. Okihiro, *Margins and Mainstreams: Asians in American History and Culture* (University of Washington Press, 1994); Roderick A. Ferguson, *One-Dimensional Queer* (Polity Press, 2019); Chela Sandoval, *Methodology of the Oppressed* (University of Minnesota Press, 2000).

19. Ferguson, *Reorder of Things*, 186–87.

20. Ferguson, *Reorder of Things*.

21. Justice William O. Douglas, concurring opinion in Jones v. Alfred H. Mayer Co., 392 U.S. 409 (1968).

22. Publications replete with articles attending to these issues include, among others, *Ethnic Studies Review*, *Critical Ethnic Studies*, *Kalfou*, and *Ethnic Studies Pedagogies*.

23. Nina Sun Eidsheim, *The Race of Sound: Listening, Timbre, and Vocality in African American Music* (Duke University Press, 2019).

24. See Richard Lischer, *The Preacher King: Martin Luther King Jr. and the Word That Moved America* (Oxford University Press, 1995), especially 243–66.

25. Elizabeth Rodriguez Fielder, *The Revolution Will Be Improvised: The Intimacy of Cultural Activism* (University of Michigan Press, 2024), 30, 33.

26. Cherríe Moraga, "I Transfer and Go Underground," in *This Bridge Called My Back: Writings by Radical Women of Color*, ed. Cherríe Moraga and Gloria E. Anzaldúa (Kitchen Table: Women of Color Press, 1983), xiv.

27. Janey Lew, "A Politics of Meaning: Reading Intersectional Indigenous Feminist Praxis in Lee Maracle's *Sojourners and Sundogs*," *Frontiers* 38, no. 1 (2017): 225–59.

28. Martha Gonzalez, *Chican@ Artivistas: Music, Community, and Transborder Tactics in East Los Angeles* (University of Texas Press, 2020), 3.

29. Miguel Montiel et al., *Resolana: Emerging Chicano Dialogues on Community and Globalization* (University of Arizona Press, 2009); Walter Rodney, *The Groundings with My Brothers* (Research Associates School Times Publications, 1996).

30. For the sake of accessibility throughout this book I use the dominant term of art *the environment* to describe what is sometimes called the "other than" or "more than" human world. Yet as Aurora Levins Morales points out, decolonial ways of knowing teach us to see that what is called the environment is actually "an intricate, living web of beings, a kinship." Aurora Levins Morales, *Medicine Stories: Essays for Radicals* (Duke University Press, 2019), 16.

31. Diana Taylor, *The Archive and the Repertoire: Performing Cultural Memory in the Americas* (Duke University Press 2003), 16.

32. Martin Luther King Jr., "A Time to Break Silence," in *A Testament of Hope: The Essential Writings and Speeches of Martin Luther King Jr.*, ed. James M. Washington (Harper Collins, 1986), 243.

CHAPTER 1. ETHNIC STUDIES AS OPPOSITION

1. Taylor, *!Presente!*, 2.
2. Charles W. Mills, *The Racial Contract* (Cornell University Press, 1997); Charles W. Mills, *Blackness Visible: Essays on Philosophy and Race* (Cornell University Press, 1999); Charles W. Mills, *Black Rights/White Wrongs: The Crisis of Racial Liberalism* (Oxford University Press, 2017).
3. Roderick A. Ferguson, *Aberrations in Black: Toward a Queer of Color Critique* (University of Minnesota Press, 2004), viii; Anders Walker, "Legislating Virtue: How Segregation Disguised Racial Discrimination as Moral Reform Following *Brown v. Board of Education*," *Duke Law Journal* 47 (1997): 399–418; George Lipsitz, *The Possessive Investment in Whiteness: How White People Profit from Identity Politics* (Temple University Press, 2018).
4. Sara Ahmed, *Queer Phenomenology: Orientations, Objects, Others* (Duke University Press, 2006), 128.
5. Christopher C. Martell et al., "Silent Covenants and Structural Barriers: State Standards Committees and the Maintenance of Race-Evasive Social Studies Standards," *AERA Open* 10, no. 1 (January-December 2024): 1–16.
6. Daniel Martinez HoSang, "Understanding the Role of the Multiracial Right—and Why It Matters," *Public Eye Quarterly* 1 (Summer 2024): 3–6.
7. Peter Hart, "King's Dream Remains Unfilled, Julian Bond Says," *University Times*, April 2, 2003, https://www.utimes.pitt.edu/archives/?p=1241. The durability of Bond's comparison shows the long history of the Democratic Party refusing to stand up for racial justice. Bill Clinton's attack on Sister Souljah in 1992 and his retraction of the appointment of Lani Guinier were designed to present himself as someone who could protect white people from Black analyses of their suffering. He drew on Ronald Reagan's demonization of Black women on welfare by producing the "end of welfare as we know it." Clinton supported legislation that defamed inner-city youths as vicious predators, ended public housing, and deregulated the home mortgage industry. Barack Obama disavowed the claims by his pastor Jeremiah Wright that the US is systematically racist, fired Shirley Sherrod when right-wing attacks lied and portrayed her as antiwhite, and bailed out the perpetrators of mortgage fraud while offering no aid to their victims. Obama incarcerated and deported more immigrants than his predecessor did. Over the objections of Indigenous water protectors, he supported oil pipeline projects that harmed the environment and violated Indigenous sovereignty. Ruth Bader Ginsberg never hired a Black law clerk and stated that NFL player Colin Kaepernick taking a knee during the national anthem to protest police killings of Black people was dumb, disrespectful, and ridiculous. Republicans refused to consider Obama's appointment of Merrick Garland to the Supreme Court, claiming it came a year before the 2016 election (too close to a possible change of government); yet Dianne Feinstein cooperated with Republican efforts to rush confirmation of Amy Coney Barrett to the court a mere few

weeks before the 2020 election, hugging Republican minority chair Lindsay Graham and praising him for conducting one of the best sets of hearings she had participated in. Derek Hyra's *Slow and Sudden Violence: Why and When Uprisings Occur* (University of California Press, 2024) reveals how the housing policies of the Clinton and Obama administrations created the desperate conditions that led to the Ferguson and Baltimore uprisings in 2014 and 2015.

8. Charles W. Mills, "White Time: The Chronic Injustice of Ideal Theory," *Du Bois Review* 11, no. 1 (2014): 27–42.

9. Michael Hanchard, "Afro-Modernity: Temporality, Politics, and the African Diaspora," *Public Culture* 11, no. 1 (1999): 245–68.

10. Charles Mills, *Racial Contract*.

11. Samuel Hoadley-Brill, "Chris Rufo's Critical Race Theory Reporting Is Filled with Errors, and He Doesn't Seem to Care," *Flux*, July 26, 2021; Benjamin Wallace-Wells, "How a Conservative Activist Invented the Conflict over Critical Race Theory," *New Yorker*, June 18, 2021.

12. Sarah Jones, "How to Manufacture a Moral Panic: Christopher Rufo Helped Incite an Uproar over Racism Education with Dramatic, Dodgy Reporting," *New York Magazine*, July 21, 2021.

13. See Cheryl E. Matias and Peter M. Newlove, "The Illusion of Freedom: Tyranny, Whiteness, and the State of U.S. Society," *Equity and Excellence in Education* 50, no. 3 (2017): 316–30.

14. See Cheryl E. Matias, *Feeling White: Whiteness, Emotionality, and Education* (Sense Publishers, 2016).

15. Kimberlé Williams Crenshaw, "Unmasking Colorblindness in the Law: Lessons from the Formation of Critical Race Theory," in *Seeing Race Again: Countering Colorblindness Across the Disciplines*, ed. Kimberlé Williams Crenshaw et al. (University of California Press, 2019); Patricia J. Williams, "*Metro Broadcasting, Inc. v. FCC*: Regrouping in Singular Times," *Harvard Law Review* 104, no. 2 (December 1990): 535–46; Patricia J. Williams, *Seeing a Color-Blind Future: The Paradox of Race* (Farrar, Strauss, and Giroux, 1997); Devon W. Carbado and Mitu Gulati, *Acting White? Rethinking Race in "Postracial" America* (Oxford University Press, 2013).

16. Anzaldúa, "Now Let Us Shift," 570.

17. Jess Clark, "Lawmaker Wants to Make Teaching Critical Race Theory Illegal," WKU Public Radio, June 3, 2021.

18. Lipsitz, *Possessive Investment in Whiteness*.

19. Karyn D. McKinney, *Being White: Stories of Race and Racism* (Routledge, 2005); Thandeka, *Learning to Be White: Money, Race, and God in America* (Bloomsbury, 2013).

20. Rita Segato, "Territory, Sovereignty, and the Crimes of the Second State: The Writing on the Body of Murdered Women," in *Terrorizing Women: Feminicide in the Americas*, ed. Rosa-Linda Fregoso and Cynthia Bejarano (Duke University Press, 2010), 74.

21. Riley Vetterkind, "Wisconsin Assembly Passes Ban on Teaching Critical Race Theory," *Wisconsin State Journal*, September 29, 2021; Sarah Schwartz and Eesha Pendharker, "Here's the Long List of Topics Republicans Want Banned from the Classroom," *Education Week*, February 2, 2022.

22. Michael Rogin, *Ronald Reagan the Movie: And Other Episodes in Political Demonology* (University of California Press, 1987), xiii.

23. Charles Mills, *Racial Contract*, 86.

24. Charles Mills, *Racial Contract*, 121.

25. Charles Mills, *Racial Contract*, 58.

26. Galeano, *Upside Down*, 34.

27. Lipsitz, *Possessive Investment in Whiteness*.

28. Derrick Bell, "*Brown v. Board of Education* and the Interest Convergence Dilemma," *Harvard Law Review* 93, no. 3 (January 1980): 518–33; Derrick Bell, *And We Are Not Saved: The Elusive Quest for Racial Justice* (Basic Books, 1987); Derrick Bell, *Faces at the Bottom of the Well: The Permanence of Racism* (Basic Books, 1992); Sherrick Hughes et al., "Derrick Bell's Post-*Brown* Moves Toward Critical Race Theory," *Race Ethnicity and Education* 16, no. 4 (2013): 442–69.

29. Charles Mills, *Racial Contract*, 132.

30. W. E. B. Du Bois, *Black Reconstruction in America, 1860–1880* (Atheneum, 1992), 704.

31. Barbara Tomlinson and George Lipsitz, "American Studies as Accompaniment," *American Quarterly* 65, no. 1 (March 2013): 1–30.

32. Ernst Bloch, *The Principle of Hope*, vol. 1, trans. Neville Plaice and Paul Knight (MIT Press, 1986), 30.

33. Bloch, *Principle of Hope*, 347, 50, 51.

34. Angelina Snodgrass Godoy, "Probing the Membrane Between Horror and Hope: Artist Claudia Bernardi," *Center for Latin American Studies Newsletter*, University of California Berkeley, 1999, quoted in Mary Watkins and Helene Schulman, *Toward Psychologies of Liberation* (Palgrave Macmillan, 2008), 122.

35. Eduardo Galeano, *Open Veins*, 283–84.

36. Bloch, *Principle of Hope*, 51.

37. Ernst Bloch, "Nonsynchronism and the Obligation to Its Dialectics," *New German Critique* 11 (Spring 1977): 26.

38. Bloch, "Nonsynchronism," 26.

39. Alvin Gouldner, *The Future of Intellectuals and the Rise of the New Class* (Oxford University Press, 1979).

40. Jennifer Sandlin and Alan Eladio Gomez, "Toward New Critical Pedagogies and Conspirituality Consumption: Exploring and Combatting the COVID-19 New-Age Grifters," *New Directions in Adult Continuing Education* 178 (Summer 2023): 41–57.

41. Christine E. Sleeter and Miguel Zavala, *Transformative Ethnic Studies in Schools: Curriculum, Pedagogy, and Research* (Teachers College Press, 2020); Michael Dominguez et al., "Why a Journal on Ethnic Studies Pedagogies?" *Ethnic Studies Pedagogies* 1, no. 1 (2023): 1–6.

42. Among these are the Chicagoland Researchers and Advocates for Transformative Education (CReATE), the California Alliance of Researchers for Equity in Education (CARE-ED), Hawai'i Scholars for Education and Social Justice, Education Deans for Justice and Equity (EDJE), Radical STEMM Educators of the Bay Area, and the Coalition for Racial Equity in the Arts + Educa-

tion (creat+e). See Lois A. Yamauchi et al., "Scholar Collectives Advocating for Social Justice in Education," *Kalfou* 9, no. 1 (Spring 2022): 225–46.

43. *Ethnic Studies Pedagogies* 1, no. 1 (2023), www.EthnicStudiesPedagogies.org.

44. Michael Yellow Bird, "Cowboys and Indians: Toys of Genocide, Icons of Colonialism," *Wicazo Sa Review* 19, no. 2 (Fall 2024): 39.

45. Arlene Davila, *Latinx Art: Artists, Markets, and Politics* (Duke University Press, 2020), 127.

46. Susan Ratcliffe, ed., *Oxford Essential Quotations,* 4th ed. (Oxford University Press, 2016), https://www.oxfordreference.com/display/10.1093/acref/9780191826719.001.0001/q-oro-ed4-00000730.

47. Sleeter and Zavala, *Transformative Ethnic Studies;* Dominguez et al., "Why a Journal"; Brian David Lozenski, "Constructing a Dual Subjectivity: Understanding the Intersection of Ethnic Studies and YPAR," *Global Journal of Transformative Education* 1, no. 1 (2019): 26–37.

48. Sleeter and Zavalla, *Transformative Ethnic Studies*. Scores on standardized tests and even improved grade point averages and rates of graduation and college attendance are not flawless or even reliable measures of effective instruction. But they provide the kinds of evidence the audit culture of the education industry has come to demand and respect, especially when results show deficiencies among students from aggrieved groups. When results such as these demonstrate strengths and successes, the opponents of ethnic studies suddenly find flaws in empirical methods and the results that flow from them. Moreover, when studies show that "reforms" like No Child Left Behind or Race to the Top fail, the proponents of ostensible evidence-based policies ignore that evidence. See Brian D. Lozenski, "Beyond Mediocrity: The Dialectics of Crisis in the Continuing Miseducation of Black Youth," *Harvard Educational Review* 87, no. 2 (Summer 2017): 161–85.

49. Judith Butler, *Precarious Life: The Powers of Mourning and Violence* (Verso, 2004), 41.

50. Lynne Layton, *Toward a Social Psychoanalysis: Culture, Character, and Normative Unconscious Processes* (Routledge, 2020).

51. C. L. R. James, *American Civilization* (Blackwell, 1993), 158.

52. Pamela Brown et al., "Trump Pardons Steve Bannon as One of His Final Acts in Office," *CNN Politics,* January 20, 2021; Rio Yamat, "Trump Pardons Nevada Politician Who Paid for Cosmetic Surgery with Funds to Honor a Slain Officer," Associated Press, US News, April 24, 2025.

53. Toni Cade Bambara, "Toni Cade Bambara," interview by Claudia Tate, in *Black Women Writers at Work,* ed. Claudia Tate (Haymarket Books, 2023), 54.

54. Iris Morales, *Revisiting Herstories: The Young Lords Party* (Red Sugarcane Press, 2023). Those commitments fueled a wide range of successful projects but did not settle the group's gender politics once and for all. In subsequent years, male leaders closed down the women's and gay caucuses in the group to advance a narrow and ultimately unsuccessful nationalism. References to the Young Lords in this book mostly concern the New York chapter. For information about the Chicago chapter, see Johanna Fernández, *The Young Lords: A Radical History* (University of North Carolina Press, 2020), and Sara Awartani,

"You Have Living Legends Among You: Commemorating the Fiftieth Anniversary of the Chicago Young Lords," *Kalfou* 6, no. 1 (Spring 2019): 127–32.

55. Neda Maghbouleh, "Twenty-Five Years of Charles Mills's *Racial Contract* in Sociology," *Sociology of Race and Ethnicity* 8, no. 4 (August 2022): 433–42.

56. Charles Mills, "Alumnus Charles Mills on Pedagogy, White Supremacy, and the Future of Philosophy," interview by *Philosophy News*, reposted to website of University of Toronto, Department of Philosophy, May 18, 2018, https://philosophy.utoronto.ca/news/charles-mills-alumnus-interview/.

57. Kimberlé Williams Crenshaw, "Twenty Years of Critical Race Theory: Looking Back to Move Forward," *Connecticut Law Review* 43, no. 5 (July 2011): 1261.

58. Robin D. G. Kelley, *Freedom Dreams: The Black Radical Imagination* (Beacon Press, 2002), 9.

59. Cedric J. Robinson, *Black Marxism: The Making of the Black Radical Tradition* (University of North Carolina Press, 2000), 5.

60. Nelson Maldonado-Torres, "Ethnic Studies in the Face of the Liberal Hydra," Ethnic Studies Rise Roundtable, January 15, 2020, https://ethnicrise.github.io/roundtable/liberal-hydra/.

61. Charles Payne, *I've Got the Light of Freedom: The Organizing Tradition and the Mississippi Freedom Struggle* (University of California Press, 2007); Shirley Sherrod, *The Courage to Hope: How I Stood Up to the Politics of Fear* (Atria, 2012); Edward Onaci, *Free the Land: The Republic of New Afrika and the Pursuit of a Black Nation State* (University of North Carolina Press, 2020); Hasan Kwame Jeffries, *Bloody Lowndes: Civil Rights and Black Power in Alabama's Black Belt* (New York University Press, 2010); Alondra Nelson, *Body and Soul: The Black Panther Party and the Fight Against Medical Discrimination* (University of Minnesota Press, 2011); Dan Georgakas and Marvin Surkin, *Detroit: I Do Mind Dying: A Study in Urban Revolution* (South End Press, 1998); Kazuyo Tsuchiya, *Reinventing Citizenship: Black Los Angeles, Korean Kawasaki and Community Participation* (University of Minnesota Press, 2014); Daniel Widener, *Black Arts West: Culture and Struggle in Postwar Los Angeles* (Duke University Press, 2010); Jeffrey Haas, *The Assassination of Fred Hampton: How the FBI and the Chicago Police Murdered a Black Panther* (Lawrence Hill Books, 2019).

62. The pairing of fate and fatalism appears in Avery Gordon, *The Hawthorn Archive: Letters From the Utopian Margins* (Fordham University Press, 2018), 56.

63. Kimberlé Williams Crenshaw, "Race, Reform, and Retrenchment: Transformation and Legitimation in Anti-discrimination Law," in Crenshaw et al., *Critical Race Theory*.

64. ArCasia D. James-Gallaway, "What Got Them Through: Community Cultural Wealth, Black Students, and Texas School Desegregation," *Race Ethnicity and Education* 25, no. 2 (2022): 173–91.

65. George Lipsitz, "'Constituted by a Series of Contestations': Critical Race Theory as a Social Movement," *Connecticut Law Review* 43, no. 5 (July 2011): 1461–78; Crenshaw, "Twenty Years."

66. Kimberlé Williams Crenshaw, "Demarginalizing the Intersections of Race and Sex: A Black Feminist Critique of Antidiscrimination Doctrine, Feminist Theory, and Antiracist Politics," *University of Chicago Legal Forum* 14 (1989): 138–67; Kimberlé Williams Crenshaw, "Mapping the Margins: Intersectionality, Identity, and Violence Against Women of Color," *Stanford Law Review* 43 (1991): 1241–99; Cheryl Harris, "Whiteness as Property," *Harvard Law Review* 106, no. 8 (June 1993): 1707–91; Bell, "*Brown v. Board of Education*"; Mari Matsuda, "Looking to the Bottom: Critical Legal Studies and Reparations," *Harvard Civil Rights and Civil Liberties Law Review* 22 (1987): 323–99; Charles R. Lawrence III, "The Id, the Ego, and Equal Protection: Reckoning with Unconscious Racism," *Stanford Law Review* 39 (January 1987): 317–88; Barbara Tomlinson and George Lipsitz, *Insubordinate Spaces: Improvisation and Accompaniment for Social Justice* (Temple University Press, 2019).

67. Tara J. Yosso, "Whose Culture Has Capital? A Critical Race Theory Discussion of Community Cultural Wealth," *Race Ethnicity and Education* 8, no. 1 (2005): 65–91; Tara J. Yosso and David D. Garcia, "'This Is No Slum': A Critical Race Theory Analysis of Community Cultural Wealth in Culture Clash's Chavez Ravine," *Aztlan: A Journal of Chicano Studies* 32, no. 1 (2007): 145–79.

68. Gustavo Esteva, "The Hour of Autonomy," *Latin American and Caribbean Ethnic Studies* 10, no. 1 (2015): 138.

69. William Parker, liner notes to David Mott and Jesse Stewart's *Anagrams* (2014), quoted in Ajay Heble and Jesse Stewart, *Jamming the Classroom: Musical Improvisation and Pedagogical Practice* (University of Michigan Press, 2023), 1.

CHAPTER 2. ETHNIC STUDIES AS INCORPORATION

1. George Lipsitz, "Teaching After the Battle in Seattle: This Is What Plutocracy Looks Like," in *What Democracy Looks Like: A New Critical Realism for a Post-Seattle World*, ed. Amy Schrager Lang and Cecilia Tichi (Rutgers University Press, 2006).

2. Michael Denning, *The Cultural Front: The Laboring of American Culture* (Verso, 1996); Lizabeth Cohen, *Making a New Deal: Industrial Workers in Chicago, 1919–1930* (Cambridge University Press, 1990).

3. Cedric Johnson, *Revolutionaries to Race Leaders: Black Power and the Making of African American Politics* (University of Minnesota Press, 2007); Katherine Lee, "An Asian American Studies Writing Pedagogy: Reformulating the Work of Writing in Asian American Studies Classes," *Journal of Asian American Studies* 26, no. 2 (June 2023): 265–76; Maylei Blackwell, *Chicana Power! Contested Histories of Feminism in the Chicano Movement* (University of Texas Press, 2011); Carlos Velez-Ibanez, *Border Visions: Mexican Cultures of the Southwest United States* (University of Arizona Press, 1996); Jason Ferreira, "From College Readiness to Ready for Revolution! Third World Student Activism at a Northern California Community College, 1965–1969," *Kalfou* 1, no. 1 (Spring 2014): 117–44.

4. Ferguson, *Reorder of Things*.

5. Ferguson, *Reorder of Things;* Noliwe Rooks, *White Money/Black Power: The Surprising History of African American Studies and the Crisis of Race in Higher Education* (Beacon, 2017).

6. James Kyung-Jin Lee, *Urban Triage: Race and the Fictions of Multiculturalism* (University of Minnesota Press, 2004).

7. Mora et al., "How Many Latino Studies Programs."

8. Stuart Hall, "When We Are All Enemies of the State," *Boston Review,* June 12, 2025. Thanks to Jordan T. Camp for discovering this speech and making it available to the public.

9. Leah Lakshmi Piepzna-Samarasinha, *The Future Is Disabled: Prophecies, Love Notes, and Mourning Songs* (Arsenal Pulp Press, 2022).

10. Okihiro, *Third World Studies;* Ferreira, "From College Readiness."

11. Kelley, "Black Study, Black Struggle."

12. David Hilliard, *Huey: Spirit of the Panther* (Thunder's Mouth, 2006), 32; I Wor Kuen, "I Wor Kuen's 12 Point Platform and Program," History Is a Weapon, 1969, https://www.historyisaweapon.com/defcon1/12pointiworkuen.html; Darrel Wanzer-Serrano, *The New York Young Lords and the Struggle for Liberation* (Temple University Press, 2015), 53.

13. Lorgia Garcia Peña, *Community as Rebellion: A Syllabus for Surviving Academia as a Woman of Color* (Haymarket, 2022), 72.

14. Nick Estes, *Our History Is the Future: Standing Rock Versus the Dakota Pipeline and the Long Tradition of Indigenous Resistance* (Haymarket, 2023), 180.

15. Jack D. Forbes, "Intellectual Self-Determination and Sovereignty: Implications for Native Studies and for Native Intellectuals," *Wicazo Sa Review* 13, no. 1 (Spring 1998): 11–23.

16. Morales, *Revisiting Herstories,* 42.

17. Estes, *Our History Is the Future,* 179.

18. John-Carlos Perea, "'Native Noise' and the Politics of Powwow Musicking in a University Soundscape," in *Music and Modernity Among First Peoples of North America,* ed. Victoria Lindsay Levine and Dylan Robinson (Wesleyan University Press, 2019); Diane C. Fujino, "Rhizomatic Organizing, Collective Leadership, and Community-Centered Pedagogy in the Early Asian American Movement," *Journal of American Studies,* September 2024, 1–34.

19. Wanzer-Serrano, *New York Young Lords,* 48; Johanna Fernández, *Young Lords.*

20. Carmichael, "Toward Black Liberation."

21. Ferguson, *Reorder of Things,* 33, 124.

22. Michael Denning, *Culture in the Age of Three Worlds* (Verso, 2004), 146.

23. Ahmed, *Queer Phenomenology,* 134.

24. Okihiro, *Third World Studies.*

25. Garcia-Peña, *Community as Rebellion,* 83.

26. James R. Barrett and David Roediger, "Inbetween Peoples: Race, Nationality, and the 'New Immigrant' Working Class," *Journal of American Ethnic History* 16, no. 3 (1997): 3–44; Noel Ignatiev, *How The Irish Became White*

(Routledge, 1996); Karen Brodkin, *How Jews Became White Folks and What That Says About Race in America* (Rutgers University Press, 1998).

27. Jennifer Ponce de León, *Another Aesthetics Is Possible: Arts of Rebellion in the Fourth World War* (Duke University Press, 2021).

28. Mayra Cazares-Minero et al., *Often Overlooked but Not Unseen: An Overview of Highly Mobile Youth in the U.S.*, brief, UCLA Center for the Transformation of Schools, 2025, https://transformschools.ucla.edu/research/often-overlooked-but-not-unseen-an-overview-of-highly-mobile-youth-in-the-u-s/.

29. Chris Barcelos, *Youth Organizing for Reproductive Justice: A Guide for Liberation* (University of California Press, 2025); University of Chicago Urban Labs, "Students in Temporary Living Situations," July 2021, https://urbanlabs.uchicago.edu/projects/students-in-temporary-living-situations.

30. Mayra Cazares-Minero et al., *1.37 Million and Rising: Understanding the National 25% Spike in Student Homelessness*, UCLA Center for the Transformation of Schools, brief, 2025, https://transformschools.ucla.edu/research/1-37-million-and-rising-understanding-the-national-25-spike-in-student-homelessness/2025.

31. Garcia-Peña, *Community as Rebellion*.

32. I spoke at this symposium and edited and contributed the article "Shattering Silences: Contradictions, and Ethnic Studies at the Crossroads" to a special issue of the journal *Kalfou* 7, no. 2 (Fall 2020): 222–48, featuring statements made at that session.

33. Readers may object that Harvard and other elite institutions deny tenure to candidates more frequently than most other Research One institutions and that because personnel matters are confidential the full story of the tenure denial cannot be accessed from the outside. My view is that this tenure case was different from others precisely because the innovative and generative nature of Garcia-Peña's scholarship, its connections to the knowledge of aggrieved racialized people, and the support she received from a wide range of allies all make it clear that the controversy involved incommensurable competing understandings of what original discovery research can and should be.

34. Lipsitz, "Shattering Silences."

35. Daniel Martinez HoSang, *Racial Propositions: Ballot Initiatives and the Making of Postwar California* (University of California Press, 2010); Walter Johnson, "Living Inside a Psyop: Three Months at Harvard," *n+1*, January 10, 2024.

36. William C. Mao and Veronica Paulus, "Harvard Dismisses Leaders of Center for Middle Eastern Studies," *Harvard Crimson*, March 29, 2025; Dhruv T. Patel and Grace E. Yoon, "Harvard Suspends Research Partnership with Birzeit University in the West Bank," *Harvard Crimson*, March 17, 2025; Sebastian B. Connolly and Julia A. Karabolli, "Harvard Divinity School Suspends Religion, Conflict, and Peace Initiative," *Harvard Crimson*, April 7, 2025; Dhruv T. Patel and Grace E. Yoon, "Harvard Will Create Process to Centralize Protest Discipline Cases Under University President," *Harvard Crimson*, April 25, 2025.

37. Ricardo Levins Morales, *The Land Knows the Way: Eco-Social Insights for Liberation* (RLM Art Studio, 2025).

38. Cedric Robinson, "Manichaeism and Multiculturalism," in *Mapping Multiculturalism*, ed. Avery F. Gordon and Christopher Newfield (University of Minnesota Press, 1996).

A BRIDGE FOR THIS BOOK

1. Robert Farris Thompson, *Flash of the Spirit: African and Afro-American Art and Philosophy* (Vintage, 1983), 19.

2. Elizabeth McAlister, *Rara! Vodou, Power, and Performance in Haiti and Its Diaspora* (University of California Press, 2002), 23. Here and elsewhere the crossroads metaphor can convey ableist assumptions, but I think "moving" can be a mental as well as a physical process, a term that connotes negotiating difficulties and taking actions in response to them that improve the situation, a practice that people negotiating disabilities know well.

3. Thanks to Neda Maghbouleh for directing me to these words.

4. Gloria E. Anzaldúa, *Borderlands/La Frontera: The New Mestiza* (Aunt Lute Books, 1987), 194–95.

5. Houston A. Baker, *Blues, Ideology and African American Literature* (University of Chicago Press, 1985).

6. Aurora Levins Morales and Rosario Morales, *Getting Home Alive* (Firebrand Books, 1986), 212–13.

7. Edna Horiuchi, "Nobuko Miyamoto: Giving Voice to Asian American Stories—Part 2," *North American Post*, March 15, 2022, https://napost.com/2022/nobuko-miyamoto-giving-voice-to-asian-american-stories-part-1/.

8. Bambara, "Toni Cade Bambara," 36.

9. Thompson, *Flash of the Spirit*, 222.

10. Patrick Bellegarde-Smith and Claudine Michel, "Danbala/Ayida as Cosmic Prism: The Lwa Trope for Understanding Metaphysics in Haitian Vodou and Beyond," *Journal of Africana Religions* 1, no. 4 (2013): 458–87.

11. Chris Andersen, "Critical Indigenous Studies: From Difference to Density," *Cultural Studies Review* 15, no. 1 (September 2009): 80–100.

12. Thompson, *Flash of the Spirit*.

13. Walter Benjamin, *One Way Street* (Belknap/Harvard University Press, 2016), 87–88.

14. Because the caduceus is associated with commerce, medical professionals favor the rod of Asclepius as their symbol. The caduceus is more useful to me as a metaphor because I view its relation to commerce to be about negotiation and the ideal of reciprocity purported (although rarely enacted) in commercial exchanges. The caduceus also appears as a sign of peace.

15. William Godwin, *Lives of the Necromancers* (Harper Brothers, 1835), https://babel.hathitrust.org/cgi/pt?id=hvd.hwl3jb&seq=11.

16. R. Levins Morales, *The Land Knows the Way*.

17. Estes, *Our History Is the Future*, 14.

18. Anzaldúa, "Now Let Us Shift," 540.

19. Judith Butler, *The Psychic Life of Power: Theories in Subjection* (Stanford University Press, 1997), 83.

20. Judith Butler, *Excitable Speech: A Politics of the Performative* (Routledge, 1997), 38.

21. Kimmerer, *Braiding Sweetgrass*, 166.

22. George Rawick, *From Sundown to Sunup: The Making of the Black Community* (Greenwood Press, 1972); Theophus Smith, *Conjuring Culture: Biblical Formations of Black America* (Oxford University Press, 1994); Nathaniel Samuel Murrell et al., eds., *Chanting Down Babylon: The Rastafari Reader* (Temple University Press, 1998).

23. Fielder, *Revolution Will Be Improvised*; Taylor, *Archive and the Repertoire*.

24. João Costa Vargas, *Catching Hell in the City of Angels: Life and Meanings of Blackness in South Central Los Angeles* (University of Minnesota Press, 2006).

25. Courtney Bowles and Mark Strandquist, "The People's Paper Co-op," in *The Art and Art Therapy of Papermaking: Material, Methods, and Applications*, ed. Drew Luan Matott and Gretchen R. Miller (Routledge, 2024).

26. Michel Foucault, *The History of Sexuality*, vol. 1, *An Introduction* (Vintage, 1980).

27. Ahmed, *Queer Phenomenology*.

28. Fielder, *Revolution Will Be Improvised*, 137.

29. Barbara Andrea Sostaita, *Sanctuary Everywhere: The Fugitive Sacred in the Sonoran Desert* (Duke University Press, 2024).

30. Jules Joanne Gleeson and Elle O'Rourke, introduction to Gleeson and O'Rourke, *Transgender Marxism*, 9–10.

31. Lisa Beard, *If We Were Kin: Race, Identification, and Intimate Political Appeals* (Oxford University Press, 2023).

32. Trouillot, *Global Transformations*.

33. Quoted in Aimee Villarreal, "Anthropolocura as Homeplace Ethnography," in *Ethnographic Refusals: Unruly Latinidades*, ed. Alex E. Chávez and Gina M. Pérez (University of New Mexico Press, 2022), 199.

34. Martin Luther King Jr., *Strength to Love* (Fortress Press, 2010).

35. Leslie Gerald Desmangles, "African Interpretations of the Christian Cross in Vodou," in *Vodou in Haitian Life and Culture: Invisible Powers*, ed. Claudine Michel and Patrick Bellegarde-Smith (Palgrave Macmillan, 2006); Claudine Michel, "Vodou in Haiti: Way of Life and Mode of Survival," in Michel and Bellegarde-Smith, *Vodou in Haitian Life*.

36. Robert Stam, "From Hybridity to the Aesthetics of Garbage," *Social Identities* 3, no. 2 (1997): 277.

37. George Lipsitz, "Neighborhood Development and Art-Based Community Making," in *Collective Creative Actions: Project Row Houses at 25*, ed. Ryan N. Dennis (Project Row Houses, 2018).

38. Rick Bonus, *The Ocean in the School: Pacific Islander Students Transforming Their University* (Duke University Press, 2020), 33.

39. Mary Pat Brady, *Scales of Captivity: Racial Capitalism and the Latinx Child* (Duke University Press, 2022).

40. Gonzalez, *Chican@ Artivistas*.
41. Bissett Perea, *Sound Relations*.
42. Bissett Perea, *Sound Relations*, 139.
43. Ferguson, *Reorder of Things*.
44. Homi K. Bhabha, "Remembering Fanon: Self-Psyche and the Colonial Condition," foreword to the 1986 edition of Frantz Fanon, *Black Skin, White Masks* (Pluto Press, 2008), xxiv.
45. José Esteban Muñoz, *Disidentifications: Queers of Color and the Performance of Politics* (University of Minnesota Press, 1999), 79.
46. Muñoz, *Disidentifications*, 11.
47. Angela Y. Davis, "Deepening the Debate over Mass Incarceration," *Socialism and Democracy* 28, no. 3 (2014): 15–23.
48. Jack Halberstam, *In a Queer Time and Place: Transgender Bodies, Subcultural Lives* (New York University Press, 2005), 23.
49. Godoy, "Probing the Membrane," 23.
50. Taylor, *Archive and the Repertoire*.
51. Mia Mingus, "About," *Leaving Evidence* (blog), accessed January 16, 2022, https://leavingevidence.wordpress.com/about-2/.
52. Kristen L. Buras, *Pedagogy, Policy, and the Privatized City: Stories of Dispossession and Defiance from New Orleans*, with Jim Randels, Kalamu ya Salaam, and Students at the Center (Teachers College Press, 2010), 39.
53. C. L. R. James, *The Black Jacobins: Toussaint L'Ouverture and the San Domingo Revolution* (Vintage, 1989); Ramón A. Gutiérrez, *When Jesus Came, the Corn Mothers Went Away: Marriage, Sexuality, and Power in New Mexico, 1500–1846* (Stanford University Press, 1991); Nayan Shah, *Contagious Divides: Epidemics and Race in San Francisco's Chinatown* (University of California Press, 2001); Nancy Yunhwa Rao, *Inside Chinese Theater: Community and Artistry in Nineteenth Century California and Beyond* (University of Illinois Press, 2025).
54. Karen Mary Davalos, "A Poetics of Love and Rescue in the Collection of Chicano/a Art," *Latino Studies* 5 (2007): 76–103.
55. Flint Water Crisis Public Archive, "Introduction to the Flint Water Crisis Public Archive," 2024, https://fwcpublicarchive.lib.uiowa.edu/introduction-to-the-flint-water-crisis-public-archive/; John D'Emilio, *Queer Legacies: Stories from Chicago's LGBTQ Archives* (University of Chicago Press, 2020).
56. Taylor, *Archive and the Repertoire*, 13.
57. Taylor, *Archive and the Repertoire*, 64.
58. Alessandro Portelli, *The Death of Luigi Trastulli and Other Stories: Form and Meaning in Oral History* (State University of New York Press, 1991).
59. Michel-Rolph Trouillot, *Silencing the Past: Power and the Production of History* (Beacon, 1995), 72.
60. Bloch, *Principle of Hope*, 13.
61. Taylor, *Archive and the Repertoire*, 143.
62. Taylor, *Archive and the Repertoire*, 19–20.
63. Antonio Gramsci, *Selections from the Prison Notebooks of Antonio Gramsci*, ed. and trans. Quinten Hoare and Geoffrey Nowell Smith (International Publishers, 1971), 192.
64. Wanzer-Serrano, *New York Young Lords*.

65. May Lin, "Khmer Girls in Action and Healing Justice: Expanding Understandings of Anti-Asian Racism and Public Health Solutions," *Frontiers in Public Health* 10 (2022): 956308; George Lipsitz, *A Life in the Struggle: Ivory Perry and the Culture of Opposition* (Temple University Press, 1995), 253–54.

66. HoSang, *Wider Type of Freedom*, 32.

67. Betty A. Reardon, "Human Rights as Education for Peace," in *Human Rights Education for the Twenty-First Century*, ed. George J. Andreopoulos and Richard Pierre Claude (University of Pennsylvania Press, 1997); Martha Matsuoka to George Lipsitz, personal communication, September 8, 2006.

68. George Lipsitz, *How Racism Takes Place* (Temple University Press, 2011), 162.

69. Maylei Blackwell, *Scales of Resistance: Indigenous Women's Transborder Activism* (Duke University Press, 2023), 247.

70. Floridalma Boj Lopez, "Mobile Archives of Indigeneity: Building la Communidad Ixim Through Organizing in the Maya Diaspora," *Latino Studies* 15 (2017): 201–18; Blackwell, *Scales of Resistance*, 286.

71. Tomlinson and Lipsitz, *Insubordinate Spaces*.

72. Halberstam, *In a Queer Time*, 32, 156, 159; José Esteban Muñoz, "Ephemera as Evidence: Introductory Notes to Queer Acts," *Women and Performance: A Journal of Feminist Theory* 8, no. 2 (1996): 5–16.

73. Angela J. Aguayo, *Documentary Resistance: Social Change and Participatory Media* (Oxford University Press, 2019).

74. Sharim Studio, "Press Events," 2025, https://www.sharimstudio.com/press-events.

75. Su'ad Abdul Khabeer, "[In] Searching Our Mothers' Archives: Building Umi's Archive Through Mourning Work," *African Journal of Gender and Religion* 29, no. 2 (2023): 1–25.

76. K.T. Ewing, "Fugitive Archives: Black Women, Domestic Repositories, and Hoarding as Informal Archival Practice," *Black Scholar* 52, no. 4 (2022): 43–51.

77. Roderick A. Ferguson, "Building Relations, Critical University Studies and Student Activism: A Conversation with Roderick A. Ferguson," interview by Kong Pheng Pha and José Manuel Santillana Blanco, *Agitate Journal*, Summer 2024, https://agitatejournal.org/article/building-relations-critical-university-studies-and-student-activism-a-conversation-with-roderick-a-ferguson/.

78. Rita Laura Segato, "Patriarchy from Margins to Center: Discipline, Territoriality, and Cruelty in the Apocalyptic Phase of Capital," *South Atlantic Quarterly* 115, no. 3 (July 2016): 615–24.

79. Kalamu ya Salaam, *Be About Beauty* (University of New Orleans Press, 2018), 32.

80. Gordon, *Hawthorn Archive*, 53.

81. R. Levins Morales, *Land Knows The Way*.

CHAPTER 3. ETHNIC STUDIES AS ACCOMPANIMENT

1. Nobuko Miyamoto, *Not Yo' Butterfly: My Long Song of Relocation, Race, Love, and Revolution* (University of California Press, 2022), 291–92.

2. Tomlinson and Lipsitz, *Insubordinate Spaces*, 23.

3. Sunni Patterson, "My City Ain't for Sale," in *We Know This Place: Poems*, ed. Sunni Patterson (Runagate Press, 2022), 33.

4. Patterson, "My City Ain't for Sale," 34.

5. Patterson, "My City Ain't For Sale," 33.

6. Sunni Patterson, "We Know This Place," in Patterson, *We Know This Place*.

7. Stuart Hall, "The Neo-liberal Revolution," *Cultural Studies* 25, no. 6 (2011): 705–28; Brownwyn Davies and Sue Saltmarsh, "Gender Economies: Literacy and the Gendered Production of Neoliberal Subjectivities," *Gender and Education* 19, no. 1 (2007): 1–20.

8. Lipsitz, *Possessive Investment in Whiteness*; William A. Darity and A. Kirsten Mullen, *From Here to Equality: Reparations for Black Americans in the Twenty-First Century* (University of North Carolina Press, 2020).

9. Patrick Chamoiseau and William Parker, "Epistolary Conversation," discussion preceding the performance of Parker's symphonic poem *Trail of Tears* at the February 2022 Sons d'hiver festival, *La Plateforme*, November 17, 2021, to January 3, 2022, laplateforme-sonsdhiver.org/chamoiseau-parker/.

10. Chamoiseau and Parker, "Epistolary Conversation."

11. For an eloquent and insightful explication of caretaking relations, see Kim TallBear (Sisseton-Wahpeton Oyate), "Caretaking Relations, Not American Dreaming," *Kalfou* 6, no. 1 (Spring 2019): 24–41. Also valuable is the insight that caring can be an individual act that helps one person but also the work of creating systems that help everyone, as articulated by Leah Lakshmi Piepzna-Samarasinha in *The Future Is Disabled: Prophecies, Love Notes, and Mourning Songs* (Arsenal Pulp Press, 2022).

12. C. Robinson, *Black Marxism*, xxx.

13. Patterson, "We Know This Place."

14. Clyde Woods, ed., *In the Wake of Hurricane Katrina: New Paradigms and Social Visions* (Johns Hopkins University Press, 2010); Sunni Patterson, "We Made It," in *Development Drowned and Reborn: The Blues and Bourbon Restorations in Post-Katrina New Orleans*, by Clyde Woods, ed. Jordan T. Camp and Laura Pulido (University of Georgia Press, 2017), ix–x.

15. Rina Benmayor, "Digital Testimonio as a Signature Pedagogy for Latin@ Studies," *Equity and Excellence in Education* 45, no. 3 (2012): 507–24.

16. Frantz Fanon, *The Wretched of the Earth* (Grove Press, 1968), 243.

17. Other examples of autonomous learning circles with connections to ethnic studies are delineated in Monisha Das Gupta, "'KNOw History/KNOw Self': Khmer Youth Organizing for Justice in Long Beach," *Amerasia Journal* 45, no. 2 (2019): 137–56; Beard, *If We Were Kin*.

18. Students of Roosevelt High School, *La Vida Diferente: Celebrating Boyle Heights' Community Treasures* (826LA, 2014).

19. Gonzalez, *Chican@ Artivistas*, 3.

20. George Lipsitz and Alliance for California Traditional Arts, *Saludarte: Building Health Equity on the Bedrock of Traditional Arts and Culture* (Alliance for California Traditional Arts, 2020).

21. George Lipsitz, "Learning How to Arrive: The Improvisational Toolkit of Artivistas in Boyle Heights," in *The Improviser's Classroom: Pedagogies for*

Cocreative World Making, ed. Daniel Fischlin and Mark Lomanno (Temple University Press, 2024); George B. Sanchez-Tello, "Reintroducing Traditional Foodways Through a School Cafeteria Mural," *Capital and Main*, March 24, 2023.

22. Loren Kajikawa, "Leaders of the New School? Music Departments, Hip-Hop, and the Challenge of Significant Difference," *Twentieth Century Music* 18, no. 1 (2021): 45–64; Yana Stainova, "An Ethnography of Joy: Entrepreneurship Among Latinx Communities in East Los Angeles," *American Anthropologist* 126, no. 4 (2024): 635–46; Russell C. Rodríguez, "Mariachi Accompaniment: Cultural Bearers for Community Conviviality," *Twentieth Century Music* 21, no. 2 (2024): 180–208; George Lipsitz, "FandangObon: Amplification, Counter-publics, and Fugitive Spaces of Belonging in Los Angeles," *American Anthropologist* 126, no. 2 (2024): 260–79.

23. I coedited and contributed an introduction to *Go to Jail*. Students at the Center, *Go to Jail: Confronting a System of Oppression* (LMO Projects, 2021).

24. Buras et al., *Pedagogy, Policy*; Diane C. Fujino et al., "A Transformative Pedagogy for a Decolonial World," *Review of Education, Pedagogy, and Cultural Studies* 40, no. 2 (2018): 69–95.

25. Fielder, *Revolution Will Be Improvised*, 30, 33.

26. George Lipsitz, "Challenging Neoliberal Education at the Grass Roots: Students Who Lead, Not Students Who Leave," *Souls* 17, nos. 3–4 (2015): 303–21; Students at the Center, *Go to Jail*.

27. Fielder, *Revolution Will Be Improvised*, 99.

28. I have hosted talks by Morgan, Jones, and Rideau at college campuses.

29. AIWA initially recruited Korean and Chinese immigrants, but as the labor force expanded with successive waves of new migrants, it later turned its attention to women from Vietnam, Laos, Bangladesh, and Nepal.

30. I have worked with AIWA on a film about the organization's work and on the film's teachers' guide. I am a coauthor with its director Young Shin of Jennifer Jiyhe Chun et al., "Immigrant Women Workers at the Center of Social Change: AIWA Takes Stock of Itself," *Kalfou*, inaugural issue (2010): 127–32.

31. Jennifer Jihye Chun et al., "Immigrant Women Workers at the Center of Social Change: Asian Immigrant Women Advocates," in *Immigrant Women Workers in the Neoliberal Age*, ed. Nilda Flores Gonzalez et al. (University of Illinois Press, 2013).

32. Young Shin, "Immigrant Women Voice, Participate and Advocate: Developing Grassroots Leadership Toward a Just and Inclusive Society," Balgopal Lecture Series Keynote Speech, University of Illinois, April 2010, copy in author's possession courtesy of Young Shin.

33. Jennifer Jihye Chun et al., "Intersectionality as a Social Movement Strategy: Asian Immigrant Women Advocates," *Signs* 38, no. 4 (Summer 2013): 917–40; Lee Romney, "Chairs Sit Well with Laborers," *Los Angeles Times*, May 26, 2004.

34. Romney, "Chairs Sit Well with Laborers."

35. Asian Immigrant Women Advocates, "Teacher's Study Guide for Gary Delgado, *Becoming Ourselves: How Immigrant Women Transformed Their World* (Film, 2013)," *Kalfou* 4, no. 1 (2017): 96–117.

36. Gordon, *Hawthorn Archive*, 52.

37. Greg Burris, *The Palestinian Idea: Film, Media, and the Radical Imagination* (Temple University Press, 2019); Alex E. Chavez, *Sounds of Crossing: Music, Migration, and the Aural Poetics of Huapango Arribeño* (Duke University Press, 2017); Gonzalez, *Chican@ Artivistas;* Deborah Wong, *Louder and Faster: Pain, Joy, and the Body Politic in Asian American Taiko* (University of California Press, 2019).

38. Charles Briggs, *Unlearning: Rethinking Poetics, Pandemics, and the Politics of Knowledge* (University Press of Colorado, 2021), 3.

39. C. Briggs, *Unlearning,* 5.

40. Fielder, *Revolution Will Be Improvised,* 51; Thomas C. Dent et al., eds., *The Free Southern Theater, by the Free Southern Theater* (Bobbs-Merrill, 1969); Taylor, *Archive and the Repertoire.*

41. Johari Jabir to George Lipsitz, personal communication, June 24, 2024; Perea, "'Native Noise.'"

42. George J. Sanchez, "Keeping the Dance Alive: Institutionalization of the Crossroads of Ethnic and American Studies," in "Beyond Interdisciplinarity: The New Goals of American Studies Programs," edited by Simon J. Bronner, *American Studies Association Newsletter* 28, no. 1 (March 2005): 1–17.

43. C. Briggs, *Unlearning.*

44. D. Wong, *Louder and Faster,* 134.

45. Muñoz, *Disidentifications;* José Esteban Muñoz, *Cruising Utopia: The Then and There of Queer Futurity* (New York University Press, 2019).

46. Muñoz, *Disidentifications,* 4.

47. Muñoz, *Disidentifications,* 5.

48. Muñoz, *Disidentifications,* 93.

49. Halberstam, *In a Queer Time,* 155.

50. Frye Jean Graveline, "Idle No More: Enough Is Enough," *Canadian Social Work Review* 29, no. 2 (2012): 293–300.

51. Noah Zaznis, "Social Reproduction and Social Cognition: Theorizing (Trans)gender Identity Development in Community Context," in *Transgender Marxism,* ed. Jules Joanne Gleeson and Elle O'Rourke (Pluto Press, 2021).

52. Frances R. Aparicio, "*Aguanile*: Critical Listening: Mourning, and Decolonial Healing," in *Critical Dialogues in Latinx Studies: A Reader,* ed. Ana Y. Ramos-Zayas and Mérida Rúa (New York University Press, 2021).

53. African American Policy Forum, "We will never forget our sisters who have lost their lives to police violence," Twitter, September 20, 2021, https://x.com/AAPolicyForum/status/1440857679451230212?mx=2.

54. Norman Conti, "Stanton Heights," *Kalfou* 5, no. 2 (Fall 2018): 372–93; Jonathan D. Gomez et al., "Cedric Robinson, Modest Audacity, and the Black Radical Tradition," *Kalfou* 3, no. 2 (Fall 2016): 288–97; Stuesse, *Scratching Out a Living.*

CHAPTER 4. ETHNIC STUDIES AND INTERSECTIONAL JUSTICE

1. Leanne Betasamosake Simpson, *As We Have Always Done: Indigenous Freedom Through Radical Resistance* (University of Minnesota Press, 2017).

2. Leah Lakshmi Piepzna-Samarasinha, *Care Work: Dreaming Disability Justice* (Arsenal Pulp Press, 2023); Piepzna-Samarasinha, *Future Is Disabled*.

3. Ferguson, *One-Dimensional Queer*, 3.

4. When Rivera was three, her mother committed suicide and tried to kill her as well. She then lived with her grandmother, who shunned her as a troublemaker and beat her repeatedly. As a youth Rivera tried to kill herself and lived most of her life on the streets. See Jessi Gan, "'Still at the Back of the Bus': Sylvia Rivera's Struggle," *Centro Journal* 19, no. 1 (Spring 2007): 125–39.

5. Morales, *Revisiting Herstories*, 83–84.

6. Morales, *Revisiting Herstories*.

7. Tourmaline, *Marsha: The Joy and Defiance of Marsha P. Johnson* (Tiny Reparations Books, 2025), 125; Wanzer-Serrano, *New York Young Lords*, 118.

8. Johanna Fernández, *Young Lords*.

9. Lawrence LaFountain Stokes, "The Life and Times of Trans Activist Sylvia Rivera," in Ramos Zyas and Rúa, *Critical Dialogues;* Beard, *If We Were Kin*.

10. Samuel Galen Ng, "Trans Power! Sylvia Lee Rivera's STAR and the Black Panther Party," *Left History* 17, no. 1 (Spring/Summer 2013): 11–41; Benjamin Shepard, "From Community Organization to Direct Services: The Street Trans Action Revolutionaries to Sylvia Rivera Law Project," *Journal of Social Service Research* 39, no. 1 (2013): 95–114.

11. Shepard, "From Community Organization," 96.

12. Gan, "'Still at the Back of the Bus.'"

13. Juana María Rodríguez, *Queer Latinidad: Identity Practices, Discursive Spaces* (New York University Press, 2003); Horacio Roque Ramírez, "'That's My Place!' Negotiating Racial, Sexual, and Gender Politics in San Francisco's Gay Latino Alliance, 1975–1983," *Journal of the History of Sexuality* 12, no. 2 (2003): 224–58; Ferguson, *One-Dimensional Queer*, 90.

14. Ahmed, *Queer Phenomenology*, 79.

15. Ferguson, *Aberrations in Black*.

16. C. Wright Mills, *White Collar: The American Middle Classes* (Oxford University Press, 2002), 80; Gramsci, *Selections from the Prison Notebooks*.

17. Ferguson, *Aberrations in Black*, ix and passim.

18. Ferguson, *One-Dimensional Queer*, 38–39.

19. Ahmed, *Queer Phenomenology*, 78, 112.

20. Jodi A. Byrd (Chickasaw), "A Return to the South," *American Quarterly* 66, no. 3 (September 2014): 615.

21. Muñoz, *Disidentifications*, 78.

22. Muñoz, *Disidentifications*, xii.

23. Ahmed, *Queer Phenomenology*, 161–62.

24. I make an extended argument about the relevance of disability justice critiques of normativity to social justice more generally in George Lipsitz, "AUMI as a Model for Social Justice," in *Improvising Across Abilities: Pauline Oliveros and the Adaptive Use Musical Instrument*, ed. the AUMI Editorial Collective (University of Michigan Press, 2024).

25. I am grateful to Sherrie Tucker and Susan Schweik for all they have taught me about disability justice. I know I still have a long way to go but am

grateful for their ideas, evidence, and arguments that I think are helping me be better about addressing disability in principled ways.

26. Patty Berne, "Disability Justice: A Working Draft," *Sins Invalid* (blog), June 10, 2013, https://webable.com/articles/disability-justice-a-working-draft-by-patty-berne-sins-invalid/; Alice Wong, ed., *Disability Intimacy: Essays on Love, Care and Desire* (Vintage, 2024); A. Levins Morales, *Story of What Is Broken;* Piepzna-Samarasinha, *Care Work* and *Future Is Disabled*.

27. Lipsitz, *Danger Zone Is Everywhere*.

28. Catherine A. Okoro et al., "Prevalence of Disabilities and Health Care Access by Disability Status and Type Among Adults—United States 2016," *Morbidity and Mortality Weekly Report* 67, no. 32 (2018): 882–88.

29. Lipsitz, *Danger Zone is Everywhere*.

30. Ferguson, *Reorder of Things*, 140; Robert McRuer, *Crip Theory: Cultural Signs of Queerness and Disability* (New York University Press, 2006).

31. George Yancy and Talila A. Lewis, "Ableism Enables All Forms of Inequity and Hampers All Liberation Efforts," *Truthout*, January 3, 2023, 2.

32. Susan Schweik, "Lomax's Matrix: Disability, Solidarity, and the Black Power of 504," *Disability Studies Quarterly* 31, no. 1 (2011): 1–21.

33. Schweik, "Lomax's Matrix."

34. Schweik, "Lomax's Matrix."

35. Sami Schalk, *Black Disability Politics* (Duke University Press, 2022).

36. Piepzna-Samarasinha, *Care Work*.

37. Angélica Guevara, "Ableness as Property," *University of Wisconsin Law School Legal Studies Research Paper Series*, Paper No. 1593 (2024): 1–44.

38. Naomi Ortiz, "Crip Ecologies: Complicate the Conversation to Reclaim Power," in A. Wong, *Disability Intimacy*.

39. Sins Invalid, *Skin, Tooth, and Bone: The Basis of Movement Is Our People: A Disability Justice Primer*, 2nd ed. (Sins Invalid, 2019), 5.

40. Nathaniel Dickson, "Seizing the Means: Towards a Trans Epistemology," in Gleeson and O'Rourke, *Transgender Marxism*.

41. Jordy Rosenberg, "Afterword: One Utopia, One Dystopia," in Gleeson and O'Rourke, *Transgender Marxism*.

42. Gary Okihiro, *Third World Studies;* Natalia Molina et al., eds., *Relational Formations of Race: Theory, Methods, and Practice* (University of California Press, 2019).

43. Kiswani et al., "Palestine Is Ethnic Studies"; Sean Arce and Theresa Montaño, "Chicanx Studies in the Movement for Ethnic Studies," *Aztlan* 47, no. 2 (Fall 2022): 121–42.

44. Fujino, "Rhizomatic Organizing."

45. Juan Flores, "'Que Assimilated, Brother, Yo Soy Asimilao': The Structuring of Puerto Rican Identity in the United States," *Journal of Ethnic Studies* 13, no. 3 (1985): 1–16.

46. Fujino, "Rhizomatic Organizing."

47. Lauren Araiza, *To March for Others: The Black Freedom Struggle and the United Farm Workers* (University of Pennsylvania Press, 2014); Matt Garcia, *From the Jaws of Victory: The Triumph and Tragedy of Cesar Chavez and the Farm Worker Movement* (University of California Press, 2012).

48. Miyamoto, *Not Yo' Butterfly*.
49. Aileen Moreton Robinson, *The White Possessive: Property, Power, and Indigenous Sovereignty* (University of Minnesota Press, 2015); Elyse Carter Vosen, "Singing and Dancing Idle No More: Round Dances as Indigenous Activism," in Levine and Robinson, *Music and Modernity*.
50. Estes, *Our History Is the Future*, 248.
51. Estes, *Our History Is the Future*.
52. Estes, *Our History Is the Future*, 211, 175.
53. Arthur Manuel (Secwépemc), *Unsettling Canada: A National Wake-Up Call* (Between the Lines Press, 2015), 16.
54. Estes, *Our History Is the Future*.
55. Robert Warrior and Paul Chaat Smith, *Like a Hurricane: The American Indian Movement from Alcatraz to Wounded Knee* (New Press, 1996), 128, 129.
56. Estes, *Our History Is the Future*.
57. Art Neville et al., *The Brothers Neville: An Autobiography* (Little, Brown, 2000).
58. Haas, *Assassination of Fred Hampton*.
59. Andersen, "Critical Indigenous Studies"; Bissett Perea, *Sound Relations*.
60. Elizabeth Ellis, *The Great Power of Small Nations: Indigenous Diplomacy in the Gulf South* (University of Pennsylvania Press, 2023).
61. Simpson, *As We Have Always Done*, 35, 229.
62. Bissett Perea, *Sound Relations*.
63. Vincent Harding, "Responsibilities of the Black Scholar to the Black Community," in *The State of Afro-American History*, ed. Darlene Clark Hine (Louisiana State University, 1989), 281.
64. Harding, "Responsibilities of the Black Scholar," 278.
65. Harding, "Responsibilities of the Black Scholar," 282.
66. Harding, "Responsibilities of the Black Scholar," 282.
67. King, Jr., "Time to Break Silence," 238.
68. Harding, "Responsibilities of the Black Scholar," 278.
69. Walter Rodney, *How Europe Underdeveloped Africa* (Howard University Press, 1984), 11, 224.
70. Vincent Harding, "The Vocation of the Black Scholar and the Struggles of the Black Community," in *Education and Black Struggle: Notes from the Colonized World* (Institute of Black World, 1974), 11.
71. Harding, "Vocation of the Black Scholar," 14.
72. Harding, "Vocation of the Black Scholar," 14.
73. Harding, "Vocation of the Black Scholar," 20.
74. Jodi A. Byrd (Chickasaw), *The Transit of Empire: Indigenous Critiques of Colonialism* (University of Minnesota Press, 2011).
75. TallBear (Sisseton-Wahpeton Oyate), "Caretaking Relations."
76. Cyanne Topaum, "'Savage States: Settler Governance in an Age of Sorrow': Lecture by Audra Simpson—Response by Cyanne Topaum," *Kritik* (blog), January 31, 2019, https://unitforcriticism.wordpress.com/2019/01/31/savage-states-settler-governance-in-an-age-of-sorrow-lecture-by-audra-simpson-response-by-cyanne-topaum-english/.

77. Yellow Bird, "Cowboys and Indians."
78. Anzaldúa's references to Indigenous categories honor them but also lack familiarity with their full reach and scope, a shortcoming I attribute to the education system's omissions at the time when she wrote, omissions that continue to this day.
79. Sostaita, *Sanctuary Everywhere.*
80. Anzaldúa, "Now Let Us Shift," 548.
81. Stuart Hall, *Familiar Stranger: A Life Between Two Islands,* with Bill Schwartz (Duke University Press, 2017), 62.
82. Hall, *Familiar Stranger,* 86.
83. Hall, *Familiar Stranger,* 144, 171.
84. Quoted in Blackwell, *Scales of Resistance,* 27.
85. George Lipsitz, *American Studies in a Moment of Danger* (University of Minnesota Press, 2001); Trouillot, *Global Transformations;* Lorgia Garcia-Peña, *Translating Blackness: Latinx Colonialities in Global Perspective* (Duke University Press, 2022).
86. Trouillot, *Global Transformations,* 94.
87. Gina M. Pérez, *Sanctuary People: Faith-Based Organizing in Latina/o Communities* (New York University Press, 2024), 72.
88. Beloved community as both practice and ideal also infuses the work of the LGBTQ antiracist social justice group Southerners on New Ground (SONG). See Beard, *If We Were Kin.*
89. Pérez, *Sanctuary People.*
90. Villareal, "Anthropolocura as Homeplace Ethnography."
91. Sostaita, *Sanctuary Everywhere,* 48–49.
92. Sostaita, *Sanctuary Everywhere,* 94–95.
93. Sostaita, *Sanctuary Everywhere,* 5.
94. Sostaita, *Sanctuary Everywhere,* 157, 109; Pérez, *Sanctuary People,* 73.
95. A. Levins Morales, *Medicine Stories,* 25.
96. Kimberlé Crenshaw's theorizing of intersectionality is a core component of critical race theory. For its relations with ethnic studies, see chapter 1 of this book as well as Crenshaw, "Twenty Years of Critical Race Theory"; Lipsitz, "'Constituted by a Series."
97. Lorena Garcia, "Intersectionality," *Kalfou* 2, no. 1 (2016): 103.
98. Kristie Dotson, "Theorizing Jane Crow, Theorizing Unknowability," *Social Epistemology* 31, no. 5 (2017): 417–30; Mari Matsuda, *Where Is Your Body? And Other Essays on Race, Gender, and the Law* (Beacon, 1997).
99. Chana Kai Lee, *For Freedom's Sake: The Life of Fannie Lou Hamer* (University of Illinois Press, 1999), 167.

CHAPTER 5. ETHNIC STUDIES AS INQUIRY AND INSTRUCTION

1. Kimmerer, *Braiding Sweetgrass,* 306.
2. Barbara Tomlinson, *Undermining Intersectionality: The Perils of Powerblind Feminism* (Temple University Press, 2019), 13.
3. Taylor, *Archive and the Repertoire.*

4. John Szwed, *Space Is the Place: The Lives and Times of Sun Ra* (Pantheon, 1997), 236.
5. Kimmerer, *Braiding Sweetgrass*, 160.
6. Dominguez et al., "Why a Journal," *Ethnic Studies Pedagogies* 1, no. 1 (2023): 1–6.
7. Tomlinson and Lipsitz, "American Studies as Accompaniment."
8. Kimmerer, *Braiding Sweetgrass*, 152.
9. Tomlinson, *Undermining Intersectionality*.
10. Michel Foucault, "Practicing Criticism: Interview with Didier Ebron," in *Politics, Philosophy, Culture: Interviews and Other Writings, 1977–1984* (Routledge, 1988).
11. Bissett Perea, *Sound Relations*, 7.
12. Bissett Perea, *Sound Relations*, 7.
13. Francesca Lopez and Christine Sleeter, *Critical Race Theory and Its Critics: Implications for Research and Teaching* (Teachers College Press, 2023); Sleeter and Zavala, *Transformative Ethnic Studies*.
14. Zavella, *Movement for Reproductive Justice*.
15. Sarah Deer, *The Beginning and End of Rape: Confronting Sexual Violence in Native America* (University of Minnesota Press, 2015).
16. Keith Feldman, *A Shadow over Palestine: The Imperial Life of Race in America* (University of Minnesota Press, 2015); Sunaina Maira, *Boycott! The Academy and Justice for Palestine* (University of California Press, 2018); Alex Lubin and Marwin Kraidy, eds., *American Studies Encounters the Middle East* (University of North Carolina Press, 2016); Christopher Lee and Melani McAlister, eds., "Generations of Empire in American Studies," *American Quarterly* 74, no. 3 (2022): 477–97.
17. Kimmerer, *Braiding Sweetgrass*, 146; Karen McCarthy Brown, "Afro-Caribbean Spirituality: A Haitian Case Study," in Michel and Bellegarde-Smith, *Vodou in Haitian Life*, 24–25.
18. Roberto Rodríguez, "Ixiim: A Maize Based Philosophy," *Journal of Latinos in Education* 18, no. 2 (2017): 126–33; Mary Watkins and Helene Shulman, *Toward Psychologies of Liberation* (Palgrave Macmillan, 2008), 154.
19. Jeremiah Reyes, "Loon and Kapwa: An Introduction to a Filipino Virtue Ethics," *Asian Philosophy* 25, no. 2 (2015): 148–71.
20. Estes, *Our History Is the Future*.
21. Taylor, *Archive and the Repertoire*, 94.
22. María López Vigil, *Oscar Romero: Memories in Mosaic* (Dartman, Longman, and Todd, 2000); Kimmerer, *Braiding Sweetgrass*, 306.
23. Muñoz, *Cruising Utopia*, 49.
24. Vosen, "Singing and Dancing"; Chun et al., "Intersectionality."
25. Taylor, *¡Presente!* Thich Nhat Hanh observes that in Vietnamese the word for "I" is relational, connoting "your servant." Thich Nhat Hanh and Daniel Berrigan, *The Raft Is Not the Shore: Conversations Toward a Buddhist-Christian Awareness* (Orbis Books, 2001), 42.
26. Robert Farris Thompson, *Flash of the Spirit*, 222; Salaam, *Be About Beauty*, 147; Ahmed, *Queer Phenomenology*, 112, 161–62.

27. Denning, *Culture in the Age of Three Worlds.*
28. Ferguson, *Reorder of Things;* Taylor, *Archive and the Repertoire;* Julietta Singh, *Unthinking Mastery: Dehumanism and Decolonial Entanglements* (Duke University Press, 2018).
29. Trouillot, *Global Transformations,* 81.
30. Cedric Robinson shows that when Europeans encountered Indigenous Peoples in the global South they had already created the savage slot by demonizing the poor inside their nations and attributing less-than-human characteristics to people in Ireland and other sites of imperial conquest. C. Robinson, *Black Marxism.*
31. C. Briggs, *Unlearning,* 45.
32. Tomlinson, *Undermining Intersectionality.*
33. Michel-Rolph Trouillot, "Anthropology and the Savage Slot: The Poetics and Politics of Otherness," in *Trouillot Remixed: The Michel-Rolph Trouillot Reader,* ed. Yarimar Bonilla et al. (Duke University Press, 2021).
34. Hall, *Familiar Stranger.*
35. Laura Briggs, *How All Politics Became Reproductive Politics: From Welfare Reform to Foreclosure to Trump* (University of California Press, 2017).
36. L. Briggs, *How All Politics.*
37. David Hilliard, "The Women's and Gay Liberation Movements," in *The Huey Newton Reader,* ed. David Hilliard and Donald Weise (Seven Stories, 2011), 157–59.
38. L. Briggs, *How All Politics,* 168–69.
39. Zavella, *Movement for Reproductive Justice,* 85.
40. Zavella, *Movement for Reproductive Justice,* 145.
41. A vast network of conjurers, *curandera/os, mambos, mackandals, altaristas, yereros, santeros,* and other traditional healers draw on folk traditions to treat illnesses and infirmities.
42. Quoted in Zavella, *Movement for Reproductive Justice,* 146; See also the home page of the Kindred: Southern Justice Healing Collective, https://kindred southernhjcollective.org/.
43. Walter Mignolo, *The Darker Side of Western Modernity: Global Futures, Decolonial Options* (Duke University Press, 2011).
44. Subcomandante Marcos, *Our Word Is Our Weapon* (Seven Stories Press, 2002).
45. Mignolo, *Darker Side of Western Modernity.*
46. Walter Mignolo, "Epistemic Disobedience, Independent Thought and Decolonial Freedom," *Theory, Culture, and Society* 26, no. 708 (2009): 161.
47. Portelli, *Death of Luigi Trastulli.*
48. Antonieta Mercado, "Civic Engagement: Learning from Teaching Community Praxis," in *Civic Engagement in Diverse Latinx Communities: Learning from Social Justice Partnerships in Action,* ed. Mari Casteñeda and Joseph Krupczynski (Peter Lang, 2018).
49. Stuesse, *Scratching Out a Living;* Ingrid R. G. Waldron, *There's Something in the Water: Environmental Racism in Indigenous and Black Communities* (Fernwood, 2018); Michelle Tellez, *Border Women and the Community of Maclovio Rojas: Autonomy in the Spaces of Neoliberal Neglect* (University of

Arizona Press, 2021); Speed, *Incarcerated Stories;* Eric Tang, *Unsettled: Cambodian Refugees in the New York City Hyperghetto* (Temple University Press, 2015); Alison Rose Reed, *Love and Abolition: The Social Life of Black Queer Performance* (Ohio State University Press, 2022); Monisha Das Gupta, *All of Us Or None: Migrant Organizing in an Era of Deportation and Dispossession* (Duke University Press, 2024).

50. Jordan T. Camp and Christina Heatherton, eds., *Freedom Now! Struggles for the Human Right to Housing in LA and Beyond* (Freedom Now Books, 2012).

51. Ryan N. Dennis, ed., *Collective Creative Actions: Project Row Houses at 25* (Project Row Houses, 2018).

52. Lipsitz and Alliance for California Traditional Arts, *Saludarte.*

53. Elsinore Bennu Think Tank for Restorative Justice, *Life Sentences: Writings from Inside an American Prison* (Belt, 2019); Students at the Center, *Go to Jail: Confronting a System of Oppression* (LMO Projects, 2021).

54. Gloria E. Anzaldúa, "Now Let Us Shift," 567–68; Brian David Lozenski, "Constructing a Dual Subjectivity: Understanding the Intersection of Ethnic Studies and YPAR," *Global Journal of Transformative Education* 1, no. 1 (2019): 26–37.

55. Trouillot, *Global Transformations,* 118.

56. Tomlinson and Lipsitz, *Insubordinate Spaces.*

57. Kimmerer, *Braiding Sweetgrass,* 20.

58. C. Briggs, *Unlearning;* Toni Cade Bambara, *The Salt Eaters* (Vintage Books, 1980), 31.

59. Butler, *Excitable Speech.*

60. Ferguson, *Reorder of Things,* 232.

61. Dominguez et al., "Why a Journal," 3.

62. Taylor, *!Presente!*

63. Lozenski, "Constructing a Dual-Subjectivity."

64. Madison High School 9th Grade Ethnic Studies, *The Story of Environmental Health Coalition* (Environmental Health Coalition, 2024).

65. UCI Public Scholarship Team and Alumni, *Writing the Future of El Sol Together: Escribiendo el Futuro de El Sol Juntos* (UCI Public Scholarship Team and Alumni, 2024), document in author's possession courtesy of Ana Rosas.

66. Aviaja Lyberth Hauptmann et al., "Growing Microbiology Literacy Through Interdisciplinary Approaches to Food Fermentations and an Indigenous Peoples' Rights Framework," *Journal of Microbiology and Biology Education* 26, no. 1 (2025): 1–11.

67. Hauptmann et al., "Growing Microbiology Literacy."

68. Anti-Eugenics Collective at Yale, "Confronting Eugenics and Its Afterlives at Yale and Beyond," accessed May 22, 2025, https://www.antieugenicscollective.org/.

69. Arlene Davila, "Making Moves in the University: Reflections on the Latinx Project," unpublished manuscript in author's possession, received June 20, 2025.

70. Jonathan D. Gomez, "Poetry as Praxis: The Culture Counts Reading Series at San Jose State University," *Aztlan: A Journal of Chicano Studies* 50, no. 2 (2025): 135–146. I am a member of the advisory board of the CCRS.

71. Tricia Rose, *Metaracism: How Systemic Racism Devastates Black Lives—and How We Break Free* (Basic Books, 2024).
72. Tricia Rose, *Way Outta No Way*, web-based project, https://www.wayouttanoway.com/.
73. Trouillot, "Anthropology and the Savage Slot," 57.
74. Arlene M. Davila, foreword to Chávez and Pérez, *Ethnographic Refusals*, xxix.
75. Benjamin, "Theses on the Philosophy of History," 255.
76. Woods, *Development Drowned and Reborn*.
77. James, *American Civilization*, 128.
78. Quoted in Gordon, *Hawthorn Archive*, 105.
79. Paula Ioanide, "The Alchemy of Race and Affect," *Kalfou* 1, no. 1 (2014): 151–68.
80. Davila, *Latinx Art*.
81. Quoted in HoSang, *Wider Type of Freedom*, 56.

CHAPTER 6. ETHNIC STUDIES AND THE CURRENT CRISIS

1. Bambara, *Salt Eaters*, 199.
2. A warm meringue surrounding a center of ice cream set on a sponge cake.
3. Toni Morrison, *Song of Solomon* (Alfred A. Knopf, 1977), 59–60.
4. Gloria E. Anzaldúa, "Preface: (Un) Natural Bridges, (Un) Safe Spaces," in Anzaldúa and Keating, *This Bridge We Call Home*, 3.
5. Benjamin, "Theses on the Philosophy of History"; C. Robinson, *Black Marxism*, 171.
6. Salaam, *Be About Beauty*, 163.
7. Irena Lara, "Healing Suenos for Academia," in Anzaldúa and Keating, *This Bridge We Call Home*, 434.
8. Gordon, *Hawthorn Archive*, 48.
9. Gordon, *Hawthorn Archive*, 48, 63.
10. Gordon, *Hawthorn Archive*, 49.
11. James Russell Lowell, "The Present Crisis," 1845, Poets.org, https://poets.org/poem/present-crisis.
12. Du Bois, *Black Reconstruction in America*.
13. Rawick, *From Sundown to Sunup*.
14. Trouillot, "Anthropology and the Savage Slot," 57–58.
15. Gordon, *Hawthorn Archive*, v.
16. Razia Iqbal, "Rashid Khalidi, America's Foremost Scholar of Palestine, Is Retiring: 'I Don't Want to Be a Cog in the Machine Any More,'" *The Guardian*, October 9, 2024, https://www.theguardian.com/world/ng-interactive/2024/oct/08/rashid-khalidi-palestine-israel-scholar-columbia-university-retires.
17. Denning, *Cultural Front*.
18. Denning, *Cultural Front*; Payne, *I've Got the Light of Freedom*.
19. William Cullen Bryant, "The Battle-Field," 1878, Poets.org, https://poets.org/poem/battle-field.

20. George Lipsitz and Russell Rodriguez, "Turning Hegemony on Its Head: The Insurgent Knowledge of Américo Paredes," *Journal of American Folklore* 125, no. 495 (2012): 111–25.

21. Denning, *Cultural Front*.

22. Meagan Parker Brooks and Davis W. Houck, eds., *The Speeches of Fannie Lou Hamer: To Tell It Like It Is* (University of Mississippi Press, 2011); Chana Kai Lee, *For Freedom's Sake*.

23. R. Levins Morales, *Land Knows the Way*.

24. Lisa Hirmer, "Everything We Have Done Is Weather Now," *Public* 35, no. 70 (2024): 51–54.

25. Robin D. G. Kelley, "American Studies (Still) in a Moment of Danger," paper presented at California State University, Long Beach, April 24, 2025, manuscript in author's possession courtesy of Robin Kelley.

Bibliography

Aguayo, Angela J. *Documentary Resistance: Social Change and Participatory Media*. Oxford University Press, 2019.

Ahmed, Sarah. *Queer Phenomenology: Orientations, Objects, Others*. Duke University Press, 2006.

Andersen, Chris. "Critical Indigenous Studies: From Difference to Density." *Cultural Studies Review* 15, no. 1 (September 2009): 80–100.

Anti-Eugenics Collective at Yale. "Confronting Eugenics and Its Afterlives at Yale and Beyond." Accessed May 22, 2025. https://www.antieugenicscollective.org/.

Anzaldúa, Gloria E. *Borderlands/La Frontera: The New Mestiza*. Aunt Lute Books, 1987.

Anzaldúa, Gloria E. "Now Let Us Shift . . . the Path of Conocimiento . . . Inner Work, Public Acts." In Anzaldúa and Keating, *This Bridge We Call Home*.

Anzaldúa, Gloria E. "Preface: (Un) natural Bridges, (Un) safe Spaces." In Anzaldúa and Keating, *This Bridge We Call Home*.

Anzaldúa, Gloria E., and AnaLouise Keating, eds. *This Bridge We Call Home: Radical Visions for Transformation*. Routledge, 2002.

Aparicio, Frances. "*Aguanile*: Critical Listening, Mourning, and Decolonial Healing." In Ramos-Zayas and Rúa, *Critical Dialogues*.

Araiza, Lauren. *To March for Others: The Black Freedom Struggle and the United Farm Workers*. University of Pennsylvania Press, 2014.

Arce, Sean, and Theresa Montaño. "Chicanx Studies in the Movement for Ethnic Studies." *Aztlan* 47, no. 2 (Fall 2022): 121–32.

Asian Immigrant Women Advocates. "Teacher's Study Guide for Gary Delgado, *Becoming Ourselves: How Immigrant Women Transformed Their World* (Film, 2013)." *Kalfou* 4, no. 1 (2017): 96–117.

Awartani, Sara. "You Have Living Legends Among You: Commemorating the Fiftieth Anniversary of the Chicago Young Lords." *Kalfou* 6, no. 1 (Spring 2019): 127–32.

Baker, Houston A. *Blues, Ideology and African American Literature.* University of Chicago Press, 1985.

Bambara, Toni Cade. "Toni Cade Bambara." Interview by Claudia Tate. In *Black Women Writers at Work*, edited by Claudia Tate. Haymarket Books, 2023.

Bambara, Toni Cade. *The Salt Eaters.* Vintage, 1980.

Barcelos, Chris. *Youth Organizing for Reproductive Justice: A Guide for Liberation.* University of California Press, 2025.

Barrett, James R., and David Roediger. "Inbetween Peoples: Race, Nationality, and the 'New Immigrant' Working Class." *Journal of American Ethnic History* 16, no. 3 (1997): 3–44.

Beard, Lisa. *If We Were Kin: Race, Identification, and Intimate Political Appeals.* Oxford University Press, 2023.

Bell, Derrick. *And We Are Not Saved: The Elusive Quest for Racial Justice.* Basic Books, 1987.

Bell, Derrick. "*Brown v. Board of Education* and the Interest Convergence Dilemma." *Harvard Law Review* 93, no. 3 (January 1980): 518–33.

Bell, Derrick. *Faces at the Bottom of the Well: The Permanence of Racism.* Basic Books, 1992.

Bellegarde-Smith, Patrick, and Claudine Michel. "Danbala/Ayida as Cosmic Prism: The Lwa Trope for Understanding Metaphysics in Haitian Vodou and Beyond." *Journal of Africana Religions* 1, no. 4 (2013): 458–87.

Benjamin, Walter. "Theses on the Philosophy of History." In *Illuminations: Essays and Reflections.* Shocken Books, 1968.

Benjamin, Walter. *One Way Street.* Belknap/Harvard University Press, 2016.

Benmayor, Rina. "Digital Testimonio as a Signature Pedagogy for Latin@ Studies." *Equity and Excellence in Education* 45, no. 3 (2012): 507–24.

Berne, Patty. "Disability Justice: A Working Draft." *Sins Invalid* (blog), June 10, 2013. https://webable.com/articles/disability-justice-a-working-draft-by-patty-berne-sins-invalid/.

Bhabha, Homi K. "Remembering Fanon: Self-Psyche and the Colonial Condition." Foreword to the 1986 edition of Frantz Fanon, *Black Skin, White Masks.* Pluto Press, 2008.

Bissett Perea, Jessica. *Sound Relations: Native Ways of Doing Music in Alaska.* Oxford University Press, 2021.

Blackwell, Maylei. *Chicana Power! Contested Histories of Feminism in the Chicano Movement.* University of Texas Press, 2011.

Blackwell, Maylei. *Scales of Resistance: Indigenous Women's Transborder Activism.* Duke University Press, 2023.

Bloch, Ernst. "Nonsynchronism and the Obligation to Its Dialectics." *New German Critique* 11 (Spring 1977): 22–38.

Bloch, Ernst. *The Principle of Hope.* MIT Press, 1986.

Boj Lopez, Floridama. "Mobile Archives of Indigeneity: Building la Communidad Ixim Through Organizing in the Maya Diaspora." *Latino Studies* 15 (2017): 201–18.

Bonus, Rick. *The Ocean in the School: Pacific Islander Students Transforming Their University*. Duke University Press, 2020.

Bowles, Courtney, and Mark Strandquist. "The People's Paper Co-op." In *The Art and Art Therapy of Papermaking: Material, Methods, and Applications*, edited by Drew Luan Matott and Gretchen R. Miller. Routledge, 2024.

Brady, Mary Pat. *Scales of Captivity: Racial Capitalism and the Latinx Child*. Duke University Press, 2022.

Briggs, Charles L. *Incommunicable: Toward Justice in Health and Medicine*. Duke University Press, 2024.

Briggs, Charles L. *Unlearning: Rethinking Poetics, Pandemics, and the Politics of Knowledge*. University Press of Colorado, 2021.

Briggs, Laura. *How All Politics Became Reproductive Politics: From Welfare Reform to Foreclosure to Trump*. University of California Press, 2017.

Brodkin, Karen. *How Jews Became White Folks and What That Says About Race in America*. Rutgers University Press, 1998.

Brooks, Megan Parker, and Davis W. Houck, eds. *The Speeches of Fannie Lou Hamer: To Tell It Like It Is*. University of Mississippi Press, 2011.

Brown, Karen McCarthy. "Afro-Caribbean Spirituality: A Haitian Case Study." In Michel and Bellegarde-Smith, *Vodou in Haitian Life*.

Brown, Pamela, Paul LeBlanc, and Kaitlin Collins. "Trump Pardons Steve Bannon as One of His Final Acts in Office." *CNN Politics*, January 20, 2021.

Bryant, William Cullen. "The Battle-Field." 1878. https://poets.org/poem/battle-field.

Buras, Kristen L. *Pedagogy, Policy, and the Privatized City: Stories of Dispossession and Defiance from New Orleans*. With Jim Randels, Kalamu ya Salaam, and Students at the Center. Teachers College Press, 2010.

Burris, Greg. *The Palestinian Idea: Film, Media, and the Radical Imagination*. Temple University Press, 2019.

Butler, Judith. *Excitable Speech: A Politics of the Performative*. Routledge, 1997.

Butler, Judith. *Precarious Life: The Powers of Mourning and Violence*. Verso, 2004.

Butler, Judith. *The Psychic Life of Power: Theories in Subjection*. Stanford University Press, 1997.

Byrd, Jodi A. (Chickasaw). "A Return to the South." *American Quarterly* 66, no. 3 (September 2014): 609–20.

Byrd, Jodi A. (Chickasaw). *The Transit of Empire: Indigenous Critiques of Colonialism*. University of Minnesota Press, 2011.

Camp, Jordan T., and Christina Heatherton, eds. *Freedom Now! Struggles for the Human Right to Housing in LA and Beyond*. Freedom Now Books, 2012.

Carbado, Devon W., and Mitu Gulati. *Acting White? Rethinking Race in "Postracial" America*. Oxford University Press, 2013.

Carmichael, Stokely (Kwame Ture). "Toward Black Liberation," *Massachusetts Review* 7, no. 4 (1966): 639–51.

Cazares-Minero, Mayra, Hui Huang, and Joseph Bishop. *Often Overlooked but Not Unseen: An Overview of Highly Mobile Youth in the U.S. Brief*, UCLA Center for the Transformation of Schools, 2025. https://

transformschools.ucla.edu/research/often-overlooked-but-not-unseen-an-overview-of-highly-mobile-youth-in-the-u-s/.

Cazares-Minero, Mayra, Hui Huang, and Joseph Bishop. *1.37 Million and Rising: Understanding the National 25% Spike in Student Homelessness*. UCLA Center for the Transformation of Schools, 2025. https://transformschools.ucla.edu/research/1-37-million-and-rising-understanding-the-national-25-spike-in-student-homelessness/2025.

Chamoiseau, Patrick, and William Parker. "Epistolary Conversation." Discussion preceding the performance of Parker's symphonic poem *Trail of Tears* at the February 2022 Sons d'hiver festival. *La Plateforme*, November 17, 2021, to January 3, 2022. https://laplateforme-sonsdhiver.org/chamoiseau-parker/.

Chávez, Alex E. *Sounds of Crossing: Music, Migration, and the Aural Poetics of Huapango Arribeño*. Duke University Press, 2017.

Chávez, Alex E., and Gina M. Pérez, eds. *Ethnographic Refusals: Unruly Latinidades*. University of New Mexico Press, 2022.

Chun, Jennifer Jiyhe, George Lipsitz, and Young Shin. "Immigrant Women Workers at the Center of Social Change: AIWA Takes Stock of Itself." *Kalfou*, inaugural issue (2010): 127–32.

Chun, Jennifer Jiyhe, George Lipsitz, and Young Shin. "Immigrant Women Workers at the Center of Social Change: Asian Immigrant Women Advocates." In *Immigrant Women Workers in the Neoliberal Age*, edited by Nilda Flores Gonzalez, Anna Romina Guevara, Maura Toro-Morn, and Grace Chang. University of Illinois Press, 2013.

Chun, Jennifer Jiyhe, George Lipsitz, and Young Shin. "Intersectionality as a Social Movement Strategy: Asian Immigrant Women Advocates." *Signs* 38, no. 4 (Summer 2013): 917–40.

Clark, Jess. "Lawmaker Wants to Make Teaching Critical Race Theory Illegal." WKU Public Radio, June 3, 2021.

Cohen, Lizabeth. *Making a New Deal: Industrial Workers in Chicago, 1919–1930*. Cambridge University Press, 1990.

Connolly, Sebastian B., and Julia A. Karabolli. "Harvard Divinity School Suspends Religion, Conflict, and Peace Initiative." *Harvard Crimson*, April 7, 2025.

Conti, Norman. "Stanton Heights." *Kalfou* 5, no. 2 (Fall 2018): 372–93.

Crane, Emma Shaw. "Lush Aftermath: Race, Labor, and Landscape in the Suburb." *Society and Space* 41, no. 2 (2023): 210–30.

Crenshaw, Kimberlé Williams. "Demarginalizing the Intersections of Race and Sex: A Black Feminist Critique of Antidiscrimination Doctrine, Feminist Theory, and Antiracist Politics." *University of Chicago Legal Forum* 14 (1989): 138–67.

Crenshaw, Kimberlé Williams. "Mapping the Margins: Intersectionality, Identity, and Violence Against Women of Color." *Stanford Law Review* 43 (1991): 1241–99.

Crenshaw, Kimberlé Williams. "Race, Reform, and Retrenchment: Transformation and Legitimation in Anti-discrimination Law." In Crenshaw et al., *Critical Race Theory*.

Crenshaw, Kimberlé Williams. "Twenty Years of Critical Race Theory: Looking Back to Move Forward." *Connecticut Law Review* 43, no. 5 (July 2011): 1253–1352.
Crenshaw, Kimberlé Williams. "Unmasking Colorblindness in the Law: Lessons from the Formation of Critical Race Theory." In *Seeing Race Again: Countering Colorblindness Across the Disciplines*, edited by Kimberlé Williams Crenshaw, Luke Harris, Daniel HoSang, and George Lipsitz. University of California Press, 2019.
Crenshaw, Kimberlé, Neil Gotanda, Gary Peller, and Kendall Thomas, eds. *Critical Race Theory: The Key Writings That Made the Movement*. New Press, 1995.
Darity, William A., and A. Kirsten Mullen. *From Here to Equality: Reparations for Black Americans in the Twenty-First Century*. University of North Carolina Press, 2020.
Das Gupta, Monisha. *All of Us Or None: Migrant Organizing in an Era of Deportation and Dispossession*. Duke University Press, 2024.
Das Gupta, Monisha. "'KNOw History/KNOw Self': Khmer Youth Organizing for Justice in Long Beach." *Amerasia Journal* 45, no. 2 (2019): 137–56.
Davalos, Karen Mary. "A Poetics of Love and Rescue in the Collection of Chicano/a Art." *Latino Studies* 5 (2007): 76–103.
Davies, Bronwyn, and Sue Saltmarsh. "Gender Economies: Literacy and the Gendered Production of Neoliberal Subjectivities." *Gender and Education* 19, no. 1 (2007): 1–20.
Davila, Arlene. Foreword to Chávez and Pérez, *Ethnographic Refusals*.
Davila, Arlene. *Latinx Art: Artists, Markets, and Politics*. Duke University Press, 2020.
Davila, Arlene. "Making Moves in the University: Reflections on the Latinx Project." Manuscript in author's possession courtesy of Arlene Davila. Received June 20, 2025.
Davis, Angela Y. "Deepening the Debate over Mass Incarceration." *Socialism and Democracy* 28, no. 3 (2014): 15–23.
Deer, Sarah. *The Beginning and End of Rape: Confronting Sexual Violence in Native America*. University of Minnesota Press, 2015.
D'Emilio, John D. *Queer Legacies: Stories from Chicago's LGBTQ Archives*. University of Chicago Press, 2020.
Denning, Michael. *The Cultural Front: The Laboring of American Culture*. Verso, 1996.
Denning, Michael. *Culture in the Age of Three Worlds*. Verso, 2004.
Dennis, Ryan N., ed. *Collective Creative Actions: Project Row Houses at 25*. Project Row Houses, 2018.
Dent, Thomas C., Richard Schechner, and Gilbert Moses, eds. *The Free Southern Theater, by the Free Southern Theater*. Bobbs-Merrill, 1969.
Desmangles, Leslie Gerald. "African Interpretations of the Christian Cross in Vodou." In Michel and Bellegarde-Smith, *Vodou in Haitian Life*.
Dickson, Nathaniel. "Seizing the Means: Towards a Trans Epistemology." In *Transgender Marxism*, edited by Jules Joanne Gleeson and Elle O'Rourke. Pluto Press, 2021.

Dominguez, Michael, Brian Lozenski, Miguel Zavala, and Maria Nubia Feliciano. "Why a Journal on Ethnic Studies Pedagogies?" *Ethnic Studies Pedagogies* 1, no. 1 (2023): 1–6.
Dotson, Kristie. "Theorizing Jane Crow, Theorizing Unknowability." *Social Epistemology* 31, no. 5 (2017): 417–30.
Du Bois, W. E. B. *Black Reconstruction in America, 1860–1880.* Atheneum, 1992.
Eidsheim, Nina. *The Race of Sound: Listening, Timbre, and Vocality in African American Music.* Duke University Press, 2019.
Ellis, Elizabeth. *The Great Power of Small Nations: Indigenous Diplomacy in the Gulf South.* University of Pennsylvania Press, 2023.
Elsinore Bennu Think Tank for Restorative Justice. *Life Sentences: Writings from Inside an American Prison.* Belt, 2019.
Estes, Nick. *Our History Is the Future: Standing Rock Versus the Dakota Pipeline and the Long Tradition of Indigenous Resistance.* Haymarket, 2023.
Esteva, Gustavo. "The Hour of Autonomy." *Latin American and Caribbean Ethnic Studies* 10, no. 1 (2015): 134–45.
Ewing, K. T. "Fugitive Archives: Black Women, Domestic Repositories, and Hoarding as Informal Archival Practice." *Black Scholar* 52, no. 4 (2022): 43–51.
Fanon, Frantz. *The Wretched of the Earth.* Grove Press, 1968.
Feldman, Keith. *A Shadow over Palestine: The Imperial Life of Race in America.* University of Minnesota Press, 2015.
Ferguson, Roderick A. *Aberrations in Black: Toward a Queer of Color Critique.* University of Minnesota Press, 2004.
Ferguson, Roderick A. "Building Relations, Critical University Studies and Student Activism: A Conversation with Roderick A. Ferguson." Interview by Kong Pheng Pha and José Manuel Santillana Blanco. *Agitate Journal,* Summer 2024. https://agitatejournal.org/article/building-relations-critical-university-studies-and-student-activism-a-conversation-with-roderick-a-ferguson/.
Ferguson, Roderick A. *One-Dimensional Queer.* Polity Press, 2019.
Ferguson, Roderick A. *The Reorder of Things: The University and Its Pedagogies of Minority Difference.* University of Minnesota Press, 2012.
Ferguson, Roderick A. *We Demand: The University and Student Protests.* University of California Press, 2017.
Fernández, Johanna. *The Young Lords: A Radical History.* University of North Carolina Press, 2020.
Ferreira, Jason. "From College Readiness to Ready for Revolution! Third World Student Activism at a Northern California Community College." *Kalfou* 1, no. 1 (Spring 2014): 117–44.
Fielder, Elizabeth Rodriguez. *The Revolution Will Be Improvised: The Intimacy of Cultural Activism.* University of Michigan Press, 2024.
Flint Water Crisis Public Archive. "Introduction to the Flint Water Crisis Public Archive." 2024. https://fwcpublicarchive.lib.uiowa.edu/introduction-to-the-flint-water-crisis-public-archive/.
Flores, Juan. "'Que Assimilated, Brother, Yo Soy Asimilao': The Structuring of Puerto Rican Identity in the United States." *Journal of Ethnic Studies* 13, no. 3 (1985): 1–16.

Forbes, Jack D. "Intellectual Self-Determination and Sovereignty: Implications for Native Studies and for Native Intellectuals." *Wicazo Sa Review* 13, no. 1 (Spring 1988): 11–23.

Foucault, Michel. *The History of Sexuality*. Vol. 1, *An Introduction*. Vintage, 1980.

Foucault, Michel. "Practicing Criticism: Interview with Didier Ebron." In *Politics, Philosophy, Culture: Interviews and Other Writings, 1977–1984*. Routledge, 1988.

Fujino, Diane C. "Rhizomatic Organizing, Collective Leadership, and Community-Centered Pedagogy in the Early Asian American Movement." *Journal of American Studies*, September 2024, 1–34.

Fujino, Diane C., Jonathan D. Gomez, Esther Lezra, George Lipsitz, Jordan Mitchell, and James Fonseca. "A Transformative Pedagogy for a Decolonial World." *Review of Education, Pedagogy, and Cultural Studies* 40, no. 2 (2018): 69–95.

Galeano, Eduardo. *The Open Veins of Latin America*. 25th Anniversary Edition. Monthly Review Press, 1997.

Galeano, Eduardo. *Upside Down: A Primer for the Looking Glass World*. Henry Holt, 2008.

Gan, Jessi. "'Still at the Back of the Bus': Sylvia Rivera's Struggle." *Centro Journal* 19, no. 1 (Spring 2007): 125–39.

Garcia, Lorena. "Intersectionality." *Kalfou* 2, no. 1 (2016): 103.

Garcia, Matt. *From the Jaws of Victory: The Triumph and Tragedy of Cesar Chavez and the Farm Worker Movement*. University of California Press, 2012.

Garcia-Peña, Lorgia. *Community as Rebellion: A Syllabus for Surviving Academia as a Woman of Color*. Haymarket, 2022.

Garcia-Peña, Lorgia. *Translating Blackness: Latinx Colonialities in Global Perspective*. Duke University Press, 2022.

Georgakas, Dan, and Marvin Surkin. *Detroit: I Do Mind Dying: A Study in Urban Revolution*. South End Press, 1998.

Gilmore, Ruth Wilson. *Golden Gulag: Prisons, Surplus, Crisis, and Opposition in Globalizing California*. University of California Press, 2007.

Gleeson, Jules Joanne, and Elle O'Rourke. Introduction to Gleeson and O'Rourke, *Transgender Marxism*.

Gleeson, Jules Joanne, and Elle O'Rourke, eds. *Transgender Marxism*. Pluto Press, 2021.

Godoy, Angela Snodgrass. "Probing the Membrane Between Horror and Hope: Artist Claudia Bernardi." *Center for Latin American Studies Newsletter*, University of California Berkeley, 1999.

Godwin, William. *Lives of the Necromancers*. Harper Brothers, 1835. https://babel.hathitrust.org/cgi/pt?id=hvd.hwl3jb&seq=11.

Gomez, Jonathan D. "Poetry as Praxis: The Culture Counts Reading Series at San Jose State University." *Aztlan: A Journal of Chicano Studies* 50, no. 2 (2025): 135–146.

Gomez, Jonathan D., Jorge Lopez-Ramirez, and Ismael F. Illescas. "Cedric Robinson, Modest Audacity, and the Black Radical Tradition." *Kalfou* 3, no. 2 (Fall 2016): 288–97.

Gonzalez, Martha. *Chican@ Artivistas: Music Community, and Transborder Tactics in East Los Angeles.* University of Texas Press, 2020.

Gordon, Avery. *The Hawthorn Archive: Letters from the Utopian Margins.* Fordham University Press, 2018.

Gouldner, Alvin. *The Future of Intellectuals and the Rise of the New Class.* Oxford University Press, 1979.

Gramsci, Antonio. *Selections from the Prison Notebooks of Antonio Gramsci.* Edited and translated by Quinten Hoare and Geoffrey Nowell Smith. International Publishers, 1971.

Graveline, Frye Jean. "Idle No More: Enough Is Enough." *Canadian Social Work Review* 29, no. 2 (2012): 293–300.

Guevara, Angélica. "Ableness as Property." *University of Wisconsin Law School Legal Studies Research Paper Series,* Paper No. 1593 (2024): 1–44.

Gutiérrez, Ramón A. *When Jesus Came, the Corn Mothers Went Away: Marriage, Sexuality, and Power in New Mexico, 1500–1846.* Stanford University Press, 1991.

Haas, Jeffrey. *The Assassination of Fred Hampton: How the FBI and the Chicago Police Murdered a Black Panther.* Lawrence Hill Books, 2019.

Halberstam, Jack. *In a Queer Time and Place: Transgender Bodies, Subcultural Lives.* New York University Press, 2005.

Hall, Stuart. *Familiar Stranger: A Life Between Two Islands.* With Bill Schwartz. Duke University Press, 2017.

Hall, Stuart. "The Neo-liberal Revolution." *Cultural Studies* 25, no. 6 (2011): 705–28.

Hall, Stuart. "When We Are All Enemies of the State." *Boston Review,* June 12, 2025.

Hanchard, Michael. "Afro-Modernity: Temporality, Politics, and the African Diaspora." *Public Culture* 11, no. 1 (1999): 245–68.

Hanh, Thich Nhat, and Daniel Berrigan. *The Raft Is Not the Shore: Conversations Towards a Buddhist Christian Awareness.* Orbis Books, 2001.

Harding, Vincent. "Responsibilities of the Black Scholar to the Black Community." In *The State of Afro-American History,* edited by Darlene Clark Hine. Louisiana State University Press, 1989.

Harding, Vincent. "The Vocation of the Black Scholar and the Struggles of the Black Community." In *Education and Black Struggle: Notes from the Colonized World.* Institute of the Black World, 1974.

Harris, Cheryl. "Whiteness as Property." *Harvard Law Review* 106, no. 8 (June 1993): 1707–91.

Hart, Peter. "King's Dream Remains Unfilled, Julian Bond Says." *University Times,* April 2, 2003. https://www.utimes.pitt.edu/archives/?p=1241.

Hauptmann, Aviaja Lyberth, Stephanie Maroney, Jessica Bissett Perea, and Maria L. Marco. "Growing Microbiology Literacy Through Interdisciplinary Approaches to Food Fermentations and an Indigenous Peoples' Rights Framework." *Journal of Microbiology and Biology Education* 26, no. 1 (2025): 1–11.

Heble, Ajay, and Jesse Stewart. *Jamming the Classroom: Musical Improvisation and Pedagogical Practice.* University of Michigan Press, 2023.

Henry, Charles P. *Black Studies and the Democratization of American Higher Education.* Palgrave Macmillan, 2017.
Hilliard, David. *Huey: Spirit of the Panther.* Thunder's Mouth, 2006.
Hilliard, David. "The Women's and Gay Liberation Movements." In *The Huey Newton Reader,* edited by David Hilliard and Donald Weise. Seven Stories, 2011.
Hirmer, Lisa. "Everything We Have Done Is Weather Now." *Public* 35, no. 70 (2024): 51–54.
Hoadley-Brill, Samuel. "Chris Rufo's Critical Race Theory Reporting Is Filled with Errors, and He Doesn't Seem to Care." *Flux,* July 26, 2021.
Horiuchi, Edna. "Nobuko Miyamoto: Giving Voice to Asian American Stories—Part 2." *North American Post,* March 15, 2022. https://napost.com/2022/nobuko-miyamoto-giving-voice-to-asian-american-stories-part-1/.
HoSang, Daniel Martinez. *Racial Propositions: Ballot Initiatives and the Making of Postwar California.* University of California Press, 2010.
HoSang, Daniel Martinez. "Understanding the Role of the Multiracial Right—and Why It Matters." *Public Eye Quarterly* 1 (Summer 2024): 3–6.
HoSang, Daniel Martinez. *A Wider Type of Freedom: How Struggles for Racial Justice Liberate Everyone.* University of California Press, 2021.
Hughes, Sherrick, George Noblit, and Darrell Cleveland. "Derrick Bell's Post-*Brown* Moves Toward Critical Race Theory." *Race Ethnicity and Education* 16, no. 4 (2013): 442–69.
Hyra, Derek. *Slow and Sudden Violence: Why and When Urban Uprisings Occur.* University of California Press, 2024.
Ignatiev, Noel. *How The Irish Became White.* Routledge, 1996.
Ioanide, Paula. "The Alchemy of Race and Affect." *Kalfou* 1, no. 1 (2014): 151–68.
Iqbal, Razia. "Rashid Khalidi, America's Foremost Scholar of Palestine, Is Retiring: 'I Don't Want to Be a Cog in the Machine Any More.'" *The Guardian,* October 9, 2024.
I Wor Kuen. "I Wor Kuen's 12 Point Platform and Program." History Is a Weapon, 1969. https://www.historyisaweapon.com/defcon1/12pointiworkuen.html.
James, C. L. R. *American Civilization.* Blackwell, 1993.
James, C. L. R. *The Black Jacobins: Toussaint L'Ouverture and the San Domingo Revolution.* Vintage, 1989.
James-Gallaway, ArCasia D. "What Got Them Through: Community Cultural Wealth, Black Students and Texas School Desegregation." *Race Ethnicity and Education* 25, no. 2 (2022): 173–91.
Jeffries, Hasan Kwame. *Bloody Lowndes: Civil Rights and Black Power in Alabama's Black Belt.* New York University Press, 2010.
Jenkins, Destin. *The Bonds of Inequality: Debt and the Making of the American City.* University of Chicago Press, 2021.
Johnson, Cedric. *From Revolutionaries to Race Leaders: Black Power and the Making of African American Politics.* University of Minnesota Press, 2007.
Johnson, Walter. "Living Inside a Psyop: Three Months at Harvard." *n+1,* January 10, 2024.

Jones, Sarah. "How to Manufacture a Moral Panic: Christopher Rufo Helped Incite an Uproar over Racism Education with Dramatic, Dodgy Reporting." *New York Magazine,* July 21, 2021.

Kahrl, Andrew. *The Black Tax: 150 Years of Theft, Exploitation, and Dispossession in America.* University of Chicago Press, 2024.

Kajikawa, Loren. "Leaders of the New School? Music Departments, Hip-Hop, and the Challenge of Significant Difference." *Twentieth Century Music* 18, no. 1 (2021): 45–64.

Kelley, Robin D. G. "American Studies (Still) in a Moment of Danger." Paper presented at California State University, Long Beach, April 24, 2025. Manuscript in author's possession courtesy of Robin D. G. Kelley.

Kelley, Robin D. G. "Black Study, Black Struggle." *Boston Review,* March 1, 2016.

Kelley, Robin D. G. *Freedom Dreams: The Black Radical Imagination.* Beacon Press, 2002.

Khabeer, Su'ad Abdul. "[In] Searching Our Mothers' Archives: Building Umi's Archive Through Mourning Work." *African Journal of Gender and Religion* 29, no. 2 (2023): 1–25.

Kimmerer, Robin Wall. *Braiding Sweetgrass: Indigenous Wisdom, Scientific Knowledge, and the Teachings of Plants.* Milkweed, 2013.

King, Martin Luther, Jr. *Strength to Love.* Fortress Press, 2010.

King, Martin Luther, Jr. "A Time to Break Silence." In *A Testament of Hope: The Essential Writings and Speeches of Martin Luther King Jr.,* edited by James M. Washington. Harper Collins, 1991.

Kiswani, Lara, Nadine Naber, and Samia Shoman. "Palestine Is Ethnic Studies: The Struggle for Arab American Studies in K-12 Ethnic Studies Curriculum." *Journal of Asian American Studies* 26, no. 2 (June 2023): 221–31.

Kuennen, Tamara. "Uncharted Violence: Reclaiming Structural Causes in the Power and Control Wheel." *Arizona State Law Journal* 55 (2023): 560–607.

Lara, Irene. "Healing Suenos for Academia." In Anzaldúa and Keating, *This Bridge We Call Home.*

Lawrence, Charles R., III. "The Id, the Ego, and Equal Protection: Reckoning with Unconscious Racism." *Stanford Law Review* 39 (January 1987): 317–88.

Layton, Lynne. *Toward a Social Psychoanalysis: Culture, Character, and Normative Unconscious Processes.* Routledge, 2020.

Lee, Chana Kai. *For Freedom's Sake: The Life of Fannie Lou Hamer.* University of Illinois Press, 1999.

Lee, Christopher, and Melani McAlister, eds. "Generations of Empire in American Studies." *American Quarterly* 74, no. 3 (2022): 477–97.

Lee, James Kyung-Jin. *Urban Triage: Race and the Fictions of Multiculturalism.* University of Minnesota Press, 2004.

Lee, Katherine. "An Asian American Studies Writing Pedagogy: Reformulating the Work of Writing in Asian American Studies Classes." *Journal of Asian American Studies* 26, no. 2 (June 2023): 265–76.

Levine, Victoria Lindsay, and Dylan Robinson. *Music and Modernity Among First Peoples of North America.* Wesleyan University Press, 2019.

Levins Morales, Aurora. *Medicine Stories: Essays for Radicals.* Duke University Press, 2019.

Levins Morales, Aurora. *The Story of What Is Broken Is Whole: An Aurora Levins Morales Reader.* Duke University Press, 2024.

Levins Morales, Aurora, and Rosario Morales. *Getting Home Alive.* Firebrand Books, 1986.

Levins Morales, Ricardo. *Tending the Soil: Lessons for Organizing.* Zine/pamphlet. RLM Art Studio, 2020.

Levins Morales, Ricardo. *The Land Knows The Way: Eco-Social Insights for Liberation.* RLM Art Studio, 2025.

Lew, Janey. "A Politics of Meeting: Reading Intersectional Indigenous Feminist Praxis in Lee Maracle's *Sojourners and Sundogs.*" *Frontiers* 38, no. 1 (2017): 225–59.

Lin, May. "Khmer Girls in Action and Healing Justice: Expanding Understandings of Anti-Asian Racism and Public Health Solutions." *Frontiers in Public Health* 10 (2022): 956308.

Lipsitz, George. *American Studies in a Moment of Danger.* University of Minnesota Press, 2001.

Lipsitz, George. "AUMI as a Model for Social Justice." In *Improvising Across Abilities: Pauline Oliveros and the Adaptive Use Musical Instrument,* edited by the Aumi Editorial Collective. University of Michigan Press, 2024.

Lipsitz, George. "Challenging Neoliberal Education at the Grass Roots: Students Who Lead, Not Students Who Leave." *Souls* 17, nos. 3–4 (2015): 303–21.

Lipsitz, George. "'Constituted by a Series of Contestations': Critical Race Theory as a Social Movement." *Connecticut Law Review* 43, no. 5 (July 2011): 1461–78.

Lipsitz, George. *The Danger Zone Is Everywhere: How Housing Discrimination Harms Health and Steals Wealth.* University of California Press, 2024.

Lipsitz, George. "FandangObon: Amplification, Counter-publics, and Fugitive Spaces of Belonging in Los Angeles." *American Anthropologist* 162, no. 2 (2024): 260–79.

Lipsitz, George. *How Racism Takes Place.* Temple University Press, 2011.

Lipsitz, George. "Learning How to Arrive: The Improvisational Toolkit of Artivistas in Boyle Heights." In *The Improviser's Classroom: Pedagogies for Cocreative World Making,* edited by Daniel Fischlin and Mark Lomanno. Temple University Press, 2024.

Lipsitz, George. *A Life in the Struggle: Ivory Perry and the Culture of Opposition.* Temple University Press, 1995.

Lipsitz, George. *The Possessive Investment in Whiteness: How White People Profit from Identity Politics.* Temple University Press, 2018.

Lipsitz, George. "Neighborhood Development and Art-Based Community Making." In *Collective Creative Actions: Project Row Houses at 25,* edited by Ryan N. Dennis. Project Row Houses, 2018.

Lipsitz, George. "Shattering Silences: Dictions, Contradictions, and Ethnic Studies at the Crossroads." *Kalfou* 7, no. 2 (Fall 2020): 222–48.

Lipsitz, George. "Teaching After the Battle in Seattle: This Is What Plutocracy Looks Like." In *What Democracy Looks Like: A New Critical Realism for a Post-Seattle World,* edited by Amy Schrager Lang and Cecilia Tichi. Rutgers University Press, 2006.

Lipsitz, George, and Alliance for California Traditional Arts. *Saludarte: Building Health Equity on the Bedrock of Traditional Arts and Culture*. Alliance for California Traditional Arts, 2020.

Lipsitz, George, and Russell Rodriguez. "Turning Hegemony on Its Head: The Insurgent Knowledge of Américo Paredes." *Journal of American Folklore* 125, no. 495 (2012): 111–25.

Lischer, Richard. *The Preacher King: Martin Luther King Jr. and the Word That Moved America*. Oxford University Press, 1995.

Lopez, Francesca, and Christine Sleeter. *Critical Race Theory and Its Critics: Implications for Research and Teaching*. Teachers College Press, 2023.

Lowell, James Russell. "The Present Crisis." 1845. Poets.org. https://poets.org/poem/present-crisis.

Lozenski, Brian. "Beyond Mediocrity: The Dialectics of Crisis in the Continuing Miseducation of Black Youth." *Harvard Educational Review* 87, no. 2 (Summer 2017): 161–85.

Lozenski, Brian. "Constructing a Dual Subjectivity: Understanding the Intersection of Ethnic Studies and YPAR." *Global Journal of Transformative Education* 1, no. 1 (2019): 26–37.

Lubin, Alex, and Marwin Kraidy, eds. *American Studies Encounters the Middle East*. University of North Carolina Press, 2016.

Madison High School 9th Grade Ethnic Studies. *The Story of Environmental Health Coalition*. Environmental Health Coalition, 2024.

Maghbouleh, Neda. "Twenty-Five Years of Charles Mills's *Racial Contract* in Sociology." *Sociology of Race and Ethnicity* 8, no. 4 (August 2022): 433–42.

Maira, Sunaina. *Boycott! The Academy and Justice for Palestine*. University of California Press, 2018.

Maldonado-Torres, Nelson. "Ethnic Studies in the Face of the Liberal Hydra." Ethnic Studies Rise Roundtable, January 15, 2020. https://ethnicrise.github.io/roundtable/liberal-hydra/.

Manuel, Arthur (Secwépemc). *Unsettling Canada: A National Wake-Up Call*. Between the Lines Press, 2015.

Mao, William C., and Veronica Paulus. "Harvard Dismisses Leaders of Center for Middle Eastern Studies." *Harvard Crimson*, March 29, 2025.

Martell, Christopher C., Lauren McArthur Harris, J'Shon Lee, Jennifer P. Chalmers, and Jami Carmichael. "Silent Covenants and Structural Barriers: State Standards Committees and the Maintenance of Race-Evasive Social Studies Standards." *AERA Open* 10, no. 1 (January-December 2024): 1–16.

Matias, Cheryl E. *Feeling White: Whiteness, Emotionality, and Education*. Sense Publishers, 2016.

Matias, Cheryl E., and Peter M. Newlove. "The Illusion of Freedom: Tyranny, Whiteness, and the State of U.S. Society." *Equity and Excellence in Education* 50, no. 3 (2017): 316–30.

Matsuda, Mari. "Looking to the Bottom: Critical Legal Studies and Reparations." *Harvard Civil Rights and Civil Liberties Law Review* 22 (1987): 323–99.

Matsuda, Mari. *Where Is Your Body? And Other Essays on Race, Gender, and the Law*. Beacon, 1997.

McAlister, Elizabeth. *Rara! Vodou, Power, and Performance in Haiti and Its Diaspora*. University of California Press, 2002.
McKinney, Karyn D. *Being White: Stories of Race and Racism*. Routledge, 2005.
McRuer, Robert. *Crip Theory: Cultural Signs of Queerness and Disability*. New York University Press, 2006.
Mercado, Antonieta. "Civic Engagement: Learning from Teaching Community Praxis." In *Civic Engagement in Diverse Latinx Communities: Learning from Social Justice Partnerships in Action*, edited by Mari Casteñeda and Joseph Krupczynski. Peter Lang, 2018.
Michel, Claudine. "Vodou in Haiti: Way of Life and Mode of Survival." In Michel and Bellegarde-Smith, *Vodou in Haitian Life*.
Michel, Claudine, and Patrick Bellegarde-Smith, eds. *Vodou in Haitian Life and Culture: Invisible Powers*. Palgrave Macmillan, 2006.
Mignolo, Walter. *The Darker Side of Western Modernity: Global Futures, Decolonial Options*. Duke University Press, 2011.
Mignolo, Walter. "Epistemic Disobedience, Independent Thought and Decolonial Freedom." *Theory, Culture, and Society* 26, no. 708 (2009): 159–81.
Mills, C. Wright. *White Collar: The American Middle Classes*. Oxford University Press, 2002.
Mills, Charles. "Alumnus Charles Mills on Pedagogy, White Supremacy, and the Future of Philosophy." Interview by *Philosophy News*, reposted to website of University of Toronto, Department of Philosophy, May 18, 2018. https://philosophy.utoronto.ca/news/charles-mills-alumnus-interview/.
Mills, Charles. *Black Rights/White Wrongs: The Crisis of Racial Liberalism*. Oxford University Press, 2017.
Mills, Charles. *Blackness Visible: Essays on Philosophy and Race*. Cornell University Press, 1999.
Mills, Charles. *The Racial Contract*. Cornell University Press, 1997.
Mills, Charles. "White Time: The Chronic Injustice of an Ideal Theory." *Du Bois Review* 11, no. 1 (2014): 27–42.
Mingus, Mia. "About." *Leaving Evidence* (blog), accessed January 16, 2022. https://leavingevidence.wordpress.com/about-2/.
Miyamoto, Nobuko. *Not Yo' Butterfly: My Long Song of Relocation, Race, Love, and Revolution*. University of California Press, 2022.
Molina, Natalia, Daniel Martinez HoSang, and Ramón A. Gutíerrez, eds. *Relational Formations of Race: Theory, Methods, and Practice*. University of California Press, 2019.
Montiel, Miguel, Tomás Atencio, and E. A. "Tony" Mares. *Resolana: Emerging Chicano Dialogues on Community and Globalization*. University of Arizona Press, 2009.
Mora, Christina G., Nicholas Vargas, and Dominic Cedillo. "How Many Latino Studies Programs Are There? Tracking Departmental Growth, Stagnation, and Invisibility, 1960–2020." *Latino Studies* 21, no. 3 (2023): 388–410.
Moraga, Cherríe. "I Transfer and Go Underground." In *This Bridge Called My Back: Writings by Radical Women of Color*, edited by Cherríe Moraga and Gloria E. Anzaldúa. Kitchen Table: Women of Color Press, 1983.

Morales, Iris. *Revisiting Herstories: The Young Lords Party.* Red Sugarcane Press, 2023.
Morrison, Toni. *Song of Solomon.* Alfred A. Knopf, 1977.
Muñoz, José Esteban. *Cruising Utopia: The Then and There of Queer Futurity.* New York University Press, 2019.
Muñoz, José Esteban. *Disidentifications: Queers of Color and the Performance of Politics.* University of Minnesota Press, 1999.
Muñoz, José Esteban. "Ephemera as Evidence: Introductory Notes to Queer Acts." *Women and Performance: A Journal of Feminist Theory* 8, no. 2 (1996): 5–16.
Murrell, Nathaniel Samuel, William David Spencer, Adrian Anthony McFarlane, and Clinton Chisholm, eds. *Chanting Down Babylon: The Rastafari Reader.* Temple University Press, 1998.
Nelson, Alondra. *Body and Soul: The Black Panther Party and the Fight Against Medical Discrimination.* University of Minnesota Press, 2011.
Neville, Art, Aaron Neville, Charles Neville, Cyril Neville, and David Ritz. *The Brothers Neville: An Autobiography.* Little, Brown, 2000.
Ng, Samuel Galen. "Trans Power! Sylvia Lee Rivera's STAR and the Black Panther Party." *Left History* 17, no. 1 (Spring/Summer 2013): 11–41.
Okihiro, Gary Y. *Margins and Mainstreams: Asians in American History and Culture.* University of Washington Press, 1994.
Okihiro, Gary Y. *Third World Studies: Theorizing Liberation.* 2nd ed., rev. and expanded. Duke University Press, 2024.
Okoro, Catherine A., NaTasha Hollis, Alyssa Cyrus, and Shannon Griffin-Blake. "Prevalence of Disabilities and Health Care Access by Disability Status and Type Among Adults—United States 2016." *Morbidity and Mortality Weekly Report* 67, no. 2 (2018): 882–88.
Onaci, Edward. *Free the Land: The Republic of New Afrika and the Pursuit of Black Nation State.* University of North Carolina Press, 2020.
Ortiz, Naomi. "Crip Ecologies: Complicate the Conversation to Reclaim Power." In A. Wong, *Disability Intimacy.*
Patel, Dhruv T., and Grace E. Yoon. "Harvard Suspends Research Partnership with Birzeit University in the West Bank." *Harvard Crimson,* March 17, 2025.
Patel, Dhruv T., and Grace E. Yoon. "Harvard Will Create Process to Centralize Protest Discipline Cases Under University President." *Harvard Crimson,* April 25, 2025.
Patterson, Sunni. "My City Ain't for Sale." In Patterson, *We Know This Place.*
Patterson, Sunni. "We Know This Place." In Patterson, *We Know This Place.*
Patterson, Sunni, ed. *We Know This Place: Poems.* Runagate Press, 2022.
Patterson, Sunni. "We Made It." In *Development Drowned and Reborn: The Blues and Bourbon Restorations in Post-Katrina New Orleans,* by Clyde Woods, edited by Jordan T. Camp and Laura Pulido. University of Georgia Press, 2017.
Payne, Charles. *I've Got the Light of Freedom: The Organizing Tradition and the Mississippi Freedom Struggle.* University of California Press, 2007.

Perea, John-Carlos. "'Native Noise' and the Politics of Powwow Musicking in a University Soundscape." In Levine and Robinson, *Music and Modernity.*

Pérez, Gina M. *Sanctuary People: Faith-Based Organizing in Latina/o Communities.* New York University Press, 2024.

Piepzna-Samarasinha, Leah Lakshmi. *The Future Is Disabled: Prophecies, Love Notes, and Mourning Songs.* Arsenal Pulp Press, 2022.

Piepzna-Samarasinha, Leah Lakshmi. *Care Work: Dreaming Disability Justice.* Arsenal Pulp Press, 2023.

Ponce de León, Jennifer. *Another Aesthetic Is Possible: Arts of Rebellion in the Fourth World War.* Duke University Press, 2021.

Portelli, Alessandro. *The Death of Luigi Trastulli and Other Stories: Form and Meaning in Oral History.* State University of New York Press, 1991.

Quijano, Anibal. "Coloniality of Power, Eurocentrism and Latin America." *Nepantla: Views from the South* 1, no. 3 (2000): 215–32.

Ramírez, Horacio Roque. "'That's My Place!' Negotiating Racial, Sexual, and Gender Politics in San Francisco's Gay Latino Alliance, 1975–1983." *Journal of the History of Sexuality* 12, no. 2 (2003): 224–58.

Ramos-Zayas, Ana Y., and Mérida Rúa, eds. *Critical Dialogues in Latinx Studies: A Reader.* New York University Press, 2021.

Rao, Nancy Yunhwa. *Inside Chinese Theater: Community and Artistry in Nineteenth Century California and Beyond.* University of Illinois Press, 2025.

Ratcliffe, Susan, ed. *Oxford Essential Quotations.* 4th ed. Oxford University Press, 2016.

Rawick, George. *From Sundown to Sunup: The Making of the Black Community.* Greenwood Press, 1972.

Reardon, Betty A. "Human Rights as Education for Peace." In *Human Rights Education for the Twenty-First Century,* edited by George J. Andreopoulos and Richard Pierre Claude. University of Pennsylvania Press, 1997.

Reed, Alison Rose. *Love and Abolition: The Social Life of Black Queer Performance.* Ohio State University Press, 2022.

Reyes, Jeremiah. "Loon and Kapwa: An Introduction to a Filipino Virtue Ethics." *Asian Philosophy* 25, no. 2 (2015): 148–71.

Robinson, Aileen Moreton. *The White Possessive: Property, Power, and Indigenous Sovereignty.* University of Minnesota Press, 2015.

Robinson, Cedric J. *Black Marxism: The Making of the Black Radical Tradition.* University of North Carolina Press, 2000.

Robinson, Cedric J. "Manichaeism and Multiculturalism." In *Mapping Multiculturalism,* edited by Avery F. Gordon and Christopher Newfield. University of Minnesota Press, 1996.

Robinson, Marc Arsell. "Black Student Unions to the Gang of Four: Interracial Alliances and Community Organizing from San Francisco to Seattle." *California History* 98, no. 2 (2021): 24–49.

Rodney, Walter. *The Groundings with My Brothers.* Research Associates School Times Publications, 1996.

Rodney, Walter. *How Europe Underdeveloped Africa.* Howard University Press, 1984.

Rodríguez, Juana María. *Queer Latinidad: Identity Practices, Discursive Spaces*. New York University Press, 2003.

Rodríguez, Roberto. "Ixiim: A Maize Based Philosophy." *Journal of Latinos in Education* 13, no. 2 (2017): 126–33.

Rodríguez, Russell. "Mariachi Accompaniment: Cultural Bearers for Community Conviviality." *Twentieth Century Music* 21, no. 2 (2024): 180–208.

Rogin, Michael. *Ronald Reagan the Movie: And Other Episodes in Political Demonology*. University of California Press, 1987.

Romney, Lee. "Chairs Sit Well with Laborers." *Los Angeles Times*, May 26, 2004.

Rooks, Noliwe. *White Money/Black Power: The Surprising History of African American Studies and the Crisis of Race in Higher Education*. Beacon, 2017.

Rose, Tricia. *Metaracism: How Systemic Racism Devastates Black Lives—and How We Break Free*. Basic Books, 2024.

Rose, Tricia. *Way Outta No Way*. Web-based project. https://www.triciarose.com/wayouttanoway.

Rosenberg, Jordy. "Afterword: One Utopia, One Dystopia." In Gleeson and O'Rourke, *Transgender Marxism*.

Salaam, Kalamu ya. *Be About Beauty*. University of New Orleans Press, 2018.

Sanchez, George J. "Keeping the Dance Alive: Institutionalization of the Crossroads of Ethnic Studies and American Studies." In "Beyond Interdisciplinarity: The New Goals of American Studies Programs," edited by Simon J. Bronner, *American Studies Association Newsletter* 28, no. 1 (March 2005): 1–17.

Sanchez-Tello, George B. "Reintroducing Traditional Foodways Through a School Cafeteria Mural." *Capital and Main*, March 24, 2023.

Sandlin, Jennifer, and Alan Eladio Gomez. "Toward New Critical Pedagogies and Conspirituality Consumption: Exploring and Combatting the COVID-19 New-Age Grifters." *New Directions in Adult Continuing Education* 178 (Summer 2023): 41–57.

Sandoval, Chela. *Methodology of the Oppressed*. University of Minnesota Press, 2000.

Schalk, Sami. *Black Disability Politics*. Duke University Press, 2022.

Schwartz, Sarah, and Eesha Pendharker. "Here's the Long List of Topics Republicans Want Banned from the Classroom." *Education Week*, February 2, 2022.

Schweik, Susan. "Lomax's Matrix: Disability, Solidarity, and the Black Power of 504." *Disability Studies Quarterly* 31, no. 1 (2011): 1–21.

Seamster, Louise. *The Flint Water Coup: Debt at the End of Democracy*. Columbia University Press, forthcoming.

Segato, Rita. "Patriarchy from Margins to Center: Discipline, Territoriality, and Cruelty in the Apocalyptic Phase of Capital." *South Atlantic Quarterly* 115, no. 3 (July 2016): 615–24.

Segato, Rita. "Territory, Sovereignty, and the Crimes of the Second State: The Writing on the Body of Murdered Women." In *Terrorizing Women: Feminicide in the Americas*, edited by Rosa-Linda Fregoso and Cynthia Bejarano. Duke University Press, 2010.

Shah, Nayan. *Contagious Divides: Epidemics and Race in San Francisco's Chinatown*. University of California Press, 2001.

Sharim Studio. "Press Events." 2025. https://www.sharimstudio.com/press-events.
Shepard, Benjamin. "From Community Organization to Direct Services: The Street Trans Action Revolutionaries to Sylvia Rivera Law Project." *Journal of Social Service Research* 39, no. 1 (2013): 95–114.
Sherrod, Shirley. *The Courage to Hope: How I Stood Up to the Politics of Fear*. Atria, 2012.
Shin, Young. "Immigrant Women Voice, Participate, and Advocate: Developing Grassroots Leadership Toward a Just and Inclusive Society." Balgopal Lecture Series Keynote Speech, University of Illinois, April 2010. Copy in author's possession courtesy of Young Shin.
Simpson, Leanne Betasamosake. *As We Have Always Done: Indigenous Freedom Through Radical Resistance*. University of Minnesota Press, 2017.
Singh, Julietta. *Unthinking Mastery: Dehumanism and Decolonial Entanglements*. Duke University Press, 2018.
Sins Invalid. *Skin, Tooth, and Bone: The Basis of Movement Is Our People: A Disability Justice Primer*. 2nd ed. Sins Invalid, 2019.
Sleeter, Christine E., and Miguel Zavala. *Transformative Ethnic Studies in Schools: Curriculum, Pedagogy, and Research*. Teachers College Press, 2020.
Smith, Theophus. *Conjuring Culture: Biblical Formations of Black America*. Oxford University Press, 1994.
Sostaita, Barbara Andrea. *Sanctuary Everywhere: The Fugitive Sacred in the Sonoran Desert*. Duke University Press, 2024.
Speed, Shannon. *Incarcerated Stories: Indigenous Women Migrants and Violence in the Settler-Capitalist State*. University of North Carolina Press, 2019.
Stainova, Yana. "An Ethnography of Joy: Entrepreneurship Among Latinx Communities in East Los Angeles." *American Anthropologist* 126, no. 4 (2024): 635–46.
Stam, Robert. "From Hybridity to the Aesthetics of Garbage." *Social Identities* 3, no. 2 (1997): 275–90.
Steusse, Angela. *Scratching Out a Living: Latinos, Race, and Work in the Deep South*. University of California Press, 2016.
Stokes, Lawrence LaFountain. "The Life and Times of Trans Activist Sylvia Rivera." In Ramos Zyas and Rúa, *Critical Dialogues*.
Students at Roosevelt High School. *La Vida Diferente: Celebrating Boyle Heights' Community Treasures*. 826LA, 2014.
Students at the Center. *Go to Jail: Confronting a System of Oppression*. LMO Projects, 2021.
Subcomandante Marcos. *Our Word Is Our Weapon*. Seven Stories Press. 2002.
Szwed, John. *Space Is the Place: The Lives and Times of Sun Ra*. Pantheon, 1997.
TallBear, Kim (Sisseton-Wahpeton Oyate). "Caretaking Relations, Not American Dreaming." *Kalfou* 6, no. 1 (Spring 2019): 24–41.
Tang, Eric. *Unsettled: Cambodian Refugees in the New York City Hyperghetto*. Temple University Press, 2015.
Taylor, Diana. *The Archive and the Repertoire: Performing Cultural Memory in the Americas*. Duke University Press, 2003.
Taylor, Diana. *¡Presente! The Politics of Presence*. Duke University Press, 2020.

Tellez, Michelle. *Border Women and the Community of Maclovio Rojas: Autonomy in the Spaces of Neoliberal Neglect.* University of Arizona Press, 2021.
Thandeka. *Learning to Be White: Money, Race, and God in America.* Bloomsbury, 2013.
Thompson, Robert Farris. *Flash of the Spirit: African and Afro-American Art and Philosophy.* Vintage, 1983.
Tomlinson, Barbara. *Undermining Intersectionality: The Perils of Powerblind Feminism.* Temple University Press, 2019.
Tomlinson, Barbara, and George Lipsitz. "American Studies as Accompaniment." *American Quarterly* 65, no. 1 (March 2013): 1–30.
Tomlinson, Barbara, and George Lipsitz. *Insubordinate Spaces: Improvisation and Accompaniment for Social Justice.* Temple University Press, 2019.
Topaum, Cyanne. "'Savage States: Settler Governance in an Age of Sorrow': Lecture by Audra Simpson—Response by Cyanne Topaum." *Kritik* (blog), January 31, 2019. https://unitforcriticism.wordpress.com/2019/01/31/savage-states-settler-governance-in-an-age-of-sorrow-lecture-by-audra-simpson-response-by-cyanne-topaum-english/.
Tourmaline. *Marsha: The Joy and Defiance of Marsha P. Johnson.* Tiny Reparations Books, 2025.
Trouillot, Michel-Rolph. "Anthropology and the Savage Slot: The Poetics and Politics of Otherness." In *Trouillot Remixed: The Michel-Rolph Trouillot Reader,* edited by Yarimar Bonilla, Greg Beckett, and Mayanthi I. Fernando. Duke University Press, 2021.
Trouillot, Michel-Rolph. *Global Transformations: Anthropology and the Modern World.* Palgrave Macmillan, 2003.
Trouillot, Michel-Rolph. *Silencing the Past: Power and the Production of History.* Beacon, 1995.
Tsuchiya, Kazuyo. *Reinventing Citizenship: Black Los Angeles, Korean Kawasaki and Community Participation.* University of Minnesota Press, 2014.
UCI Public Scholarship Team and Alumni. *Writing the Future of El Sol Together: Escribiendo el Futuro de El Sol Juntos.* UCI Public Scholarship Team and Alumni, 2024. Document in author's possession courtesy of Ana Rosas.
University of Chicago Urban Labs. "Students in Temporary Living Situations." July 2021. https://urbanlabs.uchicago.edu/projects/students-in-temporary-living-situations.
Vargas, João Costa. *Catching Hell in the City of Angels: Life and Meanings of Blackness in South Central Los Angeles.* University of Minnesota Press, 2006.
Vasilko, Kayla. "Dr. Kim Scipes: Building a Network of Compassion in a World Waiting to Be United." *Purdue Journal of Service-Learning and International Engagement* 9, no. 1 (2022): article 8.
Velez-Ibanez, Carlos. *Border Visions: Mexican Cultures of the Southwest United States.* University of Arizona Press, 1996.
Vetterkind, Riley. "Wisconsin Assembly Passes Ban on Teaching Critical Race Theory." *Wisconsin State Journal,* September 29, 2021.
Vigil, María López. *Oscar Romero: Memories in Mosaic.* Dartman, Longman, and Todd, 2000.

Villareal, Aimee. "Anthropolocura as Homeplace Ethnography." In Chávez and Pérez, *Ethnographic Refusals*.
Vosen, Elyse Carter. "Singing and Dancing Idle No More: Round Dances as Indigenous Activism." In Levine and Robinson, *Music and Modernity*.
Waldron, Ingrid R. G. *There's Something in the Water: Environmental Racism in Indigenous and Black Communities*. Fernwood, 2018.
Walker, Anders. "Legislating Virtue: How Segregation Disguised Racial Discrimination as Moral Reform Following *Brown v. Board of Education*." *Duke Law Journal* 47 (1997): 399–418.
Wallace-Wells, Benjamin. "How a Conservative Activist Invented the Conflict over Critical Race Theory." *New Yorker*, June 18, 2021.
Wanzer-Serrano, Darrel. *The New York Young Lords and the Struggle for Liberation*. Temple University Press, 2015.
Warrior, Robert, and Paul Chaat Smith. *Like a Hurricane: The American Indian Movement from Alcatraz to Wounded Knee*. New Press, 1996.
Watkins, Mary, and Helene Schulman. *Toward Psychologies of Liberation*. Palgrave Macmillan, 2008.
Widener, Daniel. *Black Arts West: Culture and Struggle in Postwar Los Angeles*. Duke University Press, 2010.
Williams, Patricia J. "*Metro Broadcasting, Inc. v FCC*: Regrouping in Singular Times." *Harvard Law Review* 104, no. 2 (December 1990): 535–46.
Williams, Patricia J. *Seeing a Color-Blind Future: The Paradox of Race*. Farrar, Strauss, and Giroux, 1997.
Wong, Alice, ed. *Disability Intimacy: Essays on Love, Care and Desire*. Vintage, 2014.
Wong, Deborah. *Louder and Faster: Pain, Joy, and the Body Politic in Asian American Taiko*. University of California Press, 2019.
Woods, Clyde. *Development Drowned and Reborn: The Blues and Bourbon Restorations in Post-Katrina New Orleans*. University of Georgia Press, 2017.
Woods, Clyde, ed. *In the Wake of Hurricane Katrina: New Paradigms and Social Visions*. Johns Hopkins University Press, 2010.
Yamat, Rio. "Trump Pardons Nevada Politician Who Paid for Cosmetic Surgery with Funds to Honor Slain Officer." Associated Press, US News, April 24, 2025.
Yamauchi, Lois E., Joni B. Acuff, Ruchi Agarwal-Rangnath, et al. "Scholar Collectives Advocating for Social Justice in Education." *Kalfou* 9, no. 1 (Spring 2022): 225–46.
Yancy, George, and Talila A. Lewis. "Ableism Enables All Forms of Inequity and Hampers All Liberation Efforts." *Truthout*, January 3, 2023, 1–14.
Yellow Bird, Michael (Mandan, Hidatsa, and Arikara). "Cowboys and Indians: Toys of Genocide, Icons of Colonialism." *Wicazo Sa Review* 19, no. 2 (Fall 2024): 33–48.
Yosso, Tara J. "Whose Culture Has Capital? A Critical Race Theory Discussion of Community Cultural Wealth." *Race Ethnicity and Education* 8, no. 1 (2005): 65–91.

Yosso, Tara J., and David D. Garcia. "'This Is No Slum': A Critical Race Theory Analysis of Community Cultural Wealth in Culture Clash's Chavez Ravine." *Aztlan: A Journal of Chicano Studies* 32, no. 1 (2007): 145–79.

Zavella, Patricia. *The Movement for Reproductive Justice: Empowering Women of Color Through Social Activism*. New York University Press, 2020.

Zaznis, Noah. "Social Reproduction and Social Cognition: Theorizing (Trans) gender Identity Development in Community Context." In Gleeson and O'Rourke, *Transgender Marxism*.

Index

abolition: abolition democracy, 40, 48, 140, 204; abolitionist time, 128; knowledge category, 177; prison abolition, 94, 145, 183
accompaniment, 109–133; counterculture inside ethnic studies, 13, 17, 18, 19–20, 21; disability justice, 142; improvisation, 94, 105; origin, 109, 165; pedagogy, 188–89; research, 182; sanctuary, 198; Sunni Patterson, 113
Afro-Latinx, 70–71, 190
Ahmed, Sara: gay liberation and racial justice, 139, 174; neoliberal incorporation, 63; perception of difference as impetus for enhanced critical capacities, 139, 157; queer identity as creative disorientation, 139, 173–74; racism as fear of imagined loss of future family line, 26, 140
Ahrens, Rosanna Esparza: *altarista*, 114–15; learning how to arrive, 114–17, 133
Alaskan Native peoples: cognitive mapping, 93; disability among, 141; fermentation practices of, 187–88; musical culture as collective responsibility among, 171; Pamyua, 153, 199
Alliance for California Traditional Arts: art projects in East Los Angeles, 116–19; *Saludarte: Building Health Equity on the Bedrock of Traditional Arts and Culture*, 183

American Indian Movement: community patrols, 151; Rainbow Coalition in Chicago, 151; survival schools, 60
American Studies, 16, 174, 176; American Studies Association, 69, 113, 128, 172
Andersen, Chris (Métis): density and difference, 152; Indigenous Data Sovereignty initiative, 84
Anti-Eugenics Collective at Yale (AECY), 189, 193
Anzaldúa, Gloria: *Borderlands: La Frontera*, 179; comforts based on exploitation of others, 3; identities not fixed, 32; *la facultad*, 179; *nepantla*, 157, 158; problem of perpetual conflict, 184; safe spaces, 200–201; snake as symbol, 86; "To Live in the Borderlands Means You," 82
archive: Afro-Latinx, 68–71; alternative archives, 8, 71, 121, 202; art, 189; contradictory nature, 96–97, 98, 101; definition, 19, 95–104; disability, 96; film, 104; K–12, 187; performance and display, 100–101; private collections, 97; queer, 97, 103; social movements, 97; official archives and ethnic studies, 81, 96, 101, 132, 179, 182, 198
Asian American: Asian American movement, 149, 150; Asian American Political Association, 148; Asian American Studies, 61, 128, 146, 147,

267

Asian American *(continued)*
150; Asian Immigrant Women Advocates, 19, 123–28, 173; crossroads, 82, 148–149; taiko, 130–31; Young Lords, 137
autonomous learning centers and circles, 7, 17, 19–20, 108–33; activism as crucible, 9; Alliance for California Traditional Arts, 116–19; community knowledge, 59–62, 101–103, 183, 187, 188; Community Transformational Organizing Strategy, 123–28; critical race theory, 50–51; disability, 145; Indigenous survival schools, 60; reproductive rights, 177, 180; story circle pedagogy, 119–23; Young Lords Party, 61

Bambara, Toni Cade: abstractionism, 185; finding significance, 83; institutions and actions, 199; movement, 45; *The Salt Eaters*, 199; vehicle and objective, 199, 207
Benjamin, Walter: memories that flash up, 194; presence of mind, 84; tradition of the oppressed, 3–4, 14, 201–2
Bernardi, Claudia: deep wounds, 95; dirty war, 38
Black Lives Matter: hashtag, 24, 45; liberal and conservative responses, 27, 44, 72; movement, 5, 105, 131, 205; organization, 24; slogan, 24; song, 149
Black Panther Party: Brad Lomax, 142–43; disability politics, 142–43; Huey Newton on gay liberation, 178; Indigenous connections, 151; intercommunalism, 65, 173; Michael Zinzun, 87; Revolutionary People's Constitutional Convention, 14, 137; Sylvia Rivera, 137; Ten Point Program, 59; *The Black Panther*, 47, 143
bridge: concept, 18–19, 79, 80–81; chapter, 80–117
Briggs, Charles: critique of abstractions, 76; dance and radio work as preparation for fieldwork, 130; disciplines as gatekeeping mechanisms, 176–77; learning outside the academy, 129–30; magic nominalism, 185; *Unlearning*, 177
Briggs, Laura: crisis in social reproduction, 177–78; Garcia-Peña tenure battle, 69; reproductive justice, 178–80
Brown, John, 35, 204
Brown University: hosting Sunni Patterson, 113; *Way Outta No Way* project, 192–93

Brown v. Board of Education, 26, 36, 49, 209
Butler, Judith: ascription, 86; subjection, 42, 86, 186
Byrd, Jodi (Chickasha): Indigenous peoples not a single racial minority, 156; links between queer and Indigenous politics, 140

caduceus: concept, 17, 18–19, 85–95; ethnic studies dilemmas, 104–6, 174–78, 199–216; intersectional justice, 135–65
Carmichael, Stokely (Kwame Ture): being ready, 205; *Black Power*, 151; dictatorship of definition, interpretation, and consciousness, 6
Chavez, Cesar: coalition with Filipinx organizers, 148; support for gay liberation, 178
Chicanx: art, 97; community education, 191; *conocimiento*, 7, 177, 179; name, 185; *nepantla*, 7, 95, 157, 158, 177; people, 153, 155; performance, 98, 149; studies, 146, 147
Christianity: Bible, 87; caduceus elements, 85, 87, 90; Catholicism, 36, 85, 95, 212; Martin Luther King, Jr., 6, 35, 90, 132, 170, 211; nationalism, 13; Oscar Romero, Saint, 109, 165; sanctuary, 162; theology, 90, 155, 162, 204
civil rights, 33, 34, 56, 203, 213; court decisions, 178, 195, 203, 213; laws, 32, 34, 36, 47–50; movement, 55, 65, 124, 162, 205
convivencia, 15, 117, 119
COVID-19: disability, 145; impact, 3, 77, 215; Indigenous communities, 194
Crenshaw, Kimberlé: age of repudiation, 49, 65; critical race theory, 46; impact on legal studies, 172
crisis: capital and 1960s, 55; climate, 3, 11, 76, 100, 159, 183, 205, 215; current, 3, 37–42, 64–83, 199–216; defined, 203; exception, 3, 203; Flint water, 97; James Russell Lowell, 203–4; mortgage foreclosures, 3; Puerto Rico hurricane response, 132; social reproduction, 177; survival strategies, 4, 111, 114
critical race rheory (CRT): actual positions, 31–32; campaign against, 11, 24–52, 129, 193; disability, 144; influenced by parallel institutions of the Black freedom movement, 46–48; oppositional potential, 81, 86; response to *Brown v. Board* and

racial liberalism, 36, 48–51; social movement origins, 46–48
crossroads: Alaska Natives music, 93; American studies, 174; Arabic word, 82; argument, 169; Aurora Levins Morales, 82; autonomous learning circles, 108; concept and framework, 19, 79, 80–85, 107; disability, race, sexuality, gender, poverty, 140, 142, 146–63, 179; Eshu Elegba (trickster), 84; ethnic studies, 54, 59, 64–67; Gloria Anzaldúa, 82; Haitian vodou, 80, 90; Houston Baker, 82; idealized motherhood, 89; intersectionality, 136, 163–65; José Esteban Muñoz, 94; learning to arrive, 116; Persian word, 82; Robert Farris Thompson, 84; Toni Cade Bambara, 83; Yuri Kochiyama, 82; Yoruba symbol, 80

Davila, Arlene: anthropology, 172, 194; the Latinx Project, 189–90
Davis, Angela, 132; social movement activist, 135; transgender activism influence on prison abolition, 145
Democratic Party, 27–28, 213, 222n7
Denning, Michael: incorporation, 63; the laboring of American culture, 210
density, 146, 152–53, 177
difference: advantage, 14, 46, 75, 128; capitalism, 110; CRT, 32; demonized, 25, 89; disability, 140–45; ethnic studies, 59, 63, 66, 91, 118; excuse for domination, 78–79, 134–65, 176, 201, 216; history, 146–50, 164, 181, 201; Indigenous, 152–153, 156; liberal management, 54, 56, 57, 63, 78; questioned, 8, 12; savage slot, 176; social movements, 137, 138, 140–44
disability: ableism, 10, 136, 143–45; antidisability, 52; arbitrary standards of normativity, 141, 142; crip ecologies of care, 144–145; disability justice, 13, 20, 50, 140–46; disability justice activists, 82, 92, 140, 142–43; disability justice needed in educational institutions, 144, 196; disproportionate presence among aggrieved groups, 141; and ethnic studies, 142, 147, 157, 193, 196, 216; impetus for study and creative problem solving, 135, 139, 144, 145–46; mass incarceration, 141; participation in broad freedom struggles, 136, 142–43; and racial segregation, 141; relation to capitalism and valorization of labor, 141; relation to LGBTQ liberation, 136, 141, 142; relation to race, 17, 21, 136, 141–43, 208; relational social construct, 21, 135, 141; Sins Invalid, 145
disciplines: advantages and disadvantages, 10, 83, 170–77, 208; boundary work, 57, 174, 176, 189, 194; concepts, 50, 89; ethnic studies influence on, 58, 75, 171, 172, 176; state-centrism, 174; theory, 176
diversity, equity, and inclusion: caricature and scapegoating of, 74, 134–35; Charles Mills on, 30; CRT, 31; electoral gambit, 27, 28, 37; institutions knuckling under to pressure, 52, 74; opposition to, 24, 33, 74, 193
domination, 1–2, 20, 21; Afro-Latinx, 71; Anglo-Protestant, 212; coloniality, 129; corporate, 50; CRT, 32, 52; epistemological, 60, 88, 97; racist, 12, 20
Du Bois, W. E. B.: cracked plate analogy, 31; indigeneity, 151; racism as intellectual enfeeblement, 37

equity-oriented collaborative community-based research, 181–83; *Collective Creative Actions*, 183; *Freedom Now!*, 183; *Go to Jail*, 183; *Life Sentences*, 183; *Saludarte*, 183
Estes, Nick: Indigenous resistance, 150; influenced by Robin Kelley, 151
ethnic studies: activist campaigns, 59–61; alienation as aesthetic pleasure, 197; antagonisms inside, 184–86; caduceus quality of, 19, 88; campus projects connected to communities, 187–93; Chicago school of sociology influence, 63–64; concepts, 7, 41, 95, 124; crossroads, 19; defined, 1–9; disciplines and interdisciplinary research, 170–73, 175; empire and imperialism, 120, 124, 138, 147, 152, 173, 174, 175, 203; fused departments vs. separate ethnic units, 58, 146–53; hostility from gatekeepers, 168, 169; incorporation and institutionalization, 9–13, 18, 53–79; inquiry and instruction, 20, 166–98; Joy de la Cruz poem about, 53–54; limits of identities, 8, 86, 136, 138, 146, 165; opposition by and against, 11, 18, 23–52, 167–69, 193; meager institutional support for, 52, 58; neoliberal suppression, 55–56, 64–66, 105–7, 205–7; parallel institutions,

ethnic studies *(continued)*
  47–51, 61–62, 70, 138; parallel knowledges, 73–74; response to 1960s crises, 55–57, 59–62
EZLN (Ejército Zapatista de Liberación Nacional): organizing philosophy and pedagogy, 180; snail metaphor, 187; Third and Fourth World Wars, 65, 180, 207

fascism: Ernst Bloch analysis and critique of, 38–39; Europe in the 1930s, 5; threat of in United States, 39, 43, 208, 215
Ferguson, Roderick: *Aberrations in Black*, 139; difference as generative, 136, 139; distribution of the sensible, 11; importance of small actions, 104, 186; incorporation of minority difference, 12; interlocking struggles, 136; queer liberation movements connected to broader social justice struggles, 135–36; sexual regulation crucial to racial subordination, 26, 139; transgender critiques of normativity, 139
Floyd, George, 4, 5, 24, 194, 214–15
Foucault, Michel: avoiding facile gestures, 170; criticism purposes, 170; domination and resistance, 84, 88
Free Southern Theater: influence on Students at the Center, 119–22; performance theory origins, 130; plays as meetings, 14; reproductive justice application, 179

Galeano, Eduardo: knowledge and change, 6; looking glass school, 1–2; power's self-sacralization, 36; society of sleepwalkers, 39
Garcia-Peña, Lorgia: Afro-Latinx identity, 70–71; awards, prizes, and fellowships, 69; *Community as Rebellion*, 68–69; dictions and contradictions, 71–72; ethnic framework history, 63; original and generative ideas, 70–72, 75–76; overtly racist attacks against, 68; peer validation and popular support, 69, 77–79; tenure battle, 67–79; *Translating Blackness*, 69; *vaivén*, 71, 159
Gaza: demonstrations about, 73, 206; persecution of protesters, 73–74; war, 13, 195
Gomez, Jay Lynn: American Studies Association panel, 128; installation art and worker dignity, 102

Gonzalez, Martha: cognitive mapping, 93; *convivencia*, 15, 117; Entre Mujeres, 93; Emma Perez influence on, 132; FandangObon work with Nobuko Miyamoto, 149
Gordon, Avery: abolitionist time, 128, 205; critique of academic fatalism and resignation, 107; living in difference, 202–3, 205
Gramsci, Antonio: contradictory conjuncture, 5; ideological hegemony, 139; origin of ideas, 99

Haiti and Haitians: activism, 43; archives, 71, 97; *balans*, 84, 173; crossroads, 80, 82; *konesans*, 84; lies about, 134; meetings, 15; music, 82; predation as example, 195; scholars of, 82–82, 132; vodou, 84
Halberstam, Jack: punk music, 131; queer archives, 103; transgender dual possibilities, 95
Hall, Stuart: feeling out of place, 158; incorporation, 59; perceptions of difference as impetus for enhanced critical capacities, 157, 158; shortcomings of grand theory, 177
Hamer, Fannie Lou: the left and the "left out," 165; Winona beating, 213–14
Harding, Vincent, 153–55; coloniality, 155; interpretation of Hopi prophecy, 154–55; move to Denver, 154; rejecting assimilation, 153–54, 155; work with Martin Luther King, Jr., 154
Harvard University: Alternative Course and CRT, 50; Board of Trustees, 73; bottom-up and top-down ethnic studies, 72–75; capitulation to donor, trustee, and political pressure, 73–74; Garcia-Peña tenure battle, 67–72, 75, 76; law school, 47, 48–50
HoSang, Daniel Martinez: Anti-Eugenics Collective at Yale (AECY), 189, 193; Chicano Park mural, 100; racism and capitalism, 2

incorporation: civil rights movement, 210–11; co-optation, 63; ethnic studies, 11, 12, 14, 18, 21, 64, 53–79, 206, 207; labor movement, 56, 210; neoliberal limits, 65; perils, 55–57, 62; subordinate inclusions, 59; transgender co-optation, 95

Indigenous: autonomous learning circles, 60, 61; autonomy, 51; caduceus thinking, 86–87, 173; Chris Andersen, 84, 152; cognitive mapping, 89, 93; cosmologies, 85, 160, 171; density and difference, 152–53; disability, 141; displacement and dispossession, 13, 32, 63, 71, 87, 150–51, 216; fermentation knowledge, 187–88; grounded normativity, 135; harvesters and farmers, 86, 88, 118; Jessica Bissett Perea, 93, 152, 194; Jodi Byrd, 140, 156; Michael Yellow Bird, 40, 156; murdered and missing women and girls, 33, 89; pedagogy, 130, 191; relations with Black freedom struggles, 149, 150–51, 152–57, 173; relations with queer politics, 140, 151; savage slot, 20, 142, 175–76, 208; settler colonialism, 147, 155–56, 172; sovereignty, 24, 100, 193; studies, 146, 147, 150; survivance, 84, 193; water protectors, 4, 209; the white possessive, 150–51

intersectionality: concept, 7, 34, 50, 165; justice, 20; political and epistemological practice, 151, 157–158, 159–64; single axis analysis, 95, 150, 163–64; theory, 176, 177, 179

Israel: Diaspora and Foreign Affairs Ministry, 71; mass slaughter and ethnic cleansing, 147, 195, 206; protests against policies, 73, 74, 195, 206; surveillance technology, 162

James, C. L. R.: authoritarian leaders, 43; influence on José Esteban Muñoz, 173; intellectuals bored, 197; work with Grace Lee Boggs and James Boggs, 149

Johnson, Marsha P., 135, 137–38

K-12 education: activist links, 109, 186; curricula and pedagogies, 9, 40–42, 133, 147, 186, 191; East L.A. High School Blowouts, 60; eugenics project, 189; grades, graduation rates, and test scores, 42; incarcerated houseless and housing insecure students, 65–66; target of right-wing mobilizations, 39, 195, 207

Kelley, Robin D. G.: fighting fascism, 215–16; *Freedom Dreams* as influence on Indigenous scholarship, 151, 152; Garcia-Peña tenure case, 69; impact on historical research, 172; social movements and knowledge, 47; Students at the Center, 121; study and struggle, 6

Kimmerer, Robin Wall: academic verbal smackdowns, 168; belonging rather than belongings, 173; contributions to botany, 172; recognizing the dark, 166; writing as an act of reciprocity, 169

King, Martin Luther, Jr.: assassination, 211; bitter but beautiful struggle, 22; caduceus thinking, 90; "Drum Major Instinct," 90; Poor Peoples March and Campaign, 151; radical revolution in values, 170, 211; songs about, 152; *Strength to Love*, 90; study war no more, 6; unities of opposites, 90; Vietnam War, 6, 155; Vincent Harding, 154; writings banned, 35

labor movements, 20, 55–56, 178, 208–12

Latinx: art, 97, 100, 102, 189–90, 193; demonization, 28, 52, 64; name, 185; K-12 students, 65–66, 69; policing, 161; reproductive justice, 179; steered toward military and police work, 28; studies, 58, 146; subprime wealth loss, 3; the Latinx Project, 189–90, 193; violence against, 3; youths, 191

Latinx Project, The (NYU), 189–90, 193

learning how to arrive, 114–17, 133

Levins Morales, Aurora: becoming the people we need to be, 163; "Child of the Americas," 82; disability justice, 140; *This Bridge Called My Back*, 7

Levins Morales, Ricardo: improvisation and action, 107; liberals and power, 74; *maskhiki*, 85; seed and soil metaphor, 8

Make America Great Again (MAGA), 44–45

Malcolm X: assassination, 211; Cyril Neville shrine, 151; Fannie Lou Hamer, 213; incorporation, 62; influence on Indigenous activists, 151

Maldonado-Torres, Nelson: desegregation of higher education, 47; Lorgia Garcia-Peña tenure case, 69

meetings: American Sociological Association, 25–26; American Studies Association, 113, 128; Asian Immigrant Women Advocates, 123–26; brush arbors, 14; Cherríe Moraga and Barbara Smith, 14; *convivencia*, 15; groundings, 15; East Los Angeles *artivistas*, 15; Fannie Lou Hamer, 213; Idle No More, 131; Japanese American Citizens

meetings *(continued)*
    League, 149; *lakou*, 15; *la resolana*, 15; learning how to arrive, 115–16; limits, 14; mass meetings, 7, 14; plays seen as meetings, 14, 121; San Jose State community projects, 191; school board meetings, 45; songs, 14; template for this book, 14
Mills, Charles: activism in Jamaica and Toronto, 46; American Sociological Association 2021 presentation, 25; attacks on CRT, 25–26; contrapuntal ensemble, 29, 178; epistemology of ignorance, 29; institutional exclusion of subaltern knowledge, 36–37; lack of empathy surfeit of self-pity, 30; racial contract, 25–26, 30, 150; sanitized history and revanchist violence, 36–37; temporality, 29–30
Mingus, Mia: activism, 140; archive, 96
Miyamoto, Nobuko, 82, 108, 149
Morrison, Toni: books banned, 35; *Song of Solomon*, 199–200
Muñoz, José Esteban: archive, 102–3; C. L. R. James futurity, 173; difference as epistemological provocation, 157; disco dance floor, 131; disidentification, 7, 94–95, 157; Marga Gomez provoking queer theory, 131; punk rock mosh pit, 131; queer performance, 140; queerness, 140; X (band), 131
"My City Ain't for Sale" (Patterson), 110–14

neoliberalism: cultural project, 37, 110, 113, 117, 129, 180; economic project, 111; market-centered view of life, 207; university conforming, 206–7
nepantla/borderlands, 7, 95, 157–58, 177
Newton, Huey P.: queer liberation, 137, 178; Sylvia Rivera, 137
non-normativity: generative potential of, 135, 177; source of criminalization of, 139
normativity: citizenship, 189; critiques of, 139, 140, 145, 178; disability, 140, 143, 145; eugenics, 136; fascism, 39; gender, 64, 131, 139, 183; grounded, 135; political force, 139; racism, 136, 140, 143; sexual, 28, 31, 139, 140; single axis, 139; social construct, 135

Palestine: archive, 132; censorship against, 147; ethnic cleansing, 147; Gaza encampments, 206; self-determination, 147; settler colonialism, 147; slaughter, 147, 195, 206; surveillance towers, 162
Pamyua: fermentation class, 188; Inuit Soul Music group, 153–54
parallel institutions: Black freedom movement, 48, 50; CRT, 48, 50; ethnic studies, 48, 62, 70, 81; STAR, 136; Young Lords, 61
Patterson, Sunni: appearances at universities and professional conferences, 113, 128; critique of neoliberal racial capitalism, 110–114; education and activism, 112–13; "My City Ain't For Sale," 110, 111, 114; "We Know This Place," 111, 113, 157, 193; "We Made It," 113
Perea, Jessica Bissett (Dena'ina): cognitive mapping, 93; COVID-19 and previous epidemics, 194; density and difference, 152; music as broad social practice and epistemology, 171; musical world making without stateness, 93; Native Alaskan Music, 171
Perea, John-Carlos (Mescalero Apache) and Chicano powwow and fish camp science pedagogies, 130
Pérez, Gina: sanctuary, 161–63
performance studies, 22, 130
Portelli, Alessandro: archives and oral history, 97; research as experiment in equality, 181–82
Puerto Rico: artists, 82; hurricane devastation, 76, 132, 161, 215; Roberto Clemente book banned, 35; sanctuary movement, 162; studies, 60; Sylvia Rivera, 136–37; UFW recruits, 149; Young Lords Party, 46, 59–61, 99, 137; Yuri Kochiyama, 82

queer: activism, 137–39, 142, 173; archive, 102–103; disability connections and parallels, 136, 140–43, 145; disidentification, 95; epistemological orientation, 86, 90, 94, 139–40, 144, 147, 190; feminists, 86, 157; identities, 138–39, 144, 157, 165, 173–74; queer of color politics, 135–39, 145; race as queer matter, 139, 173–74; rights, 193; sexual identities, 140; subjugated identities, 90; theory, 94, 102–3, 131, 157

racial contract: activism, 46; Asian American movement, 150; autonomous learning circles, 51; Charles Mills formulation, 25–31; CRT, 31–37, 42,

46, 50; ethnic studies, 166; Indigenous identity, 150, 176; research and teaching, 68–72
racial liberalism: administrative disposition, 72–73; limits, 30, 49, 156, 172; response to 2020 protests, 5–6, 210; tenets of, 66
repertoire, 18–19, 98–99; autonomous learning circles, 100, 128, 196, 208; ethnic studies, 104, 189; mobile, 102; performance, 103, 121; Restorative Cultural Arts Practice/Praxis, 119; struggle, 70, 100–101, 161, 202; Sunni Patterson, 114
reproductive justice: collectives, 9; Fannie Lou Hamer, 214; freedom, 137; healing justice, 4, 7, 20, 50, 179; health, 172; rights, 23, 178, 193, 195, 201, 203; services, 99, 131; ways of knowing, 179–80
Rivera, Sylvia: biography and activism, 135–39; Black Panther Party contacts, 137; co-founder of STAR, 137–38; Sylvia Rivera Law Project, 138; Young Lords Party contacts, 137
Robinson, Cedric J.: Black Radical Tradition, 112; collective consciousness, 202; conditions of our existence, 77; penetrating comprehension of Black opposition, 47
Romero, Oscar: accompaniment, 109, 165; being more as opposed to having more, 173; preferential option for those left out, 165
Rose, Tricia: *Metaracism*, 192; *Way Outta No Way*, 192–93

Sacco, Nicola, and Bartolomeo Vanzetti, 212–13, 214
Salaam, Kalamu ya: Afrodiasporic asymmetry, 173; American Studies Association meeting, 113; archive of resistance, 96; changing ways, 107; fighting, 202; Students at the Center, 122, 123
San Francisco, California: Asian American service organizations, 61; disability rights sit-in, 142; Native studies program at San Francisco State College, 61; powwow and fish camp science pedagogy at San Francisco State University, 130; Proyecto ContraSIDA por Vida, 139; University of San Francisco Medical Center, 127

San Jose, California: Culture Counts Reading Series, 190–91; the Cultural Work of Poetry Project, 190–91; Healing Youth Justice Platica and Poetry project, 190–91; Restorative Healing and Justice Mentorship Program, 191; Santa Clara County Public Defender's Office, 190–92
sanctuary, 9, 92, 139, 214; becoming sanctuary people, 161, 163, 198; Indigenous traditions, 162; intersectionality, 20, 161, 162; mobile practices of care, 162; religious commitments, 160–61, 162; sanctuary movement, 163–69
savage slot, 20, 142, 175–76, 208
scenes of argument, 167–78
Segato, Rita Laura: performances of immunity and impunity, 33; personality structures created by domination, 106
social movements: arts, 119, 121, 132; Asian American Political Association, 148; attacks on ethnic studies, 25, 31–43, 55, 107; co-optation, 45, 208–11; CRT, 46–47, 48, 51; ethnic studies, 4, 178, 183, 197, 200; incubators of new knowledge, 7, 11, 46, 87; intersectional, 137, 149, 177; new possibilities, 45, 46, 215
Sostaita, Barbara Andrea: on *nepantla*, 157; on sanctuary, 161–63
story circle pedagogy, 113, 119–23, 133, 179, 191, 192
Students at the Center (New Orleans), 96, 113, 119–23, 179, 183

Taylor, Breonna, 4, 5, 24, 214–15
Taylor, Diana: archive, 95–98; performance studies, 22; repertoire, 95, 98–104; snail as symbol, 187; what can we do, 23
Tomlinson, Barbara: accompaniment, 109; feminist disavowal of ethnic studies, 176; first, middle, and last word, 185; scenes of argument, 167–70, 178
transgender: children, 35; critiques of normativity, 139; epistemologies, 145–46; Marsha P. Johnson, 137–38; Sylvia Rivera, 136–39; valorization of gender fluidity, 95
Trouillot, Michel-Rolph: academic shock and malaise, 193, 205; anthropology, 172; archival silences, 97; border anxiety, 159–60; categories, 175; culture concept, 89; grand metanarratives,

Trouillot, Michel-Rolph *(continued)*
176–77; newness, 184–85; savage slot, 175–76; state-centric scholarship, 174–75

Trump, Donald: appeal, 43; electoral success, 26–29, 43; racist policies, 27, 194–95; repression, 39, 74, 194; supporter grifters, 44–45

United Farm Workers union, 148–49, 178

War on Poverty, 104–5

whiteness: disavowal, 34, 37, 54, 141, 172; family line of inheritance, 140; Indigenous dispossession, 153; political project, 36, 52, 155; social construct, 31, 50; systemic and structured advantage, 25, 26, 29, 31, 40, 152; unearned privileges, 18, 33, 44; white anti-racism, 35

wokeism, 18, 23, 27

Young Lords: gender politics, 46; parallel institutions, 60, 61; repertoire, 99; Sylvia Rivera, 137; Thirteen Point Program, 59

Zavella, Patricia: reproductive justice, 179–80

AMERICAN CROSSROADS

Edited by Earl Lewis, George Lipsitz, George Sánchez, Dana Takagi, Laura Briggs, and Nikhil Pal Singh

1. *Border Matters: Remapping American Cultural Studies,* by José David Saldívar
2. *The White Scourge: Mexicans, Blacks, and Poor Whites in Texas Cotton Culture,* by Neil Foley
3. *Indians in the Making: Ethnic Relations and Indian Identities around Puget Sound,* by Alexandra Harmon
4. *Aztlán and Viet Nam: Chicano and Chicana Experiences of the War,* edited by George Mariscal
5. *Immigration and the Political Economy of Home: West Indian Brooklyn and American Indian Minneapolis, 1945–1992,* by Rachel Buff
6. *Epic Encounters: Culture, Media, and U.S. Interests in the Middle East since 1945,* by Melani McAlister
7. *Contagious Divides: Epidemics and Race in San Francisco's Chinatown,* by Nayan Shah
8. *Japanese American Celebration and Conflict: A History of Ethnic Identity and Festival, 1934–1990,* by Lon Kurashige
9. *American Sensations: Class, Empire, and the Production of Popular Culture,* by Shelley Streeby
10. *Colored White: Transcending the Racial Past,* by David R. Roediger
11. *Reproducing Empire: Race, Sex, Science, and U.S. Imperialism in Puerto Rico,* by Laura Briggs
12. *meXicana Encounters: The Making of Social Identities on the Borderlands,* by Rosa Linda Fregoso
13. *Popular Culture in the Age of White Flight: Fear and Fantasy in Suburban Los Angeles,* by Eric Avila
14. *Ties That Bind: The Story of an Afro-Cherokee Family in Slavery and Freedom,* by Tiya Miles
15. *Cultural Moves: African Americans and the Politics of Representation,* by Herman S. Gray
16. *Emancipation Betrayed: The Hidden History of Black Organizing and White Violence in Florida from Reconstruction to the Bloody Election of 1920,* by Paul Ortiz
17. *Eugenic Nation: Faults and Frontiers of Better Breeding in Modern America,* by Alexandra Stern
18. *Audiotopia: Music, Race, and America,* by Josh Kun
19. *Black, Brown, Yellow, and Left: Radical Activism in Los Angeles,* by Laura Pulido
20. *Fit to Be Citizens? Public Health and Race in Los Angeles, 1879–1939,* by Natalia Molina
21. *Golden Gulag: Prisons, Surplus, Crisis, and Opposition in Globalizing California,* by Ruth Wilson Gilmore
22. *Proud to Be an Okie: Cultural Politics, Country Music, and Migration to Southern California,* by Peter La Chapelle

23. *Playing America's Game: Baseball, Latinos, and the Color Line*, by Adrian Burgos, Jr.
24. *The Power of the Zoot: Youth Culture and Resistance during World War II*, by Luis Alvarez
25. *Guantánamo: A Working-Class History between Empire and Revolution*, by Jana K. Lipman
26. *Between Arab and White: Race and Ethnicity in the Early Syrian-American Diaspora*, by Sarah M. A. Gualtieri
27. *Mean Streets: Chicago Youths and the Everyday Struggle for Empowerment in the Multiracial City, 1908–1969*, by Andrew J. Diamond
28. *In Sight of America: Photography and the Development of U.S. Immigration Policy*, by Anna Pegler-Gordon
29. *Migra! A History of the U.S. Border Patrol*, by Kelly Lytle Hernández
30. *Racial Propositions: Ballot Initiatives and the Making of Postwar California*, by Daniel Martinez HoSang
31. *Stranger Intimacy: Contesting Race, Sexuality, and the Law in the North American West*, by Nayan Shah
32. *The Nicest Kids in Town: American Bandstand, Rock 'n' Roll, and the Struggle for Civil Rights in 1950s Philadelphia*, by Matthew F. Delmont
33. *Jack Johnson, Rebel Sojourner: Boxing in the Shadow of the Global Color Line*, by Theresa Rundstedler
34. *Pacific Connections: The Making of the US-Canadian Borderlands*, by Kornel Chang
35. *States of Delinquency: Race and Science in the Making of California's Juvenile Justice System*, by Miroslava Chávez-García
36. *Spaces of Conflict, Sounds of Solidarity: Music, Race, and Spatial Entitlement in Los Angeles*, by Gaye Theresa Johnson
37. *Covert Capital: Landscapes of Denial and the Making of U.S. Empire in the Suburbs of Northern Virginia*, by Andrew Friedman
38. *How Race Is Made in America: Immigration, Citizenship, and the Historical Power of Racial Scripts*, by Natalia Molina
39. *We Sell Drugs: The Alchemy of US Empire*, by Suzanna Reiss
40. *Abrazando el Espíritu: Bracero Families Confront the US-Mexico Border*, by Ana Elizabeth Rosas
41. *Houston Bound: Culture and Color in a Jim Crow City*, by Tyina L. Steptoe
42. *Why Busing Failed: Race, Media, and the National Resistance to School Desegregation*, by Matthew F. Delmont
43. *Incarcerating the Crisis: Freedom Struggles and the Rise of the Neoliberal State*, by Jordan T. Camp
44. *Lavender and Red: Liberation and Solidarity in the Gay and Lesbian Left*, by Emily K. Hobson
45. *Flavors of Empire: Food and the Making of Thai America*, by Mark Padoongpatt
46. *The Life of Paper: Letters and a Poetics of Living Beyond Captivity*, by Sharon Luk
47. *Strategies of Segregation: Race, Residence, and the Struggle for Educational Equality*, by David G. García

48. *Soldiering through Empire: Race and the Making of the Decolonizing Pacific,* by Simeon Man
49. *An American Language: The History of Spanish in the United States,* by Rosina Lozano
50. *The Color Line and the Assembly Line: Managing Race in the Ford Empire,* by Elizabeth D. Esch
51. *Confessions of a Radical Chicano Doo-Wop Singer,* by Rubén Funkahuatl Guevara
52. *Empire's Tracks: Indigenous Peoples, Racial Aliens, and the Transcontinental Railroad,* by Manu Karuka
53. *Collisions at the Crossroads: How Place and Mobility Make Race,* by Genevieve Carpio
54. *Charros: How Mexican Cowboys are Remapping Race and American Identity,* by Laura R. Barraclough
55. *Louder and Faster: Pain, Joy, and the Body Politic in Asian American Taiko,* by Deborah Wong
56. *Badges without Borders: How Global Counterinsurgency Transformed American Policing,* by Stuart Schrader
57. *Colonial Migrants at the Heart of Empire: Puerto Rican Workers on U.S. Farms,* by Ismael García Colón
58. *Assimilation: An Alternative History,* by Catherine S. Ramírez
59. *Boyle Heights: How a Los Angeles Neighborhood Became the Future of American Democracy,* by George J. Sánchez
60. *Not Yo' Butterfly: My Long Song of Relocation, Race, Love, and Revolution,* by Nobuko Miyamoto
61. *The Deportation Express: A History of America through Mass Removal,* by Ethan Blue
62. *An Archive of Skin, An Archive of Kin: Disability and Life-Making during Medical Incarceration,* by Adria L. Imada
63. *Menace to Empire: Anticolonial Solidarities and the Transpacific Origins of the US Security State,* by Moon-Ho Jung
64. *Suburban Empire: Cold War Militarization in the US Pacific,* by Lauren Hirshberg
65. *Archipelago of Resettlement: Vietnamese Refugee Settlers across Guam and Israel-Palestine,* by Evyn Lê Espiritu Gandhi
66. *Arise! Global Radicalism in the Era of the Mexican Revolution,* by Christina Heatherton
67. *Resisting Change in Suburbia: Asian Immigrants and Frontier Nostalgia in L.A.,* by James Zarsadiaz
68. *Racial Uncertainties: Mexican Americans, School Desegregation, and the Making of Race in Post–Civil Rights America,* by Danielle R. Olden
69. *Pacific Confluence: Fighting over the Nation in Nineteenth-Century Hawai'i,* by Christen T. Sasaki
70. *Possible Histories: Arab Americans and the Queer Ecology of Peddling,* by Charlotte Karem Albrecht
71. *Indian Wars Everywhere: Colonial Violence and the Shadow Doctrines of Empire,* by Stefan Aune

72. *Plantation Pedagogy: The Violence of Schooling across Black and Indigenous Space*, by Bayley J. Marquez
73. *The Danger Zone Is Everywhere: How Housing Discrimination Harms Health and Steals Wealth*, by George Lipsitz
74. *The Violence of Love: Race, Family, and Adoption in the United States*, by Kit W. Myers
75. *Health as Property: Racial Capitalism and Sexual Liberalism in Los Angeles*, by Nic John Ramos
76. *Ethnic Studies at the Crossroads*, by George Lipsitz

Founded in 1893,
UNIVERSITY OF CALIFORNIA PRESS
publishes bold, progressive books and journals
on topics in the arts, humanities, social sciences,
and natural sciences—with a focus on social
justice issues—that inspire thought and action
among readers worldwide.

The UC PRESS FOUNDATION
raises funds to uphold the press's vital role
as an independent, nonprofit publisher, and
receives philanthropic support from a wide
range of individuals and institutions—and from
committed readers like you. To learn more, visit
ucpress.edu/supportus.

www.ingramcontent.com/pod-product-compliance
Lightning Source LLC
Chambersburg PA
CBHW020453300426
44174CB00032B/328